FALANGE

FALANGE

A History of Spanish Fascism

STANLEY G. PAYNE

STANFORD UNIVERSITY PRESS
Stanford, California

Stanford University Press
Stanford, California
© 1961 by the Board of Trustees of the
Leland Stanford Junior University
Printed in the United States of America
Cloth ISBN 0-8047-0058-3
Paper ISBN 0-8047-0059-1
Original edition 1961
Last figure below indicates year of this printing:
79

To the memory of
JAIME VICENS VIVES (1910–1960)
A great Spanish historian

PREFACE

The Spanish Civil War has long been a subject of lively controversy in the English-speaking world, in part because the victory in that epic struggle went to the authoritarian nationalist tendency that lost out in the greater conflict of 1939–45. Yet few things in modern European politics have been less clearly understood than the foundations of the Franco regime which were laid during the Civil War.

This study deals with only one aspect of Spain's turbid political world of the nineteen-thirties—her experience with fascism. It has been obvious for many years that the fascist movements of the thirties were not cut of whole cloth, and that the various fascist parties differed considerably in character and composition; the Spanish essay in fascism is here viewed as a peculiarly Spanish phenomenon, the product of Spanish conditions and Spanish feeling. Its ideological content was usually less definitive than its emotional tone, and it was above all in the temper of his political spirit that the Falange's founder, José Antonio Primo de Rivera, stood out amid the passions and hatreds of the Republic. The first half of this book is therefore dominated by the *Jefe,* and I have tried to present, without adulation or recrimination, what I believe is the first fully balanced view of his career.

Since the outbreak of the Civil War the Falange has lived under the shadow of the Caudillo, Francisco Franco. The Generalissimo has been a most singular figure, a careful little man who has survived constant shifts of the political kaleidoscope. I have tried to describe as accurately as possible just how he has used a fascist party, and how it in turn has lived off his regime.

The later years of the Franco regime have been treated in less detail because the government had a relatively uneventful internal history in the decade 1945–55. Since the basic structure of the regime was forged in the period 1936–43, the central focus of this study has been placed on those years.

Perhaps no one will ever present the whole truth about Spanish fascism and the complex struggles of the Civil War period, but I have tried to be as balanced as possible and as objective as the circumstances permit. Every possible kind of printed source material has been consulted and listed in the Notes and Bibliography. I have also tried, where feasible, to return to the original Thucydidean method of historical investigation, talking with significant figures in my story whenever they were living and available, and collecting private notes and documents from a great number of people. In the latter part of the book, in dealing with topics on which very little public material is available, I have had to rely heavily on such personal sources. The dangers inherent in this procedure are clear, but I have tried to make reasonable allowances for egocentric bias and distortion.

The Spanish gentlemen to whom I am indebted for the collection of information are many, and it would not be possible to name them all. I must, however, acknowledge a very heavy debt of gratitude to Don Dionisio Ridruejo and Don Manuel Hedilla Larrey; this book could not have been adequately written without their help. Important assistance was also given to me by the late distinguished president of the Basque government, José Antonio de Aguirre, by Don Rodolfo Llopis, Secretary of the Spanish Socialist Party, and by the venerable but energetic Carlist historian, Don Melchor Ferrer. I would also like to acknowledge the generous assistance of José Andino, Miguel Angel Astiz, Pedro Gamero del Castillo, Patricio González de Canales, José María Iribarren, Miguel Maura, Narciso Perales, Carlos Juan Ruiz de la Fuente, the brothers José and Luis Rosales, the Baleztena family of Pamplona, and my friends Jon Bilbao and Francisco Javier Lizarza.

This study was begun while I was a doctoral candidate at Columbia University under Professor Shephard B. Clough, to whom I owe a good deal for his aid and encouragement, as well as his helpful criticism. Much of the research and writing was made possible by a predoctoral fellowship from the Social Science Research Council in 1958–59. Parts or the whole of the manuscript were given careful attention by the following friends and mentors: Professors Francisco

García Lorca, Juan J. Linz, Garrett Mattingly, and John Wuorinen of Columbia University; Mr. Joaquín Maurín; Professor Richard A. Webster of the University of California; Mr. Cyril J. Fox of Queens College; Dr. Josef L. Altholz of the University of Minnesota; and Mr. John D. Donohue, Jr. To all of them, my sincere thanks.

STANLEY G. PAYNE

Minneapolis, Minnesota
May 1961

NOTE TO THE 1967 PRINTING
Since the volume was originally published in 1961, I have corrected several errors that have come to my attention. In the 1967 printing, the previously misleading reference to Pedro Gamero del Castillo's activity has been revised (pp. 225-26).

S.G.P.

CONTENTS

PREFACE   vii

I. THE BACKGROUND   1

II. THE BIRTH OF NATIONAL SYNDICALISM   10

III. THE EMERGENCE OF JOSE ANTONIO PRIMO DE RIVERA   21

IV. THE FOUNDING OF THE FALANGE   38

V. POETRY AND TERRORISM   49

VI. THE STRUGGLE OVER TACTICS AND COMMAND   59

VII. THE PARTY OF JOSE ANTONIO   74

VIII. THE ELECTIONS OF 1936   89

IX. THE FALANGE INTO THE HOLOCAUST   101

X. THE FALANGE EARLY IN THE CIVIL WAR   116

XI. JOSE ANTONIO IN ALICANTE   132

XII. THE FALANGE MILITIA   142

XIII. POLITICAL INTRIGUE IN SALAMANCA   148

XIV. THE FALANGE AS STATE PARTY, 1937–1939   174

XV. THE "NEW SPAIN" OF THE CAUDILLO   199

XVI. POLITICS DURING WORLD WAR II   225

XVII. PLAYING OUT THE STRING   239

NOTES   269

BIBLIOGRAPHY   299

INDEX   309

I

THE BACKGROUND

THE VIOLENT TENSIONS of twentieth-century European history have centered around two poles: strife between social classes and warfare between nations. Strikes and demonstrations by the working class were widespread on the eve of World War I, and that upheaval simultaneously brought a quickening of the nationalist spirit which had been growing for generations. During the war class consciousness was buried beneath an outburst of nationalism that transcended it, but the reasons for the class struggle remained. After the war, working-class rebellion was apparent all over Europe, and everywhere chauvinist zealots, combined with the entrenched interests, rallied support for the nation irrespective of class. The strength of these rival allegiances thus favored the growth of hybrid "national socialist" or "corporatist" movements designed either to blend nationalism and socialism or to use the first to control the second.

Given authoritarian form, the combination of nationalism with socialism or corporatism usually became known as "fascism." The attraction fascism had for European countries with serious political and social problems now seems obvious. It drew its main strength from the fear and insecurity of the middle classes, who turned to the corporate coordination of economic forces in the name of the nation as the only new creed which could control the proletarian rebellion. The success of fascist movements varied widely, depending on the vigor of a country's political institutions and the strength of its economic structure. Italian Fascism, for instance, groped toward a pragmatic reconciliation of socialist and nationalist aspirations; German National Socialism talked of socialism only to submerge it beneath nationalism.

The last of the larger west European nations to develop a native fascist movement was Spain. For several generations her social and political development had varied so far from the European norm that socialism and nationalism after the European pattern had been very slow in maturing. The mediocre rate of economic growth, due largely to a low level of popular education and to a general cultural isolation, temporarily stunted the growth of organized class consciousness, but when the class struggle came, it came with a vengeance. After the turn of the century, anarchist assassinations, police retaliations, and peasant uprisings in the south occurred with increasing frequency. The bloody riots and church-burnings which upset the country in the summer of 1909 were but a modest prelude to Spain's first nationwide general strike, which took place in 1917.

Since 1875 Spain had nominally been ruled by a constitutional monarchy, and there had been a number of notable improvements. A cultural renaissance in the early twentieth century created the nation's greatest literary age since the days of Cervantes. Such thinkers as José Ortega y Gasset once more brought vitality to Spanish philosophy. Political life also increased in vigor, as more and more citizens participated in it. The nation seemed more active than at any time in its modern history.

The rise of organized social rebellion, however, threatened in the long run to overshadow these achievements. It was Spain's misfortune that limited change was not sufficient to solve her problems; it merely exacerbated them, creating new ones in the process. Economic development was not widespread, and its benefits were confined to certain regions and classes. Industrial and agricultural equipment was primitive, productivity was slight, and the standard of living did not rise rapidly, even though it started from a very low level; Spanish workers in 1914 were paid the lowest real wages in western Europe outside of Portugal. In the circumstances, the growth of the first scattered Socialist and Syndicalist movements into mass organizations took place rapidly and created a distinct class consciousness in the proletariat, which demanded revolutionary social and economic changes. A feeling of despondent extremism was especially pronounced among the landless peasantry of southern Spain, many of whom had been despoiled of their common lands by the aristocracy and middle class during the past two centuries.

The bulk of the Spanish bourgeoisie saw no need to make concessions to the workers. In most regions the middle classes were lethargic; their economic acumen was usually slight and, except for the ruthless action of a financial oligarchy, they lacked initiative. Above all, they were self-centered. They took little positive interest in the present or future of their country, and sought no direct solution for the nation's economic imbalance until the problems which it caused were thrust forcibly upon them in the nineteen-twenties. For a time Spain's very backwardness shielded her from modern social conflict, but so stark a background merely made the class struggle more violent when it came.

The tardiness of Spanish political and economic institutions in adapting to the requirements of modern life created tension between regions as well as between classes. The nation's most advanced region, Catalonia, spoke a popular language distinct from Castilian and had a tradition of self-rule dating from the Middle Ages. The growth of the Catalan middle class, the pressure of economic development, and the abuses of centralized misgovernment from Madrid, together with the indispensable catalyst of a Catalan literary renaissance, combined to create a separatist movement with middle-class leadership. The same kind of regional nationalism, springing from some of the same causes, was a political force in the Basque country.

A substantial segment of the middle class was profoundly opposed to every new influence which had appeared in Spanish life. Though monarchism was fast becoming discredited, powerful traditional institutions like the Church had many defenders. Hence the changes taking place in Spain had an ambivalent meaning. To some, the growth of representative government meant the beginning of a new era of liberal progress. To others, the extremists of both the Left and the Right, the new era marked the start of an intensified struggle; the Leftists wanted to bring the process of growth and reform to a revolutionary climax, while the Rightists were determined to subject it once more to the authoritarian controls of an earlier period.

There was little articulate nationalist feeling in Spain similar to the organized middle-class nationalism which swept many other continental countries in the nineteenth century. No one had been able to arrest the slow decay of Spain's overseas empire, even though such a process of dissolution was diametrically opposed to the pattern of expansion then characteristic of European states. There was no spirit of *revanchisme* or of irredentism, for Spain had been too deeply sunk in economic sloth and governmental incompetence to nourish positive ambitions. Her wars and territories had been lost either too long ago or too far away to excite popular feeling. After 1898 there were no real foreign threats to Spain; she was not involved in a single international incident capable of arousing collective excitement.

This does not mean that Spaniards were deficient in sentimental national feeling, but only that they were unresponsive to organized nationalism expressed in explicit ideologies or political movements. The Spaniard is perhaps the most traditionalist of Europeans, and tenaciously resists any attack on his customs or social relationships. This backward-looking patriotic traditionalism, especially dominant among the Castilian middle class and the northern peasantry, had little in common with the dynamic modern nationalism of central Europe, which harped on future growth and expansion as well as on the glories of the past.

The most vigorous example of traditionalist patriotism resisting forces of change was the Carlist community, which based its program on the major historical institutions of the nation, an intolerant Church and a nonconstitutional monarchy. Purporting to champion national tradition against modern perversion, the Carlists were in fact clerical reactionaries and monarchical corporatists who based their system on the particularism of the old regime. Their regionalist, neo-medieval monarchism bore no resemblance to modern nationalism, which was devoted to welding the nation into an instrument for new glory and accomplishment.

The first brief expression of twentieth-century Spanish nationalism came from the orthodox Right rather than from the Carlists. After the fall of the conservative leader Antonio Maura in 1909, his followers organized a youth movement called the Juventudes Mauristas, which was dedicated to national regeneration. The Maurist youth decried the irregularities of parliamentary bargaining and called for reform on a nationwide basis, at the same time emphasizing the need for a drastic curtailment of Leftist subversion. However, they had no nationalist mystique, and their pronouncements often sounded somewhat like those of the old Conservative Party.[1]

A more liberal kind of nationalist spirit, itself not untinged with xenophobia, was exhibited by some of the "Generation of Ninety-Eight." Such outstanding esthetes as Miguel de Unamuno and Antonio Machado probed into the marrow of Spanish being and came up with a new appreciation of the Castilian style and spirit, which they found full of harsh, sober colors and rugged contrasts, modulated by the deep flesh tones of earth and hillside, and shaded by the night of clerical black and a certain death-obsession. The *noventayochistas* were sure that Spain was different from the rest of Europe and had a distinct path to follow. But they could contribute to Spanish nationalism no more than an esthetic attitude without social or political content.

The military juntas which sprang up in 1917 were one form of nationalist or patriotic reaction. The rebellious junior officers who set up professional committees in that year were not explicitly nationalistic, and they offered no real program or ideology. But like similar rebels in other countries, they pronounced against favoritism and corruption in politics and demanded that the nation's energies be put to better use.

The years 1917–23 were full of bitter social dispute. Andalusian peasants scribbled "Viva Lenin" on whitewashed walls while hundreds of people were being killed in political assassinations at Barcelona. The disastrous defeat of Spanish arms in Morocco speeded a process of political decay already encouraged by the policies of a clever and ambitious but short-sighted King. Conservatives and liberals alike were eager for reforms which would fortify the state and decrease internal strife.

Thus the stage was set for General Primo de Rivera's *coup* in 1923, which first gave official expression to twentieth-century Spanish nationalism. Miguel Primo de Rivera was neither an intellectual nor a politician; he was simply an Andalusian general, and a somewhat old-fashioned one at that. He was impatient with constitutions, legal technicalities, and sociological theories. He liked order and simplicity. Though he came from the land-owning petty aristocracy, he had been given the spare and modest upbringing of most Spaniards. Even when dictator of Spain, Primo de Rivera found it hard to get used to expensive silk shirts. He liked wine, talk, and tobacco, and the more he drank, the more he talked. He was especially fond of women, and his taste extended from the elegant courtesans of Paris to the more earthy hetaerae of Madrid, who shared his not infrequent drinking bouts. He had come to power after half a decade of confusion and violence, and he declared that his concern was for Spaniards, not for mere politicians or legal theories.

The only ideological basis for Primo's seven-year regime was patriotic feeling. Pronouncing the parliamentary system corrupt and inefficient, he first put the national government into the hands of a staff of colonels. After a few years, this arrangement was converted into a more conventional cabinet structure. The aim of his regime—the nonpartisan union of all Spaniards—was superficially realized in a new political party, the amorphous Unión Patriótica. This organization was set up in 1925 to help fill Primo's authoritarian caricature of a representative assembly.

The Unión Patriótica was by no means conceived as an authoritarian fascist party. In theory, it was a constitutional association, designed merely to provide support for the government during a difficult period of transition. According to the dictator, the Unión Patriótica "should be made up of all those who accept the Constitution of 1876. That is to say, of all those who accept and revere the precepts contained in the fundamental code of the nation."[2] Primo de Rivera always betrayed a guilty conscience about his usurpation of power. He publicly admitted that his *coup* was "illegal," adding the words "but patriotic."[3] He even called it "a violation of discipline, which is the true sacrament of the Army."[4] In an attempt to gain popular support, the qualifications for membership in the Unión Patriótica were later broadened to require only that members be men of general good will.[5]

Thus Primo de Rivera really had no party, no ideology, and no political system. The Unión Patriótica was nothing more than a collection of conservatives whose duty was to approve the dictatorship while waxing strong in patriotic rhetoric. The regime's economic program called for nothing more drastic than public works and more tariff protection. There was no program for social reform save the ambitious arbitration device of *comités paritarios,* in which the Socialist Union (UGT) was legally represented in Spanish government for the first time. The Primo de Rivera regime was not a new order, but the old order on its last legs. It relied heavily on the Church for moral support.

The only political concept the General ever formed was that politics, politicians, and parliamentarianism were bad, while authoritarian control and national unity were good. He recognized that the nation needed economic development in order to create a base from which it could transcend the class struggle, but he left economic planning in the hands of younger cabinet ministers, notably José Calvo Sotelo and Eduardo Aunós. For the time being, this cautious paternalism seemed to satisfy the middle classes and the Socialists. The Anarchists, the only dissident group who remained hostile, were sternly suppressed.

Primo de Rivera expressed strong admiration for the Mussolini regime. The dictator and the King visited Rome during the first months of Primo's rule, and Spain signed a treaty of friendship and arbitration with Italy in 1926. Beyond that Primo could not go, for the political and ideological structure of Italian Fascism was too artfully contrived to fit his own shrewd but simple hand.

The only note of radical nationalism during Primo's regime was struck by a strange esthete, Ernesto Giménez Caballero. Of all the fascist writers who proliferated throughout Europe in the nineteen-twenties and -thirties, Giménez Caballero was perhaps the most bizarre.* A professional *littérateur,* he had gyrated wildly between the poles of modern political ideologies during his brief writing career. By 1930 his imagination was entirely captive to "Roman" Fascism. National Socialism interested him much less, though some of the first Nazi propaganda in Spain, prepared by party members resident in Madrid, was printed on the same press that turned out his own *Gaceta Literaria.*[6] The ideal behind Giménez Caballero's fulminations was the "Universal Kingdom of Spain," something that had ended over one hundred years earlier. Spain was "the country chosen by God."[7] Thus he wrote, "the Spaniard was born to command and not to be a proletarian."[8] The trouble with Spain was that it had

---

* Unless otherwise qualified, the word "fascist" and derivative terms will be used in their broadest sense, to indicate adherence to an authoritarian, corporatist, nationalist form of government.

ceased to be Spanish; salvation would come by reasserting the essence of Spanishness. By this Giménez did not intend to preach a return to the past, as did many of the Carlists. The content of his nationalism was modernistic and radical and based on esthetic, not spiritual, norms.

Violence, he thought, was necessary to establish a new hegemony: "There is no murder in war. There is only he who strikes second or cannot strike any more."[9] "Spain is and ought to be at war."[10] Modern Spanish Anarchism was at once "the repository of the heroic tradition of the conqerors" and "the most authentic refuge for popular Catholicism in Spain."[11] "[Anarchist] gunmen are not vulgar criminals. . . . Those who respect the truly Hispanic revere those gunmen."[12] In 1934, at a patriotic rite near Covadonga, Giménez Caballero summed up his doctrine very clearly: "We are going to exalt national sentiment with insanity, with paroxysms, with whatever need be. I prefer a nation of lunatics."[13]

Though the *Gaceta Literaria* translated such foreign sensations as Curzio Malaparte's *Technique of the Coup d'État,* Giménez Caballero's frantic rhetoric drew very little attention from the predominantly liberal Spanish intelligentsia. Whatever prestige the journal had was purely literary. Spanish "fascism" could not thrive under the provincial authoritarianism of the Primo de Rivera regime.

Six years of that strange assortment of political devices which was *primorriverismo* produced confusion and general dissatisfaction. By 1929 public finance was in a parlous state. The World War I surplus had been dissipated and no new funds were available for public works. The peseta fell to its lowest rate of international exchange since 1899. The Socialists were growing tired of their political compromise with the regime, and their rivals in the Anarcho-Syndicalist movement were only marking time until a fresh outburst could be made. The upper classes, whose position Primo de Rivera had stepped in to save, were equally dissatisfied. Fearing that the nation's economic position would deteriorate further, they wanted to get rid of the overhead charged by the regime. The King, in whose name Primo de Rivera was supposed to be ruling, showed signs of eagerness to resume some degree of personal control. Furthermore, Primo's health began to fail. When his fellow generals proved reluctant to reaffirm his authority early in 1930, he was obliged to resign.

What followed was little better. Two brief governments of semi-dictatorship, led successively by a general and an admiral, produced no political peace and ran into the worldwide economic depression. Alfonso XIII contemplated a return to constitutional monarchy, but he was now seven years too late. He was blamed for both the failures of the dictatorship and the increasing frustrations of 1930. Even the moderate middle classes began to desert the Monarchy, and republican groups gained greatly in strength. The "forces of order" became seriously alarmed; there was even some apprehension over a possible rebellion by the Left. Amid this turmoil, the Court tried to win popular support by announcing that full municipal elections would be held on April 12, 1931. The turmoil mounted. In the larger cities, the elections were almost entirely swept by the republicans, who demanded that monarchy come to an end. By April 14 Alfonso XIII found himself with scarcely a single positive supporter in the land. The fruitless decades of Spanish constitutional monarchy had left a hollow edifice. Even the Right made no move to save it. Several leading generals had become republican sympathizers and the Monarchy had no sword. In a gracious gesture, the King left Spain. The Republic was proclaimed the same day.

II

THE BIRTH OF NATIONAL SYNDICALISM

THE PAINLESS BIRTH of the Republic gave rise to rejoicing and good feeling in many places, even though few Spaniards were ardent liberals. Such a peaceful change of regime seemed to augur a happy, progressive future for a troubled land which had never changed systems of government without bloodshed and tragedy. During the first days of the Republic dissenting voices were few.

While the public indulged in a mood of expectant euphoria, two new expressions of Spanish nationalism in Madrid went largely unnoticed. One was a tiny group called the Spanish Nationalist Party. The other was a weekly paper called *La Conquista del Estado,* whose director was Ramiro Ledesma Ramos. The Spanish Nationalist Party had been formed by a fat, leather-lunged neurologist from Valencia, José María Albiñana. His proclaimed program was the defense of all existing institutions: "The Spanish National Party has no other base than the very broad one of Tradition."[1] Albiñana could point to a sudden rash of Anarchist outbreaks as a mere hint of what Republican liberalism would bring. His platform was grounded on respect for the military and a rigorously nationalistic line in every aspect of government.[2] Albiñana hated all liberal intellectuals, and they responded by ignoring him. Since no one took seriously his talk about being "above parties," he was discredited from the beginning, and he quickly gained the reputation of a reactionary rhetorician in the pay of the landowners. The only effective segment of his minuscule following was the organized group of militiamen and street brawlers known as "Legionarios de Albiñana."

When the Monarchy fell in April 1931, Albiñana's little band tried one or two street fights with the exultant Left and were immediately eliminated. Republican liberals were riding so high that even the upper middle classes were not interested in wasting time with a nationalist monarchical agitator. Albiñana lamented:

> Though enthusiastic and resolute, we could not even pay the rent for our Center, because the moneyed classes did not help us. To ask money in Spain for any work that does not bring immediate personal reward is to pass a fearsome calvary. The absence of the slightest sense of cooperation is one of the greatest ills of our country.[3]

Albiñana was arrested for seditious activities and later exiled to the barren region of Las Hurdes. José María Gil Robles, head of the conservative Acción Popular party, petitioned in the Cortes for Albiñana's release, but the Right was still unimpressed with the doctor's political potential.[4] The hundreds of people who visited Albiñana in Las Hurdes did so largely out of personal sympathy; almost no one joined his now illegal party.[5]

Ramiro Ledesma Ramos, who was also trying to force himself onto a dimly lit corner of the political stage, was of an entirely different type. A postal clerk and sometime student of philosophy, Ledesma was an abrupt, taciturn, and unsociable young man; at the age of fifteen he had fled to Madrid from the province of Zamora, where his father had been a poor village schoolmaster.

Ledesma's first love was German philosophy, and he managed to gain a degree in philosophical studies at the University of Madrid.[6] During the late nineteen-twenties he published some respectable but unimaginative essays on aspects of modern German thought in Ortega y Gasset's *Revista de Occidente* and Giménez Caballero's *Gaceta Literaria*.[7] However, by the time Ledesma was twenty-five, formal philosophy had lost much of its appeal for him. He wanted to escape from the lifeless world of metaphysics into the febrile atmosphere of radical, ideologically oriented politics; he had a passionate longing to apply abstract ideas to practical affairs.

Coming from the deeply traditional society of Old Castile, Ledesma knew how incompatible the emotional temper of the Spanish people was with orthodox liberalism or scientific socialism. He ab-

horred both the atomistic individualism of liberal systems and the
fatalistic impersonality of Marxism. His sympathies were not with
the intellectual Left, certainly not with the international Left, but
with the Spanish Left. He yearned for emotional identification with
a Spanish proletarian movement, a truly nationalistic workers' revolution.

In a way, his notion was in keeping with the spirit of the times,
embracing as it did both nationalism and collectivism. While everywhere else the world depression was threatening the foundations of
liberal democracy, the Nazi Party had revived with great *éclat*. It
seemed that the hour for Mussolini's system had truly arrived, and
Salazar was about to install a corporatist republic in Portugal. Ledesma reasoned that since Spanish nationalist revolutionary ideology
must be original and not imitative, its system could be called neither
corporatism nor national socialism. On the other hand, the most
purely revolutionary force in Spain was Anarcho-Syndicalism, which
led him to conclude that the neo-Leftist quality of the nationalist
revolution and the nationalist quality of the neo-Leftist revolution
could best be synthesized in the term "National Syndicalism."[8] This
realignment of national forces took shape in the mind of Ramiro
Ledesma, a penniless postal clerk, in the winter of 1930–31.

During the last year of the Monarchy, calls for national unity had
frequently been made by Spain's intellectual leaders. The most per-
ceptive and influential among them, Don José Ortega y Gasset, repeatedly called for an all-embracing "national front," a party of parties to represent all Spaniards almost as a corporate entity.[9] This was
poor, weak stuff to Ledesma, hanging on the fringe of the Spanish
intellectual world. His mind had traveled beyond the realm of *orte-
guismo,* and liberal nationalism meant nothing to him. The nationalism of the Right meant still less. Ledesma several times described
the loudest nationalist leader, Albiñana, as "reactionary" and probably despised him more than any other public figure of the day.[10]

At the time Ledesma's political notions were beginning to crystal-
lize, he had few friends with whom to associate. Unkempt, opinion-
ated, and asocial, he did not attract most intellectuals. But he was
single-minded in his desire to create a fascist party, and he ultimately
acquired ten disciples and collaborators, all about his own age (twen-

ty-five). With their uncertain help he began to publish a political weekly, *La Conquista del Estado,* on March 14, 1931, just one month before the Monarchy collapsed. The youngest of Ledesma's collaborators, his secretary, Juan Aparicio, has written that the only things the members of the little band had in common "were their youth and their university background."[11] In addition, they were all dissatisfied with the government, impatient with the backward Right and the doctrinaire Left, and eager to do something about Spain's domestic stagnation and third-rate position in world affairs.

Their greatest lack was money. Ledesma had managed to get the paper started on a handout from the monarchist propaganda fund of Admiral Aznar's government, which preceded the downfall of the Monarchy. Aznar's political informants apparently hoped to use Ledesma's group to create division among the liberal intellectuals.

Ledesma and his colleagues signed their first manifesto by candlelight in an office consisting of four virtually unfurnished rooms. It emphasized the following points:

> The new State will be constructive, creative. It will supplant individuals and groups, and the ultimate sovereignty will reside in it and only in it. . . . We defend, therefore, Panstatism. . . .
>
> [We advocate] exaltation of the Universities, . . . the supreme creative organ of scientific and cultural values. . . .
>
> [We advocate] articulation of the varied districts of Spain. The basic reality of Spain is not Madrid, but the provinces. Our most radical impulse must consist, then, in connecting and encouraging the vital forces of the provinces. . . .
>
> Syndication of economic forces will be obligatory and in each instance bound to the highest ends of the State. The State will discipline and will guarantee production at all times. . . .
>
> · · ·
>
> Our primary goal is revolutionary efficiency. Therefore we do not seek votes, but audacious and valiant minorities. . . . We favor the politician with a military sense of responsibility and combativeness. Our organization will be founded on the basis of syndical cells and political cells.[12]

During these early months, Ledesma's propaganda was more than a little confused. He applauded some aspects of Carlism, then eulogized the Anarchists at the opposite end of the political spectrum.[13]

His rhetoric often amounted to little more than up with the new and down with the old:

> Long live the new world of the twentieth century!
> Long live Fascist Italy!
> Long live Soviet Russia!
> Long live Hitler Germany!
> Long live the Spain we will make!
> Down with the bourgeois parliamentary democracies![14]

Ledesma tried to appeal to every non-Marxist revolutionary force in Spain. He commended the Anarcho-Syndicalists for being the first group in Spain "to free themselves from the bourgeois love of [individual] liberty," but criticized them for refusing to set their goals in national terms.[15] Nonetheless, he saw the Anarcho-Syndicalist CNT as "the most efficient level for subversion" existing in 1931–32, because their revolutionary ardor was unsullied by connections with any branch of international Socialism.[16] Ledesma planned a number of provocative demonstrations with his handful of supporters, but to no avail. No one was impressed by his writings either, and *La Conquista del Estado* was in financial trouble from the beginning.

Ledesma's political ideas were based on pure thought and unrelated to practical reality. No matter how passionate and fascistic, or how virulent and materialistic, his talk became, he always remained an intellectual theorist. Ledesma found not an Absolute Idea, but an Absolute Passion in nationalism. His emotion sprang from his mental struggles, so that in a sense even his irrationality was calculated.

The basic problem of Spain's Republican leaders during those months was to make parliamentary democracy take root in a land hitherto dominated by an intransigent Right and at the same time to stand off the Left, which scorned the slow give-and-take of parliamentary government. The Republic had been brought about not by a great popular initiative on the part of Republicans, but by the utter collapse of the Monarchy. In order to establish a secure democracy in a land where only a minority of the population were liberal democrats, work and patience were needed. Ledesma's penchant for abstract opinions made it impossible for him even to understand the nature of this task.

To finance *La Conquista del Estado* was a constant trial. After his original monarchist subsidy, Ledesma appears to have received a few meager handouts from the world of high finance, notably from the Bilbao bankers. The gradual drying up of these sources ended an internal debate within Ledesma's clique over the propriety of accepting funds from the far Right. It also ended *La Conquista del Estado*, whose last number appeared on October 25, 1931.

By this time Ledesma's ten had already begun to split up. One joined the Republican liberals, another the moderate Radical Party, and a third the clerical Spanish Confederation of Autonomous Rightist Groups (CEDA). A fourth went back to the Left, while a fifth, it would seem, later entered a mental institution.[17] Giménez Caballero, who occasionally collaborated with Ledesma, had walked out some months before.

Despite its short life, Ledesma's paper bore the essential germs of what later became known as Spanish national syndicalism. Its writers refused the formal label of fascism and never used the term in referring to themselves. They were fumbling to develop a Spanish ideology, second-hand though it might be. Their writings on state-controlled nationalism, the legitimacy of violence, the glory of empire, national syndication of labor, land expropriation, and the incorporation of the masses set off a very slow chain reaction among university students and on the far Right which belied the original insignificance of the propagandists. Unfortunately for Ledesma, this reaction was long in coming, and was contingent on a series of events beyond his control.

In June 1931 a group of similar size and aim was formed in the ancient Castilian capital of Valladolid, under the leadership of Onésimo Redondo Ortega. Born into a peasant family, Redondo came from a thoroughly clerical background and grew up in the highly conservative environment of rural Castile. In 1928 he served for one year as reader of Spanish in the Catholic college of Mannheim, Germany, where he became acquainted with Nazi ideology.[18] Although the peculiar characteristics of German National Socialism were not easily compatible with Spanish Catholicism, Redondo was impressed by the possibilities of a revolutionary modern nationalist movement.*

Young, vigorous, handsome, and passionate, Onésimo Redondo was obsessed by three goals: national unity, the primacy of traditional "Spanish values," and social justice. His religion was the stern Catholicism of Torquemada, and his ideal was to drive the money changers from the temple.[19] Redondo despised tolerance; he burned to revive the martial spirituality of Spain's warrior monks of the Middle Ages.

During 1930–31 Redondo spent nearly twelve months working as an organizer for a syndicate of *remolacheros* (sugar beet growers) that had recently been established in Valladolid province. Though the organization's efforts came to a temporary standstill owing to a lack of funds, they gave Redondo an introduction to national syndicalism.[20] Throughout his career as a nationalist agitator, he continued to work on behalf of the *remolacheros* of Valladolid.

Redondo was thus deeply engaged in the defense of the small farmer of Old Castile. He resented the bourgeois separatists of Vizcaya and Catalonia, the Leftist workers of the large cities, the finance capitalists of Madrid and Bilbao, and the meddling anticlerical politicians of the liberal parties. He wanted a rebellion that would reaffirm Spanish tradition in a manner adequate for the modern world, a rebellion that would restore to the toiling Catholic classes of solid, provincial Spain their proper dominance over the deluded liberals and godless radicals of the cities. He thought economic life should be controlled by nationwide syndicates, thoroughly organized but partially autonomous. All the agnostic, divisive, and relativistic forces which had gained ascendancy in 1931, or even in 1875, should be swept away.

Catholic Action, for which he had once been a propagandist, now seemed far too pale and compromising. Redondo wanted a revolutionary national youth movement, politically radical, economically nationalistic, religiously conservative, but violent in its style and

* Employing the customary line of the clerical fascist during those years, he declared that Adolf Hitler represented "Christianity facing Communism." (*El Estado Nacional*, No. 19, Mar. 20, 1933.)

tactics.* With the support of several acquaintances of vaguely similar backgrounds and aspirations, he founded a weekly paper in Valladolid entitled *Libertad*. Its first number appeared on June 13, 1931, just three months after the inception of *La Conquista del Estado*.

According to Redondo, the remedy for Spain's ills lay "in the people," that is, the honest and devout working people, and above all the peasant farmers and small shopkeepers of Old Castile, whom he called on to save the rest of Spain.[21] He was certain that Castile had done the best job in Spain of preserving its spiritual integrity in the face of the egotistical, "pornographic," "Jewish" influences corrupting the land.[22]

Redondo's propaganda had no more coherence than Ledesma's. On the one hand, he demanded the economic destruction of the bourgeoisie; on the other, he raged against the anticlerical laws of the new Republic.† He even declared that Spain already lived in a state of civil war and exhorted the young to gird themselves for battle:

> Our young men ought to exercise themselves in physical struggle, ought to love violence as a system. National violence by the young is just, is necessary, is convenient. One of our permanent goals is to cultivate the spirit of a morality of violence, of military shock.[23]

On August 9, 1931, Redondo founded a political group, the Juntas Castellanas de Actuación Hispánica, in order to translate some of his emotions into action. Its first members were a few rambunctious students and a handful of Redondo's followers around Valladolid.

Although Redondo and Ledesma had been aware of each other's work from the very beginning, several months passed before they officially took notice of each other. The leaders had little in common: the conservative Redondo deplored Ledesma's pan-radicalism, and Ledesma sneered at Redondo's religiosity. However, in September

---

* "This can only be done by a movement steeped in a true Spanish [*españolista*] frenzy, launched by the young, and dedicated to combatting at every turn not only the uncontrolled wave of materialism, but also the irresponsible hypocrisy of the bourgeoisie." (*Libertad*, No. 29, Dec. 28, 1931.)

† *"Coeducation is a ministerial crime against decent women. It is a chapter in the history of Jewish atrocity against free nations, a crime against the health of the people for which the traitors responsible ought to pay with their heads."* (*Ibid.*, No. 17, Oct. 5, 1931. All italics are Redondo's.)

1931 Ledesma was fast running out of money and desperately needed collaborators in order to keep his movement alive. On the other hand, Redondo was isolated in Valladolid and knew virtually no one in Madrid. The two men obviously needed each other. For all their differences, they were both nationalist, and anti-Marxist authoritarian revolutionaries, and it was in their best interests to combine forces.

In its penultimate issue on October 10, *La Conquista del Estado* announced the impending formation of the Juntas de Ofensiva Nacional Sindicalista, a fusion of the Madrid and Valladolid groups. The new organization was to be controlled by a national council, which in practice became a duumvirate, with Ledesma and Redondo remaining in more or less mutually autonomous command of their respective groups.

The members of the JONS, who were known as "Jonsistas," belonged to the first official political organization in Spain bearing a national syndicalist label. For their emblem they chose the yoked arrows of the Catholic Kings, a fitting symbol for those who dreamed of reviving Spain's imperial grandeur.[24] It was during this period, also, that Ledesma coined several slogans—such as *¡Arriba!* and *España, Una, Grande y Libre*—which later became standard in the propaganda of national syndicalism.[25] To demonstrate their radical aims, the Jonsistas adopted as their colors the red-black-red banner of the Anarchists.

With Ledesma's rasping tongue silenced owing to lack of funds, the only spokesman for the minuscule movement was Redondo. The Valladolid agitator poured out his moralistic frenzy in a steady stream, always emphasizing that the JONS was in no way tied to either the Monarchy or the Church.[26] According to Redondo, "nationalism" was utterly pragmatic with regard to formal political structure, and was bound to scorn all explicit programs or ideologies. Spain's two great ills were "foreignization and the cult of formulas."[*] Redondo demanded a "popular dictatorship," which would create its own leader and its own program out of the process of its own dialectic.[27]

---

[*] *El Estado Nacional* (a weekly review for the discussion of political theory, directed by Redondo), Feb. 20, 1932. The use of "formulas" assured "the selection of the worst policy." (*Ibid.*, Feb. 27, 1932.)

As Ledesma later admitted, "During all the year 1932, the activity of the JONS was almost nil."[28] Redondo's university students in Valladolid engaged in demonstrations against Marxism, but these soon degenerated into futile brawling, and the leader of the group was obliged to leave town.[29] Ledesma still had no money and no prospects. It was impossible to interest any of the reactionary, anti-Republican bankers in financing him. Though the liberal cabinet then ruling the country began to run into difficulties, Left and Right alike ignored the existence of national syndicalism.

The miniature movement possessed little ideological coherence or physical organization. Its leadership rested on the implicit compromise established by Ledesma and Redondo. A real test of their cooperation came in the summer of 1932, when a handful of military men prepared a hasty *coup* against the Republic. Ledesma regarded them as reactionaries and hence remained on the sidelines. Redondo, however, saw an opportunity for establishing the "national dictatorship" he always talked of, and took a very minor part in the conspiracy. When the rebellion failed, Redondo barely escaped across the Portuguese border, one jump ahead of the Republican police.

During its first two years of existence Spanish national syndicalism accomplished nothing more than a certain airing of ideas, which might better be described as noisy suggestions. Redondo and Ledesma rarely agreed and still more rarely made sense. In effect, there was neither a national syndicalist movement nor a national syndicalist program at the beginning of 1933.

The practical ignorance of the little group was staggering. Except for Redondo, with his brief experience among the small farmers of Valladolid, no one in the JONS seems to have had the slightest acquaintance with practical economics. As far as labor economics were concerned, ignorance reigned supreme. No theory of syndical organization was worked out, and no one had the vaguest idea what national syndicalism would really mean in practice.

Like many central European fascists, Ledesma and Redondo were petit-bourgeois types. Redondo, with his provincial background, could take to radicalism easily because modern upper-middle-class economic attitudes had never effectively penetrated his rural world. Ledesma, whose experience had been divided between the post office and the philosophy classroom, had led a typical white-collar functionary's life. Both acted from personal emotion. Both sought great ends and were impatient with means. Both lived in a world of passionate vision, which bordered on illusion.*

At the end of 1932 the efforts of the Jonsistas appeared futile. In making economic revolution one of their principal issues, they had cut themselves off from the wealthy and respectable Right-wing parties. Their nationalism had alienated the organized Left. They proposed, at least in their more lucid moments, to establish a national syndicalist dictatorship against the Left, but without joining the Right or suspending their ridicule of the Center. It is little wonder that there were few to heed them. Their only chance for success seemed to lie in a national catastrophe.

---

* "Ramiro . . . could never find the frontiers which separate the fluidity of real life from imagined existence, which only possesses us in fleeting moments of enchantment. . . . One cannot well ascertain if Ramiro dreamed in order to act or longed for action in order to dream. Nor could he himself." (Emiliano Aguado, *Ramiro Ledesma en la crisis de España,* p. 114.)

III

THE EMERGENCE OF
JOSE ANTONIO PRIMO DE RIVERA

THE ONLY RIGHT-WING GROUP not swept off balance by the sudden birth of the Republic in 1931 was the Comunión Tradicionalista, the political organization of the Carlists. The Carlist stronghold lay among the archconservative, hyper-Catholic peasantry of Navarre. Carlists had been predicting the downfall of the "illegitimate" line of the Bourbon dynasty for generations, and they regarded the abrupt end of Alfonso XIII's reign as almost Biblical justice. Only a few weeks after the birth of the Republic, at a secret meeting in Leiza (about 20 miles from San Sebastián) Carlist leaders agreed to reorganize the Carlist militia (known as "Requetés" or "Boinas rojas") for the purpose of protecting Traditionalist interests from Republican depredation and perhaps striking a blow for the cause, should the occasion arise.[1] The Carlists expected nothing from the Republic, but they continued to scorn the pragmatic Right. They were content to drill their militia and await developments.*

The majority monarchists, the *alfonsinos,* were slower to react. It was several months before their leaders began drawing together the strands of support which the King had left behind. In negotiations with Alfonso at Paris, it was finally agreed to organize a monarchist party, the Renovación Española, which would operate legally under the Republic and thus serve as a cover for efforts to restore the throne.[2] The party's open political activity was slight, for as one of its leading members later admitted, its only goal was to overthrow the Republic.[3] Pressure from the Renovación Española was partly responsible for

---

* Part of the militia was later sent to Italy for further training, along with the customary Carlist complement of priests (Jaime del Burgo, *Requetés en Navarra*).

the *coup d'état* attempted by a handful of officers in August 1932. The *coup* was a miserable failure and showed what scant support the monarchist Right could expect from the nation as a whole.

Genuine monarchist sentiment was virtually dead among the Spanish middle classes in 1932. What most of the Spanish bourgeoisie wanted was a guarantee against any future agitation by the lower classes, a check on incendiary anticlericalism, and an assurance that the political revolution of 1931 would not become an economic revolution in 1933 or 1934.

With both monarchism and corporatism disqualified by their lack of broad appeal, direction of the forces of conservatism tended to devolve temporarily upon certain prominent members of the religious laity. This trend was almost unavoidable, for the most important disputes in the Constituent Cortes concerned those sections in the new constitution which disestablished the Church and banned it from education.

One of these new conservative leaders was Don Angel Herrera, editor of the influential Jesuit-financed *El Debate* and a leader of Catholic Action. Herrera took a moderate and practical position. He believed it the duty of the Church and its believers to submit to the prevailing government so long as it did not deprive them of necessary liberties. Regarding monarchism as a dead issue in Spain, he endeavored to mobilize the forces of Spanish Catholicism behind a pragmatic, parliamentary-oriented political movement, tied to the interests of the Church but respectful of the Republican regime.[4]

It was partly through Herrera's efforts that Acción Popular, the political arm of Catholic Action, became the center of a new federation representing the forces of the Spanish Right. Its title, the Spanish Confederation of Autonomous Rightist Groups (CEDA), suggested the moderate, pragmatic, and even heterogeneous nature of the group behind it. José María Gil Robles, a pudgy, balding young lawyer from Salamanca, emerged as the leader of this force, which received the full support of the Church.[5] Gil Robles and his followers showed no interest in contesting the legitimacy of the Republican regime; their only goal was to restore the lost privileges of the Church and to re-establish the social and economic status quo of 1931. Accordingly, they planned to revise the national constitution and to reverse the liberal legislation of the first year of the Republic. The CEDA was a careful, moderate, bourgeois party, with few vocal nationalists and no stomach for violence. It reassured the bulk of the Spanish middle class, which did not want to go either backward or forward.

The absence of well-organized opposition from the Right was not enough to provide a period of untroubled gestation for the new regime, which was under assault from the very beginning. The process began in the Constituent Cortes, where the conservatives walked out, the extreme Left refused to cooperate, anticlerical politicians attempted to right ancient wrongs, and Socialists endeavored to carve out their own version of working-class representation. As the months passed, the clerical dispute became increasingly bitter, and a modest land reform proposal created an enormous uproar. The Anarchists tried to set up a little republic of their own, and the world depression exacerbated the existing social disputes. Workers grew restive, monarchists plotted rebellion, and the cabinet bogged down completely. When the Socialists left the government, the liberal Republic was doomed.

No one had expected so much of the Republic as the intellectuals. Republican almost to a man and predominantly liberal in spirit, they had been eager to serve the new Spain. Ortega y Gasset set the pace by organizing his Group for the Service of the Republic, a body of professional men who offered their services to help draft laws and even to administer government departments. It was hoped that political justice would bring social justice, and that progress and enlightenment would turn Spain into a model republic. But Spanish reality was more resistant to the mold of theory than anyone had dreamed. The disillusionment was extreme. Remembering the republic he had hoped for, Ortega y Gasset could look at the real Republic in 1933 and exclaim, "It wasn't this!"

The *orteguistas* had not forgotten the notion of a national party-above-parties, which they had advocated in 1930, and during 1932 several members of the group talked of reviving this plan. Chief among them was Alfonso García Valdecasas, a Professor of Law and formerly one of the principal *orteguista* deputies in the Constituent Cortes.[6] Late in 1932 Valdecasas and his friends established the

Frente Español, a party dedicated to saving the Republic from the dogmas of the intransigent Right, the radical Left, and the doctrinaire Center. Their platform had some appeal to nationalists, and one or two intellectuals left Ledesma's camp to join the new movement, but on the whole the Frente Español never amounted to more than a sounding board for a few ex-liberals who were looking to some sort of national consolidation for new political norms. It is significant only because it indicates certain new directions that the Center and the Right were beginning to consider in 1932.

The far Right did not profit from the frustrations of Spanish liberalism in 1931–32. The conservative counterattack was being led by the moderate, semi-Republican, religiously oriented CEDA. Nonetheless, certain industrialists and financiers were becoming increasingly worried about the potentialities of the working-class movement. Intermittently, they discussed the possibility of creating some kind of nationalistic socialist front. Furthermore, the scattered partisans of General Primo de Rivera still harbored dreams of restoring political and economic stability to Spain by authoritarian means. Some of them looked to Mussolini for inspiration. However, these conservative desires and ambitions would never have found public expression in 1933 had it not been for a high-minded and resourceful young man, José Antonio Primo de Rivera, the eldest son of the late dictator. It was he who eventually brought together the divergent currents of Spanish fascism during the Republic.

José Antonio Primo de Rivera was born in 1903 into an upper-middle-class family with a strong military tradition. The Primo de Riveras were socially prominent in Andalusia, having intermarried with large landholders and merchants around Jerez de la Frontera. José Antonio's great-uncle, General Francisco Primo de Rivera, had been awarded the newly created title of Marqués de Estella for bringing the Second Carlist War to a close in 1878. When his father died in 1930, José Antonio became the third Marqués in that line.

José Antonio was very different from his father, who had been a jovial, sensual man, little troubled by intellectual problems.[7] Like so many patrician Spaniards, José Antonio was educated in the law. He also received considerable instruction in literature and modern languages, and was an amateur poet. Although very popular and even something of a social charmer, he was known for his modesty and was never accused of presuming on his station as the dictator's son.[8] He was first put to work at the age of sixteen in the business firm of a maternal uncle, where he handled a share of the English-language correspondence. He was a good student and did graduate work in law before completing his military service. He was basically a serious young man.[9]

At the University of Madrid José Antonio took an interest in student politics, but despite his family background he spurned the backward Catholic students' organization and tended to favor the liberal faction in university affairs.[10] He was careful never to identify himself with any sort of political activity during the seven-year dictatorship. Nonetheless, he was emotionally very much involved with his father's career, glorying in the dictator's successes and watching with dismay as his regime foundered. As the years drew on, José Antonio formed his own interpretation of the regime's mild but authoritarian policies. He later showed himself to have been strongly influenced by his father's scorn for all politicians and his faith in what he called "intuicismo" or "intuitionism."[11] José Antonio came also to scorn the liberal intelligentsia which had attracted him as a student. The more they attacked and ridiculed his father, the more antagonistic he became toward their insistence on middle-class liberal democracy and parliamentary forms.

When the regime began to totter in 1928 and 1929, José Antonio put aside his literary pursuits and became seriously interested in public affairs.[12] He began reading Spengler, Keyserling, Marx, Lenin, and Ortega, as well as the Spanish traditionalists. He speculated at length on the ambivalence of modern freedom, which enfranchised the masses but offered no shelter for cultural values; which vastly increased national wealth but so grossly maldistributed it that only a cataclysmic class revolution seemed able to remove the inequities. To him the liberal emphasis on abstract equality and internationalism seemed to obliterate the national, regional, and individual differences that had made European culture so rich.

By the end of 1929 the Spanish upper classes were ready and eager to let Primo de Rivera go. They had never supported his vague plans for reform, and they now feared that his continued presence as head of the government would only bring new and greater difficulties. The ailing dictator's resignation in January 1930 thus came as a relief to those who had profited most from his rule. He was bundled off to Paris, where he died within a few months.

José Antonio was deeply moved by his father's end and revolted by the hypocrisy of many erstwhile aristocratic supporters. Without hesitation, he undertook the political defense of the dictator. Primo de Rivera's most acute commentator has written that "in the main, the dictatorship fostered class cleavage and class particularism and made more difficult, almost impossible, the coexistence of the disparate elements of Spanish society."[13] José Antonio was incapable of such an objective estimation of his father's record. He whitewashed the regime completely, and even tried to pretend that the disastrous financial policies of the dictatorship had helped stabilize the public treasury.[14]

After Primo de Rivera fell, certain conservative forces which still favored his idea of a non-party directorship for the nation joined with the strongest supporters of the Monarchy to form the Unión Monárquica Nacional. This new organization was more than merely monarchist; it held to a certain vague conception of a monarchical government that would formulate, above the party system, national policies for preserving present institutions and effecting needed reforms. As the pressure from Leftists and Republicans grew stronger, most of the vested interests threw their support behind the Unión Monárquica, whose superficial interest in a few reforms offered them a convenient disguise.[15]

José Antonio was asked to become Vice-Secretary General of the Unión Monárquica; he accepted the post on May 2, 1930, one month after the formation of the group. He declared that he looked upon this first venture into politics as an obligation, since all but two of the ministers who had served his late father were Unión members.[16] José Antonio had no real concern with the Bourbon Monarchy, and Alfonso XIII's secretary had broken off personal relations with him after the fall of Don Miguel; but he was so accustomed to an aristocratic environment that he did not rebel against the unimaginative conservatism of the Unión Monárquica. His father had served the

traditional institutions, and so would he, despite his personal bitterness against the leading Rightists for their undignified haste in helping get rid of Don Miguel. He announced that his only political aim
was to defend his father's record and to continue his work, regardless
of circumstances.[17]

However, José Antonio's wide reading and energetic temperament
were beginning to suggest to him that modern society and government could no longer be held together simply by the paternalistic
defense of nineteenth-century institutions. Firmly believing that his
father's ideas had been right, he began to realize that Don Miguel
had pursued them in the wrong way. In February 1930, during a
lecture at the Ateneo of Albacete on the juridical subject "What Is
Just?," José Antonio had suggested that the just and fair could be
ascertained only by considering the entire range of particular norms
which might bear on a given problem.[18] Taken in a political sense,
this would seem to recommend a thoroughly open-minded, pragmatic approach. But no matter how tolerant José Antonio tried to
be, he could hardly remain free of political prejudice when the very
name Primo de Rivera was anathema to the liberals and the Left.*

Not until several months after the fall of the Monarchy did José
Antonio resolve to enter politics as a candidate for office. Unable to
bear the attacks on his father's record that abounded in the Constituent Cortes, he decided to run for election to that body; he sought the
support of the Right as a candidate from Madrid in the by-election of
October 1931. He announced that he wanted to go to the Cortes solely

> to defend the sacred memory of my father. But I do not present
> myself for personal vanity nor because of a taste for politics, which
> every instant attracts me less. . . . God well knows my vocation is
> amid my books, and that to separate myself from them to throw
> myself momentarily in the sharp vertigo of politics causes me real
> pain. But it would be cowardly or senseless if I dozed quietly
> while in the Cortes, before the people, accusations continue to be
> hurled against the sacred memory of my father.[19]

---

* After José Antonio spoke in Albacete the leading Socialist jurist, Luis
Jiménez de Asúa, canceled an engagement in the same hall, saying that he
would not occupy the chair just used by a Primo de Rivera (*La Nación,* Feb. 26,
1930).

During the campaign part of the Rightist press maintained a glacial tone, not wishing to compromise itself with any more Primo de Riveras.[20] Despite this handicap José Antonio made a reasonable showing. His opponent, the revered liberal academician Bartolomé Manuel de Cossío, beat him by a margin of two to one, but that was better than many people had thought a Primo de Rivera could do in the Socialist Madrid of 1931.*

After his electoral defeat, José Antonio returned to private life and devoted himself to building up a respectable private law practice. In his leisure hours he tried to sort out his political and social ideas, which were in a very confused state.[21] At times he seemed very discouraged and sometimes spoke to friends about emigrating to America.

Meanwhile, he grew more and more antagonistic toward the old political and social regime in Spain, the regime his father had tried to save through mild reform but which had discarded his father and then collapsed before the liberal wave of 1930–31. Even when campaigning for the Unión Monárquica, José Antonio declared that one of his father's greatest achievements was overthrowing the rule of the political bosses who had dominated the Spanish provinces.[22] He took a similar attitude toward the enormous social and economic abuses sanctioned by the Spanish Right. According to him, the only thing wrong with the late dictator's public development program and system of workers' representation was that, for lack of opportunity, they had not been carried far enough.

On the other hand, José Antonio could not tolerate the doctrinaire liberal theorists and intellectuals. This attitude, firmly rooted in family sentiment, was sometimes expressed in the bitterest terms. Defending his dead parent from their barbs, he had sneered, "Behold the ridiculous *intellectuals,* stuffed with pedantry. . . . How are they ever going to see—through their myopic eyeglasses—the solitary gleam of divine light?"[23]

The incessant wrangling of the Republicans and the slowness of their approach to basic problems combined to complete José An-

---

* Ramiro Ledesma applauded the result, claiming that José Antonio's ballots reflected a "national" reaction against the bourgeois Constituent Cortes. (*La Conquista del Estado,* Oct. 10, 1931.)

tonio's alienation from political liberalism. He declared that intellectual positivism and political liberalism were in mortal crisis, and that the death of liberalism would be followed not by reaction but by revolution.[24] Europe had entered the social age, in which traditional conservatism and old-guard liberalism were equally bankrupt.

If the Right was incompetent and the Center inadequate, the Left could not attract a man of José Antonio's aristocratic background. He considered revolution almost inevitable, especially for so backward a country as Spain. But radical change could take many directions, and José Antonio, as an esthete and an aristocrat, had no intention of becoming either a Marxist or an Anarchist. Instead, he wanted to take up his father's burden of national reform, on the same basis of authoritarianism and revolution-from-above at which Primo de Rivera had clumsily aimed. The difference was José Antonio's belief that the process of national authoritarian reconstruction must be made more radical and thoroughgoing in order to succeed.

Patriotic sentiment was familiar to José Antonio, who had grown up within the Spanish military hierarchy. Though his English literary training sometimes made him skeptical about the capabilities of the Spanish people, he accepted nationalism as the emotional lever necessary to engage popular enthusiasm for a non-Marxist program of revitalization. Furthermore, he was repelled to see his father's efforts to create national solidarity being undone by the regional autonomy statutes of the Republic Cortes.

José Antonio was an enthusiastic student of Ortega y Gasset and other theorists who advocated an elite. This belief in the role of what later came to be called the "creative minority" was consonant with the simplistic political notions on which his father's dictatorship had rested. A small group of national-minded reformers had swept away the political chaos of 1923 by authoritarian means. The same solution, he thought, could be imposed on the problems of 1933, except that it had to be more potent and supported by a real political movement.

By the beginning of 1933 José Antonio's political ideas coalesced in a plan for leading an audacious minority which would inaugurate radical political and economic reforms by authoritarian means, employing the ideological framework of nationalism to enlist the moral enthusiasm of the young. If successful, such a movement would not only save the political integrity of Spain but raise the country to a more prominent position in the new nationalist European order. For José Antonio, this was Spanish fascism.

Practical plans were slow to take shape in his mind. He hesitated for months trying to decide whether he should throw himself into the current of corporatist interest which had begun to run through sections of the Spanish Center and Right.[25] His basic problem was to decide what kind of men he could best work with and what sort of cooperation he could expect from them. José Antonio was not bent on founding a new group of his own; indeed, he lacked the resources for such a task. He was drawn toward both the liberal leader Manuel Azaña and the conservative José María Gil Robles, but he decided that neither could provide the radically new initiative he wanted. The issues of *La Conquista del Estado* had aroused a certain interest, and when one of his law clerks joined the JONS José Antonio sent him to talk with Ledesma; but from his clerk's report the Jonsista leader seemed too brash and undisciplined, too cold and materialistic.[26] José Antonio was searching for a political creed that would appeal to esthetic sentiment and the generous instincts—an idealistic, poetic style of nationalism.

Adolf Hitler's rise to power on January 30, 1933, quickened the interest of the Spanish Right in the nature and goals of fascistic nationalism. The first person to take advantage of the curiosity thus aroused had commercial rather than political ends in view. This individual was Manuel Delgado Barreto, a capable journalist then serving as editor of the Madrid daily *La Nación*, which had been founded in the twenties to serve as the mouthpiece for the Primo de Rivera regime and was still patronized by former leaders of the Unión Patriótica. Delgado decided to capitalize on the new wave of interest by establishing a weekly called *El Fascio*, which would be devoted to the discussion of things more or less fascist. He advertised this venture throughout the circles of the extreme Right and obtained enough advance subscriptions to assure the success of the paper.[27] To supply copy he enlisted the services of Ledesma and his colleagues, who gladly accepted an opportunity to make free propaganda for themselves. Delgado also asked José Antonio Primo de Rivera and a few other nationalist writers, including Rafael Sánchez Mazas and Giménez Caballero, to contribute articles.

The first number of *El Fascio* was to appear on March 16, 1933. No one who wrote for it was greatly enthusiastic; most of the contributors realized that the paper was chiefly a middle-class business venture, and Ledesma even decried the mimicry of the title itself. José Antonio, partly against his better judgment, contributed a vague article about the nature of the nationalist state, which was supposed to establish some sort of permanent system that he never managed to explain clearly. The other articles ranged in style from the weird outpourings of Giménez Caballero to the rasping dialectic of Ramiro Ledesma. Some of the articles read almost like translations of the more abstract points of Nazi and Fascist doctrine.[28]

El Fascio did not survive the day of its birth. With Germany just fallen into the hands of National Socialism and with fascist movements on the march in Austria and even in France, the liberals in power did not want to take chances in Spain. The entire first edition of *El Fascio* was confiscated, and further publication of the paper was banned by the government.[29]

By this time it was well known that José Antonio was interested in fascism and entertained political ambitions in that direction. He now began to put out serious feelers of his own, seeking to unify some of the flutters of sympathy and interest aroused among the Right. When Juan Ignacio Luca de Tena, editor of the influential monarchist *ABC*, wrote a sympathetic criticism of *El Fascio*, José Antonio engaged in a friendly polemic with that newspaper. In his first letter he outlined an abstractly idealistic view of fascism:

> Fascism is not a tactic—violence. It is an idea—unity.
> Fascism was born to inspire a faith not of the Right (which at bottom aspires to conserve everything, even the unjust) or of the Left (which at bottom aspires to destroy everything, even the good), but a collective, integral, national faith. . . .
> A fascist state is not created by the triumph of either the strongest or the most numerous party—which is not the right one for being the most numerous, though a stupid suffrage may say other-

wise—but by the triumph of a principle of order common to all, the constant national sentiment, of which the state is the organ. . . .

If anything truly deserves to be called a workers' state, it is the fascist state. Therefore, in the fascist state—and the workers will come to realize this, no matter what—the workers' syndicates are directly elevated to the dignity of organs of the state. . . .

One achieves true human dignity only when one serves. Only he is great who subjects himself to taking part in the achievement of a great task.[30]

Luca de Tena's reply was apt, if rather eulogistic. After defending *El Fascio*'s right to exist, he pointed out that José Antonio's schema was excessively idealistic and not supported by political reality:

Only place "socialist" where you say "fascist," and the partisans of Marxism could subscribe to a very similar concept. . . .

What is born in the heart cannot be imported. And I suspect that your fascism has sprung from your great heart rather than from your brilliant intelligence.[31]

During the spring of 1933 José Antonio corresponded with family friends, political associates of his father, representatives of the Spanish financial world, radical-minded monarchists, Jonsistas, and nationalistic ideologues of varying descriptions. Each group had its own ideas, often extremely vague, about the form a fascist movement should assume. Among the interested parties, José Antonio was taking the most definite stand, and he emerged as the most likely candidate to head an organized movement. García Valdecasas was too lukewarm and academic, Ledesma too unstable.

However, some of the businessmen who had expressed interest in helping finance a new nationalist movement showed little enthusiasm about backing another Primo de Rivera. They argued that a fascist leader must be a man of the people, like Mussolini, or a front-line soldier, like Hitler; if the workers were to be seduced, they must be seduced by one of their own kind.

A candidate whom Bilbao financiers had wanted to consider was the pragmatic, middle-of-the-road Socialist leader Indalecio Prieto. Having made his way up selling newspapers on the streets of Bilbao, Prieto fitted the working-class description they desired. As a practical politician, he had never lost contact with Vizcayan finance and industry, and within the Socialist Party he had tried to combat the irresponsible agitation of idealistic revolutionaries. In return, Bilbao capitalists had not been above sheltering him from police during the last days of the Monarchy. In 1932 they hoped he might become sufficiently disgusted with the wild talk and obstructionism of the Left wing of the Socialist Party to consider developing an alternative "national" socialism. But Prieto proved to be a dedicated working-class leader and a stout progressive. He refused to sponsor any variant of social fascism, although he later showed a certain personal interest in the national syndicalist movement.[32]

Another possibility was Demetrio Carceller, the director of a petroleum company in the Canary Islands, who had risen from the proletariat to a significant position in the business world. Carceller was talented, possessed great drive and energy, and was not averse to entering politics. However, the total lack of concrete political preparation behind the ideas of the financiers eventually caused him to lose interest; besides, he was primarily interested in making money.[33]

José Antonio was well aware of the suspicion with which he was viewed by business circles, and disclaimed any desire to make himself the *caudillo* of Spanish fascism. He told friends that he would like to help form a more authentic and popular kind of political movement, but not one purely of his own making. He declared that he had "too many intellectual preoccupations to be a leader of masses." "My intellectual vocation is one of the least suitable for the role of *caudillo*," he said.[34]

On March 24, 1933, José Antonio authorized an old friend and distant relative, Sancho Dávila, to act as his representative in organizing those among the upper classes around Seville and Cádiz who were sympathetic to a nationalistic fascism. Dávila did not find the assignment easy. On April 2, José Antonio wrote to his cousin Julián Pemartín, who was helping Dávila:

> It is true that the working out of this idea is something that will probably be reserved for a man of popular extraction. Being *caudillo* has something of the prophet about it, requiring a large dose of faith, health, enthusiasm, and anger that is not compatible with refinement. For my part, I would serve for anything better

than for a fascist *caudillo*. The attitude of doubt and sense of irony, which never leaves those of us who have some degree of intellectual curiosity, incapacitates us for shouting the robust, unflinching cries that are required of the leaders of masses. Hence, if in Jerez, as in Madrid, there are friends whose liver suffers from the thought that I should want to make myself *Caudillo del Fascio,* you may reassure them with respect to me.[35]

José Antonio had found a solid collaborator in Julio Ruiz de Alda, a famous aviator who had accompanied Ramón Franco on the first nonstop transatlantic flight to Buenos Aires in 1926.[36] The Spanish Air Force had been a fertile breeding ground for radicalism in the twenties, but the Left had no appeal to Ruiz de Alda. A hearty, direct, military type, he had served as president of the National Aeronautic Federation, and had filled minor technical posts during the dictatorship. He was attracted by nationalist appeals and distrusted the established parties. After the founding of the Republic, he wrote to the Catalan politician Francesc Cambó, declaring that the republican system was entirely wrong and that a "totalitarian system" was needed. He made contact with Ledesma in 1931 and was briefly enrolled in Ledesma's group, but he never had anything to do with the later JONS.[37]

Ruiz de Alda had helped set up the Spanish Company of Aerial Photogrammetric Works, which was to make an aerial survey of Spain in order to supply the data for a study of national water resources. This scheme fell through in 1932 when government aid was suspended, partly because of the radical Right-wing sentiments of Ruiz de Alda and his principal associates, the monarchist Ansaldo brothers. Embittered at this treatment, they established an "Aviation Armaments" group to lobby for nationalization of the virtually nonexistent aircraft industry.[38] By early 1933 various Right-wing figures had begun to sound out Ruiz de Alda on the subject of a national fascist party. As one of the obvious candidates for leadership in such a party, he was interviewed by Giménez Caballero for *El Fascio*.

In these circles Ruiz de Alda made the acquaintance of José Antonio. They considered themselves more sincere and idealistic than the opportunists and reactionaries around them, and discovered with mutual satisfaction that they could work together. They wanted to found a fascist movement, but on their own terms, not on those of the Bank of Bilbao.*

Ruiz de Alda was level-headed and a good organizer. He was utterly inept as a public speaker, but his solid, methodical talents helped control José Antonio's sometimes unbridled rhetoric. The latter's grandiloquent concept of nationalism as *destino en lo universal* seemed too deterministic for Ruiz de Alda's simple activism. The aviator would have preferred to say "unity of mission," but his tongue was no match for José Antonio's.[39]

It took the two several months to concert their efforts fully, and for some time they worked along separate but parallel lines. The first title José Antonio put forward for the proposed group was Movimiento Español Sindical, a vague and abstract term. Ruiz de Alda wanted to label propaganda leaflets "F.E.," which might stand for either Fascismo Español or Falange Española (Spanish Phalanx). Rightist financiers soon placed adequate financial resources at the command of the two men, and by the early summer of 1933 they had begun to circulate around the capital a considerable number of tracts advertising their idealistic brand of national syndicalism.[40]

This new activity, combined with the increasing energy of the Jonsistas in Madrid, frightened the Dirección General de Seguridad, which was being pressed by the Socialists not to take chances. Between July 19 and July 22, 1933, hundreds of suspected fascists were arrested all over Spain.[41] Ruiz de Alda and José Antonio prudently removed themselves from circulation for a few days, but Ledesma was detained, along with a heterogeneous collection of Jonsistas, Anarchists, monarchists, Albiñanistas, retired officers, and ex-*upetistas* from the dictatorship. Ninety of the more important suspects were held for a week or two, until the police finally satisfied themselves that there was no "fascist plot" to worry about.

---

* In the *El Fascio* interview, Ruiz de Alda said that he favored "a radical and violent movement, directed to the coming generation, with a deep social base integrating workers and intellectuals. A movement directed by resolute spirits ready for sacrifice, so that it would not result in a simple act of class defense or of cowardly capitalism. . . ." (Ruiz de Alda, *Obras completas*, pp. 205–9.)

José Antonio and Ruiz de Alda resumed their organizational planning in August. They hoped to persuade García Valdecasas to dissolve his Frente Español and join hands with them. Valdecasas was
definitely interested, but hesitated to become actively involved. At
the end of the month the three had a conference with Ledesma in
Bilbao, at which they explored the possibility of uniting forces with
the JONS under a new name. Ledesma later admitted that he was
"perhaps too intransigent" on this occasion.* He proposed that José
Antonio and Ruiz de Alda devote their efforts to expanding the
JONS, which would then be directed by a new triumvirate headed
by José Antonio. José Antonio, however, insisted on an entirely new
party, one capable of attracting his late father's more conservative
supporters as well as other elements which still disdained the JONS;
he proposed that this party be called "Fascismo Español." Ledesma
said that such second-hand titles and attitudes were out of the question and broke off the talks.[42]

By late September José Antonio and Ruiz de Alda had completed
their organizational work, and they decided to launch their movement at the next change in the national political weather.[43] They
had not long to wait. In October a caretaker government was ordered
to adjourn the Cortes, and elections were scheduled for mid-No-
vember. The temporary limitations on political propaganda imposed
earlier in the year were lifted, and full freedom of speech was to be
allowed during the electoral campaign.

Favored for his family connections and his proven opposition to
liberal idealogy in public life, José Antonio was offered a place on
the Rightist lists in Madrid and in Cádiz.† He rejected the offer from
Madrid, since election there might have bound him to the cautious

---

*   ¿Fascismo en España?, p. 111. Within his own coterie Ledesma sneered
at the "ingenuous" nature of José Antonio's propaganda, which he claimed was
directed exclusively toward old elements connected with the dictatorship, the
horde of newly retired Army officers, and the big provincial landowners. (See
¿Fascismo en España?, p. 104.)

    † Shortly before, José Antonio had launched a movement to force the
prominent liberal moderate Ossorio y Gallardo from the presidency of the
College of Lawyers in Madrid. Ossorio later resigned. (Angel Ossorio, Mis
memorias, pp. 217–18.)

policy of the clerical CEDA.[44] The Cádiz candidacy, which had been arranged with the help of his old oligarchical family friends, came with fewer strings attached. He accepted this proposal, since it offered a fairly certain seat in the Cortes and a platform for his own propaganda. He decided to announce his political candidacy and the organization of the new movement at the same time.

IV

THE FOUNDING OF THE FALANGE

José antonio's new national syndicalist movement was launched at a political meeting held at the Teatro Comedia of Madrid on Sunday afternoon, October 29, 1933. Free use of the theater had been offered by its owner, a friend of the Primo de Rivera family. National radio coverage had been arranged, and three speakers, José Antonio Primo de Rivera, Julio Ruiz de Alda, and Alfonso García Valdecasas, addressed the meeting.* About two thousand people were present, most of them sympathetic Rightists; Ramiro Ledesma and a group of Jonsistas took seats near the front.[1]

The highlight of the day, without question, was José Antonio's address. Its heavily rhetorical and tensely poetic style set the tone for the Falange's early appeals; and as the first official statement of the party's goals, it is worth quoting at length:

> Finally, the liberal state came to offer us economic slavery, saying to the workers, with tragic sarcasm: "You are free to work as you wish; no one can compel you to accept specified conditions. Since we are the rich, we offer you the conditions that please us; as free citizens, you are not obliged to accept them if you do not want to; but as poor citizens, if you do not accept them you will die of hunger, surrounded of course by the utmost liberal dignity." . . .
> Therefore socialism had to appear, and its coming was just (for we do not deny any evident truth). The workers had to defend themselves against a system that only promised them right and did not strive to give them a just life.
> However, socialism, which was a legitimate reaction against

* García Valdecasas later claimed that he was only asked to take part in a meeting of "Spanish affirmation" and did not know that José Antonio and Ruiz de Alda intended to proceed immediately to the foundation of a political movement. (Conversation in Madrid, Nov. 18, 1958.)

liberal slavery, went astray because it resulted, first, in the materialist interpretation of life and history; second, in a sense of reprisal; and third, in the proclamation of the dogma of class struggle.

.   .   .

The *Patria* is a total unity, in which all individuals and classes are integrated; the *Patria* cannot be in the hands of the strongest class or of the best organized party. The *Patria* is a transcendent synthesis, an indivisible synthesis, with its own goals to fulfill; and we want this movement of today, and the state which it creates, to be an efficient, authoritarian instrument at the service of an indisputable unity, of that permanent unity, of that irrevocable unity that is the *Patria*.

And we already have the principle for our future acts and our present conduct, for we would be just another party if we came to announce a program of concrete solutions. Such programs have the advantage of never being fulfilled. On the other hand, when one has a permanent sense of life and history, that very sense gives solutions beyond the concrete, just as love may tell us when we ought to scold and when we ought to embrace, without true love having set up a minimum program of embraces and reproaches.

Here is what is required by our total sense of the *Patria* and the state which is to serve it:

That all the people of Spain, however diverse they may be, feel in harmony with an irrevocable unity of destiny.

That the political parties disappear. No one was ever born a member of a political party; on the other hand, we are all born members of a family; we are all neighbors in a municipality; we all labor in the exercise of a profession. . . .

We want less liberal word-mongering and more respect for the deeper liberty of man. For one only respects the liberty of man when he is esteemed, as we esteem him, the bearer of eternal values; when he is esteemed as the corporal substance of a soul capable of being damned and of being saved. Only when man is considered thus can it truly be said that his liberty is respected, and more especially if that liberty is joined, as we aspire to join it, to a system of authority, of hierarchy, and of order.

.   .   .

Finally, we desire that if on some occasion this must be achieved by violence, there be no shrinking from violence. Because who has said—while speaking of "everything save violence"—that the supreme value in the hierarchy of values is amiability? Who has said that when our sentiments are insulted we are obliged to be accommodating instead of reacting like men? It is very correct indeed that dialectic is the first instrument of communication. But no other dialectic is admissible save the dialectic of fists and pistols when justice or the *Patria* is offended.

· · ·

But our movement would not be understood at all if it were believed to be only a manner of thinking. It is not a manner of thinking; it is a manner of being. We ought not merely to propose to ourselves a formal construction, a political architecture. Before life in its entirety, in each one of our acts, we must adopt a complete, profound, and human attitude. This attitude is the spirit of sacrifice and service, the ascetic and military sense of life. Henceforth let no one think that we recruit men in order to offer rewards; let no one imagine that we join together in the defense of privileges. I should like to have this microphone before me carry my voice into every last working-class home to say: Yes, we wear a tie; yes, you may say of us that we are *señoritos*. But we urge a spirit of struggle for things that cannot concern us as *señoritos*; we come to fight so that hard and just sacrifices may be imposed on many of our own class, and we come to struggle for a totalitarian state that can reach the humble as well as the powerful with its benefits. We are thus, for so always in our history have been the *señoritos* of Spain. In this manner they have achieved the true status of *señores*, because in distant lands, and in our very *Patria,* they have learned to suffer death and to carry out hard missions precisely for reasons in which, as *señoritos,* they had no interest at all.

I believe the banner is raised. Now we are going to defend it gaily, poetically. There are some who think that in order to unite men's wills against the march of the revolution it is proper to offer superficially gratifying solutions; they think it is necessary to hide everything in their propaganda which could awaken an emotion or signify energetic or extreme action. What equivocation! The peoples have never been moved by anyone save the poets, and woe to him who, before the poetry which destroys, does not know how to raise the poetry which promises!

In a poetic movement we shall raise this fervent feeling for Spain; we shall sacrifice ourselves; we shall renounce ourselves, and the triumph will be ours, a triumph—why need I say it?—that we are not going to win in the next elections. In those elections vote for whoever seems to you least undesirable. But our Spain will not emerge from [the Cortes], nor is our goal there. The atmosphere there is tired and murky, like a tavern at the end of a night of dissipation. That is not our place. Yes, I know that I am a candidate; but I am one without faith and without respect.

I say this now, when it can mean that I lose votes. That matters not at all. We are not going to argue with habitués over the disordered remains of a dirty banquet. Our place is outside, though we may occasionally have to pass a few transient minutes within. Our place is in the fresh air, under the cloudless heavens, weapons in our hands, with the stars above us. Let the others go on with their merrymaking. We outside, in tense, fervent, and certain vigilance, already feel the dawn breaking in the joy of our hearts.[2]

Although it was clear that the new movement would attract wider support than the JONS, it was not taken seriously by the political press. *El Sol,* the nation's leading liberal newspaper, aptly dismissed it as "A Poetic Movement," one largely concerned with style and outward forms: "We reject it in the first place for wanting to be fascist . . . and in the second, for not truly being it, for not being a deep and authentic fascism."[3] Most of the Right concurred, although *Acción Española,* the clerical-corporatist-monarchist intellectual review, received the movement very favorably. An article by the Traditionalist leader Victor Pradera pointed out its similarities to Carlist corporatist antiparliamentarianism.[4] Only the clerical reactionaries saw possibilities in the organization.

The Martínez Barrio government took an almost benevolent attitude toward the new movement. Police protection was provided for the Teatro Comedia meeting, which passed entirely without incident.* José María Carretero, the leading pundit of the intransigent Right, wrote: "It seems a bit suspicious that the first public fascist meeting should end in an atmosphere of peaceful normality. On leaving the theater and stepping out into the clear, quiet street, I had the feeling of having attended a lovely literary tea at the Ateneo."[5]

The movement did not receive a name until November 2, when the official organizational meeting took place. Either Ruiz de Alda or Sánchez Mazas suggested the ultimate choice, "Falange Española," a term which had been in the air for some time.[6]

The Falange was the fifth party of the radical Right to be formed

---

* Martínez Barrio was one of the leading Masons in Spain. This caused Giménez Caballero (who had been introduced to José Antonio through Ruiz de Alda) to declare that Masonry favored the foundation of the Falange and hoped to control it through intrigue. (Ramiro Ledesma, *¿Fascismo en España?,* p. 125.)

in Spain. Among the others, the Comunión Tradicionalista (the Carlists) maintained its customary isolation, and neither the JONS nor the *Albiñanistas* counted for anything.* The leaders of the monarchist Renovación Española had no use for fascism, but because of the great dispersion of political forces in Spain they considered it more prudent to infiltrate the Falange from within than to ignore it. Hence a considerable number of monarchist zealots took up membership in the Falange during the winter and spring of 1934. They were tacitly led by Juan Antonio Ansaldo and his brother, both leading activists in Renovación Española, professional aviators, and personal friends of Julio Ruiz de Alda.[7]

A fairly large number of people joined the movement during its first two or three months. Whereas the JONS claimed only a few hundred adult members in all Spain, the Falange soon signed up several thousand. This initial success was in large part due to the aura of conservative *primorriverismo* and paternal nationalism associated with José Antonio's name; a disproportionately large number of those who were first attracted to the party appeared to be disgruntled conservatives, retired Army men, and ex-*upetistas*. This conservative element was balanced only by a nucleus of students who were fascinated with José Antonio's rhetoric. An aura of vagueness surrounded the political program of the Falange; it was commonly supposed to be Spanish fascism, but each member had his own notion of what that meant.

At this stage the party leaders were hardly more enlightened. José Antonio had formulated no concrete goals, no day-by-day party program, and no general outline of party tactics; he continued to talk of a "poetic movement." Ruiz de Alda was no help with regard to ideology, and it proved impossible to obtain the cooperation of García Valdecasas. Within a fortnight after the organizational meeting Valdecasas married a marquesa and went off on a long honeymoon; he never returned to the party. Fearing that the movement would either fall apart or degenerate into street-gang violence, he had decided to have no part of it.[8]

* Albiñana was elected to the Cortes in 1933 on the Rightist list from Burgos, but that was scant solace; his following, never large, had virtually disappeared. Much of the *pistolero* element went over to the Falange.

During the first months of the Falange José Antonio spent most of his time trying to spell out the theoretical premises of his political attitudes, although even among party members there were few who cared to listen to him. According to his philosophy, the individual achieved true significance only when occupied in some noble collective task: "Life is not worth the effort if it is not to be burnt up in the service of a great enterprise."[9] Great enterprises were formed only by the free and enthusiastic union of individuals. Individuals bound together by historical tradition, material cooperation, and mutual destiny formed a nation.

A nation could guarantee the freedom of individuals because law and justice could arise only from its historical development and could be enforced only by its superior moral authority.[10] Going one step further, the nation could fulfill its function and maintain the integrity of its institutions only by offering individual citizens a common destiny, to be achieved through a transcendent, national enterprise. That is, the nation was really possible only as Empire. When the nation lost its sense of a transcendent vocation and common destiny, when classes and regions pursued goals of their own, the ethical fabric of national life went to pieces. Social strife, economic misery, and political discord would end only when Spaniards once more forged a common destiny for themselves in the world.

The economic correlative of a common destiny was some form of national coordination—a nationwide syndical system, for example—which would guarantee economic justice and increase material production. At first, José Antonio's ideas on economic reconstruction went little beyond this; in 1933-34 he was still preoccupied with drawing up the outlines of his nationalist vision.

José Antonio's "destiny in the universal," which he had derived from a concept of Ortega's, had few practical implications.[11] He never made it clear whether the phrase implied a restoration of Spanish cultural dominance or a resuscitation of the Spanish Empire. Although dreams of empire were patently absurd considering Spain's meager resources, José Antonio was not above dreaming. He was apparently convinced that Europe was entering an area of conflict that would bring great territorial realignments on the Continent and in North Africa. Personally, José Antonio was a repressed Anglophile and even admired Kipling.* But as an intellectual, he had absorbed all the antiliberal propaganda of his generation, and, like Ledesma, he believed that the end of the Western liberal order was at hand. If Spain could rejuvenate herself in time to follow the dynamic new nationalist trend, she might greatly increase her territorial holdings and international influence. In private conversations José Antonio later came to talk confidently of absorbing Portugal.[12]

José Antonio wanted Spain to make a great historical leap, vaulting feudal backwardness and liberal capitalism at the same time. Apparently he never imagined that it might be the possibilities and not the impracticalities of liberalism that were exciting disturbance in Spain, which had never known an honest system of liberal representation. Rather than trying to help the nation resolve its differences, José Antonio and his colleagues proposed to jam the mechanism of parliamentary government and replace it with an abstract system that few people supported and even fewer understood. He thought that an elite or "creative minority" could lead the nation to greatness. He forgot that an elite can control a resistant majority only by the ruthless and terroristic exercise of power.

José Antonio easily won a seat in the Cortes in the elections of 1933, placing second on the Rightist list at Cádiz.[13] Alienated by the corruption of Andalusian politics, he did not play an active role in the new Cortes.† Nevertheless, he took great care to make a good impression there, except when it came to the defense of his father's reputation or record, a matter on which he remained intransigent. He prepared his infrequent speeches carefully, and was very pleased when he could impress such leading orators of the Left as Prieto and

---

* José Antonio's favorite poem was "If," which he used to recite in English.

† Cádiz was managed for the conservatives by Ramón Carranza, Marqués de la Pesadilla (literally, Marquis of the Nightmare), one of the last of the old-style political bosses (caciques). Since the Anarcho-Syndicalist CNT had considered boycotting the elections, Carranza simply increased their incentive with a personal bribe. The voting power of the Left was crippled and the conservative list won easily. (Cánovas, Apuntes; Foltz, pp. 68–69; conversation with Pedro Sáinz Rodríguez, one of the leading political manipulators of the radical Right during the Republic, in Lisbon, May 1, 1959.)

José Antonio later began a comic political novel in English (his second language), entitled "The Anarcho-Carranzists." (Foltz, p. 69; Jacinto Miquelarena in Dolor y memoria, pp. 239–41.)

Azaña. His eloquence and personal charm won a number of friends for him in the national parliament. The clerical reactionary Ramiro de Maeztu remarked that in elegance of figure and gesture, the leader of the Falange reminded him more of the young Ramsay MacDonald than of Mussolini or Hitler. José Antonio's antagonistic comrade Juan Antonio Ansaldo used to tell him that he looked the perfect image of a proper president for the International Anti-Fascist League.[14]

At the time the Falange was founded, the originators of national syndicalism in Spain, the JONS, were just beginning to prosper. According to Ramiro Ledesma, "The year 1933 was the real year of the JONS."[15] An effort to form a student syndicate at the University of Madrid in the spring of that year was immensely successful; four hundred students joined immediately.[16] A syndicate of taxi drivers was also set up, and one hundred young activists were organized into squads of four to do battle in the streets.[17] Furthermore, a few elements of the moneyed Right came forward once more to provide a meager subsidy for Ledesma's radical agitation, and he was given enough money to begin publishing a new monthly review of JONS propaganda.* By the summer of 1933 national syndicalist units were operating in eight cities of Spain. None of the groups had more than a few dozen members, but two of them (Valencia and Zaragoza) began to publish weekly reviews.[18] Although he still had fewer than five hundred followers (apart from University students), Ledesma saw the future brighten for the first time.

The party's prospects were soon swept away, however, by the first wave of interest in the Falange, with its superior financial resources and propaganda facilities. As Ledesma later admitted, "The entry of new militants and the upward course of the JONS slackened most noticeably from the very beginning of FE."[19]

Both parties suffered from the victory of the moderate Right in

---

* Small sums were evidently paid by the ex-smuggler Juan March, the richest man in Spain; by Antonio Goicoechea, head of the Renovación Española; by José Félix de Lequerica, the chief political agent of the Bilbao industrialists; and by the Bank of Vizcaya, which was partly controlled by the Jesuits. (Foltz, p. 64.)

the elections of 1933. It became apparent that if Spanish conservatives could achieve their aims by parliamentary means, they would never support the authoritarian parties. After the fall of Azaña, both Ledesma and José Antonio had hoped to woo embittered liberals, but few of them had lost their faith. The largest group of all, the workers, grew more intransigent by the day. With so little potential support, two competing national syndicalist movements in Spain could hardly survive.

During the winter of 1933–34, there was considerable pressure on Ledesma to agree to a fusion of the JONS and the Falange.* *Jonsismo*'s main prop, its student following, had begun to fall away, seduced by José Antonio's rhetoric and the more lavish propaganda of the Falange. As incidents attending the sale of party papers in Madrid mounted, all available attention became focused on the Falange, and the prospects of the JONS were "paralyzed."[20] The sources of financial support that had temporarily been opened to the JONS closed once more; the business world was prepared to sustain only one fascistic movement, and the Falange was the larger and safer party. At the same time, the leaders of the Falange were having difficulty maintaining discipline, and José Antonio thought that fusion with the JONS would make it easier to control the amorphous reactionaries in the Falange. For his part, Ledesma finally decided that

> the enormous defects of the FE were, perhaps, of a transitory character, and could be overcome. As for that alluvial mass (the Falange), it lacked vigor and a unified historical consciousness, so that it should not have been difficult to displace it from the areas of control. On the other hand, the JONS, utilizing the resonant platform of the FE, could popularize its ideas with relative ease.[21]

Ledesma thought that Ruiz de Alda's military mentality and quasi-totalitarian aspirations were very favorable to *Jonsismo,* and would tilt the balance of internal power.

---

* Ledesma threw all the blame for the separation of the two groups on José Antonio's ideological confusion and his political compromises with reactionaries. (Letter of Nov. 14, 1933, to Francisco Bravo, the JONS leader in Salamanca, in Bravo, *José Antonio,* pp. 63–64.) Meanwhile, Ernesto Giménez Caballero had decided to eulogize José Antonio as the new Caesar in his next book.

On February 11, 1934, the National Council of the JONS, representing the nine local Jonsista groups then in existence, met in Madrid to consider a merger with the Falange.[22] A majority of the fifteen-member Council voted to consider terms of unification, while condemning certain "grave errors" in the Falange which they proposed to rectify. Since José Antonio and Ruiz de Alda were also anxious for union, there was very little difficulty in arriving at terms. It was agreed that the new movement would henceforth be called Falange Española de las Juntas de Ofensiva Nacional-Sindicalista, or, in moments of fatigue, F.E. de las J.O.N.S. All the Jonsista slogans and emblems (the yoked arrows, the red and black flag) were officially adopted by the new organization.* The unified movement would be directed by a triumvirate composed of José Antonio Primo de Rivera, Ramiro Ledesma Ramos, and Julio Ruiz de Alda. José Antonio insisted that Ledesma take membership card No. 1 in the Falange, because of his seniority. José Antonio became No. 2, Redondo No. 3, Ruiz de Alda No. 4, and so on. Each local unit of the Falange was to be called a *Jons*.[23]

In a general sense, the two groups had been very similar, and the union worked well, although the monarchists and conservatives who had signed up to work for "Spanish fascism" were not enthusiastic about the revolutionary dialectic of the JONS. The only member to desert Ledesma's small following was Santiago Montero Díaz, a history teacher and ex-leader of Communist youth who headed the JONS group at the University of Santiago de Compostela. In announcing his resignation in a letter to Ledesma, he declared that national syndicalism could thrive only on the basis of "revolutionary rivalry" with Marxism. The "Rightist limitations" of the Falange would be mortal, he said. "Despite all the merely verbal declarations to the contrary, the membership, content, and political tactics of the Falange are in open opposition to the national revolution."[24]

* All the major Falange slogans, such as "España, Una, Grande y Libre," "Por la Patria, el Pan y la Justicia," and "¡ Arriba !," were coined by Ramiro Ledesma in *La Conquista del Estado*. (See Francisco Bravo Martínez, *Historia de Falange Española de las J.O.N.S.*, p. 23.) The phrase "¡ Arriba España !" is said to have been coined later by the rhetorician Sánchez Mazas. (Ximénez de Sandoval, p. 222.)

Although the personality differences between Ledesma, the intellectual proletarian, and José Antonio, the aristocratic esthete, were never overcome, the Jonsistas strengthened the Falange a great deal.* Ledesma was correct in believing that the revolutionary rhetoric of the JONS would eventually prevail over the monarchist-*upetista* sentiment in the Falange. In the first month after the merger Falange propaganda began to adopt a tone and content characteristic of Ledesma and Redondo; this helped fill the gap between the verbal incompetence of Ruiz de Alda and the fine spiritual tension of José Antonio's talk. Falange ideology henceforth took its esthetic tone from José Antonio and much of its practical content from Ramiro Ledesma.

Forced to compete with Ledesma for internal leadership, José Antonio began to place increasing emphasis on revolutionary aims. He was pushed still further in this direction by the hesitations of the older conservative supporters of the Falange. Although their money was vital, José Antonio began to realize in 1934 that he would have to work himself free of them; if he did not, they would eventually cripple his party and abandon him, just as they had his father. But the break did not occur immediately, for the party was just entering a year of internal crisis.

* Numerically, however, they added little. Whereas the Falange membership was about two thousand, the Jonsistas, not counting their students, numbered little more than three hundred in all Spain. (¿*Fascismo en España?*, p. 178 n.)

V

POETRY AND TERRORISM

WHEN JOSÉ ANTONIO SPOKE in the Comedia of a "poetic move-ment," he was not merely coining a phrase; he was determined to give the Falange a literary and esthetic appeal. After the establishment of *FE*, the movement's first official weekly, in December 1933, he seemed to worry more about finding the proper tone for the party organ than about urgent practical problems. In the turbulent years that followed, this esthetic preoccupation never left him.*

His intimate associates were personal friends and second-rate writers rather than dedicated national syndicalists. One of the activists ridiculed them as José Antonio's "court of poets and *littérateurs*."[1] But he was deaf to criticism, and in 1934 and 1935 his circle at the Ballena Alegre ("Happy Whale"), a Madrid literary cafe, continued to expand. One of his chief cronies was Rafael Sánchez Mazas, a journalist and sometime poet from Bilbao who became "the provider of rhetoric for the Falange."[2] Other young poets in the circle were José María Alfaro, Agustín de Foxá, Samuel Ros, and Dionisio Ridruejo.

José Antonio's interest in cultivating an esthetic approach to politics was not altogether unnatural. All the national syndicalist ideologues had paid homage to Unamuno, Ortega, Angel Ganivet, and Pío Baroja, whom they deemed their "precursors" among the Generation of Ninety-Eight.† Ledesma had once hoped to attract men of

* The establishment of *FE* is described in Arrarás, I, 681–85. Even in the violent weeks preceding the outbreak of the Civil War, when the party had been outlawed and its leadership imprisoned, José Antonio warned the party members who were publishing the clandestine Falange sheet *No Importa* that they would have to suspend publication if they could not improve its format. (Bravo, *José Antonio*, pp. 194–201.)

† Pío Baroja, Spain's foremost living novelist, had written in his *César o nada*: "More than a democratic, federalist organization we need iron, military

this stripe. José Antonio may have been particularly eager to win the approbation of Spanish intellectuals because of the slights his father had suffered from them. In 1934 he wrote a personal letter to Ortega y Gasset, thinking that the philosopher must have been impressed by the intellectual tone of the Falange's appeals.[3] Ortega had not been impressed. Unamuno was initially better disposed toward the Falange than Ortega, even though he had condemned the original JONS; and in March 1935, on the occasion of a meeting in Salamanca, he received José Antonio in his home. He soon changed his mind, however, and accused the party of contributing to the "dementalization" of the young.[4] Ultimately, José Antonio was forced to combat the disdain of Spain's leading intellectuals in his "Homenaje y reproche a Ortega y Gasset" and other writings. His failure to win support from men of Ortega's stature only increased his desire to create a new intelligentsia around national syndicalism.

All the members of the Falange literary group (except the *bilbaíno* Sánchez Mazas and the *gallego* Montes) were from Castile, and like virtually all the writers of the post-1898 generation, they came from the middle and lower-middle classes.[5] Having grown up in the more traditionalist regions of Spain, they provided the Falange with a vocabulary of mystical exaltation, sacrifice and violence, national mission and emotional revolution, a mixture that proved intoxicating to the young. From the beginning, it was the students who responded most fervently to Falange propaganda; it was they who made a political idol of José Antonio, and they who provided the idealism and the first martyrs that gave spirit and strength to the party. No more than a significant minority of the nation's students were ever enrolled in the Falange, but their enthusiasm compensated for their lack of numbers.

In 1931 the most ardently Republican segment of the Spanish population consisted of politically minded university students and the intelligentsia. The Association of Catholic Students always held a nominal majority of the students, most of whom came from upper-

---

discipline. . . . democracy, the Republic, Socialism, at bottom have no roots in our land. . . . The only thing that is right for us is to have a leader. . . . What Spain needs is the Loyola of extra-religious individualism." (Quoted by Giménez in *JONS*, No. 8, January 1934.)

class homes.[6] But the more dynamic and energetic students belonged to the Federación Universitaria Española (FUE), a Socialist-liberal student association, which was founded in 1927 and had become a national political force by 1931. The hard experiences of the Azaña government disillusioned some of the young Socialists, and in 1932 a spirit of revolt began to spread through the FUE. In March 1933, when nearly four hundred secondary-school and university students in Madrid signed up with a JONS syndicate, it became clear that the FUE could no longer hope to retain the allegiance of all nonclerical students.

Just as university students had been the first to give public approval to Ledesma's *La Conquista del Estado,* they provided the active core of the Falange's first syndicate, the Sindicato Español Universitario (SEU). In fact, many of them were the same students. Matías Montero Rodríguez de Trujillo, who had sent the first written pledge of support received by Ramiro Ledesma,* was one of three students who helped Ruiz de Alda draw up statutes for the SEU.[7]

The Falange's poetics also drew some of the more daring upper-class students away from the FUE.[8] When the SEU was organized, late in November of 1933, it already had many members in Madrid, and it soon won followings in the provincial universities, notably in Seville. Its main enemy was the FUE, which it set out to destroy by taunts, propaganda, and physical provocation. In a lecture to the Madrid SEU a few months later, Ruiz de Alda declared: "Our aim is to defeat the FUE, to make it disappear, either by absorbing it, by tearing it apart, or by taking it over. . . . Make the Catholic Student Association fight."[9] In the university there could be no neutrals.

From their first days the national syndicalists had talked a great deal about violence. In the Comedia meeting, José Antonio spoke of engaging the Left in a "dialectic of fists and pistols," and Ruiz de

---

* In a letter dated February 9, 1931, he had written: "Sincerely convinced that your ideology opens a path to salvation from the contemporary politico-social confusion, I enroll myself herewith and pray that you send me pamphlets explaining in detail what the party is going to do. I am a pre-medical student and am at present seventeen years old, but will soon be eighteen." (Quoted in Jato, p. 45.) The immaturity of the young men about to be caught up in Spain's political holocaust was both tragic and pathetic.

Alda declared that Leftists would be treated as "enemies in a state of war." José Antonio explained that although violence was of minor importance in the Falange program, it was definitely justified in the right time and place.[10] "Violence is not censurable in itself," he said, but only "when it is employed against justice."[11]

Perhaps the Falange leaders had not thought their talk would be taken seriously by the Left; if so, they were mistaken. The Socialists were touchy and worried after losing the 1933 elections; the Marxists had engaged in street violence during that campaign and were ready for trouble.* The Left in general, having accomplished little from their participation in a coalition government for more than a year, greatly feared a reaction from the Right. Germany had gone to the Nazis during the previous winter, Dollfuss was preparing to suppress the Viennese Socialists, and the French parliamentary regime was foundering. Spain seemed to be the last great hope of western European Socialism. The Socialists could afford to ignore *Jonsismo*, but the Falange was something more serious: it was capable of making a lot of noise, and it apparently had financial and political backing. The Falange manifesto meant fighting, and the Socialists grimly prepared to fight.[12] In these months the Madrid press carried many notices advertising firearms.

After the first appearance of *FE*, the Falange weekly, the Socialists put so much pressure on kiosk dealers that the paper was banned from ordinary retail trade. SEU students had to hawk the journal personally on the streets. Several squads of activists were formed to protect the vendors from Leftist assailants, and on one occasion José Antonio and Ruiz de Alda took part in the selling to encourage their youngsters.

The Left had already drawn first blood when a Jonsista government employee was stabbed to death in Daimiel on November 2, 1933.[13] One month later, Ruiz de Alda barely escaped being attacked while passing through the town of Tudela en route to Pamplona; his car was seized and burned by the assailants.[14] A major brawl

---

* *El Sol*, Nov. 21, 22, 23, 27, 1933. Political violence during the second Republic had first come from Albiñana's *legionario* gunmen even before the Republic was formally installed.

attended the sale of the fifth issue of *FE* on January 11, 1934; during the scuffle, a twenty-two-year-old Falange sympathizer was shot and killed.[15] Similar incidents began to occur around the Universities of Zaragoza and Seville, where the SEU was strong. Before the month was out, four more Falangists had been slain in different parts of the country.[16]

The climate in the University of Madrid grew very tense, with raid and counter-raid carried on by the FUE and the SEU. A few students began to attend classes carrying hollow books containing guns.[17] On February 9, Matías Montero, one of the three founders of the SEU, was shot five times and killed while returning home from selling copies of *FE*.[18] Montero had been one of the most fervent Falangists in Madrid, and one of the very few who had some grasp of the ideological or historical dimensions of Spanish nationalism.[19] He was twenty years of age, and received a very moving burial.*

This succession of apparently unavenged attacks on the nascent fascist movement caused certain commentators to nickname the party "Funeraria Española" and its leader "Juan Simón the Gravedigger."[20] After an unavenged *pistolero* assault on one of José Antonio's electoral campaign meetings in Cádiz, *ABC* had declared that the new party looked more like Franciscanism than Fascism.[21] The conservatives and reactionaries on the fringes of the party demanded more aggressive tactics. The Spanish Right began to act as if it wanted its money back unless the forces of local fascism could make a stronger showing.

José Antonio's only reply to the Montero killing was a note for the press which stated: "Falange Española in no way resembles a criminal organization, and it does not intend to copy the methods of such organizations, no matter how many provocations it may receive."

---

* *El Sol*, Feb. 17, 1934. Montero's funeral was a dramatic affair, with several hundred Falangists and nearly one thousand other friends and sympathizers attending. At the interment, José Antonio pronounced a laconic elegy before the faithful: "Comrade Matías Montero Rodríguez! Thank you for your example. May God give you his eternal rest and deny rest to us until we learn to win for Spain the seed that you have sown. For the last time: Matías Montero Rodríguez!" (*Obras*, p. 157.)

ABC complained in return: "Spanish public opinion expected something more energetic than a protest in the newspapers, such as immediate reprisals—but instead, nothing."[22]

This criticism only increased José Antonio's disgust with the hidebound conservatives. His own attitude toward the legitimacy of violence was ambiguous. He later explained that the "dialectic of fists and pistols" of which he had spoken was little more than a rhetorical metaphor.[23] Although he had stated in the first number of *FE* that the end justifies the means ("Violence can be legal when employed for an ideal which justifies it"), he was dead set against the use of political terrorism by the Falange. This was in part to differentiate the movement from other anti-Leftist groups, such as the Albiñanistas and the Sindicatos Libres, which employed salaried gunmen. Personally, José Antonio abhorred the idea of indiscriminate physical violence. When the Falange headquarters were raided by Madrid police on January 3, 1934, twenty clubs were found, but no firearms.[24]

The rank and file of the Falange, however, were not influenced by such fine moral considerations; as one member has said, "The first boys to join were more athletic than ideological."[25] When *ABC* declared its "astonishment, in which many people concur, on seeing the state of defenselessness in which the FE leaves its spirited youth," the "spirited youth" agreed.[26] The activists were not prepared to be mowed down like regimented eighteenth-century infantrymen, and a definite restlessness was spreading among them. To placate them, José Antonio was eventually forced to countenance "the law of reprisal," but he would not personally associate himself with its workings.

Physical action was the special concern of the party militia, whose first leader was Colonel Arredondo, a middle-aged officer retired under the 1932 Army law. An old *upetista* with no understanding of twentieth-century radicalism, he tried to drill his young men like a group of Prussian guardsmen. Other party officials of similar background were equally incapable of taking advantage of the emotional fervor of the Falangist youth. Besides Arredondo, there was Alvargonzález, the coordinator for the provinces, and Colonel Emilio Tarduchy, who concentrated on social propaganda. Tarduchy did little, and Alvargonzález confined his efforts to composing grandiosely rhetorical circulars, a task he enjoyed immensely. Chaos threatened to rule in the Falange's provincial organization.[27]

In mid-winter José Antonio began to complain to Ruiz de Alda and other associates that it had probably been a great mistake to found the movement in the prevailing climate of conservative backwardness and Leftist violence; he said they should have waited longer and made more thorough preparations. Ruiz de Alda was less pessimistic and pointed out the encouraging number of new members the party had enrolled.[28] But both of them knew that the initial growth of the Falange reflected no more than a certain vogue, and that their loftier concept of the movement was not shared by the average member.

It was in these circumstances that José Antonio welcomed fusion with the JONS, despite what he called its "crudeness."[29] Ledesma's national syndicalism would undermine the power of the *upetista* element and add backbone to the Falange. Ledesma immediately set about reorganizing the party hierarchy and getting rid of the over-age officeholders; it was soon decreed that all leaders and active members had to be between eighteen and forty-five years of age, although the rule was not enforced immediately.

José Antonio and Ramiro Ledesma planned to make the first major meeting of the unified movement an expression of party solidarity. For the site of the meeting they chose the former JONS stronghold of Valladolid, which now had the second-largest party membership in Spain. Besides serving to advertise the Falange in the provinces, a meeting in Valladolid would help to compensate Redondo for having to remain in the background while the other leaders laid their plans in Madrid.

On March 14, 1934, busloads of Falangists from all over northern Spain converged upon Valladolid's Teatro Calderón. The setting had been well prepared by Redondo's group: the meeting opened in the electric atmosphere of a hall full of Falange banners and emblems, and when the four leaders entered, they received the fascist salute from the more than three thousand enthusiasts who packed the building.[30]

José Antonio, as usual, delivered the major speech of the day. After some rhetorical flourishes on the landscape of Castile (in a style reminiscent of Unamuno, Azorín, or Antonio Machado), he denounced the Right:

> They suppose that we, too, are reactionaries, for while they murmur in their casinos and long for their lost privileges, they nourish the vague hope that we are going to be the shock troops of the reaction, that we are going to snatch their chestnuts from the fire and exhaust ourselves in re-establishing those who now contemplate us so comfortably. . . .

Then he dwelt on Redondo's preoccupation with the charge that the Falange was copying foreign ideologies:

> What characterizes this desire, this enterprise of ours, is the temperature, the spirit. What does the corporative state matter to us, what does it matter if Parliament is suppressed, if we are simply going to produce by different means more of the same cautious, pale, hesitant, and smiling young men, incapable of firing themselves with enthusiasm for the *Patria* and even, no matter what they may say, for religion?
>
> Be very careful with this talk about the corporative state; be very careful with all those cold things many will say to convince you that we are simply another party. Onésimo Redondo has already pointed out the danger of such talk. We cannot satisfy our aspirations merely by giving the state a different configuration. What we want is to restore to Spain a sense of optimism, a faith in herself, a clear and energetic sense of common life.[31]

As the meeting broke up, shots were heard in the street outside the theater. Police tried to keep the Falangists inside the building while they quelled the disturbance, but José Antonio and Ruiz de Alda led some of their militants out to do battle with the would-be assailants. Although one Falange student died of injuries received in the brawl, the meeting was a definite success and provided a kind of baptism of fire for the newly unified party.[32]

On the way back to Madrid, José Antonio proposed that from that day forward all Falangists employ the familiar form of speech (*tuteo*) to each other.[33] He himself was already widely known simply as José Antonio, and it was by this familiar name that he soon became known throughout the political world.[34]

Two more Falangists were killed in Madrid during March.[35] Following the inquest on the second slaying, an attempt was made on

José Antonio's life. A bomb shattered the windshield of his car while he was driving through the center of Madrid, but the occupants somehow escaped injury. José Antonio leaped out of the damaged vehicle in time to fire several pistol shots after his fleeing assailants.[36]

It was obvious that some more effective reply would have to be given to these attacks. One of the SEU students addressed a letter to José Antonio saying, "If FE continues in this literary, intellectual tone, it will not be worth risking one's life to sell it."[37] José Antonio announced he had no intention of diminishing the literary vigor of the party paper, but he privately recognized that it was necessary to provide more active direction in the street.

This task was given to Juan Antonio Ansaldo, the seasoned political conspirator from Renovación Española who had joined the Falange in April. Directing the Falange's "reprisals" and *attentats* was no easy task, for the parties on the radical fringe of Spanish politics were honeycombed with intrigue, and innumerable agents served more than one party. So many of Ansaldo's early *coups* were betrayed that he adopted the practice of locking his participants together in a room during the hours between instruction and execution. One traitor was caught and was promptly shot. Ansaldo soon proved an effective leader, and by May 1 his terrorist units were well organized. There were no Socialist excesses in Madrid on May Day, 1934.[38]

Sunday, June 10, marked a new high in political violence, however, as both sides scored fatally. An eighteen-year-old Falangist had been killed by young Socialists in a picnic spot outside Madrid, and Ansaldo's squad was quick to reply. Later that evening, as a bus transporting Socialist Youth excursionists unloaded them in a working-class district of Madrid, a car driven by Falange gunmen waited behind it. The gunmen had no assurance that these young people had been connected with the earlier killing, but that no longer mattered. The car slowly passed the crowd of young people on the sidewalk, spraying them with bullets. A brother and sister were killed and four other young Socialists wounded.*

While the Falange gunmen were at work, José Antonio was

---

* *El Sol*, June 11, 1934. This became a *cause célèbre* for the Left, and the Communists later claimed that these were the first fatalities caused by Falange gunmen (*Mundo Obrero*, Jan. 18, 1936; *Claridad*, June 20, 1936). Rafael Al-

attending a cocktail party in the fashionable Chamartín district of
Madrid. A medical acquaintance and his wife, upon leaving the
gathering a few minutes early in an American automobile resembling
José Antonio's, were both wounded by gunmen lurking outside.[39]
Having failed on this occasion, five Leftist gunmen passed the Falange headquarters in a taxi some ten days later and fired on members lounging by the entrance, wounding two of them.[40]

There was no end to such reprisals. On July 1 Manuel Groizard,
a young doctor who was Ansaldo's chief lieutenant in the "Blood
Falange" ("Falange de la Sangre"), as the terrorist unit was now
called, was badly wounded by gunmen of the Socialist Youth, who
held him responsible for the latest killing.[41] On July 8 five men were
wounded in a newspaper-vending fray, as a result of which *FE* was
banned from Spanish streets.[42] Attempt followed attempt, assassination met assassination, in regular procession. It was impossible even
to keep an accurate list of the victims. Against José Antonio's will
and even his expectations, the natural dialectic of his chosen movement was forcing the Falange into a career of violence.

---

berti, a talented young poet with Leftist leanings, wrote several verses in honor
of the girl, Juanita Rico.

For the *attentat,* party gunmen had borrowed the car of the young *señorito*
Alfonsito Merry del Val, the scion of a prominent family in the diplomatic
corps. Although the automobile was identified, nothing could be proved in a
full-dress trial, and Merry del Val was released. His guilt is admitted in Jato,
p. 109.

THE STRUGGLE OVER TACTICS AND COMMAND

B Y MID-1934 IT WAS CLEAR that the Falange had made no significant impression on Spanish politics. The initial flood of letters pledging support for it had subsided to a trickle. Oppressed by the government of the victorious Right and harassed in the streets by the defeated Left, the Falange was little more than a splinter group too weak for effective action.

The Cedo-Radical coalition then ruling Spain correctly assumed that the national syndicalist movement was trying to block any moderate conservative solution to Spain's problems.* Accordingly, the government took every opportunity to harass the Falange. Its various centers were periodically searched by police, and *FE* vendors were eventually banned from the streets of Madrid. After an incident in front of the party headquarters in Seville during the April 14 Republic Day parade, the Falange center was closed and all its occupants arrested, along with a few of the Leftists involved.[1] José Antonio protested in the Cortes, but to no avail.[2]

The kind of treatment the party might expect was further demonstrated in June 1934, when José Antonio himself was called up for impeachment by the Cortes on the charge of unlawfully possessing firearms. All spring the police had been conducting a campaign to reduce the large number of firearms held without license by private citizens.† In these troubled times, however, almost every political

---

* This coalition was a tactical alliance between the clerical CEDA and the corrupt, conservative, middle-class Radical Party, which no longer had even the slightest "radical" tinge. Although the CEDA was the largest party in the Cortes, the Left blocked Gil Robles from the premiership, which was held by the Radical leader, Alejandro Lerroux.

† *El Sol,* June 7, July 4, July 13, 1934. During a three-hour personal search in downtown Madrid, one hundred and three firearms were removed from passing pedestrians.

leader of note employed a bodyguard, and José Antonio was no exception; after the first attempt on his life, picked Falange militiamen maintained a twenty-four-hour guard around his residence.[3] Largely out of political animosity, the Center-Right faction in the Cortes planned to strip him of legislative immunity and try him for a serious misdemeanor.[4] José Antonio eventually escaped impeachment through the intercession of the moderate Socialist leader Indalecio Prieto, who had a considerable liking for the young Falange leader and grave doubts about the propriety of the proceeding. After Prieto gave a strong speech in his behalf, José Antonio hurried over to Prieto's bench to thank him for his personal generosity and political impartiality.[5]

Instead of being grateful for their leader's deliverance, the militant faction in the Falange was incensed to see José Antonio cooperating with a Socialist leader. The gap between the "intellectual Falange" and the "militant Falange" had grown wider since Ansaldo had taken over direction of the militiamen and *pistoleros*. These militants had long been irritated by José Antonio's apparent distaste for violence, and this incident in the Cortes was too much for them; they demanded a radical change.[6]

Coached by Ansaldo, they planned to burst into José Antonio's office and demand that he adopt a more violent, inflexible line or resign from the party. Should he refuse to accept this ultimatum, they intended to force him. Their lust for violent self-expression could not be contained much longer.*

On July 10, with activist resentment close to the boiling point, the police made another raid on Falange headquarters, arresting sixty-seven members, including José Antonio and the Marqués de la Eliseda, the party's two representatives in the Cortes.[7] The two leaders were released immediately, but they demanded to be allowed to share the fate of the other Falangists. In obtaining the release of most of the other prisoners, José Antonio made such a vigorous, defiant speech to the authorities that his popularity among the impressionable activists shot up one hundred per cent.

---

* As Ansaldo later admitted, "Then one lived a great deal on flashy appearances, and young people anxious for adventure changed parties (or leaders) like they changed shirts." (*¿Para qué . . . ?*, p. 95.)

José Antonio knew that Ansaldo, who wanted to turn the Falange into an activist squad for the monarchists, was intriguing against him. It was rumored that Ansaldo planned to have him killed in his own office. When José Antonio asked whether this was true, Ansaldo frankly and cynically admitted that it was. José Antonio thereupon demanded that his fellow triumvirs join him in expelling Ansaldo from the Party. Ledesma realized that dangerous factions had to be kept under control, and soon agreed. But Ruiz de Alda was an old friend of Ansaldo's, and at first he refused to eject him; the ex-aviator assented only after José Antonio threatened to resign if he did not obtain satisfaction. Ansaldo was expelled before the end of July.[8] Only a few dissidents accompanied him into exile in France, where he continued his monarchist plotting.

Ansaldo's expulsion removed the most dangerous opposition element in the Falange, but it did not weaken the activist squads. José Antonio had no trouble with the new militia leaders, who were men of known personal loyalty, and by mid-1934 the party militia was working efficiently; the names of dead Socialists and Communists mounted until the Falange had evened the number of crosses.

The Falange had begun its career with considerable backing and sympathy from certain areas of the Right. This support, however, was dissipated first by the literary tone of Falange propaganda (the Right wanted a terrorist organization to fight the Left), and then by the increasingly radical social justice line adopted in the second half of 1934 (the Right wanted nationalism without socialism or authentic syndicalism). José Antonio attacked negative *señoritismo* as vigorously as Ledesma had, declaring that national syndicalism would demand great sacrifices from the privileged classes. Most of the *upetistas* lost interest in the Falange during 1934, and financial contributions dropped sharply.

Ramiro Ledesma claimed that the Falange spent 150,000 pesetas in its first three months of existence. The JONS had survived on less than 10,000 pesetas from May 1933 to February 1934, but after the fusion the Falange required no less than 40,000 pesetas per month.[9] Money was inefficiently handled, and even from the beginning it was a constant struggle to keep the party going; as support from the *upe-*

tistas declined party expenditures had to be curtailed sharply. Although José Antonio had an independent income, his personal resources were by no means sufficient to finance a political party. The party's most ardent supporters were students, who lacked the means to contribute.

The Falange leaders had to drum up subsidies from a variety of sources. A principal contributor, at least for the first year, was the wealthy young Marqués de la Eliseda, who sat in the Cortes.[10] Eliseda was a very conservative sort of clerical corporatist, but he found the verve of the young Falangists attractive. Furthermore, the Bilbao financiers intermittently subsidized national syndicalism.[11] They gave little money, but it helped. Juan March, the biggest and most ruthless businessman in Spain, also contributed a trifle.[12]

José Antonio was careful not to lose his personal contacts among the wealthy monarchists who were the real power behind the radical Right. Renovación Española, their political front, looked askance at the Falange because national syndicalism refused to endorse the Bourbon monarchy; but Renovación's leader, Antonio Goicoechea, was a good friend of José Antonio's and wanted to cooperate with him. Goicoechea and Pedro Sáinz Rodríguez, the secretary of Renovación, sometimes helped the Falangists coax contributions from wealthy monarchists.

The monarchists were aware of José Antonio's personal antipathy to Alfonso XIII, and even to the institution of monarchy.[13] Nevertheless, they were interested in using the Falange if it could be controlled. For his part, José Antonio remarked to comrades, "It is necessary to be bribed . . . the better to deceive the bribers."[14] In the summer of 1934 José Antonio and Sáinz Rodríguez worked out a ten-point written agreement on "The New Spanish State," which condemned liberalism, pledged action toward achieving "social justice," endorsed a corporative assembly and the abolition of parties (which parties were not specified), and authorized the use of violent methods.

On the basis of this agreement, a seven-point pact was signed between Goicoechea and José Antonio on August 20. It stipulated that the Falange would not attack in its propaganda or hinder in any way the activities of the Renovación Española or the monarchist movement in general. In exchange Renovación Española would endeavor to provide financial aid for the Falange as circumstances permitted.[15] The Falange lived up to its part of the agreement, but after a few months Renovación Española ran into financial difficulty and it became necessary to discontinue the subsidy.[16]

In August 1934 the Falange leaders set up a workers' organization, the Confederación de Obreros Nacional-Sindicalistas (CONS). Ramiro Ledesma, long eager to organize a proletarian revolution, had been pressing his fellow triumvirs toward such a move for some time. However, the principal reason for this *démarche* seems to have been the subsidy agreement just signed with Renovación Española: it had been stipulated that if the subsidy should exceed 10,000 pesetas per month, forty-five per cent of the funds were to be spent on "an anti-Marxist syndicalist workers' organization."

The Confederation of Nationalist-Syndicalist Workers began without members, but that mattered little to Ledesma, who had always thrived on abstractions. While José Antonio was occupied with Cortes appearances and speaking tours, Ledesma remained at his desk in Falange headquarters dreaming of great things and planning the construction of the CONS. The Falangists soon opened an office to serve as syndicate headquarters and began to print propaganda. The previous JONS syndicate of Madrid taxi-drivers served as the first CONS syndicate, and a similar association was planned for waiters.* With only a few dozen members each, these small groups could hardly be compared with the massive Leftist unions. They represented a beginning, however, and other syndicates were soon set up in Valladolid and Zaragoza.

Superficially, the nascent CONS bore a certain resemblance to the Sindicatos Libres, the Catholic company unions established around 1920 with official government backing. To discourage comparison, the CONS directors later circulated propaganda sheets declaring their full agreement with all the economic claims of the Left, explaining that the CONS was different only because it proposed to bring nationalist sentiment into the proletarian revolution. The Sindicatos Libres were specifically denounced in CONS propaganda. The lead-

---

* Taxi-drivers were rather numerous among party members, at least in Madrid.

ers of the small Catholic unions replied in leaflets of their own, calling the Falange directors traitors to religion and the nation.[17]

The CONS had one fleeting brush with success. During 1934
unemployment had grown worse throughout Spain, and resentful
workers were eager for any succor; by September 1 small crowds
of unemployed men were beginning to gather around the Falange
center in Madrid. The CONS leaders had no idea what to do with
them, since their organization lacked the slightest power for exerting economic pressure. At length it was decided that all unemployed
workmen to appear at CONS headquarters would be given certificates supposedly entitling them to employment on public works
projects. Thus equipped, a number of workers were sent out to various municipal construction projects in search of work. The first group
to reach a construction site was quickly engaged in a brawl; most of
the men already employed in public works were members of the
Socialist UGT, and they breathed fire at the very mention of the
Falange. The certificates, of course, were patently illegal, and the
CONS leaders were forced to suspend their futile stratagem in a
public announcement.[18]

After this first incident the UGT exerted heavy pressure on both
workmen and employers to boycott the CONS; since both classes
already distrusted the Falange, it was not difficult to isolate the new
national syndicalist organization. Unable to do anything for its own
members, the CONS made no impression on the tightly organized
Spanish working class.

The situation was the same in the provinces. When the Falange
managed to organize a construction workers' syndicate in a provincial city, the syndicate usually collapsed under a combination of pressure on the workers from the UGT-CNT and refusals by employers
to risk further labor strife by dealing with an unpopular union.[19] The
CONS served only to demonstrate that the national syndicalists actually had a few small syndicates, at least in theory.[20] Prior to the
Civil War, these were unable to escape utter insignificance.

The Falange was virtually immobilized during the summer of
1934, with monarchists pulling to the Right, Ledesma pulling to the
Left, and the gunmen demanding more direct action. Although he

was generally taken for the head of the party, José Antonio was only one triumvir among equals. In these circumstances he permitted himself the luxury of personal pessimism, admitting publicly on one occasion that the Falange might fail as a political movement.[21]

While neither Ledesma nor Ruiz de Alda agreed with José Antonio on fundamental tactics, they disagreed with each other as often as they joined to oppose José Antonio. Thus few divisions of opinion could turn the Falange from the course José Antonio wanted it to follow. After he had won back the activists it had been easy to eliminate Ansaldo. The monarchist faction was powerless alone, and it could expect no assistance from Ledesma, a very Left-wing nationalist.

The main differences of opinion in the summer of 1934 concerned immediate political strategy. Both Ledesma and Ruiz de Alda wanted a more aggressive policy. Although Ledesma agreed that there was some wisdom in José Antonio's plan to stage a series of seven or eight small provincial meetings during the spring, he had refused to participate in them.[22] Ruiz de Alda also became impatient at the slowness of the party's progress and its unaggressive political tactics; his dissatisfaction was obvious by late summer.[23]

Ruiz de Alda had been greatly annoyed when José Antonio forced him to permit the expulsion of his fellow flier, Ansaldo. Knowing this, Ledesma suggested to Ruiz that they might also gid rid of José Antonio, or at least force him to take a back seat, thus freeing the Falange from the restraint of his liberal temperament. Ruiz de Alda was tempted, but suspecting that Ledesma was merely seeking more power for himself, he refused.[24]

Despite varied opposition, José Antonio's personal stature in the Falange continued to grow. The students idolized him. With proven physical courage, personal charm, vigor, and eloquence, he seemed to be a potential *caudillo*. The silent, unprepossessing Ruiz de Alda and the hard, cold Ledesma would stand no chance in a popularity contest with him. He had bested his more immediate critics, and to most young Falangists he was the living symbol of his party. His law office doubled as the Falange's national headquarters, for the regular center was kept closed a good part of the time by the police. Whereas Ledesma and Ruiz de Alda were occasionally forced to go into hiding,

José Antonio's parliamentary immunity allowed him to remain fully active and in the public eye.

During the late summer and early autumn of 1934, a group of proponents of the *jefatura única* arose within the party. They argued that internal contradictions could not be resolved, a united front maintained, and a clear-cut ideology achieved unless the movement were given an unequivocal hierarchy of authority. They believed that a triumvirate, unwieldy even under the best conditions, was radically unsuited to control a theoretically authoritarian group so heterogeneous as the Falange. However, for every local leader who advocated the *jefatura única,* another opposed it. Almost to a man, the advocates of a *caudillo* for the movement were supporters of José Antonio. No other leader had a personal following to propose him for the leadership, and only José Antonio was capable of generating the kind of enthusiasm a *jefe* would have to sustain.

At the beginning of October three CEDA ministers were brought into the government, and the Socialists began to plot rebellion in deadly earnest. News of a revolt was expected daily. With Spain teetering on the brink of revolution, José Antonio's supporters argued that the fragile national syndicalist movement would split up unless it were given strong direction immediately.*

The First National Council of the regional and national leaders of the Falange was scheduled to meet in Madrid on October 4. Council delegates had been asked to submit memoranda on a variety of doctrinal and tactical problems, but the principal item on the agenda was the question of reorganizing the party command.[25] The ardent advocates of the *jefatura única* thought José Antonio's candidacy would meet little competition.

Early in the first session a motion was made declaring it vital to the success of the movement that a *jefe único* be chosen immediately. Not all the proponents of an authoritarian state were anxious to suffer

---

* They were also worried by the ample evidence of spying and infiltration by Leftist agents within the Falange. A series of articles had appeared in *Mundo Obrero,* the Communist organ, entitled "Falange Española de las J. O. N. S., an organization of crime in the service of capitalism." Though much of the material printed was false, confidential information also appeared. The informant, a CONS secretary, fled before he was discovered. (Ledesma, *¿Fascismo en España?,* pp. 194–97.)

the benefits of authoritarian control within the party, but great pressure was placed on them by the need for a united front in the face of the threatened Leftist *coup,* which everyone was expecting in the near future. The motion establishing the *jefatura única* barely passed, seventeen to sixteen; the antiliberal, antiparliamentary, antimajoritarian Falange voted to establish the *caudillaje* by the narrowest of liberal parliamentary majorities.[26]

Once the office of *Jefe* had been established, there was only one candidate who could fill it. Ledesma had already seen several of his former Jonsista collaborators go over to José Antonio's camp, and he knew that he stood no chance in a popularity contest. He therefore seized the initiative and proposed that the Council unanimously acclaim José Antonio as *Jefe Nacional.* This was done without hesitation, and on October 4, 1934, José Antonio Primo de Rivera became the National Chief of Falange Española de la J.O.N.S.[27]

The National Council was still in progress when the Left's rebellion against the Republic broke out on October 6. That some sort of proletarian rebellion was being prepared had been an ill-kept secret, and the Catalán nationalist revolt which accompanied it had also been anticipated. The Falange had been eager to do all it could to contain the Leftists and the separatists, but the central government had earlier refused its formal offer of aid.[28] Nonetheless, the party's provincial militia leaders had standing orders to cooperate fully with local governments and military officials in case of a rebellion. When the hour struck, Falangists took an active part in repressing the rebels at Oviedo and Gijón. Five of them were killed.[29]

Proud as he was of the Falange's role in crushing the revolt, José Antonio foresaw a series of similar upheavals in the near future. Once again he vigorously criticized Rightist government, declaring that the October victory would be rendered sterile by "*cedorradical* mediocrity."[30] In the Cortes, he explained what he considered the crux of the problem:

> The [strength of the] revolution . . . lies in the fact that the revolutionaries have had a *mystique*—a satanic *mystique,* if you prefer—but a mystical sense of revolution, and to counteract that mystical sense of revolution neither society nor the government has been able to present a mystical sense of a permanent duty valid for every circumstance.

... Do men become revolutionaries to gain two pesetas more or work one hour less? ... No one risks his life for material possessions. ... One must be full of mystical fervor for a religion, for a fatherland, or for a new sense of the society in which one lives. Because of this the miners of Asturias have been strong and dangerous.[31]

The most distinguished applicant for admission to the Falange during 1934 was José Calvo Sotelo, General Primo de Rivera's former finance minister and the darling of the moneyed Right. During his Parisian exile Calvo had been introduced to the doctrines of conservative corporatism by Charles Maurras and Léon Daudet.[32] In 1933, when he was permitted to return to Spain after being awarded a seat in the Cortes, he hoped to join forces with the Falange and thus unite monarchist wealth with syndicalist theory and youthful activitism. Such a consummation would have reassured the Right about the nature of the Falange, and the great Andalusian landlords waited expectantly.

However, after being elected *Jefe Nacional* José Antonio let it be known that national syndicalism was not big enough for both him and Calvo Sotelo.[33] He had an intense personal dislike for Calvo, who, he said, "had a head only for figures and couldn't understand a single poem."[34] He also thought Calvo was one of the men who had betrayed his father's ideals to the vested interests. Worst of all, Calvo Sotelo was the known representative of the wealthy monarchists whom José Antonio had come to consider an *ancien régime* fatal for Spain; the thought of these monarchists exerting financial control over the Falange made him gnash his teeth in frustration.

During the latter part of 1934, Calvo Sotelo made plans to set up a broadly inclusive Rightist-nationalist-corporatist front. At Jaén he spoke of the desirability of fusing the CEDA, Renovación Española, and the Falange.[35] José Antonio replied immediately with a declaration in *ABC* stating categorically that the Falange would have nothing to do with any such formation.

Once the Falange leaders had decided to reject Calvo Sotelo and the monarchical corporatists, they were forced to define the essentially secular, revolutionary character of their movement. Ramiro Ledesma was appointed president of a new Junta Política, whose first task was to prepare a definitive redaction of the Falange's program. The

Twenty-seven Points drafted by the Junta were largely the work of Ledesma, although they were corrected for style by José Antonio.* Released to the world in November 1934, the Twenty-seven Points were a systematized statement of the national syndicalist propaganda of the past three years. The state was declared to be a "totalitarian instrument" at the service of the nation, and all the other Falangist ideas—Empire, youth, military appeal, social justice, economic reform, and mass education—were dealt with in turn.

The Twenty-fifth Point, dealing with the Church, created a storm of controversy. The statement said only that the Church would not be permitted to interfere in secular matters, while explicitly declaring that the Falange was faithfully Catholic and fully reverent toward the religious ends of the Church. José Antonio had explained all this before. In the first number of *FE* he had written:

> The Catholic interpretation of life is, in the first place, the true one, and it is, in addition, historically the Spanish one.
>
> . . .
>
> So any reconstruction of Spain must bear a Catholic meaning.
> This does not mean that persecution of those who are not Catholic is going to be revived. The time of religious persecution has passed.
> Neither does it mean that the State is going to assume directly any religious functions which correspond to those of the Church.
> Even less does it mean that interference or machinations from the Church will be tolerated, with possible damage to the dignity of the State or to the national integrity.
> It means that the new State will be inspired with the Catholic religious spirit traditional in Spain and will give the Church the consideration and the aid which it deserves.

The clerically minded had always looked askance at the Falange, and early in 1934 Gil Robles had declared in the Cortes, "The Falange is not Catholic."[36] That the wealthy clericalist Francisco Moreno Herrera, the Marqués de la Eliseda, had remained so long in the party can be explained only by the doctrinal confusion evident in the move-

---

* According to Ledesma, the draft was "later modified by José Antonio in the triple sense of improving the form, making the expressions more abstract, and softening or deradicalizing some of the points." (¿*Fascismo en España?*, p. 213.)

ment throughout the greater part of 1933–34. When the Twenty-seven Points appeared, Eliseda announced that he was through; if national syndicalism were not more clerical than this, he intended to leave and take his money with him. His religious conscience was not soothed by the fact that priests had played significant roles in the Falange organizations at Oviedo, Pamplona, and one or two other places.[37] Eliseda had hoped to encourage a union of the far Right, but the Falange leaders now denied that their movement belonged to the Right.[38] José Antonio declared publicly that the Falange was not "a fascist movement"; reactionary corporatists were beginning to espouse "fascism," and the comparison with them was becoming odious.

In an *ABC* announcement of November 30, 1934, Eliseda condemned the Falange and went back to the monarchists. The Falangists were annoyed at his ostentatious defection, but they would miss only his bank account. José Antonio replied acidly in *ABC* one day later, stating that the Falange's position concided with that of Spain's most Catholic kings and with that of the doctors of the Church, "among whom the Marqués de la Eliseda does not figure up to now." Most Falangists were believers and some belonged to Catholic organizations, but virtually none of them followed Eliseda's gesture.[39]

In alienating Calvo Sotelo and Eliseda the Falange burned its last bridge with the Right. By the end of 1934 the Right could afford to ignore national syndicalism altogether, for all its factions had begun to endorse some sort of corporatism. The largest of the monarchist groups, Calvo Sotelo's new Bloque Nacional, aspired "to the conquest of the State, in order to build an authentic, integral, corporative state. . . ."[40] Even the moderate CEDA officially stated that it intended to amend the Republican constitution to provide for a corporative assembly selected by heads of families and members of professional groups rather than by the numerical masses.[41] Members of the clericalist youth movement (Juventudes de Acción Popular) wore green shirts and adopted a fifty per cent fascist salute, raising the arm part way. The Falange no longer had a clear monopoly on fascism, even though the green-shirted JAP was not a very energetic group. Anyone in Spain could now choose the brand of watered-down fascism which suited him best.

Ledesma and other Falange leaders were extremely dissatisfied with the party's dilemma. Although harassed by the *cedorradical* government, the Falange had helped defend it from the Left in October; spurned by most of the Right, the Falange had not attempted an all-out revolutionary appeal to the Left. Unable to inspire the slightest benevolence in any proletarian group, the Falange had cut itself off from all possible sources of support on the Right.

The immediate reaction to the October revolt strengthened all the parties of the Right; for about sixty days following the revolt the Falange enjoyed its first significant influx of new members since November 1933. The political climate was favorable, but the Falange made little or no use of its opportunities. Ruiz de Alda wanted to take advantage of the disturbed atmosphere in Asturias, which was still occupied by a tense and uncertain military force, to use that area as the base for an uprising against the procrastinating government.[42] Ledesma also urged José Antonio to use the Falange to fill the revolutionary gap left by the temporary defeat of the irresolute rebels.[43] He expected José Antonio to use his former family connections to win over the military for some kind of *coup*.

The Falange Chief dismissed these suggestions as impractical thinking colored by emotionalism. In November 1934 the Falange had no more than five thousand regular members and no basis for winning popular support. To attempt anything grandiose under those conditions was irrational, and José Antonio did not share Ledesma's fondness for intellectualizing the irrational. Furthermore, he had neither love nor trust for the officer corps of the Spanish Army. They had cut the ground out from under his father in 1930 and had ignored their oath to the monarchy in 1931. Almost no one had supported Sanjurjo's rebellion in 1932, and no one seemed interested in trying to intervene in the revolutionary situation in 1934. José Antonio therefore considered it both dangerous and futile to become a political ally of the military.* He still insisted on a slow, organized approach to political problems and countenanced no radical tactics.

---

* Eloy Vaquero, the Minister of the Interior at that time, insists that he received reports warning him that Falangists were trying to win support in the Army. The warnings were probably based on rumor. (Conversation in New York, May 17, 1958. Such reports are also mentioned in Vaquero's journal, *Mensaje,* Vol. II, No. 6, p. 4.)

This would have been very well had time been working on the side of the party, but facts seemed to indicate the opposite. After the last of the monarchists left, the Falange simply went broke. By the end of 1934 the party's funds were not enough even to pay for the electricity at the national headquarters. José Antonio glumly told Ruiz de Alda that it might be necessary to make concessions to the Bloque Nacional, but they decided that the Falange was too impoverished to bargain decently; it seemed better simply to withstand the cold.[44] The year 1935 opened grimly for the Falange. With recruitment falling off and no new sources of money in sight, national syndicalism seemed to have no future in Spain.

Pondering these gloomy prospects, Ramiro Ledesma decided that the Falange had run its course. Influenced by the attitude of some of his former Jonsista collaborators, he prepared to split the party wide open and rebuild the JONS from the Falange syndicate groups. He intended to revolutionize the national syndicalist movement or leave it altogether. He tried to encourage Onésimo Redondo, who had been content with a back seat throughout the previous year, to join him. Manuel Mateo, an ex-Communist who then headed the Falange syndicates, went to Valencia in an effort to convince the old JONS nucleus there to walk out on the official Falange.

But Redondo hesitated, as did most of the original Jonsistas. There seemed to be no future in dividing the movement at this juncture; if the main ship was foundering in a heavy sea, smaller boats would stand no better chance. When even Mateo backed out, Ledesma was left standing alone, having gone too far to withdraw.

On Sunday, January 16, 1935, José Antonio called a formal meeting of the Junta Política and officially expelled Ramiro Ledesma Ramos from the national syndicalist movement.[45] Ledesma, still hoping that the CONS would follow him, quickly tried to stir up the thousand or so workers and service employees connected with the Falange syndicates in Madrid.

The next day José Antonio appeared at the CONS office. He was not dressed in the Falange's dark proletarian blue, but in a parliamentarian's grey suit, with a white shirt and tie. Some of the workers lounging outside tried to prevent him from entering, but he pushed his way through. He then made a short, intense speech explaining the present situation in the party, the goals he had set for the national syndicalist revolution, and the type of discipline and ethical conduct he expected from those engaged in that struggle. The *Jefe's* flashing eye and vivid oratory could be quite convincing at close quarters. He bested Ledesma with the quality the latter most badly lacked—a courageous and inspiring personality.*

Redondo, Ruiz de Alda, and all the minor leaders hastened to reaffirm their loyalty. The Falange was now José Antonio.

* After an unsuccessful attempt to start a new splinter group, Ledesma returned to the post office. Four years of political agitation had only returned him to obscurity. His tortured personal quest finally came to an end during the first months of the Civil War: he was shot by the Republican government as a fascist in October 1936.

THE PARTY OF JOSE ANTONIO

José antonio came into his own as a political leader in 1935. He had eliminated his opponents, and the Falange was his own instrument. If he sometimes spoke of the trials and humiliations of a political chief,[1] he also spoke of the exhilaration of public leadership.[2] Although he could never be a *Duce* or a *Führer*, José Antonio was the *Jefe*, and the hero of his young men.[3] Even his political enemies privately acknowledged his charm and sincerity.[4] His only personal regret was that he was unable to shake off completely the *señorito* label attached to his background and family name.*

José Antonio was now in a position to express his liberal "elitist" attitudes in directing the party. Shortly after founding the Falange he had said:

> Until now fascism has been supported by the lower middle class. The workers will be convinced afterward. The comfortable classes must bring their historic prestige to the support of fascism. They will have to recover their lost status by means of sacrifice and effort.
>
> If we triumph, you may be sure that the *señoritos* will not triumph with us. They must find worthy employment for their talents, regaining the worthy position they squandered in idleness.[5]

During 1935 José Antonio refined this elitist theory. In a major speech at Valladolid in March, he sharply distinguished the Falange's

---

* To personal friends, he lamented: "Even for a considerable period of time, to the masses I shall continue to be a *señorito*, the son of the Dictator." (*Serrano Súñer, Semblanza de José Antonio, joven*, p. 54.)

The Falange students of Madrid, who saw him most, never wavered in their attachment to José Antonio, but even they were a trifle disturbed by the picture his enemies painted of him as an Andalusian *señorito*. Once when a stylish, overly social portrait of the *Jefe* was exhibited in the show window of a fashionable photography shop, they decided it would be necessary to smash it. Fortunately, the Socialist youth beat them to it. (Jato, p. 129.)

aims from the "romantic" Nazi method of "racial instinct" in a super-democracy.[6] According to José Antonio, Spain needed a strong state dominated by a revolutionary elite because she was incapable of generating a natural middle-class elite on the liberal French or English pattern.[7] A militant minority would guide the revolutionary movement over its entire route: "In order to realize this goal [the national revolution], it is necessary not to organize masses, but to select minorities—not many, but few, though ardent and convinced; for so everything in the world has been done."[8] The minority would reform the economic structure, elevate the lower classes, and abolish artificial privilege; the superior, not the popular, voice was to command.

It was doubtful that José Antonio had the temperament of a fascist, in the conventional sense of the term. He continued to dine, albeit secretly, with liberal friends; he was too willing to admit that the opposition was human, too friendly in personal relations, to fit the pattern.

His more intemperate followers could say, "Neither Unamuno nor Ortega nor all our intellectuals together are worth one rabid twenty-year-old, fanatical with Spanish passion,"[9] but José Antonio merely joked, "We want a happy, short-skirted Spain."[10] Party activists thought up elaborate plots for assassinating Prieto and Largo Caballero, but José Antonio would not countenance them. At one demonstration he threw his arms around a young Leftist who got in the way, to protect him from his own Falange following. He would not permit irresponsible talkers like Giménez Caballero to speak at Falange meetings, nor would he allow anyone to shout "Down with ——" or "Die ——" during party rallies:

> The anti-somethings, no matter what their something may be, seem to be imbued with residues of Spanish *señoritismo*, which is actively, yet unreflectively, opposed to anything its subject does not participate in. I am not even anti-Marxist, or anti-Communist, or ... anti-anything. The "antis" are banished from my lexicon, like all other barriers to ideas.[11]

Counselors like Francisco Bravo had to keep telling him to be "fascist," to be more stern and distant.[12] It was the firm opinion of Madrid liberals that "José Antonio, as he is known to intimates, is a fascist *malgré lui*. ... He is a parliamentarian unknown to himself."[13] In the words of the Reuters correspondent, "tall, thirty, soft-voiced, courteous, José Antonio was one of the nicest people in Madrid." "He looked very unreal in his role of a Fascist leader."[14]

Ramiro Ledesma offered one of the most acute analyses of the *Jefe*, which defined his seemingly impossible contradictions as a political leader:

> It is characteristic of Primo de Rivera that he operates on a series of insolvable contradictions traceable to his intellectual formation and the politico-social background from which he emerged. His goals are firmly held, and he is moved by a sincere desire to realize them. The drama or the difficulties are born when he perceives that these are not the aims in life which truly fit him, that he is the victim of his own contradictions, and that by virtue of them he is capable of devouring his own work and—what is worse—that of his collaborators. Behold him organizing a fascist movement, that is, a task born of faith in the virtues of impetus, of an enthusiasm sometimes blind, of the most fanatical and aggressive national patriotic sense, of profound anguish for the social totality of the people. Behold him, I repeat, with his cult of the rational, . . . with his flair for soft, skeptical modes, with his tendency to adopt the most timid forms of patriotism, with a proclivity to renounce whatever supposes the call of emotion or the exclusive impulse of voluntarism. All this, with his courteous temperament and his juristic education, would logically lead him to political forms of a liberal, parliamentary type. Nonetheless, circumstances hindered such a development. To be the son of a dictator and live tied to the social world of the highest bourgeoisie are things of sufficient vigor to influence one's destiny. They swayed José Antonio in that they forced him to twist his own sentiments and search for a politico-social attitude that might resolve his contradictions. He searched for such an attitude by intellectual means, and found it in fascism. Since the day of this discovery he has been in sharp conflict within himself, forcing himself to believe that this attitude of his is true and profound. At bottom he suspects that it is something that has come to him in an artificial, transient way, without roots. That explains his vacillation and mode of action. It was these vacillations which made him at times prefer the system of a triumvirate, curbing his aspiration to the *jefatura única*. Only when, because of the internal crisis, he saw his pre-eminence in danger did he determine to take it over. It is strange and even dramatic to watch a man not lacking in talent struggle valiantly against his own limitations. In reality, only after overcoming these limitations can he hope one day to achieve victory.[15]

There is no evidence the Falange had any official contact with the Nazi or Fascist parties before 1936. On the one hand, the Spanish movement was somewhat embarrassed by the derivative nature of its ideology, and on the other, the Germans and Italians could find little reason to pay it any heed.

Il Popolo d'Italia had greeted Delgado Barreto's *El Fascio* with a scornful article about cheap, third-class imitations of foreign ideologies. This blast was unsigned, but Guariglia, the Italian envoy in Madrid, feared it might have been written by the Duce himself.[16] During the next months Guariglia labored to dissipate the antagonism created by such statements. Just before the founding of the Falange, he managed to get José Antonio a thirty-minute interview with Mussolini during the future *Jefe*'s brief vacation in Italy.[17] Although José Antonio wrote a prologue to the Spanish translation of Mussolini's *Il Fascismo* and hung an autographed photo of the Duce beneath his own father's portrait in his office,[18] he had no real personal respect for the Italian leader. He told his intimates that Mussolini had neither created a new juridical system nor effected a revolution, but had merely constructed a myth that the Spanish movement might exploit to its own profit.[19]

José Antonio's only contact with the Nazis, or, for that matter, with German civilization, was made during the spring of 1934 when he visited Berlin while en route to England for a vacation. On that occasion, only minimum notice was accorded him as a foreign fascist leader. He neither attempted to obtain, nor was offered, an audience with Hitler. He was received by a few minor Nazi dignitaries, but no more.[20] In Germany José Antonio was pleased neither by the language, the people, nor the Nazi party. He found the Nazis to be a depressing group, rancorous and divided. He returned to Spain with his once high estimation of National Socialism badly damaged.[21]

He now fully realized that the Falange would profit little by any association with other fascistic parties, whatever their relative sincerity or efficiency; it was up to the Spanish leaders to develop a uniquely Spanish fascist movement, and thus differentiate themselves in the mind of their native public. Most party luminaries felt the same way. One of Ledesma's principal complaints against José Antonio had been the unfair one of mimicking foreign movements. As the Falange leader most closely connected with traditionalist Catholic sentiment, Redondo was constantly preoccupied with this problem. Ruiz de Alda joined the Jonsista leaders in rejecting foreign ideology as authoritative.

At the big party rally in Valladolid, José Antonio had emphasized that every nation had a different way of realizing its aspirations. Stating this by analogy, he referred to certain verse forms in the poetry of the sixteenth century that had originated in Italy but were later developed even more fully in an authentically Spanish style. The comparison may have suggested more than he meant, but it illustrated what he had in mind. José Antonio later declared that "Fascism is a universal attitude of return to one's [national] essence," and insisted that every nation had its own native style of political expression.[22]

The 1934 visit to Berlin was José Antonio's first and last formal meeting with any foreign political groups. Since fascistic movements were nationalist by definition, he declared there could be no such thing as a "fascist international." When one was actually formed a year later in Montreux, Switzerland, he refused to attend it or to acknowledge it publicly. He did not change his position even under the wheedling of Italian Fascist agents.*

Party propaganda soon ceased to call the party "fascist," and José Antonio began to lean over backward to distinguish the Falange from other movements.[23] In the Cortes, he declared: "It happens that fascism has a series of interchangeable external characteristics, which we by no means want to adopt."[24] On December 19, 1934, he announced in *ABC*, "What is more, Falange Española de las J.O.N.S. is not a fascist movement." This was nothing less than a complete reverse of terminology.

José Antonio publicly admitted that a fascist-style movement might become merely outward show.[25] He explained that the Falange sometimes made great use of emblems and ceremony only to stimulate the sluggish nationalist sentiment in the country.[26] Al-

---

* Cesare Gullino, an Italian journalist, was sent to try to persuade José Antonio to go to Switzerland. The Falange leader did attend the second Montreux conference (1935), but only for a day or two as a private observer during another vacation. (Conversation with Gullino, Madrid, Jan. 6, 1959.)

though the Falangists staunchly defended Italian policy from the beginning to the end of the Abyssinian adventure, they refused to accept Mussolini's label. Their own fervid nationalism was, in fact, the only consistently sustained point in the party program.

The more self-sufficient the Falange became, the more it stressed far-reaching economic reform, which it called "revolution." The *Jefe* admitted in private discussion that there was little difference between his economic views and those of moderate Socialists like Indalecio Prieto.[27] However, he explained:

> When we speak of capitalism, . . . we are not talking about property. Private property is the opposite of capitalism: property is the direct projection of man on his possessions; it is an essential human attribute. Capitalism has been substituting for this human property the technical instrument of economic domination.[28]

The only really radical point in the Falange's economic program was a proposal to nationalize credit, an operation which José Antonio thought could be accomplished in fifteen days. He thought it would "humanize finance."

The Falange Chief was particularly well informed on agrarian problems, and his suggestions were commended even by acknowledged experts.[29] José Antonio tried to collect information on agricultural affairs in every province of Spain. He understood that poor land required large units of cultivation, while fertile soil might be more widely distributed. He believed that large holdings forming natural units of cultivation should be protected, while excessively small peasant strips should be consolidated; some sections, he thought, would have to be taken out of production altogether. The state would encourage the growth of new industries to absorb the resulting transfer of excess population.

In a big meeting at Salamanca on February 10, 1935, and again before Madrid's "Círculo Mercantil," on April 19, 1935, he stressed that national syndicalism did not propose a socialized economy but only a certain amount of state socialism for vitally needed reforms. He repeated his earlier statement that Mussolini's corporatism represented no more for Spain than a point of departure.[30]

The nationalist content in the Falange's propaganda was in large part conditioned by the reaction against the Catalan and Basque autonomy statutes provided by the Republic. The regionalist problem was one of the principal dilemmas in Spain. Because of their bitterness against the central government, Catalan nationalists had participated with the Left in the 1934 rebellion.

Although the Falange condemned regional separatism, it did not reject regional differences. José Antonio went out of his way to commend the unique qualities of Catalonia, Galicia, and the Basque Provinces. The Falange did not oppose limited local administrative autonomy, but it denounced the separation of an entire region from the national sovereignty.

Unlike most of his followers, José Antonio was no blind nationalist. He had been educated in the Anglophilia of the liberal aristocracy and admired much of the Anglo-Saxon world, especially the British Empire. Ruiz de Alda mentioned Gibraltar in every second speech, but José Antonio was not primarily concerned with that kind of nationalism. He knew that Spaniards would have enough trouble ordering their lives at home, and once remarked to the Reuters representative, "You see, Mr. Buckley, there are a group of typical Spaniards talking, talking eternally. It is very difficult indeed to organize our race for constructive work."[31]

> I say to you that there is no fruitful patriotism which does not arrive through criticism. And I must tell you that our patriotism has also arrived by the path of criticism. We are not moved in any way by that operetta-style patriotism which sports itself with the current mediocrity and pettiness of Spain and with turgid interpretations of the past. We love Spain because it does not please us. Those who love their *patria* because it pleases them love it with a will to touch, love it physically, sensually. We love it with a will to perfection. We do not love this wreck, this decadent physical Spain of today. We love the eternal and immovable metaphysic of Spain.[32]

If this hard task of self-development were once accomplished, José Antonio thought, it might be possible for Spain to fall heir to portions of the empires of Britain and France, whom he believed to be caught in an irreversible decline into bourgeois decadence. However, this was for the distant future. José Antonio's empire-building began with the hard daily tasks at home.[33]

The Falange's organizational structure was complete by the end of 1934. Party members were divided into two categories, "first line" and "second line." The "first line" comprised the regular, active members named on the official party lists. "Second line" adherents were merely auxiliary Falangists, "fellow travelers," collaborators who remained in the background. In time they were to render important services to the party, but this was not yet apparent in 1935. The most active members joined the Militia, which provided the combative element in the party.

At the beginning of 1935 the "first line" numbered no more than five thousand. There were seven hundred and forty-three registered members in Madrid, four or five hundred in the city of Valladolid, and about two hundred in Seville. Significant nuclei existed in Santander and Burgos, but the party had done poorly in Catalonia, Galicia, and the Basque Provinces. Still, there were Falange cells in almost every provincial capital, and some of the rural areas, such as Badajoz and Cáceres, later boasted over five hundred affiliates per province, although this density was rare. Outside the capital, the Falange's main strength lay along the Seville-Cádiz and Valladolid-Burgos axes.

The Falange increased its membership during 1935, but it remained insignificant compared to the major parties. By February 1936 the *primera línea* numbered no more than ten thousand, supplemented by an equal or greater number of under-age SEU members. By no method of computation could the party's immediate following have been fixed at more than twenty-five thousand.[34] The Falange was still the smallest and weakest of the independent forces in Spanish politics.

The Falange's enemies made a great deal of propaganda about the supposed *señorito* composition of the party. Actually, students comprised the largest single source of Falange support. However, a law passed in 1934 forbade students to belong officially to political parties, and the large SEU following was therefore unable to bolster the anemic Falange membership rolls.[35] Of the regular members, only a small minority came from the upper classes. According to the official list of the Madrid *Jons,* the membership in the capital as of February 1936 was drawn from the following groups:

Laborers and service employees	431
White-collar employees	315
Skilled workers	114
Professional men	106
Women[36]	63
Students[37]	38
Small businessmen	19
Officers and aviators	17

Below José Antonio, the party was directed by a National Council and the executive advisory group, the Junta Política. All command positions were appointed from above, but the suggestions of subordinates were usually respected. Local leaders were simply *jefes locales*; above them were *jefes provinciales,* and above these *jefes territoriales.* Each *jefe* had a secretary of corresponding rank. The Secretary-General of the party, José Antonio's chief executive assistant, was a lifelong friend and fellow lawyer, Raimundo Fernández Cuesta.

The party was strikingly immature, with sixty or seventy per cent of the Falangists under twenty-one years of age. These youngsters were badly indoctrinated, as even José Antonio realized. When Unamuno warned José Antonio that the Falangists with whom he had talked had no clear conception of what they really wanted, the Falange Chief replied that they had "a great deal more heart than head."[38] They were not ideologues.* All they knew of their program was that it was radical, ultranationalistic, and stood for social reform. They knew that the party planned some sort of new economic order because José Antonio had told them so, but they had only vague ideas about the nature of that order. Their enemies were the Left, the Center, and the Right; they hated the Left and the separatists most of all

---

* Dionisio Ridruejo, the Falange propaganda chief from 1938 through 1940, has estimated that less than ten per cent of the members had any notion of party ideology. (Conversation in Madrid, Nov. 4, 1958.)

The first book of theory written by a Falangist was J. Pérez de Cabo's *¡Arriba España!* (Madrid, 1935). In the prologue, José Antonio declared that this, the only general exposition, was a far from perfect treatment of Falange ideology.

because these groups disparaged the concept of the *patria*; in their minds separatism was linked with decadence. Supernationalism was the beginning and the end of their creed.

They were a gay, sportive group, high-spirited, idealistic, little given to study, drunk on José Antonio's rhetoric, and thirsting for direct action. Their only goal was an everlasting nationalist dynamism. As José Antonio told them,

> Paradise is not rest. Paradise is against rest. In Paradise one cannot lie down; one must hold oneself up, like the angels. Very well: we, who have already borne on the road to Paradise the lives of the best among us, want a difficult, erect, implacable Paradise; a Paradise where one can never rest and which has, beside the threshold of the gates, angels with swords.[39]

José Antonio's worst defect as a party leader was his difficulty in choosing capable subordinates. A sycophantic camarilla grew up around him in Madrid, composed of old personal friends, fascistic poets, his former law clerks, and other flatterers. The *Jefe* was far too indulgent in his personal relationships to maintain the coldly objective attitude required of a political leader. He found it very hard to believe ill of friends and associates and sometimes let himself be swayed against his better judgment.

The Madrid directors of the second rank (press chiefs, militia leaders, SEU heads, provincial directors) jealously guarded their own pre-eminence in the party. They distrusted Onésimo Redondo, since he was the outstanding leader in the provinces. They tried to convince José Antonio that Redondo's initial reluctance to break with Ledesma and discontinue his local press showed a lack of loyalty to the *Jefe*. Furthermore, they complained, Redondo had never left the path of clerical reaction, and his continued authority over the important Valladolid group augured ill for the party. Meanwhile, they encouraged the two leading student activists who were plotting a rebellion against Redondo among the young Valladolid militants.

In the summer of 1935 Redondo informed José Antonio that he would tolerate no more of this; he intended to expel the two dissident activists and whoever sided with them. José Antonio realized the danger in letting Redondo's authority be undermined from below, and disregarding the Madrid clique he authorized Redondo to proceed as he saw fit. Relations between Madrid and Valladolid remained strained throughout 1935.[40]

During the course of that summer José Antonio was forced to intervene in party affairs at Málaga and Santander, where the Falange's provincial organizations had fallen under the control of local Rightist cliques. In each case, the *Jefe* dismissed the Rightist leaders and placed working-class Falangists in charge of the provincial organization.[41]

Several times the Falange tried vainly to draw support away from the Left by intrigue. The party had inherited the old Jonsista hope of securing a degree of cooperation with the Anarchist-affiliated, anti-Marxist Confederación Nacional del Trabajo. The CNT affiliates complained of reports linking their activities with those of the Falange.[42] Indeed, some of the CNT slogans were interchangeable with headlines in *Arriba,* the Falange's new organ.*

However, José Antonio was not interested in the FAI-controlled CNT so much as in the moderate, responsible *treintistas*—dissident syndicalists who had split off when the Anarchists began to take over. Angel Pestaña, the *treintista* leader, was said to think well of José Antonio, who returned the compliment. The Falange Chief made his first effort to deal with Pestaña during a visit to Barcelona only a few weeks after founding the party. Pestaña was wary and the two never actually met; further contacts were made by Ruiz de Alda and Luys Santa Marina, a leader of the Barcelona Falange. Pestaña remained too distrustful to agree to any collaboration. A major attempt was made to interest him at the end of 1935, but he and his coterie demanded an entirely separate voting list in the coming elections. Tentative agreement was reached on a brief statement of joint principles—which affirmed a national working-class movement and condemned anticlerical violence—but on nothing more fundamental. Thinking that the Falange had more money than it really did, Pestaña wanted it to defray expenses for a *treintista* candidacy in Catalonia, which was quite impossible.[43]

---

* The headline in *Solidaridad Obrera* (the CNT daily in Barcelona) for June 25, 1936, was: "To the purely materialist concept, which converts the people into a herd preoccupied only in satisfying their physiological necessities, we must oppose the force of the spirit, the dynamic potency of the ideal."

The Right-Center cabinet that controlled Spain's government in 1935 tried to discourage extremism from both sides, and it was sometimes almost as hard on the Falange as on the Leftist parties. The national syndicalist papers were constantly censored and frequently fined; entire editions were sometimes confiscated outright. The party's provincial centers were closed following any spectacular outburst of violence, and authorization to hold public meetings was sometimes withheld until the last minute, and occasionally denied altogether.

During 1935 hardly a single newspaper in Spain considered the Falange worth any noticeable amount of news or editorial space.* Gil Robles' dictum, "The *señoritos* will never accomplish anything," reflected the public attitude regarding Falange.[44] On August 20 of that year José Antonio complained, "There is a closed understanding against us that extends from the Government to the extreme Right."[45] He lamented:

> In vain have we traveled up and down Spain wearing our voices shrill in speechmaking, in vain have we edited newspapers; the Spaniard, firm in his first infallible conclusions, . . . [is] denying us, even in the guise of alms, what we would have most esteemed: a bit of attention.[46]

Falange spokesmen raged against the moderate conservatives of the CEDA, which controlled most of the votes and financial contributions of the middle classes. The CEDA youth movement, the green-shirted JAP, which was hardly aggressive, was dismissed by the Falange as a bad joke. José Antonio declared, "This is the only case in which the debris of a party is its youth."[47] *Arriba* published side by side, and over interchangeable legends, a picture of a JAP picnic and a photo of hogs scrambling for the slop trough. José Antonio announced he had given up all hope that Gil Robles would ever rise to the stature of a national leader. In October 1935 he predicted that the liberal Azaña would be returned to power within a year—which is precisely what happened.

The national headquarters of the Falange had to change domicile twice during the year because of complaints. By Christmas-time

---

* The only possible exception was Juan March's *Informaciones,* for which Giménez Caballero wrote. Even the *upetista* paper *La Nación* had turned its back on the Falange.

party leaders once again found themselves unable to scrape up the monthly rent.[48] Such vexations forced José Antonio to admit privately that the movement faced five or ten years of intensive organizational work and campaigning before it could hope to exert any influence in national affairs.[49] Even in the most optimistic view, the future of the Falange under the Republic looked like a long, hard, upward struggle.

Only this dim outlook for the party led José Antonio to contemplate discarding his well-considered disinclination to engage in a political intrigue with the military. The Falange had to find some way out of its present *cul-de-sac*.

Toward the end of 1933 a conspiratorial group had been set up among the younger members of the officer corps of the Spanish Army. Called the "Unión Militar Española" (UME), its sole aim was to overthrow the Republic. It had no positive goal aside from the very vague one of restoring "order" and "authority" to Spain. The first director of organization was the Falangist Captain Emilio Tarduchy, a former partisan of the Primo de Rivera regime. Regarded as too sectarian, he was soon replaced by a captain on the General Staff named Barba Hernández.[50] During 1934 the UME established cells in many garrisons, but it attracted only young, ambitious, frustrated officers who lacked seniority. The UME was unable to influence events during the October crisis because none of the important military men would pay any attention to it. The lieutenants and captains in the organization were joined only by disgruntled retired officers anxious to get into "politics." As more of the conservative *primo-rriverista* officers drifted out of the Falange during 1934, they moved over to the UME.

José Antonio had flatly stated his opposition to consorting with the military, saying that generals could never be trusted.[51] The danger to the Spanish government from the attempted revolt of 1934 led him to change his attitude. After the rebellion José Antonio had to confess that the Falange was too weak to influence events by itself. In November 1934 he had prepared a letter for the military, doubtless at the prompting of Ledesma and Ruiz de Alda. In it he stressed the lack of national feeling in the Left and the political incapacity of the parliamentary Right:

Whether you desire it or not, soldiers of Spain, during these years in which the Army guards the only essence and the only vocation revealing an historical permanence in its full integrity, it will be the duty of the Army once more to *replace a nonexistent* State.

He strongly emphasized the danger of political failure on the part of the military. They might fail through excessive timidity, which could prevent them from fully abolishing the liberal state, or through excessive ambition, which could lead them to think that they could rule the nation with a purely military dictatorship. He repeated that only an "integral, totalitarian, national state" could permanently solve Spain's problems.[52]

There is no evidence as to whom this communication was sent. At any rate, it evoked no response. For his part, José Antonio was still very cautious about developing such contacts, realizing that he could gain no permanent political satisfaction at the hands of the military.

Faithful to his belief in the historical decisiveness of an audacious minority, José Antonio tried to contrive a plan for an all-Falange *coup,* aided only by a few trusted officers formerly connected with his father. In mid-June he called a special meeting of the Junta Política at a mountain resort west of Madrid. There he outlined a plan to concentrate all available Falange militiamen in Toledo, where they would be armed from a secret cache of weapons and provided with an expert officer to lead them. From Toledo they would march on Madrid while Falangists and a few disaffected military men staged a lightning *coup* on the government centers.[53] The political counselors were only momentarily enthusiastic, and the plan was soon dismissed as impossible. José Antonio's imagination had run away with him.[54] Influential Army leaders would not cooperate, since collaboration was vetoed by no less a personage than General Francisco Franco, head of the General Staff.[55]

José Antonio was already in touch with Captain Barba Hernández, who helped dissuade him from the scheme. He asked the UME representative whether the officers were ready to grant the Falange full political power in any government that might be established by joint Falange-UME action. Barba Hernández gave a categorical refusal, saying that the national syndicalist movement did not have a following sufficient to warrant such pre-eminence. José Antonio tentatively agreed to an arrangement giving the Falange priority of propaganda in order to effect a new political realignment,[56] but it was already clear that neither the Falange nor the UME was in any position to consider seriously a *coup* against the Republic.

VIII

THE ELECTIONS OF 1936

THE SECOND NATIONAL COUNCIL of Falange Española convened in Madrid on November 15, 1935. Many problems of tactics and doctrine were to be discussed, but the essential problem concerned the party's role in the next elections, which would probably take place during the coming winter. There was considerable talk in the air of forming a National Front of all the Right to combat the Popular Front which the Left was preparing.

Ought the Falange to join the conservatives and reactionaries in such a grouping? José Antonio put the question to each Counselor. They could not simply ignore the elections, for the party was nearly isolated and its treasury, as usual, was empty. Some sort of contact seemed necessary. No one dreamed that the elections would be a prelude to civil war; it was generally supposed that they would shape the political situation for several years to come.

José Antonio and Ruiz de Alda both favored participation in the National Front, provided it was based on complete equality between member organizations and designed only to maintain the integrity of the *patria*, with no ulterior political complications. The various Counselors were considerably divided among themselves as to whether the Falange should participate in a Front. Ultimately, José Antonio's will prevailed, and participation was authorized on the terms previously outlined.[1]

The Right had little desire to include the Falange on its lists. The Falange had no electoral strength anywhere, and its presence would frighten many conservatives. When José Antonio condemned in the Cortes the pitiful exploitation of agricultural labor and charged that at the present rate of transfer and amortization Spain would be some one hundred sixty years in achieving land reform (which could yet prove true), *ABC* and all the Right had denounced him as a "Bolshevik."* José Antonio retorted:

> Bolshevism is essentially an attitude of materialism before the world. . . . He who arrives at Bolshevism makes his point of departure a purely economic interpretation of history. Hence, anti-Bolshevism is very clearly the position which contemplates the world from a spiritual perspective. . . . We who today . . . sacrifice comforts and advantages in order to achieve a readjustment in the world, without failing the spiritual aspect, are the negation of Bolshevism. . . . On the other hand, those who clutch desperately at the continued enjoyment of gratuitous luxuries, those who consider the satisfaction of their most petty whims so much more urgent than the relief of the hunger of the people, are the real Bolsheviks, and with a Bolshevism of frightful refinement—the Bolshevism of the privileged.[2]

That autumn José Antonio earned the undying enmity of the Cedo-Radical politicians for his attitude toward two financial scandals which further discredited bourgeois government in Spain. Certain Radical Party politicians (including Lerroux's adopted son) had been discovered rigging a special monopolistic gambling device (*Straperlo*), and a West African navigation company was caught receiving enormously padded government payments for minor services to Ifni and other colonies.[3] José Antonio was delighted to see the government with its fingers so clearly caught in the cookie jar. He gleefully helped assemble all the damning details, paraded them in the Cortes, and dared the moderates to return an honest verdict on the government. He publicly asked Gil Robles to dissociate himself from the Lerroux coterie, if he truly had the honor of the nation at heart. The American ambassador recorded the concluding scene of this scandal in the Cortes:

> About six A.M. the vote was taken. Lerroux was exonerated, his obscure secretary condemned. . . . But scarcely was the result announced when a shrill voice rang from the deserted diplomatic gallery:
> "Viva Straperlo!"

---

* José María Carretero, reaction's leading pundit, wrote a little blurb that year entitled *Don Juan de España,* in which he denounced José Antonio as a "socialist" and expressed continuing disillusion with the Falange.

The deputies glared up into the impish face of José [Antonio] Primo de Rivera, who, with the exuberance of a mischievous child, was smiling down upon his elders. The deputies scowled angrily and filed out into the deserted street.[4]

Although he knew that he could expect little affection, José Antonio began negotiations for an electoral alignment with the CEDA in December. The first contacts with the CEDA appeared reasonably promising. During the previous year the SEU had been able to reach a satisfactory understanding with the Catholic students' association about university elections.[5] Moreover, in December the promoters of the Sindicatos Libres made increased efforts to ensnare the CONS in a larger system of anti-Marxist worker syndicates.[6] There was some talk about the Falange being given twenty seats on the Rightist list, which seemed too good to be true. Many provincial leaders were elated and began to prepare local candidacies. They were some time in being disabused of their optimism.

The complexion of the situation changed considerably when José Antonio entered into practical discussions with Gil Robles. The latter told the Falange's leader that it was illogical for an avowed anti-parliamentary group like the Falange to ask for significant representation on a parliamentary list. On the other hand, Gil Robles said, a moderate group like the CEDA, committed to parliamentary norms, was dependent on as large a Cortes delegation as it could muster.[7] José Antonio admitted the logic of this reasoning, but said that it would be very hard for his followers to accept no more than single seats on three or four provincial lists, particularly since the Rightist Front was ignoring the moderate but nonpartisan conditions for collaboration that he had wanted to stipulate. To the immense chagrin of some Falangists, José Antonio renounced the very small leavings offered by the Right.[8] A mere two or three seats was insulting to the party leaders, and the acceptance of such meager representation could never be explained to the rank-and-file militants. The Falange would have to go it alone.

Although José Antonio referred to the elections as "the masked dance," the Falange had begun to prepare its own lists of candidates. Instructions and material for a preliminary "Campaign of Penetration and Propaganda" had been sent out as early as October 15, before the

National Council meeting. Candidacies were listed in Madrid and in eighteen provinces where there was some scant possibility that a nominee might be elected. José Antonio stood for election in the capital and in six other regions. Among the other Falange candidates for one or more districts were Onésimo Redondo, Julio Ruiz de Alda, Raimundo Fernández Cuesta, Rafael Sánchez Mazas, Manuel Hedilla (*jefe provincial* of Santander), José Sáinz (*jefe provincial* of Toledo), Sancho Dávila (*jefe territorial* of Andalusia), and Jesús Muro (*jefe territorial* of Upper Aragon).[9] The party had a great deal of difficulty even obtaining registration in some areas, owing to obstruction from the conservatives.[10] At Burgos, José Antonio had to restrain local leaders from going ahead with a candidacy in conjunction with wealthy Rightist fringe elements.[11]

In its electoral propaganda the Falange stressed land reform, the promotion of local industry, and full employment. At Santander, José Antonio promised that if the Falange should come to power, credit facilities would be nationalized within fifteen days.[12] On another occasion he was reported as saying, in a moment of excitement, that one of the Falange's first governmental acts would be to hang Juan March, the multimillionaire smuggler.[13]

The most telling part of the Falange's propaganda was its ridicule of the negative nature of the Frente Nacional, with its "supposition that the union of various dwarfs suffices to make a giant."[14] Falange tracts alleged that "the parties [of the Frente Nacional] only grouped themselves together for fear of the common enemy. They did not see that against an aggressive faith one must oppose a combative, active belief, not an inert slogan of resistance."[15] "It does not suffice to come singing hymns." At Cáceres, José Antonio cried: "Less 'Down with this' and 'Against that,' and more 'Arriba España'!" He emphasized that the old battle cry was not "Abajo los moros!" but "Santiago y cierra España!"[16]

The elections were being administered by a caretaker government headed by the moderate leader Manuel Portela Valladares. Alcalá Zamora, the President, had personally chosen Portela to try to form a political third force during the electoral campaign period; he hoped that such a force might keep the Republic from foundering on the extremism of the Left or Right. Portela had no success whatever in this endeavor. It was much too late to overcome the polarization of Spanish politics.*

As the election date neared, the conservatives became increasingly displeased with the Falange. The Right declared that the only result of the Falange's obstinacy in presenting its own candidates would be a subtraction of votes from the conservative lists, which would play into the hands of the Left. The only interest stimulated by the Falange ticket in Madrid was a press campaign encouraging the party to withdraw. *ABC* flattered the Falangists by saying that their activists were worth several times as much as the more timid conservative youth, but it urged them to take the long view since they were anti-parliamentary in ideology:

> Falange Española is not in a position to expect that the four candidates it presents [in Madrid] will win seats. To persist nonetheless in the struggle will reduce not only the electoral body in favor of the candidates of the united Right, but also the spiritual force with which Falange Española can present itself to public opinion after the elections.[17]

By the end of January a regular procession of society ladies and civic leaders had marched into José Antonio's office to request that the Falange retire from the campaign.

The Falange Chief received the cold shoulder from his former Right-wing colleagues during his personal campaign for re-election in Cádiz. He would have liked to renew the independent alliance of 1933, but this time the conservatives wanted no part of him. The local *caciques* charged that he had not effectively represented their interests in Madrid, explaining that he had failed to join properly in promoting a certain sugar refinery and a new alcohol law that would have benefited their area. José Antonio had not been a good pork-barreler. The Falange in Andalusia was without funds and without hope.[18]

Despite alternate pressure and scorn from the Right, the party

* It is said that Portela asked the Falange to join a national third force if it were really sincere about being above Left and Right. According to this account, Portela offered José Antonio the Ministry of Agriculture in the new cabinet that would issue from victory, but José Antonio was not interested. (Ximénez de Sandoval, p. 622.)

retained its electoral lists and its independence. The only agreements made during the campaign were certain vague accords on the provincial level, which provided that the Falange militia would support the military should the Left win the election and the Army declare a state of war. In his last major speech of the campaign José Antonio warned: "If the result of the balloting is contrary, dangerously contrary, to the eternal destiny of Spain, the forces of the Falange will cast those ballots into the lowest depths of scorn."[19]

Huge campaign posters showing the pontifical countenance of Gil Robles stared down on Spanish cities as the balloting took place on February 16, 1936. But despite all the money expended by the Rightist bloc, the Left won a clear, if not numerically overwhelming, victory. Frightened conservative politicians tried to persuade Francisco Franco and other leading generals to declare martial law, but Franco refused to act.[20]

The Falange mustered less than five thousand votes in Madrid and about four thousand in Valladolid, which were, respectively, 1.19 and 4 per cent of the total vote in those cities. José Antonio received only 6,965 votes in his bid for re-election at Cádiz. The total party vote was slightly over forty thousand.[21] Not a single Falangist was elected, and José Antonio was reduced to the status of a private citizen.

The Popular Front victory came as something of a shock to all the non-Leftist forces, even the Falange. In December, José Antonio had prophesied a narrow margin for the Popular Front, but he was surprised by the scope of the Leftist victory.[22] From the pages of *Arriba* he attempted to rally his forces. His first reaction was to encourage the militants by declaring that the party had a total following of one hundred thousand, if one added to its electoral votes the mass of party enthusiasts under twenty-one. He seemed to fear the effects of another season in the wilderness.

However, the new perspective was not entirely dark for the Falange. The conservative wager on free elections had failed, as José Antonio said it would, and Manuel Azaña had been returned to power, as José Antonio had predicted. Moderate measures having failed, the nonliberal groups could now hope to wrest control from the Left and Left-Center only by resorting to radical methods.

The general reaction among the Falange militants was one of

euphoria. For two and a half years the national syndicalist movement had been repressed by the heavy hand of the dominant Right. Membership and money had been denied the Falange because the methods of the CEDA had prevailed. Now that the Gil Robles–Herrera policy of moderation, compromise, and parliamentarianism had been shattered, there was no immediate future for the Right in the Cortes.* Cocky young Falangists felt that their hour had arrived. As the *jefe local* of Seville wrote:

> After the elections of February, I had absolute faith in the triumph of the Falange because we considered the Right, our most difficult enemy, ruined and eliminated. Its disaster constituted for us a fabulous advance and the inheritance of its best youth. Furthermore, we held the failure of the Popular Front to be an absolute certainty, because of its internal disorganization and its frankly antinational position, openly opposed to the feelings of a great mass of Spaniards. Our task consisted simply in widening our base of support among the working class.[23]

Some Leftists complained that the young Falangists, who had failed to elect even the proverbial dogcatcher, were behaving as though they had actually won the contest.

José Antonio himself was not so self-confident as his young followers. He had his moments of hope and optimism, but he knew that in itself the defeat of the orthodox Right did little to promote the future of the Falange. The elections had changed nothing in the basic nature of his party; if anything, they had merely emphasized its isolation and lack of support. Moreover, he now understood better and feared more greatly the growing chasm between the Left and the Right. He knew that the Right, although momentarily confused, would make a strong effort to regain its position. And if the moderate methods of Gil Robles were abandoned for the extremism of Calvo Sotelo, it was not at all clear that the Falange would profit by the change.

---

* The Bloque Nacional had said the same thing, but it was no more than a coalition of splinter groups from the radical Right largely representing five big banks and several dozen *latifundistas*. The Bloque Nacional was only slightly bigger than the Falange, and had considerably less élan; its only virtue was that it had a great deal more money.

The Falange had long proclaimed the inefficacy of parliamentary tactics and had preached national syndicalist revolution. But since there was no necessary connection between these two ideas, the Right could now admit the first without accepting the second. Ever since the founding of the party, the Right had labored to capture the Falangists as shock troops of reaction; under the new order in Spanish politics, this desire would only be greater.

By 1936 José Antonio believed that the entrenched conservatives could be even more dangerous for the Falange than the proto-Marxist Left. He told *Arriba* editorialists to concentrate their fire on the discredited Right and to go easy on the liberal leaders of the Popular Front. José Antonio wanted to be sure that his followers would not forget who was actually responsible for the perilous situation in which Spain found herself. He proposed that Azaña be given a final opportunity to carry out a national liberal revolution. Four months earlier he had written:

> It will be useless to try to find . . . greater sloth and futility than that shown by the Spanish Right. . . . [The return of] Azaña is in sight. . . . Azaña will once more have in his hands the Caesarian opportunity of realizing, *even against the cries of the masses,* the revolutionary destiny that will have twice elected him.[24]

On the day after the elections *Arriba* declared that "Spain can no longer avoid fulfilling her national revolution." José Antonio said that even universal suffrage had accomplished a few desirable things: it had repudiated the conservative *bienio negro,* checked Basque separatism, and encouraged "the least frenetic" elements of the Left. He reiterated the emphasis of one of his electoral speeches:

> In the depths of our souls there vibrates a sympathy toward many people of the Left, who have arrived at hatred by the same path which has led us to love—criticism of a sad, mediocre, miserable, and melancholy Spain.[25]

. . .

> The present moment is dangerous, but it is tense and alive; it could end in catastrophe, but it could also end with positive results.[26]

On February 21, in a circular issued to local leaders throughout Spain, José Antonio stated:

The *jefes* will see that no one adopts an attitude of hostility toward the new government or of solidarity with the defeated Rightist forces. . . .

Our militants will utterly ignore all blandishments for taking part in conspiracies, projects of *coup d'état,* alliances with forces of "order," and other things of similar nature.[27]

All new members would be required to pass through a definite period of probation before receiving any place of responsibility in the party. Now, more than ever, no one was to be permitted to buy his way into the Falange.

José Antonio retained his distrust of military conspirators, and he was not invited to the first conversations of scheming officers in Madrid. He still wanted to avoid being caught up in a revolt led either by the UME or by intriguing generals. Although he kept in contact with such groups, he reserved a free hand for another sort of maneuver.[28]

The Falange's fundamental goal on the morrow of the elections was the same as Ramiro Ledesma's in 1931: to nationalize the revolutionary aspirations of the Spanish Left. José Antonio emphasized that Falange leaders must make even greater efforts to attract dissidents from the CNT and the Socialist Party.[29] One or two unstable sectors of the Andalusian CNT were won over in the months that followed, but José Antonio had an even more important plan.

Of all the leaders of the Spanish Left, the one he most admired was Indalecio Prieto. José Antonio respected Prieto for his political capacity, his grasp of economics, his moderation, his refusal to indulge in the antinational radicalism of the Left Socialists, and his personal generosity. He had long lamented the fact that it was seemingly impossible to attract men like Prieto to the Falange. He fully recognized the great value of having a leader with a working-class background at the head of a nationalist revolution. José Antonio resolved to make a serious effort to reach an understanding with Prieto.

Through mutual acquaintances the Falange Chief got in touch with Juan Negrín, a member of the *prietista* faction within the Socialist Party. He let it be known that he was interested in uniting the Falange with the moderate, national-minded elements among the Socialists. José Antonio even suggested that Prieto assume the leadership of a united Socialist Falange, in which the former *Jefe* would accept a subordinate position. Such an organization might hope to win over the *treintistas* and all the noninternationalist, anti-Marxist members of the CNT.

But Prieto refused to negotiate; he had already set himself against any dealings with the Falange. After the victory of the Popular Front, the Largo Caballero radicals were making Prieto's own position within the party very insecure; he had no room to maneuver freely. José Antonio's overtures were repulsed.[30]

This scheme proved to be another of José Antonio's unattainable projects. There was no opening for the Falange on the Left. Given the power structure of Spanish politics, it was only natural that the weak and insignificant Falange should gravitate in the perilous direction of the Right. Whether this gravitation should actually take place would depend on the success of the Right in launching its counter-attack.

During the weeks after the elections the size of the party swelled considerably. The most restless and discontented *Japistas* moved in the direction of national syndicalism. Young Rightists eager for action were inevitably attracted to the most dynamic-sounding group outside the Popular Front. Although no figures are available, it is likely that the membership of the Falange doubled within a few months.

During March and April a certain veering to the Right by the Falange became inevitable. As enrollment leaped ahead conservatives once more stepped up their financial contributions. The virtually complete polarization of political forces resulted in an increased wave of street brawls and acts of violence. The Falange had to bear the brunt of the skirmishing for the non-Leftist forces; this, after all, was what the conservatives wanted to pay for.

Soon after the elections Portela Valladares had summoned José Antonio to the government offices in the Puerta del Sol. The prime minister, then on his way out, informed the Falange Chief that the Left was behaving itself fairly well and that the Falangists would henceforth be held responsible for any violence occurring in the country. José Antonio replied that what was really needed were arms to protect the Falangists from Leftists.[31]

The *Jefe* was dismayed at the rapid degeneration of political and economic order in Spain. In so turbulent an atmosphere, it was impossible to carry out constructive work even if an opportunity should present itself. The Socialist Youth were about to join the Communist Youth, and the Leftist militia were sure that their hour had arrived. They looked on the Falange as the most dangerous physical arm of the forces of reaction, and they had no intention of letting it grow any stronger.

There had been no real letup in the street violence which had plagued the radical fringe of Spanish politics since the winter of 1934. The wheel of fire now began to move more rapidly, and the number of Falange dead passed twenty, then thirty, with corresponding losses to the Left. The party adopted the policy of hiring mercenary *pistoleros,* at least in Madrid, to guard its leaders and carry out raids and reprisals.* The Falange militia and its Leftist opponents rapidly took on the character of armed bands. On March 1, 1936, in order to strengthen the party's forces, José Antonio ordered all members of the SEU to enlist themselves in the Falange militia.[32]

Nonetheless, José Antonio did not wish to contribute irresponsibly to the destruction of order in Spain. Four Falangists were killed by Leftists in Seville within three weeks, and still the *Jefe Nacional* did not authorize direct reprisals. Finally, after a fifth Falangist was slain, the local leadership in Seville took the initiative and began a series of assaults on prominent Leftists.[33]

In this state of affairs, the new prime minister, who liked José Antonio, feared further attempts might be made on the Falange leader's life. Azaña sent a mutual friend to warn José Antonio that Socialist and Communist gunmen were planning to eliminate him. The *Jefe* replied arrogantly that not his but Azaña's life was in danger,

---

* Ansaldo admits this (p. 78) but many Falangists have stoutly denied it. The Reuters correspondent was acquainted with one of the gunmen, an unemployed mechanic who hadn't found work for two years until he was hired by the Falange (Buckley, p. 129).

Most of the professional *pistoleros* were ex-legionnaires from Morocco. When police arrested some of them in April 1936, *Mundo Obrero* printed what purported to be case histories. On the other hand, Narciso Perales, a young militant from Seville who received the party's highest decoration for his bravery there, insisted that the young people in Seville did all their own dirty work. (Conversations in Madrid, Jan. 9 and 13, 1959.)

because should anything happen to José Antonio, Falange activists would take revenge on the prime minister.[34]

Within a fortnight the situation got completely out of hand. SEU activists decided to strike an audacious blow against the Left on their own initiative. On March 11 they sent a band of gunmen to assassinate the eminent Socialist Professor of Law, Jiménez de Asúa. They missed their man but killed his bodyguard.[35]

With the tide of violence rising daily, the weak liberal government finally tried to control the situation by suppressing the Falange, which it considered one of the principal sources of disorder. Early on the morning of March 14, 1936, the Falange Española de las J. O. N. S. was declared outlawed. All members of the Junta Política who could be located in Madrid were arrested and jailed in the Cárcel Modelo.[36] Only one or two of them managed to escape.

THE FALANGE INTO THE HOLOCAUST

AFTER THE POPULAR FRONT victory, many Army officers began to consider resorting to force, but it was extremely difficult for them to work together. Most men in the officer corps were of moderately liberal, petit-bourgeois background, and they were not inspired by fascistic ideology or by reactionary nostalgia for the monarchy. The UME was only a small minority, and most of the more important generals distrusted each other. During March and April various ineffective plots were fomented, but they were confined to local garrisons, and had no broad support. In April two different groups were uncovered in Madrid and several leading officers arrested.

The strongest nucleus of conspiracy developed in the Pamplona garrison. The commander there was General Emilio Mola, the last national police chief for the Monarchy and more recently the military commander of Morocco. Toward the end of April Mola made contact with the UME cell among his forces. The cell placed itself under his orders and began to feel out other garrisons in the north and east. The need for establishing some sort of central conspiratorial network became increasingly plain in May, for although the UME was willing to work through and under Mola, the honorary leader of all the military conspirators was General Sanjurjo, the nominal chief of the abortive 1932 revolt. On May 30, Sanjurjo, living ineffectually in Portuguese exile, gave his blessing to Mola's *de facto* position as leader of the plot.

So far only junior officers had expressed much interest in the conspiracy. During June Mola devoted his efforts to consolidating his support and drawing in more generals. To attract commanding officers was difficult, for most of them were generally satisfied with their station and not anxious to rebel against the government. The majority of the officer corps remained undecided, and reacted only gradually to the rampant civil disorder. Mola originally scheduled the Army rebellion for June 20, but it had to be postponed for lack of support.

The conspirators were determined to establish an all-military directorate that would force the Republic into a more conservative mold. They did not intend to destroy the republican form of government, nor even necessarily to establish a corporative chamber. Furthermore, they were determined to have nothing to do with politicians and took none of them into their confidence.[1]

Faced with so much indecisiveness in the military, Mola began to worry about means of beating down the workers in Madrid. In this situation civilian auxiliaries began to seem valuable. The only non-Leftist militia groups available were those of the Falange and the Comunión Tradicionalista. Negotiations with José Antonio were opened on May 29, and Manuel Fal Conde, the Carlist leader, was approached early in June. In general things went so badly for Mola that on July 1 he almost resigned. However, other officers soon offered their support and the Falange definitely decided to join the conspiracy.

There was no political unity behind the revolt. The attitude of the very prudent and extremely influential General Franco remained in doubt until late in the day, while the Carlists stayed outside the conspiracy until July 12. Despite the latter's adherence, most of the leading conspirators, such as Mola, Goded, Cabanellas, and Queipo de Llano, entertained a decided antipathy to the monarchical form of government. Even Franco agreed that the Moroccan troops would act only under the flag of the Republic.[2] This prolonged confusion became apparent when the rebellion began.

The events of February and March 1936 brought about the death of José Antonio's short-lived party, but they marked the beginning of a new process, bathed in blood and steeped in frustration, which was to make an enlarged, reorganized Falange into Spain's *partido del Estado*.

After March 14 the Falange's position became impossible. With José Antonio and the principal leaders imprisoned, the party organization disrupted, and the membership driven underground, all political prospects for the movement vanished. A clear choice remained:

either give up the struggle entirely or attempt a direct *coup*, singly or in collaboration, against the Republican regime. Obviously, only the latter alternative seemed reasonable. After March 14 it became almost inevitable that the Falange, either alone or with allies, would make some sort of assault on the government.

The Cárcel Modelo, Madrid's new "model prison" in which José Antonio and the national leadership were incarcerated, was indeed an exemplary institution. The directors, who were enlightened, progressive, and humane, granted every sort of privilege to the inmates, including ample opportunities for receiving visitors. It was not difficult for the Falangists to reconstitute their chain of command by means of an elaborate system of messengers who connected José Antonio with the clandestine executive network still at liberty. A party center was set up in Madrid and administered jointly by the permanent organizational secretary, Mariano García, and whichever national leader happened to be at liberty during any given period. Raimundo Fernández Cuesta, the Secretary-General, was sometimes able to serve in this capacity, but José Antonio finally had to delegate much of his authority to his younger brother Fernando. Fernando Primo de Rivera proved to be an able executor, even though he had not thrown in his lot with the party until the political crisis that followed the elections.

Since the Falange could not function as a legal party, José Antonio ordered that the party sections be reorganized into secret cells of three in order to make the Falange a more effective weapon for subversion.[3] José Antonio had never entirely given up the notion that a small, determined, and efficient band of revolutionists might be able to seize power by a bold stroke, if worst came to worst. His first directives from prison ordered local leaders to prepare their groups for a *coup d'état* by the Falange's own forces, unhampered by alliance with anyone. During the next two months several schemes to provoke a *coup* were considered, but none of them offered any prospect of success.[4]

These furtive maneuvers were played out against a background of violence. When mild weather arrived street fighting opened up with an intensity not seen in Spain since the apogee of political terrorism at Barcelona in 1921. The extremists had thrown their last scruples to the winds. Blacklists of the Falange's principal enemies were prepared by the activist squads.[5] When a municipal judge sentenced a Falange youth for his role in the Asúa *attentat,* party *pistoleros* caught the judge alone within forty-eight hours and cut him down with a spray of bullets.[6] In one "reprisal," Falange terrorists kidnaped the president of the Socialist Casa del Pueblo in the town of Carrión de los Condes; the unlucky Leftist leader was hanged in an isolated spot together with a subordinate. Some forty Falangists, several conservatives, and well over fifty liberals or Leftists were killed within a period of ninety days.[7] *Mundo Obrero,* the Communist organ, demanded the "integral elimination" of the Falange and printed large pictures of "the bloodstained *señorito,* José Antonio Primo de Rivera."[8]

From prison, Ruiz de Alda published an article called "The Justification of Violence" in *No Importa,* a clandestine Falange paper that appeared three times during May and June. Ruiz declared that Spain was already living in a state of civil war, that it was too late to step back now, and that no holds should be barred. He received hundreds of telegrams of congratulation addressed to the Modelo by enthusiastic Rightists thirsting for vengeance on the Left.[9]

Spanish wealth was happy to finance Falange terrorism and even incited the militia to do a more effective job.* The Right had shut the Falange out of the elections only to ask for militia protection as the hour of balloting had drawn near. The Republic had its Assault Guards; the Falangists were still slated to be the shock troops of the reaction. The number of activists steadily increased as JAP members joined the SEU and passed automatically into the Falange militia. The JAP leader, Ramón Serrano Súñer, now collaborated with José Antonio and permitted some of his green-shirted youth to switch their affiliation. Gil Robles publicly distinguished between "good" and "bad" terrorists:

---

* Constancia de la Mora, a younger member of an influential monarchist-conservative clan, wrote: "My father and his friends gave money [to Falange activists] and stood back to watch the results. (*In Place of Splendor: The Autobiography of a Spanish Woman,* p. 215.)

José Antonio doubted that the new contributions to the Falange were being properly used for constructive purposes. (Letter to Onésimo Redondo, June 17, 1936, in *Epistolario,* pp. 502–3.)

Among these there are two classes of persons: those who take the path of violence honestly, believing that in this manner national problems can be resolved, and those who take it because their party cannot now apportion posts and prebends. The first, absolutely respectable, can constitute magnificent auxiliaries on the day when, disenchanted, they return to the common fold.[10]

By this Gil Robles meant that the conservatives would feel more comfortable if the violence were to end, but that as long as it should continue they would endorse the anti-Leftist *pistoleros* and condemn the gunmen opposing them.

By this time José Antonio had lost hope of checking the spread of violence. On April 16 one of his cousins was killed when gunmen opened fire on Falangists escorting the bier of a Civil Guard slain in Madrid by Leftists.[11] Such events convinced him it was better to let the revolution run on freely toward its inevitable climax. He publicly approved the Carrión de los Condes incident in the clandestine *No Importa*. Nevertheless, he vetoed an elaborate scheme for the assassination of Largo Caballero which was referred to him for consideration; this, apparently, was too provocative for him.

On May 6 and May 14 the new prime minister, Casares Quiroga, declared in the Cortes that the illegal Falange was the government's main enemy. He explained that people not officially connected with the party were also being arrested because the police now had Falange files listing the arch-reactionaries who were secretly aiding the movement.[12]

By the first of June, the Falange had suffered approximately its seventieth loss by death in street warfare since the founding of the party.[13] The growth of violence had become so rapid and confused that it was difficult to follow.[14] Some areas were on the brink of complete social chaos. The Anarchists and Left Socialists demanded their economic revolution immediately. Largo Caballero expected to become the heir of the Popular Front and did not want to be put off any longer. Innumerable strikes were under way simultaneously, and the newspapers kept box scores on those that sustained themselves longest. Many observers feared that Spain was reaching its breaking point.

Several plans to accomplish José Antonio's escape from prison

were considered, but none of them came to fruition.[15] In legal stratagem to secure his freedom, his name was entered on the conservative
list in the special run-off election for Cuenca province.[16] This move
was arranged by José Antonio's Rightist friends, notably his intimate
friend Ramón Serrano Súñer, the head of the JAP, and the monarchist
Goicoechea.[17]

The Cuenca list was made up largely of local conservative leaders.
However, one luminary besides José Antonio appeared on it—General Francisco Franco. On the night after the February elections,
Franco had hesitated to heed Gil Robles' plea for military intervention; a few days later the victorious Left relieved him of his post as
Chief of Staff and relegated him to the very minor position of military
commander of Tenerife in the Canary Islands. Franco had doubted
both the willingness and the capacity of the military to carry out an
effective *coup,* and he had refused to associate himself closely with
any of the multitudinous garrison conspiracies being developed by
the UME and by other generals. He now wanted to fortify himself in
a civilian political post and await developments.

However, José Antonio refused to let his name appear on a list
that contained both Franco and other Rightists. He did not want to
be identified with the generals' clique. Gil Robles, on the other
hand, favored the candidacy of both men, thinking that it might
promote a healthy balance for the perilous times ahead. José Antonio
sent his brother Miguel to Gil Robles' office, where Miguel threatened
that unless Franco would withdraw, he would publish a circular on
behalf of the Falange condemning him.[18] Furthermore, pressure
from the Left against Franco's name was overwhelming. Before
this, the Right had to back down. Serrano Súñer, Franco's brother-
in-law, flew to Tenerife to advise the General to withdraw his candidacy.[19] Faced with such varied opposition, Franco gave way and
retired from the contest.

The Minister of Justice urged local authorities to conduct the
election strictly as a run-off, with no new names allowed, but José
Antonio remained on the conservative list.[20] His candidacy evidently
did quite well when the voting occurred, although no reliable statistics are available. The Left, however, was determined not to
permit him an unobstructed contest. In several districts his vote was

not counted on the grounds that his name had not been entered in the first election. José Antonio's total thus placed him at the bottom of the Rightist list instead of near the top, where it probably would have put him if all his votes had been counted.[21] Serrano Súñer denounced this in the Cortes and presented a complicated set of district totals to show that José Antonio deserved a seat, but to no avail.[22]

During May the political preferences of the conservative public in Madrid were indicated in a private poll of its readers taken by the clerical newspaper *Ya*. Queried regarding their choice for the presidency of the Republic, they gave José Antonio a slight margin over their other favorites, Calvo Sotelo, Gil Robles, and General Sanjurjo.[23] The swing toward "fascism" by the Spanish Right was definitely beginning. In some of the provinces, young ladies of the upper classes ostentatiously wore Falange emblems on their dresses.[24]

Meanwhile, the government drew its coils tighter around the Falange leader. During April and May José Antonio was tried on a series of four charges, three of them legal excuses to prolong his detention. Two of these brought convictions that condemned him to some four months of imprisonment.[25] The fourth, tried on May 28, charged him with illicit possession of arms, since a full six weeks after his arrest his home had been searched and two loaded pistols found. José Antonio made an angry, impassioned defense, declaring that the arms had been planted and that the whole proceeding was a frame-up (as it clearly was, at least in intent). Nonetheless, he was found guilty, and his sentence was lengthened. José Antonio flew into a towering rage. He threw an ink pot at the clerk, then tore off his advocate's robes and stamped on them, declaring that if this were the best Spanish justice could do, he wanted no more of it.*

Since José Antonio was the government's star prisoner, police officials grew nervous about the possibility of his escape. On June 5 guards came to remove him to the provincial jail at Alicante, whence flight would be more difficult. The other Falange prisoners in the

---

* *El Sol*, May 29, 1936; *The Times* (London), May 29, 1936. José Antonio later repented his outburst, saying that he had set a very bad example for the young, who needed more, not less, discipline. (Jato, pp. 226–27.)

Modelo raised an enormous row when the *Jefe* was taken out. José Antonio shouted that he was on the way to his execution, but he arrived in Alicante without incident.[26] Some of the lesser Falange leaders were released, but all the more important ones remained behind bars. Ruiz de Alda and several score more were kept in the Cárcel Modelo, while others, like their *Jefe,* were sent to provincial prisons for safekeeping.

The possibility of José Antonio's removal from Madrid had not been unforeseen. Plans had already been laid to forestall the disruption this might cause in the clandestine chain of command, and the *Jefe* still managed to keep in touch with developments from his distant cell on the southeast coast.

The Falange's position was now growing desperate. Each day brought new arrests. Another six months of government persecution and the party would be ruined. Clearly, the Falange had to enlist the aid of someone, and before much time had passed.

> In these days an essential change of orientation was registered in the political line taken by José Antonio and the Falange. Until then an innate lack of confidence in the possibility of a military stroke, and a profound aversion toward what would be its consequence, had reigned as the fundamental orientation of [José Antonio's] thoughts and activities."[27]

In the new situation a great effort was made "to galvanize the enthusiasm of the discontented, timid, and ambitious [among the military], who were capable, because of their position, of weighing heavily in an armed rebellion."[28] This began as vague proselytizing in the officer corps, with no concrete coalition in sight.

As more and more leaders were arrested, it became very difficult to maintain the Falange's chain of command; this was not owing to willful insubordination, but simply to the confusion and isolation created when the organization was forced to go underground. The resulting lack of cohesion threatened to lead the party into awkward entanglements with various poorly conceived plots being elaborated by Army officers and reactionaries. Many Falangists were lost in the web of intrigue being spun throughout Spain. In the province of Alava, for example, the local *jefe provincial,* Ramón Castaños, had begun to plot with Carlists and other extreme Rightists. While visiting the monastery at Nanclares de la Oca in order to ask for contributions, Castaños declared that as early as April 1 the conspirators had collected 120,000 pesetas in Alava province with which to buy arms. He was arrested by the authorities after two months of intrigue.[29]

José Antonio continued to fear confusion or compromise with the organized Right. His basic problem was to gain honest collaborators for a rebellion while avoiding political entanglement with other groups. The Falange leaders feared that the monarchists would steal their thunder. José Calvo Sotelo, in a significant speech to the Cortes, announced himself willing to accept the title "fascist" if other people should wish to apply it to his political philosophy. Although the Falange leaders had often denied the appropriateness of the term when it had been employed against them by the Left, they reacted angrily to Calvo Sotelo's espousal of it. They protested that this was simply another maneuver by the Right to use the Falange and to take advantage of its impetus "on the eve of victory." Propaganda leaflets were circulated in Madrid condemning Calvo Sotelo's mimicry.*

Meanwhile, José Antonio had established contact with the Carlist leadership in France. Manuel Fal Conde, the national leader of the Carlist militia (the Requetés), was impressed by the possibility of obtaining the Falange's cooperation in a *coup* then being considered by the Carlists. Since both groups propounded a rigorously antiparliamentarian style of government, and since neither had compromised itself with the orthodox conservatives, a bargain seemed possible. Fal Conde apparently offered José Antonio equal representation in the first political directorate that would issue from a successful *coup*.

José Antonio had come to believe that the Carlists were his only possible collaborators on the Right. Their record was clean, and they would stand by their word. They were not given to double-dealing,

---

* Ansaldo, p. 122. This was the last word in the José Antonio-Calvo Sotelo rivalry, which ended shortly afterward with the latter's assassination by the Left. At this time there was even an attempt to copy the SEU. A certain Haz de Estudiantes Españoles published a manifesto in May, using Falange emblems. (Jato, p. 227.)

and they were devoted to tearing out the liberal state root and branch. José Antonio did not propose to tie himself to Carlist apron strings, but the immediate future was so dark any honorable collaborator was welcome. If the suggested terms would be respected, José Antonio agreed to bring the Falange behind any Carlist revolt, provided only that sufficient notice were given.[30] These were hopes at best. The Carlists were as weak as the Falange, and it was more than doubtful that either or both of them could stage a successful revolt without the support of the Army.

At this time José Antonio was only beginning to learn the details of the Army's conspiracy; the Falange had been working in the dark, disoriented by the great differences among local political situations. Evidence that the military conspiracy was in earnest brought him no comfort; it forced him instead toward a painful recognition of the Falange's prospects.

For three years the Falange had preached the overthrow of the Republic and the establishment of an authoritarian political system. Now that powerful forces had begun to conspire against the Republic, there was some chance that at least the negative part of the party's program would be implemented—but not by the Falange. A successful revolt by the Army, or the Right, or both would certainly produce an authoritarian system of some sort, but this would by no means be a national syndicalist revolution. The Falange militia was poorly armed and at best equipped only for sporadic street fighting.[31] It was in no position to dispute supremacy with the Army, if the Army really planned to rebel.

Once the military conspiracy became a concrete fact, the Falange could only go along with it or be crushed by a militant Right or a victorious Left. Supported in his reluctance by Ruiz de Alda, José Antonio hesitated to accept this bitter truth, but other party leaders were eager to jump into the Army plot.[32]

The *Jefe Nacional* first made official contact with General Mola on May 29. The agent was one of his principal messengers, Rafael Garcerán, a former law clerk in José Antonio's office. A series of messages was exchanged between the imprisoned Falange chief and the leader of the military conspiracy during the weeks that followed. José Antonio even sent to Mola "confidential information on persons and the organic functioning of the party."[33] As he had previously done with the UME, José Antonio tried to impose political conditions on the military which the latter refused to accept. It was not easy to strike a bargain. Local Army outbreaks threatened in Valencia and elsewhere, but there was no understanding with the Falange.

The Falange leaders remained pessimistic and distrustful about the attitude of the military. Although preliminary orders regarding the manner in which the Falange militia would take part in the rebellion were sent out on May 30, Fernando Primo de Rivera, directing the party organization in Madrid, was quite gloomy. Describing Fernando's attitude, the *jefe provincial* of Burgos wrote:

> He did not believe the military would rise. He had no faith in them, and when I assured him about Burgos . . . he told me: "Very well, that may be true for Burgos, Alava, and Logroño, and somewhere else, but in general we can do nothing with the military. In Madrid the cause is lost."[34]

José Antonio wrote to one of his contacts in northern Spain, "If everything continues to be prepared the way it is going now, we shall have a regime that will have Spain tired out [*aburrida*] within six months."[35] In the last issue of the clandestine *No Importa* (June 20), he entitled his editorial "Watch the Right. Warning to *madrugadores* [sharpers or opportunists]: the Falange is not a conservative force." José Antonio urged party militants to be wary of the old conservatives, who would try to regain their lost power by provoking the military to a reactionary *coup* and expending the Falange as shock troops in the process.

On June 24 a circular released to the local leaders said in part:

> The plurality of machinations in favor of more or less confused subversive movements that are being developed in various provinces of Spain has come to the attention of the *Jefe Nacional.*
>   . . . Some[local chiefs], swayed by an excess of zeal or by a dangerous ingenuousness, have rushed ahead to outline plans of local action and to compel the participation of comrades in certain political plans.
>
>   .   .   .
>
>   . . . The political projects of the military . . . are usually not distinguished for their relevancy. Those projects are almost all

based on an initial error: that of thinking that the ills of Spain are due to simple disarrangements of interior order and will disappear when power is handed over to those [reactionary civilian politicians] previously referred to, who are charlatans lacking any historical understanding, any authentic education, and any desire that the *Patria* break forth once more on the great paths of her destiny.

The participation of the Falange in one of those premature and ingenuous projects would constitute a grave responsibility and would entail *its* [the Falange's] *total disappearance, even in case of triumph.* For this reason: because all those who count on the Falange for such undertakings consider it . . . only as an auxiliary shock force, as a species of juvenile assault militia, destined the day after tomorrow to parade before these conceited oligarchs re-established in power.

Let all the comrades consider precisely how offensive it is to propose that the Falange take part as a supernumerary in a movement that is not going to lead to the establishment of the national syndicalist state.[86]

The various *jefes provinciales* were to report within five days whether or not their independence had been compromised by such agreements.

Four days later José Antonio revealed his fears in a letter to an old friend, the liberal politician Miguel Maura. Some weeks earlier Maura had proposed a "national liberal dictatorship" as the only way to control the potential death struggle between the Left and the Right. No one had paid any attention.[87] The Falange leader commented to Maura:

But I fear you shall soon see how the terrible lack of culture or, better said, the mental laziness of our people . . . will end up giving us either an essay in cruel and filthy Bolshevism or a flatulent representation of shortsighted patriotism under the direction of some bloated figure from the Right. May God free us of the one and of the other.[88]

The Falange's only hope was to outsmart the military. On June 29 José Antonio sent out another circular to party leaders, in which he gave instructions for Falange participation in a military revolt:

(A) The *jefe provincial* or *territorial* will deal only with the military commander in his district, and no other person.

(B) All Falange units will maintain their own identity, independence, and chain of command.

(C) If considered absolutely necessary, one-third, but no more, of the Falangists may be placed under the orders of the Army in any given locality.

(D) The local *jefe militar* must promise his Falange counterpart that the Army will retain control of the civil government for at least three days after establishing its victory before turning such functions over to civilian politicians.

(E) Unless these orders are specifically renewed, all plans shall be considered canceled as of 12:00 P.M., July 10.[89]

José Antonio requested Mola to set another date for the revolt, definitely and quickly, if he wanted the Falange to participate. Mola shifted his feet; his rebels would need some sort of auxiliary aid to take Madrid in a quick *coup,* but he knew how tenuous his little conspiracy was, and he had no faith in the military value of the Falange.

However, it was now evident that part of the plot was known to government authorities, and swift action became essential. Mola revised the date of the military *coup* to July 9–10. Unfortunately for the plotters, José Sáinz, the Falange's *jefe provincial* in Toledo, was arrested on July 6 carrying instructions for the uprising. This caused Mola to cancel the date once more, although the situation was increasingly critical.

On July 9 José Antonio extended the validity of his previous instructions until noon of July 20. He continued to bargain with Mola, but the latter made no concrete concessions. Mola was determined that the rebellion would be controlled by the Army, with no political obligations involved. There is no evidence the Falange ever received any political guarantees; most of the surviving leaders testify that there were none whatever. The only proviso which José Antonio secured was the one on which the Army insisted anyway, namely, that power would not be handed over immediately to the conservative politicians. This meant that the conservatives would not be able to dominate the Falange or vice versa; the Army would be in a position to control them both.

What José Antonio apparently hoped to gain from this was only the possibility that in the confusion following the *golpe,* the Falange could force its way into a commanding position. As a result of its own participation, and of the increased prestige it had obtained among the impotent Right during the past fifteen weeks, the Falange might find itself in a much more favorable position *vis-à-vis* the conservative parties. José Antonio was still convinced of the political incapacity of the generals, but he hoped that they would unwittingly provide an opportunity for his "audacious minority" of revolutionaries. José Antonio did not expect to see his party in power within a matter of weeks, or even months, but he did expect a swift and successful military *coup* against the Republican government to enhance considerably the stock of national syndicalism.[40]

By this time the party was at the mercy of events. Each day brought more arrests of Falangists in Madrid and in the provinces; they were being rounded up by the scores and the hundreds. The chain of command had virtually broken up. On July 10 Fernández Cuesta, directing the secret Falange secretariat in Madrid, sent out urgent orders to all *jefes provinciales* to send a person of great loyalty to the capital at once; the leadership wanted to be sure that the recent instructions had been received. A contact appeared from only one province.[41]

The tense situation was hard on everyone. In Valencia both the military garrison and the Falange group were very edgy. The Falangists jumped the gun on the night of July 11 by taking over the city's radio station to announce that "the national syndicalist movement will soon begin in the streets." This touched off a night of rioting and burning by the Left in Spain's third largest city.[42] Mola still hesitated to set a new date for the revolt. Until the last minute, there was no assurance that the Army leaders would not back out, leaving the Falange in the lurch. Party leaders became increasingly anxious.

In Madrid hatred and violence increased by the hour. The Republican Assault Guards bore the brunt of maintaining order. On July 12 Lt. José Castillo, an ardent Leftist Guards officer who had shot one or two Falangists in street fights, was murdered by UME gunmen. His companions determined to avenge him on their own initiative. The following night a detachment of Assault Guards went to the home of José Calvo Sotelo. Since the defeat of Gil Robles, Calvo

Sotelo had become the leading spokesman of the organized Right. He had repeatedly declared his unremitting opposition to the republican form of government and had publicly accepted the threats flung at him by the Left. There were no threats that night. Calvo Sotelo was taken away in an Assault Guard truck, shot, and deposited in a suburban cemetery.

This lit the fuse. All the Right cried vengeance. Wealthy citizens began to flee the capital as though it harbored the plague; during the next five days a constant stream of limousines headed for the French and Portuguese borders.

In Alicante José Antonio could no longer contain himself. On July 14 he sent Garcerán to Pamplona with a final message for Mola: if the conspirators would not agree to act within seventy-two hours, he would begin the rebellion with the Falange in Alicante. He insisted that many UME men were now impatient to go over to the Falange.[43] To lead a rebellion with the Alicante militia would have been suicidal, but this bluff was José Antonio's last hope of forcing Mola's hand.

Mola was still skeptical of the Falange's potential. Since the nearest large contingent of Falange militia was at Burgos, Mola asked José Andino, their *jefe provincial*, how many men they were ready to provide now that their leader had proclaimed them ready to act. Andino replied that he could have six thousand men ready in four hours, which was a considerable exaggeration.[44]

The principal gleam of light in Mola's world was the promised support of the Carlists, which he had obtained only during the past three days. The Carlists had promised to provide ten thousand trained militiamen to assist in the drive on Madrid. Many of the officers connected with the conspiracy were still unreliable, but further delay would be fatal. The revolt in Morocco was scheduled for July 18, with the rest of the Army to join in within forty-eight hours. Elena Medina, an upper-class girl who served as one of Mola's messengers, hurried to Cuesta with final instructions hidden in the buckle of her dress.[45]

The General's decision reached José Antonio in Alicante on the morning of July 16.[46]

THE FALANGE EARLY IN THE CIVIL WAR

T HE REBELLION BEGAN prematurely in Morocco at approximately
2 P.M. on July 17. The two senior commanders refused to participate, but they were quickly arrested and later shot. All of Spanish
Africa, including the only efficient units of the poorly organized
Army, fell into rebel hands within twenty-four hours.[1]

By the time the *coup* was finally made, the government had become so accustomed to false alarms that it could hardly believe the
truth.[2] In the late afternoon of July 18, military garrisons in Spain
began to declare a state of war; not until that evening did the Madrid
government begin to realize that it might have a serious rebellion on
its hands. It tried to call to the capital several unreliable Civil Guard
units, to prevent them from joining the rebels. Labor leaders had
already demanded that the workers be armed to defend the Republic.[3]
This request was at first firmly denied by the liberal government.

Mola issued his proclamation of revolt in Pamplona at dawn on
Sunday, July 19. Within a few hours the leading cities of Old Castile
and Aragon were in Army hands. Falange squads helped the troops
quell resistance from the workers' militia in Valladolid and Zarogoza.
Seville, Cádiz, Córdoba, and Granada had already been seized or
were soon to be taken.

The first response by the Republican government was to dissolve
the old cabinet. Diego Martínez Barrio, a conservative moderate, was
entrusted with the new ministry. By telephone Mola was formally
offered government posts for several of the leading generals. But the
rebels, bent on winning full power from the government, would
accept no compromise.[4]

Faced with a mortal struggle against the military command, the
Republican leaders began to realize that complete disaster threatened.

They reluctantly consented to the arming of workers in one or two of the largest cities. In Madrid, poorly armed but greatly aroused proletarians stormed the two thousand soldiers who had retreated into the semifortified Montaña barracks.[5] At Barcelona the Anarchists and the Assault Guards completely crushed the rebellion in two days of hard fighting.[6] By Monday, July 20, the outcome was very much in doubt everywhere. Garrisons in Galicia had begun to come out for the rebels, but not a sound was heard from the Levante. It took the military governor of Valencia a long time to make up his mind. When he did, it was too late to do anything but surrender to the Republican forces.

The Army had suspected that the rebellion might fail in Madrid, but it had not expected the same thing to happen in three-fifths of the nation.[7] Furthermore, the revolt in the Navy was largely a failure.* Government ships blockaded the straits, and it was impossible to transfer the vital Moroccan Army to the peninsula; only one boatload of Legionnaires (*Tercios*) got across to Algeciras before the barrier was established.

As the lines began to stabilize, the rebels could have counted on no more than forty thousand troops in the peninsula, perhaps less. The Republic may have had as many as five or ten thousand loyal soldiers and Assault Guards, as well as the unnumbered tens of thousands of half-armed men in the workers' militia. Most of the Civil Guard had gone over to the Army.

According to plan, Mola's northern Army group, aided by Falangist and Carlist auxiliaries, began a rapid drive on Madrid. They hoped to seize the capital before the situation got beyond their control, although the equivalent of only one Army division was all they could spare for the effort. Scattered units were sent to occupy the mountain passes that controlled the route to Madrid, but they were met by Republican militia intent upon the same object. A fierce fight developed

* Many naval officers favored the rebellion, but their sailors were more politically conscious than the Army recruits. In a number of cases, they simply put their officers to the knife and tossed the bodies into the sea. After a sharp struggle, that part of the fleet stationed at El Ferrol was won for the rebels, but it was only a part of the total. The rebel eulogists Víctor María de Solá and Carlos Martel list 85,000 tons of loyalist warships, 52,000 tons for the rebels. (*Estelas gloriosas de la escuadra azul,* p. 127.)

for control of the vital gaps. As the rebel commander, Colonel García Escámez, prepared a final assault to hurl back the government forces, he received the following message from his chief, Mola: "Impossible to send ammunition. I have 26,000 cartridges for all the Army of the North."[8]

The simple truth was that the greater part of the Spanish Army stationed in the peninsula was too poorly equipped even to fight a strong police action. Mola was in despair. According to his secretary, he was preparing to withdraw his forces for a last-ditch stand in the north when he received a message from General Franco which radically changed the entire situation.[9]

Up to this point, the rebellion had been carried forward almost exclusively by the officers of the Spanish Army. They had not been swayed by the proposals of the Falange, the demands of the Carlists, or the possible attitudes of foreign powers. There is no evidence that either the German or the Italian government was even aware that a *coup* was coming, much less guilty of having incited it. The only previous foreign contact was made through one Johannes Bernhardt, a leader of the Nazi Party in Morocco, who had organized a sizable nucleus among the German colony there and was in touch with the local representatives of the Falange. The German commercial company with which Bernhardt was connected had privately offered financial credits and air transport facilities to the Moroccan Army. This offer was flatly refused by the Spanish military.

As planned, General Franco had been flown from Tenerife to Melilla on July 18. He had been slated to take charge of the Moroccan Army and bring it over to the peninsula. Since the rebels had lost control of the straits, Franco was blocked in. Faced with a complete collapse of the rebel effort, the stubby general changed his tack immediately. He sent Bernhardt, one of his staff colonels, and the local Nazi *Ortsgruppenleiter* to Berlin by air to request that German supplies and transport facilities be sent with the utmost dispatch.[10] Meanwhile, Mola had delegated a civilian collaborator, the Marqués de Portago (later Valdeiglesias), to ask for rifle ammunition in Berlin. The German authorities were naturally taken aback by the faulty liaison of the rebel leaders.[11]

At the same time, urgent petitions for aerial assistance were made to Mussolini. The Duce's 1934 agreement with monarchist conspirators had not directly concerned the Spanish Army.[12] The military revolt took the Italians by surprise. Since the Ethiopian affair had barely ended, the first impulse of the Italian government was to avoid getting involved in the western Mediterranean. However, Mussolini could not long resist a chance to participate in another "crusade" against Bolshevism; his son-in-law acceded to Franco's third and most urgent request.[13] A number of bombers were sent to Morocco before the end of July.[14]

The Germans had now decided that Franco was the Army chief with the more important contacts and the more effective troops. Furthermore, one or two influential persons already acquainted with the General had been boosting the rebel cause in Berlin.[15] A few transport planes were dispatched to Morocco before the first of August, and several days later an entire squadron was transferred. The ground crews arrived at Cádiz on August 6.[16]

The arrival of these first transport planes enabled Franco to begin slowly transferring his troops to Andalusia and flying small quantities of ammunition to Mola; this was the occasion of his jubilant telegram to the commander of the Army of the North. Finally, on August 5 two or three Italian bombers helped Nationalist warships disperse the government blockade, thus permitting the first rebel military convoy to cross the sea.[17]

It was the decisive intervention of the Germans and the Italians that turned the Army rebellion into a civil war. Without their contributions, the Republican forces might very possibly have gained control of the situation within a few weeks.[18] With this aid, the rebels were able to build up matériel for a drive on Madrid. The capital's working class responded valiantly, and the assault was finally brought to a halt at the city limits during the first days of November.[19] Subsequent efforts to take Madrid also failed, ending with the defeat of an Italian auxiliary force at Guadalajara in March 1937.[20]

The rebels had long since been forced to renounce any hope of speedy victory. They now settled down to the task of building a military and governmental machine capable of subduing the greater part of the Spanish nation in what promised to be a prolonged and hard-fought struggle.

The critical nature of the military situation left the Falangists very little time for politics during the first weeks of the conflict. They had taken part in the rebellion in almost every section of Spain, although faulty liaison sometimes impeded their efforts to aid the military. Units of the Falange militia or the Carlist Requetés often occupied large sections of the still poorly defined front, while Army leaders searched desperately for new manpower.

The political situation was extremely confused, no less in the heterogeneous rebel camp than in the foundering Republic. The military directors had no clear goals; they all talked in vague terms about saving the Republic, restoring order, and effecting reforms. The first messages of Mola from the north and of Franco from Africa said nothing about overthrowing the present form of government; they spoke only of strengthening discipline and repressing the Left. Garrisons throughout Spain had rebelled with the cry "¡Viva la Republica!"

Spain's basic problem, the class struggle, was social and economic in origin. On this the generals were both eloquent and contradictory. They declared that reforms were surely needed, but the only concrete social policy indicated in the first Army manifesto was a statement unequivocally abolishing the Republican land reform.[21]

Gonzalo Queipo de Llano, the noisiest and one of the most radical of the generals, had won Seville in a bold and brilliant *coup* on the afternoon of July 18. From his new Sevillian fief he declared that a military directorship of twenty-five years might be necessary to restore order and discipline to the unhappy Spanish people.

During the first two or three weeks of fighting, the dimensions of the conflict were not fully revealed. To handle immediate problems a Junta de Defensa Nacional was set up in Burgos on July 25. Its ruling board was composed of colonels and generals with subordinate civilian assistants; its nominal chairman was the white-bearded Mason, General Cabanellas, the commander of the Seventh Division. The generals would have preferred to appoint civilians to some of the more prominent positions, but they could not be sure of the loyalty of many public figures, and they feared that the elevation of obscure individuals would further alienate the masses.[22]

The Falange had no official standing whatever with the Junta; it was merely an autonomous civilian force contributing to the rebel effort. Since the rebellion had failed completely in the Levante, José Antonio was now an isolated prisoner far behind the Republican lines with no hope of escape. Not only the *Jefe* but virtually all the top Falange leaders had disappeared shortly before or after the outbreak of the rebellion. Ruiz de Alda and Fernández Cuesta were as securely imprisoned as José Antonio. Onésimo Redondo, who had been sounding the call to violence for a full five years, was killed instantly when he was stopped by a truckload of Socialist militiamen on the Valladolid highway. The Falange hence found itself utterly without leadership or official representation.

It was at first impossible to coordinate party activities. With supplies scarce and transportation from region to region both perilous and hard to arrange, a kind of natural regional autonomy prevailed.

However, as sides were drawn up for civil war, the party began to assume greater significance. The orthodox Right had never developed a *mystique* adequate to sustain a civil war, and it offered no new ideology to justify the present conflict. Discredited by their past failures and present impotence, the old political groups virtually ceased to function. Only the Requetés and the Falangists were able to respond to the call for direct action. Fortunately for the Falange, the political appeal of the Comunión Tradicionalista was limited. Only the most clerical and conservative joined the Carlists, while the bulk of the middle classes preferred the Falange.[23] The party seemed to offer a dynamic new political orientation for all those who wanted to join the fight against the Left on a civilian basis. Membership increased enormously and soon passed all manageable proportions.* Within a few months the old cadres were nearly swamped by the influx. As the first wave of emotion swept the Right, everyone hastened to put on blue shirts. Even financial institutions offered to support the Falange, hoping to be remembered in return.[24]

Although the avalanche continued, pressure from the fighting front remained so great that the nominal leaders of the party had little time to work at achieving some sort of organizational coherence. There was a distinct threat that the party might become an amorphous, directionless mass, manipulated by elements from without or

---

* Two thousand Falange militiamen are said to have volunteered for party service during the first twenty-four hours of recruiting at Zaragoza. (*El Heraldo de Aragón*, July 25, 1936.)

disrupted from within by a flood of lower–middle-class ex-conservatives. The new members had but the scantiest indoctrination; most
of them knew only that the Falange stood for something "new" and
"social."[25] There was not even a national chain of command. As one
Falangist said,

> In the beginning we did not worry about a National Command,
> because the problem of supplying kilometers and kilometers of the
> war front weighed us down, being an immediate question of life
> and death. That is, we devoted ourselves to the war without think-
> ing of anything else.[26]

Falange leaders "had no clear idea" what political goals they might
achieve in so turbulent a situation.* They hoped simply to enroll as
many members as possible in order to provide support for themselves
in any situation that might arise.

By the end of August the two centers of Falange strength in rebel-
held territory were Valladolid and Seville. Valladolid had the larger
party following, but Seville was temporarily of equal significance,
being the anchor on the line of communication with the all-powerful
African Army during its march north. In Andalusia party control
had momentarily fallen into the hands of Joaquín Miranda, the *jefe
provincial* of Seville. After contact was re-established with the north,
he invited a number of Falange leaders from other regions to a conference in his city. This took place on August 29.[27] Besides Miranda,
the three principal figures in attendance were Agustín Aznar, the
unofficial head of the party's militia; Antonio Cazañas, the *jefe territorial* of Morocco; and Andrés Redondo, who not only had succeeded
his brother but had stepped up to the rank of *jefe territorial* of Old
Castile. Don Andrés was a banker and no authentic Falangist, but
as the heir of the fallen *jefe* of Valladolid he managed to extend his
power in the subsequent confusion. Cazañas was important at this
time because a fair number of the younger officers in the Morocco
garrison had joined the Falange.

---

* Canales, p. 5. On September 11, one of the German representatives reported, "At the moment one has the impression that the members of the Falangist militia themselves have no real aims and ideas; rather, they seem to be
young people for whom mainly it is good sport to play with firearms and to
round up Communists and Socialists." (*Germany and the Spanish Civil War*,
Doc. No. 80, pp. 84–89.)

Most of the leaders present favored calling a meeting of the surviving members of the National Council as soon as possible, in order to straighten out the snarls in the chain of command and establish some sort of official leadership. Such action would surely have to be taken if the party were ever to develop the many areas of contact between itself and the Army, reduce points of friction, and ensure uniformity in the solution of similar problems in the various provinces. A host of other problems—such as those connected with propaganda, the future of the CONS, and the Falange's police duties— cried for solution.

The party had always been extremely weak in the secondary ranks of its leadership. The technical competence of the local chiefs was limited, and they lacked a full grasp of the problems of the war. There was little culture or personality among them, and for the most part they were quite unable to provide direction for their amorphous groups. More important, there was considerable jealousy among the northern *jefes provinciales* toward the potential new triumvirate of Redondo-Miranda-Cazañas, even though it had not yet actually taken shape.[28] Nor was this the only source of resentment within the party; the bitterest suspicion was shown by the surviving remnants of the Madrid Falange, who keenly resented this transfer of pre-eminence to provincial leaders.

When the surviving members of the National Council met in Valladolid on September 4, a disproportionate influence was exercised by Agustín Aznar, the former Madrid *jefe provincial* of militia. Aznar had assumed provisional control of all the Falange militia, which was now playing an important part in the rebel military effort. As the nominal militia chief, Aznar was the only titular national office-holder present. Although he was the most militant of the Falange chiefs, having directed much of the street fighting in Madrid, he was also the most devoted to José Antonio, whose character and personality differed so sharply from his own.

Aznar's only aim seems to have been to hold the party leadership open for the eventual return of the *Jefe*. He and other survivors from the Madrid group, such as Rafael Garcerán, worked from the sidelines to block any move toward providing a new permanent leadership for the party. The personal initiative of the other Councilors was so slight that it was not hard to accomplish this goal. Jesús Muro, José Sáinz, José Moreno, Rodríguez Acosta, and other provincial leaders continued to fear that Redondo and Miranda might try to impose a new provisional national leader upon them.[29] The expedient devised to resolve the dilemma was the formation of a temporary Junta de Mando of seven members, headed by a chairman, to exercise executive leadership for the party.

Manuel Hedilla, the former *jefe provincial* of Santander, was nominated for the post of *jefe* of the Junta de Mando. He had served during the spring of 1936 as one of the national inspectors who had held the party together during its hectic four months of underground existence. He was courageous and tenaciously honest but lacked political culture or personal preparation for assuming high responsibilities. The Aznar clique believed that Hedilla would make an honest executive secretary, but that his personal capacity was too modest to permit him to entertain further ambitions with regard to party command. Hedilla was respected by his fellows, and his lack of notable talent saved him from anyone's envy. His nomination was approved.

The naming of a Junta de Mando was hardly a satisfactory expedient, for it immobilized party leadership for any long-range planning or organizational work. Being only a temporary arrangement, the Junta might lack the authority to make an effective agreement with the military on spheres of influence, should such an opportunity ever arise. However, given the serious shortage of executive talent in the party after the fighting began, little more was to be expected. Effective leadership could not be found in any quarter, for José Antonio had no collaborators of like stature.

Manuel Hedilla could not possibly fill the boots of the absent *Jefe*. He had no formal education, and no executive experience outside the party. He was not an intellectual or a political theorist but a former ship's mechanic. He had neither facility for rhetoric nor what one would call an outstanding personality. An Italian journalist said of him:

> One cannot say that his appearance reveals uncontrovertible signs of a leader, and nothing would indicate that he could show himself tomorrow to be that statesman for whom Spain waits. I should

rather call him an excellent lieutenant, an energetic and scrupulous executor of orders, indeed the man needed in this hour when all power is concentrated in the hands of the military. . . . The lack of a true leader constitutes the great handicap of Falangism.[30]

But Hedilla had his virtues as a leader. He was honest, forthright, hard-working, and had great moral firmness and constancy. He understood the Falange program, and he did not intend to be turned aside from it. At the same time, he felt the pressing military needs of the hour, and he lent all the force at the Falange's disposal to help meet the requirements of the Army.

During the first months, decisions in the Junta de Mando were taken by majority vote, and business was handled as well as could be expected. Hedilla set up his headquarters in Salamanca after the military government was established there on October 1. According to all accounts, he lived with his family in a simple and unostentatious fashion, working diligently to give whatever structure he could to the often incoherent party organization.

Most of the honest and patriotic elements in the party accepted Manuel Hedilla's leadership. Sancho Dávila, *jefe territorial* of Andalusia, who was still in Republican hands at the time of the first Council meeting on September 4, soon escaped by way of the Cuban legation in Madrid. At the second meeting of the National Council, held a few weeks later, he allied himself with the Aznar faction, which ratified the formation of the Junta de Mando. Other Falange leaders who later escaped from the Republican zone also approved the new arrangement.*

Facilities for propaganda expanded enormously after the war began. Party dailies blossomed in Pamplona, Valladolid, Seville, Zaragoza, and Oviedo, to be followed later by organs in Santander, Bilbao, Málaga, and other cities. Until the spring of 1937, and even beyond that date, the propaganda was very often demagogic in tone:

* Such as Vicente Cadenas, *Jefe Nacional* of Press and Propaganda, Roberto Reyes, *Delegado Nacional* of Social Justice, and Vicente Gaceo, national secretary of the now defunct Junta Política. Hedilla admits, however, that there was "quite a bit of disorder and considerable personal ambition" even during the first weeks of the war, despite the aura of moral purity feverishly being cultivated. (Conversation in Madrid, Jan. 20, 1959.)

> Open arms to the worker and peasant!
> Let there be one nobility: that of work!
> Let idlers be exterminated![31]

Party rhetoric was slanted largely toward the lower classes and was full of loud promises of social justice. Onésimo Redondo, in his only public address between the date of his liberation and his sudden death, declared over Radio Valladolid:

> The Falange bears a doctrine firm and impregnate with the most profound and extensive concern: that of redeeming the proletariat. . . .
> Let us conquer for them, above all, the satisfaction and security of daily life: bread.
> . . . If the capitalists, the rich, attended today by a facile euphoria, . . . occupy themselves as heretofore with incorrigible egoism, with a single interest, without turning their heads to the side or the rear to contemplate the wake of hunger, scarcity, and pain which follows them and closes in upon them, they will be traitors to the *Patria*.[32]

The Falange demagogy was not a materialist demagogy full of tangible promises; it was a fascist demagogy that preached unity and sacrifice as well as social justice and economic readjustment. In an interview for Italian correspondents on March 11, 1937, Hedilla outlined a militantly nationalistic program. He declared that the Falange's goals were to capture the Red masses, to eliminate their leaders, and to organize the Falangist militants serving at the front into a National Militia which would survive the war and create a militarily strong Spain.[33]

The party press devoted considerable space to favorable reports on the Nazis, the Italian Fascists, and the minor fascist movements. Periodic outbursts of anti-Semitism even occurred; these were doubly stupid because there were no Jews for Spain to contend with, but the "Protocols of the Elders of Zion" were piously dusted off by obscure Falange ideologists.[34]

However, the Falange propagandists took pains to separate themselves from racism and statism *per se*, to escape identification with the other nationalistic fascist parties. Although derivations from Italian Fascism were not denied,[35] the Falangists preferred to com-

pare their ideology to the nationalist policy of Spain's Catholic Kings
of the late fifteenth century. Their propaganda differed radically
from that of most European fascist groups in its emphasis on Catholicism and Christianity. This religious theme continued to swell
as the war progressed, and it tended to soften the party's warlike
pronouncements. Hedilla declared in a newspaper interview in
October 1936:

> The pagan sense of the cult of Fatherland and subordination to
> race, force, and so forth, that one finds among some foreign move-
> ments of a similar type is substituted in ours by a strong dose of
> religious spirituality, which is very much in accord with our tra-
> ditions.[36]

Since Church leaders were characterizing the struggle as a holy
crusade, the Falangists began to outdo themselves in declaring that
all Spanish institutions must be imbued with a specifically Catholic
spirit.[37] Fermín Yzurdiaga, the Pamplona priest who directed *Arriba
España,* became the party's most active propagandist and rose to the
post of chief of Press and Propaganda after April 1937. Hedilla's
address over Radio Salamanca on Christmas Eve, 1936, went so far
as to proclaim a twisted version of brotherly love. He said, in part:

> Its [Falange's] doctrine is immortal. It is the expression of Divine
> Justice in the secular world. . . .
>   I direct myself to the Falangists who take charge of political
> and police investigations in the cities and above all in the small
> towns. Your mission is to purge chiefs, leaders, and assassins. But
> prevent with full rigor anyone satiating personal hatreds and let
> no one be punished who because of hunger or despair has voted
> for the Left. We all know that in many towns there were—and
> still are—Rightists that were worse than the Reds. . . . [Falange's
> goal is] to sow love.[38]

Falange publications were subject to the same censorship as all
printed material in rebel Spain. Hardly a single edition of a Falange
newspaper appeared without visible marks of hasty deletion. The
military censors were not so much disturbed by abstract demagogy
as by tendencies to claim public authority or prescribe the practical
ends of the state in political or social matters.

Nonetheless, a good deal of friction was created within the rebel camp by the frequently strident tone of the Falange's revolutionary pronouncements.* When Gil Robles appeared briefly in Burgos during August 1936 to confer with other Rightist leaders, he was virtually driven out of town by the local Falange. Other Cedistas began to fear for their lives. A former personal secretary to Gil Robles was killed in Galicia over a local political dispute. Giménez Fernández, the agrarian leader, hid from Falange gunmen in Cádiz province.[39] The Carlists and other conservatives referred to the Falangists as "our Reds" and "FAIlangists."

This antagonism within the party was greatly heightened by the influx of ardent liberals and Leftists; when trapped in rebel territory, many of them joined the Falange as a means of saving themselves from the predatory hunters of the Right. After Málaga fell to the nationalists on February 10, 1937, one thousand new members joined the Falange within twenty-four hours, a good many of the newcomers being Leftists.† In Logroño and Navarre the liberals joined the Falange *en masse* as a means of thwarting the Carlists. In Andalusia and Estremadura Falange organizers followed the military advance guard into workers' districts, signing up Leftists and incorporating them into the militia. After their defeat in 1937 many of the Communist miners in Asturias were brought into the party, if only on a formal basis.[40]

The Leftists who fled into the party did not always escape persecution. In Andalusia party chiefs sometimes went back over the records of their new members; those with only moderately Leftist records were sent to join militia units at the front, but those whose previous activities had been of a more militant nature were sometimes shot.[41]

On the whole, the Falange continued to welcome ex-Leftists and liberals to the fold, although it was sometimes necessary, as at Sala-

---

* Furthermore, most Falangists antagonized their constrained bedfellows of the Right by rigidly opposing the use of any symbols of the Bourbon Monarchy, such as the red-and-yellow flag.

† Gollonet and Morales, *Málaga*, p. 165. The United Press correspondent Charles Foltz watched Communists and Anarchists tear up their party cards as they crossed the threshold of the Falange recruiting office. (*Ibid.*, p. 77.)

manca, to suspend such admissions temporarily because so many were joining.[42] Posters and announcements read: "The past means nothing to us. . . . There is room in our ranks for all those comrades who respond to our slogans and the desire to redeem the *Patria*."[43] As late as six months after the war ended, so many of those arrested in the wholesale purges conducted by the military courts were found to have enrolled in the Falange that a special order was finally published on September 9, 1939. It stipulated that everyone arrested in the future would have to be asked if he were a member of the party. If the reply was affirmative, Falange authorities would at once be notified of the proceedings.[44]

The problem of providing effective leadership for the rebel war effort could be solved only by naming a supreme military commander. Cabanellas had never been more than a figurehead, and the Burgos Junta was only a temporary group. Cabanellas had been named to conciliate the moderates, but the Right never trusted him because of his strong Masonic background.* Therefore, a series of intrigues to appoint a military chief unfolded during September 1936. The whole process of nomination and appointment was in the hands of the higher officers, and no civilian influence was visible.[45] Once it had been decided that a commander-in-chief would supersede the Junta, it became clear that the victor in this personal struggle would be placed in a position of supreme political power.

There were only two practical candidates: Mola and Franco. Mola had planned the rebellion, Franco had taken advantage of it. However, very few people were aware of the peculiar nature of Franco's role in the conspiracy. His rank prior to the February elections had been higher than Mola's and his general prestige was greater, even though Mola was equally respected in military circles. Franco had the reputation of being a very shrewd politician. Furthermore, he had providentially come into command of the decisive section of the Army, the Moroccan units. It was here that the rebels' real military power lay.

---

* The Burgos Falange created a special bodyguard for Cabanellas but gave them secret orders to see that the General made no false moves, according to José Andino, their *jefe*. (Conversation in Madrid, Feb. 6, 1959.)

The most influential officer among the younger commanders from Africa was Colonel Juan Yagüe. It was he who had organized the rebellion in Morocco. Yagüe had joined the Falange before the fighting began, but his sympathies were divided between the Army and the party.[46] There was much bad blood between Yagüe and Mola, whereas Yagüe and Franco were old comrades from the Tercios.* Yagüe not only lent his aid to Franco's supporters but campaigned actively and effectively among his fellows on behalf of the commander of the Army of the South.

By this time it was obvious that foreign aid would play a decisive role in the war. Almost all the vital German-Italian support had been received by Franco, for his troops were making the assault on Madrid. Mola admitted that Franco had greater recognition abroad and was a better diplomat than he.[47] He decided not to oppose Franco's candidacy for head of the armed forces as long as the position was to be purely military and restricted to the duration of the conflict.

Besides Yagüe, Franco's strongest promoters were his brother Nicolás, the veteran General Orgaz (a conspirator with fifteen years of experience), General Millán Astray (the half-crazed founder of the Tercios), and General Kindelán (head of the rebel Air Force). Kindelán has written that the decision to make Franco Generalissimo of the Armed Forces was reached at a meeting of the "Junta de Defensa" on September 21.[48] The only real opposition came from Cabanellas, who wanted no *mando único,* but the other officers were now ready to dispense with that old gentleman's services. Since Mola did not protest, Franco was voted military commander-in-chief.

However, the Burgos Junta failed to announce Franco's appointment immediately, and the General's backers became worried. They prepared a draft decree which Kindelán read at the next meeting of the Burgos Junta on September 28. In it there was a clause naming Franco Chief of State as well as Commander-in-Chief of the Armed Forces. Mola now protested, but the Franco candidacy had gone too far to be stopped. No faction could match the determination of the

* Mola's secretary says that it was Mola who insisted on depriving Yagüe of the command for the attack on Madrid and even threatened to shoot him. (Conversation with José María Iribarren, Pamplona, Dec. 16, 1958.)

Franco backers, and an organized, organic command was a vital necessity. The decree was approved by the Junta and was read officially three days later, on October 1, 1936.

Having been elevated to power, Franco quickly took steps to ensure his remaining there. With everyone else busy directing the war, the figure of the five-foot-three-inch Galician loomed gigantic against a background of blurred mediocrity.

The Falange as a whole had no preference for Commander-in-Chief, but Franco did have one or two admirers among the party leadership. The most important was Andrés Redondo, the banker who had temporarily ceased foreclosing on local peasants to boost himself into his late brother's job and then increase his rank to *jefe territorial*.[49]

However, a group of "legitimists" had begun to form around the surviving friends and personal associates of José Antonio. They considered the new developments dangerous for the political future of the party. On October 2, the day after Franco had been named Commander-in-Chief, the Seville *FE*, then the leading Falange newspaper in Spain, dedicated its entire third page to favorable articles on the *Generalísimo*. Agustín Aznar and Sancho Dávila, the leaders of the Falange in Madrid and Andalusia, respectively, were furious. They raged bitterly at Patricio Canales, the editor of *FE*, for having dedicated so much space to the man they called the Falange's chief enemy.[50]

JOSE ANTONIO IN ALICANTE

WHEN THE FIGHTING BEGAN, José Antonio had been imprisoned in Alicante for six weeks. On the eve of the revolt he wrote a final manifesto to the nation.[1] It said not one word about national syndicalism or revolutionary youth, but simply called upon patriotic Spaniards to support the rebellion.* Its author could only hope for the best.

The conspirators had expected to free José Antonio in their first stroke and then send him immediately to Madrid by air.[2] However, the entire rebellion failed miserably in the Levante, although that was one of the regions in which Mola had expected complete success. Some of the military leaders there suffered a complete paralysis of will. Their belated rebellion in Valencia was crushed by a thoroughly aroused workers' militia, and, as a result, the small garrisons around Alicante were largely quiescent. Officers pledged to lead the Alicante *cuartel* into the streets lost their nerve during the crisis, and nothing happened. Seeing that the military had failed utterly in this region, the Falange militia stationed nearest José Antonio made an effort of their own to rescue him, with the help of local monarchists. This, too, was ill-prepared. The rescuers were discovered and subdued by Assault Guards before they even got near the prison.[3]

José Antonio was now cut off from the outside world and was gradually deprived of sources of information. After August 16 he was denied further visits from Rightist friends in the vicinity. Though the reports he received were incomplete, José Antonio perceived the general lines of the conflict taking shape that summer. He realized

---

* Some have even thought that José Antonio could not have written such a manifesto. The author of the standard military history of the Civil War, Manuel Aznar, is among them. (*Historia militar de la guerra de España*, p. 40.)

that nothing good could result from an exhausting civil war, which would warp the course of the nation's development for years to come. He was appalled to think that the force of the Falange might be expended in a long and enervating struggle between Right and Left in which the nation as a whole would come out the loser. The aftermath of such a conflict would be the exact negation of that spirit of national unity he had preached. If the Left won, it would destroy all hope for restoring Spain to its historical Catholic solidarity. If the Right won, there would be black reaction, maintained only by force and smothering the vital energies of the nation. As he had rightly feared, the Falange was more and more to be ground between the upper and the nether millstones.

Among José Antonio's papers is preserved a very interesting draft of a letter which he prepared during that month of August 1936. It says, in part:

Situation: I have not sufficient facts as to who is doing better. Therefore, a purely moral synthesis.

A: If the Govt. wins. (1) Shootings; (2) predominance of the workers' parties (of class, of discord, of war); (3) consolidation of certain Spanish castes (unemployed functionaries, Republicanization, etc.).

It will be said: The Govt. is not to blame. The ones who rebelled are the others.

No, a rebellion (especially one so extensive) is not produced without a profound motive.

Social reaction?

Monarchical nostalgia?

No, this rebellion is, above all, of the middle classes. Even geographically, the regions in which it has most firmly taken root (Castile, León, Aragon) are regions petit-bourgeois in character.

The determining cause has been the insufferable policy of Casares Quiroga.

. . .

One cannot increase indefinitely the pressure in a boiling pot. The situation had to explode. And it exploded. But now:

B: What will happen if the rebels win?

A group of generals of honorable intentions but of abysmal political mediocrity. Elementary clichés (order, pacification of spirits . . .).

Back of them: (1) Old Carlism, intransigent Carlism, boorish, disagreeable. (2) The conservative classes, with their own interests, shortsighted, lazy. (3) Agrarian and financial capitalism, that is to say: the termination for many years of any possibility of building a modern Spain; the absence of any national sense of long-range perspective.

And then, after a few years, as a reaction, the negative revolution once more.

The only way out:

An end to hostilities and the commencement of an era of political and national economic reconstruction, without persecutions, without a spirit of reprisal, that can make of Spain a peaceful, free, and industrious nation.

My offer:

1. General amnesty.

2. Reinstatement of the functionaries declared expelled since July 18.

3. Dissolution and disarmament of all the militias. . . .

4. Lifting of the state of siege. If, for reasons of public order, this is not considered possible, modification of the law of Public Order to provide: (1) that government imprisonment may not last more than fifteen days, nor be imposed more than twice each six months; (2) that the closing of political centers are to be subject to the same norms; (3) that government fines are to be imposed only after proper resolution and, not being imposed in application of prosecuting orders, are not to be effective until all legal recourse is exhausted; (4) that revision of the penalties can be carried out during the abnormal period, in order to accommodate them to the precepts effective prior to July 18.

5. Declaration of the permanence in office of all public employees, save for the provisions of the organic regulations of the various bodies already effective on July 18.

6. Suppression of all political intervention in the administration of justice. This will be dependent on the Supreme Tribunal, constituted just as it is, and will be ruled by the laws effective prior to February 16.

7. Immediate implementation of the law of Agrarian Reform.

8. Authorization of religious teaching, subject to the technical inspection of the state.

9. Formation of a government presided over by Diego Martínez Barrio, of which the Señores Alvarez (D. Melquiades), Portela, Sánchez Román, Ventosa, Maura (D. Miguel), Ortega y Gasset, and Marañón form a part.

10. Preparation of a plan for national pacification and reconstruction.

11. Cloture of the Cortes for six months and authorization to the Government to legislate within the lines of the approved program.

José Antonio later drew up a list of cabinet members for a government of "national pacification," which contained the following names:

President: Martínez Barrio
State: Sánchez Román [one of Spain's most eminent jurists]
Justice: Melquiades Alvarez [a conservative liberal on the nineteenth-century pattern]
War: the President
Marine: Miguel Maura
Interior: Portela Valladares
Agriculture: Ruiz Funes [a man with special qualifications in this field]
Finance: Ventosa [a very able Catalan financier]
Public Instruction: Ortega y Gasset
Public Works: Prieto
Industry and Commerce: Viñuales [an outstanding economist]
Health and Labor: Marañón [an eminent liberal physician, historian, and writer][4]

Some days afterward Martín Echeverría, the Subsecretary of Agriculture, passed through Alicante, and José Antonio asked to be permitted to talk with him. According to his later testimony, the Falange leader told Echeverría:

I am watching Spain go to pieces. I can see that a triumph of one side not controlled by anyone else may bring a return to the Carlist wars, a regression in which all gains in the social, political, and economic order are carried away, the entry into a period of darkness and torpor.[5]

He asked to be allowed to fly to Burgos to mediate with the Nationalists, leaving his relatives in Alicante as hostages. Echeverría skeptically transmitted the offer to the central government, which refused to accept it.[6]

After the reconstitution of the Falange command early in September, serious efforts were made to secure the freedom of the *Jefe*. The first plan centered around an elaborate political intrigue in Alicante that failed utterly in execution.[7] The German consulate in Alicante played a central role in this scheme. Von Knobloch, the consul, was an ardent Nazi. He told his superiors that

> the liberation of José Antonio is vital to Spanish Fascism, which must bring about a National Socialist revolution of the people now, during the Civil War, since otherwise, after victory, reactionary elements . . . would hinder Franco in the execution of his program.[8]

Von Knobloch knew little about José Antonio, but he realized that the Falange leader was the only person who could face the clerical-monarchist-military elements in rebel Spain with any chance of success. He petitioned the Wilhelmstrasse for authority to exert diplomatic pressure on the Civil Governor of the province. However, the German Foreign Office had no desire whatever to become entangled with the personal fate of José Antonio Primo de Rivera, and even the Nazi Party declined to back the Falange in such matters.* Von Knobloch's requests were bluntly refused.

Intrigue having failed, the Falange chiefs now initiated a more direct plan to secure their leader's release: they proposed to develop a commando squad for a lightning descent on Alicante. All the top Falangists gave their support to this project, disregarding the fact that José Antonio's return might give swaggerers and opportunists cause for alarm:

> Among some leaders of the Falange there was considerable fear of José Antonio because they knew that he would disapprove of their conduct and that they would be resoundingly removed from their positions.[9]

But no one could oppose an all-out attempt to rescue the *Jefe*. Even the Generalissimo cooperated, although with caution:

> For Franco it was a very delicate question, given the scant political confidence which the Falange had in him. If he took charge of the operation and it failed, the responsibility would fall on his

---

* Ernst von Weizsäcker, chief political secretary to the Foreign Office, wrote on October 26, "There is no question of any authorization of Knobloch by the party to work there toward a National Socialist revolution in Spain." (*Germany and the Spanish Civil War*, Doc. No. 108, p. 120.)

shoulders. If he did nothing, he would be guilty by omission. . . . He left the initiative to the Falange and helped as much as he could.[10]

A training camp was set up outside Seville, but the whole plan came to nothing because of the technical complications involved and the general incapacity of the leadership.[11] It was necessary to turn again to political intrigue.

Early in October Hedilla went to Franco to ask for funds to support a trip to France by the Falangist writer Eugenio Montes. The money was readily granted, Montes' object being to get in touch with leading Spanish and French personalities in France and attempt to win their intervention on José Antonio's behalf. These efforts went on over a period of six weeks and involved such dissimilar figures as José Ortega y Gasset, the French cabinet member Yvon Delbos, and the wife of the Rumanian ambassador to Spain. Indalecio Prieto was the chief contact on the Republican side. But once more, it was impossible to achieve anything concrete. There seemed to be no direct way to influence the fate of the *Jefe*.[12]

The last person from the outside world to visit José Antonio was Jay Allen, an American reporter who interviewed him toward the end of October. It was clear that the Falange leader was poorly informed on current events; he asked Allen for news, saying that he could not be sure what was happening in the rest of Spain. The reporter parried by inquiring what José Antonio would say were he told that Franco's forces merely represented old conservative Spain fighting selfishly to retain its traditional privileges. José Antonio replied that he doubted whether that was true, but that if it was, the Falange had always worked for something very different. Allen then recounted the gory exploits (both true and false) of the Falange's execution squads in recent months. José Antonio said that he believed, and wanted to believe, that none of this was true, but he pointed out that his young men now had no real leader and had suffered great provocation. Reminded that he himself had introduced the term "pistol dialectics" in his founding speech, José Antonio retorted that the Left had struck first. He declared that if the Franco-led movement were in truth reactionary, he would withdraw the

Falange from it and would shortly end up in another prison. José Antonio still appeared confident of receiving his freedom within a short time. Allen thought his performance "a magnificent bluff."[13]

It was, indeed, for the personal drama of José Antonio was swiftly drawing to a close. As the Civil War grew bloodier and positions became more entrenched, pressure arose in certain quarters to settle the case of the Falange chieftain. The more extreme groups urged action against José Antonio, and several newspapers in the Republican zone began to agitate for a quick hearing. The decision to bring José Antonio to trial was taken by local political authorities. Jesús Monzón, the Civil Governor of Alicante, was a Communist and eager to be rid of the Falange leader. Prieto has written,

> On learning that my agents had approached Don Miguel Primo de Rivera [José Antonio's younger brother, imprisoned with him] . . . in order to find testimony by José Antonio which would be unfavorable to the military rebellion, he [Monzón] ordered a police investigation of these efforts in order to see if it were possible—as he publicly confessed—"to have a political weapon against him."[14]

The formal charge brought against José Antonio was that of helping prepare the revolt against the Republic. His brother and sister-in-law were prosecuted with him. The preliminary arraignment took place November 13, 1936, before a "people's court" of the kind recently instituted by the Republican legal system. During the course of his defense José Antonio read his strongest editorials from *Arriba* condemning the Right and distinguishing it from the Falange. He pointed out that the military groups around Alicante had made no attempt to free him and noted that newspapers in rebel territory had published lists of cabinet members for the future rebel government without ever, to his knowledge, having included him. José Antonio declared himself innocent

> by the very simple fact of being there in the jail, a situation that has been directly desired by the forces of the Right in rebellion. They wanted to take advantage of the spirit and combative energy of the boys of Falange Española, to thwart my control over them.[15]

He then went on to mention the letters and offers of mediation he had addressed to Echeverría and Martínez Barrio.

None of this really impressed the jury, and the verdict was almost a foregone conclusion. The only direct account of the final session was written by a local reporter:

Alien to the beehive of people packed together in the chamber, José Antonio Primo de Rivera reads a copy of the closing statement of the prosecutor, during a brief respite authorized by the Court. He does not bat an eyelash. He reads as though those pages dealt with some banal problem which did not concern him. Not the least trace of a squint or a raised eyebrow, not the slightest gesture alter his serene face. He reads intently, with full attention, without being distracted by the incessant buzzing of the chamber for an instant.

．　．　．

Primo de Rivera hears the courtroom ritual like a person listening to the rain. It would not appear that this affair, all this frightful affair, moves him. While the prosecutor reads, he reads, writes, and arranges his papers, all without the slightest affectation, without nervousness.

Margarita Larios hangs on the reading and on the eyes of her husband Miguel, who waits, perplexed by the reading, which must seem to him eternal.

The prosecutor reads on, before the emotion of the public and the attention of the jury.

José Antonio raises his head from his papers when the accusation against the prison officials is dismissed and he sees them depart freely amid the approving clamor of the public.

Yet that expression, not of surprise, but only, perhaps, of a brief hope, lasts no more than a moment.

Immediately he begins to read aloud, with tranquility and composure, his own closing statement, to which the public listens with close attention.

．　．　．

Margot raises a small handkerchief to her eyes, which are filling with tears.

Miguel listens, but he does not look at the prosecutor; his eyes are turned toward the face of his brother, which he searches avidly for an optimistic gesture or a sign of discouragement. But José Antonio continues to be a sphinx who only becomes animated when it is his turn to speak in defense of himself and the other two people on trial.

His remarks are clear and direct. Gesture, voice, and word fuse in a masterpiece of forensic oratory to which the public listens carefully, with evident signs of interest.

．　．　．

At last the sentence.

A split sentence, in which the jury has fixed the penalties according to the differing responsibilities of the accused.

And here the serenity of José Antonio Primo de Rivera was shattered before the eyes of his brother Miguel and his sister-in-law.

His nerves broke.

The scene that followed may be imagined.

His emotion, and the pathos of it, touched everyone.[16]

José Antonio was condemned to die before a firing squad. Miguel Primo de Rivera was sentenced to thirty years in prison and his wife, Margarita, to three years. The case was reasonably clear, although partially based on circumstantial evidence; death is the customary penalty for conspiring to overthrow the state. An appeal was made to the highest government authority, and the Republican cabinet itself reviewed the decision. The members of the cabinet were not of one mind, and some strongly opposed the execution of the Falange chief. But as so often happened with deliberations held under the Spanish Republic, the authorities dallied too long. According to Largo Caballero, the Prime Minister, they had not reached a final decision when word was received that the Governor of Alicante had already executed the sentence.[17]

On the nineteenth of November, José Antonio wrote his personal testament. He noted sadly the understanding and sympathy shown by some of those present in the courtroom when he listed what had been his ideals for the Falange; once more he lamented the political vacuum in which his party had been compelled to struggle. He was left to reflect on just how much his insistence on fascistic form was contributing to the nation's tragedy.*

However, José Antonio refused to cast any reproach on the current activities of the Falange or the conduct of the war. He retracted

---

* After José Antonio's death, Prieto collected the Falange leader's private papers and was impressed by what he found. Prieto later wrote: "The philosophical affirmation that there is some truth in all ideas has a long history. This comes to my mind on account of the manuscripts which José Antonio Primo de Rivera left in the Alicante jail. Perhaps in Spain we have not examined with serenity our respective ideologies in order to discover the coincidences, which were perhaps fundamental, and measure the divergences, probably secondary, in order to determine if the latter were worth being aired on the battlefield." (Prologue to *Palabras de ayer y hoy,* p. 17.)

the charges of betrayal made in his courtroom defense as mere tactical maneuvers. He could not see his way clear to condemn the failures and frustrations of his associates, nor even what may have seemed the treachery of his military allies. The outcome of the war was uncertain, and his personal opportunities were now over. José Antonio had always used his initiative as he thought best for a given moment. After writing a brief personal testament, he saw no point in saying more. His record he left without commentary.

During that next-to-last day of his life, José Antonio composed a dozen short notes to his closest relatives and associates.[18] He also said good-bye to the members of his family still in Alicante.[19] The execution took place shortly after dawn on November 20. José Antonio was placed beside four other political prisoners also condemned to die. His last words were ones of consolation to the men who were to be shot alongside him. There was no romantic flourish, only a laconic dignity.[20]

The Civil War was very hard on the Primo de Rivera family. Besides José Antonio and his brother Fernando, killed in the August 22 prison massacre in Madrid, an uncle and five cousins perished in the conflagration of those years.[21]

XII

THE FALANGE MILITIA

DURING THE GREATER PART of the Civil War three-quarters of the Falange's energy was spent preparing militiamen for military and paramilitary duties. One of the basic problems of the party command in the early months was to give adequate organization and leadership to this effort. Most of the leaders of the Falange militia had no military training, and party militants were often sent to the front under the command of amateur volunteer officers. The leaders soon realized that unless they could somehow train party men for command at the front, their whole initiative might be lost.

In some regions, such as Aragón, the local chiefs had merely named professional officers to the militia. This was clearly necessary in certain areas near the front. But large numbers of auxiliaries had to be dispatched to fill sectors which the regular Army was incapable of manning. By September 7, 1936, seven weeks after the rebellion began, the Army reported that four thousand volunteers were serving with the Fifth Bandera of Aragón alone.[1] All these men were outside the direct control of party leadership. This would not be satisfactory if the Falange were to maintain some sense of political cohesion throughout the war effort.

In José Antonio's provisional agreement with Mola it had been stipulated that no more than one-third of the Falange forces in any given area would serve under regular Army command. However, the *Jefe Nacional* of Militia, Luis Aguilar, was killed in Madrid at the beginning of the war, and his provisional successor, Agustín Aznar, did not concern himself with most of the technical, organizational problems of militia leadership. Aznar spent most of his time perpetrating acts of personal violence, avenging himself on enemies, developing plans to rescue José Antonio, and bolstering the position of his political clique.

When the military government began to talk of organizing a school for "provisional lieutenants," it became clear that Falange leaders had to develop some initiative in this respect or see their militia swallowed up by the regular Army. Despite the anti-Falange atmosphere prevailing at military headquarters in Salamanca, a fair number of the younger officers at the front were vaguely pro-Falangist. If the party leaders were capable of concerted action, they might yet be able to build up a fully autonomous and independent militia. The regular Army needed every man at the front and had no troops to spare for coercing the Falange's Junta de Mando.

Of the more important rebel officers, only Colonel (soon General) Yagüe sympathized with the goals of the Falange. He and the militia leaders from Valladolid (Girón, Vicén, Castelló) made several trips to Salamanca to convince the Junta de Mando of the need to train a real Falangist officer corps.[2] Hedilla apparently failed to see the full importance of this physical arm of the party. He first suggested that the Falange need not control posts above that of sergeant and could continue to draw its regular officers from the Army.

Much time was wasted, but the Junta de Mando was finally persuaded that something had to be done. The party decided to establish two small "military schools" for militia officers—one at Pedro Llen, near Salamanca, and the other near Seville. The Seville branch was staffed with the best instructors the organization could muster from its own ranks. The military teachers at Pedro Llen were loaned to the Falange through the offices of the German Embassy in Salamanca.* The Junta hoped later to develop independent technical staffs in engineering, chemistry, medicine, and other fields.†

The Falange military schools were not a success. The most capable candidates were attracted by the benefits and prestige of the regular Army's officer courses. Many militiamen had hastened to marry and needed the increased pay offered by the regular Army. Since the new

* In a report of Dec. 10, 1936, the German ambassador, Faupel, showed considerable concern over the lack of military training in the Falange militia. (*Germany and the Spanish Civil War,* Doc. No. 148, pp. 159–62.)

† Meanwhile, an even more ambitious effort in this line by the Requetés was being brutally quashed by the military. The Carlist leader, Fal Conde, was summarily exiled from rebel Spain.

militants lacked political indoctrination, they were not always impressed by the Falange's ideological conflicts with monarchists and conservatives, and the spirit of comradeship prevailing among the rebel officers at the front diminished other differences. Most of the Falange youth from Burgos, Zaragoza, Valladolid, and Granada ignored the schools. The branch at Seville lasted through only a portion of its first course, and its directors proposed that the whole project be scrapped. They suggested that the Falange accept a regular quota of the assignments for the training of the Army's *alféreces provisionales*.[3]

The problem was partially solved on December 22, 1936, when Franco's Cuartel General decreed the unification of all civilian militia units. Henceforth, all auxiliary forces would be subject to regular military discipline and the official Army code. Their commanders would be regular officers.[4]

This was largely a paper unification. No commander was named for nearly a month, and most militia units continued to go their own way.[5] The problems at military headquarters were too numerous to allow constant attention to the militia. The Pedro Llen training school, such as it was, was allowed to continue, although on January 28, 1937, provision was officially made for the preparation of officer candidates from the militia in the regular courses of *alféreces provisionales*.[6]

It would be difficult to exaggerate the lack of direction and organization in the various Falange units. There was really none whatever. Everything was done on a local basis. *Centurias* were recruited and equipped by the provincial and regional leadership. No one in the Falange headquarters at Salamanca had any idea how many battalions were in existence, nor what their approximate location or relative strength might be. This was largely the fault of the men who constituted the national command. Their short-range views on how to handle the political situation, their devotion to petty detail in the party bureaucracy, combined with personal factionalism, prevented constructive action. Aznar demonstrated utter incapacity to the end. He had no broad understanding of the war and no general talent for organization. He was not interested in the real problems of leadership, and saw no need to be. It would be impossible to explain his lack of initiative in strictly logical terms.

When the party fell into a profound internal crisis during the spring of 1937, even Aznar realized that something had to be done.[7] So that he would not have to do it himself, some of the best militia leaders, such as Vicén and Castelló, were recalled from the front. They were given the task of preparing some sort of technical organization for the militia, and the work began in March. Before the Falange had a chance to accomplish much, its whole political position blew up. In the shambles, the entire upper class of officer candidates at Pedro Llen was temporarily placed under arrest and their direction was taken over by the regular Army.[8]

On the whole, it cannot be said that the Falange militia ever achieved great efficiency as a fighting force. Very often "it was regarded almost with derision by the various units of the Army and by the Reds."[9] Draft dodgers later joined the Falange to escape the full rigor of military discipline, and morale was uneven. Furthermore, the military pursued a definite policy of pre-empting the ablest units for the regular forces, leaving only the dregs for the party's *banderas*. Records of the Burgos Falange show that 9,120 volunteers joined the militia in that province prior to April 19, 1937. Four hundred and ninety of these were listed as casualties. Of the remainder, 4,252—the more valiant half—were co-opted by the Cuartel General for the regular Army. The other 4,378, the less skillful and combative, remained in the militia to help win for it a name as a third-rate fighting force.

Nonetheless, portions of the Falange troops acquitted themselves well on a variety of fronts, although there has since been much bickering between different military groups about dividing up the glories of the war. It is true that the Requetés, man for man, were more aggressive and effective. However, the Falangists also served on occasion as shock troops. At the beginning of the conflict, when the rebels had difficulty manning their front, Mobile Brigades were formed in Aragón and Andalusia; these were mixed units composed of picked militiamen and trained Legionnaires.[10] Several of them

were cut to pieces in the drive on Madrid.[11] The Falange of Aragón
lent valiant assistance on the northeastern front. The resistance of
a section of the Twenty-fifth Bandera at Alcubierre, on April 9, 1937,
was especially noteworthy.[12] The Second Bandera acquitted itself
well during the bloody struggle for Codo peak during August of
that year.[18] Other banderas distinguished themselves in the fighting
at Teruel and Huesca.[14] Several militia leaders won renown during
the first year of fighting. Outstanding among them were Fernando
Zamacola, of Estremadura, who received the Army's highest decoration,[15] and the Castilians Girón and Fernández Silvestre.[16]

Owing to their disorganization, full records were never available
regarding the total number of volunteers contributed by the Falange.
At the end of 1936, the party claimed that fifty thousand militiamen
were serving at the front, with thirty thousand more in the rear
guard.[17] A reversal of these figures might bring one nearer the truth,
since the militia usually performed paramilitary duties not directly
connected with front-line service. Conservative British observers
noted the almost total predominance of the Falange in the rear
guard.[18] In April 1937 General Monasterio, the titular chief of the
united militias, is said to have stated that the militias then contained
126,000 Falangists, 22,000 Requetés, and 5,000 men from other
groups.[19]

The first recruits were drawn from such Falange centers as Valladolid, Burgos, Zaragoza, and Seville, and from outlying areas such
as Morocco and the Canaries.[20] However, the party was soon accepting recruits from all available sources. Definite pressure was put
on ex-Reds to "redeem" themselves through service at the front. A
circular was sent through León and Zamora stating that voluntary
enlistment for active duty was a clearer sign of loyalty than was
ideological purity.[21] The percentage of ex-Leftists in the militia was
at least as high as in the regular Army organization. In Asturias,
where the danger was great and the militia took part in heavy fighting, twenty per cent of the *centurias* were genuine Falangists, sixty
per cent were ex-conservatives and political indifferents, and twenty
per cent were ex-Reds.[22]

Falange leaders also gave generously of their time in recruiting
for other units. The Galician Battalion, which played so important

a role in Asturias, was originally recruited as a joint enterprise by the Falange and the Army.* Furthermore, the Falange provided volunteers for the Spanish units slated for incorporation into the picked Fascist corps of the Italian contingents serving in the war. In Estremadura many young ex-Communists were enrolled to aid the Italians in their drive on Málaga.†

All this activity was bound to have some effect. Although progressively denuded of its best elements and kept under the thumb of the regular Army, the Falange militia never entirely lost its identity. The better contingents succeeded in obtaining military commanders who were sympathetic to national syndicalism. It has been estimated that a very large proportion of the *alféreces provisionales,* who eventually led the victorious nationalist Army, began their service with Falange groups. Whatever the actual percentage, a goodly number of the tens and tens of thousands of men who passed through the Falange militia developed a certain sympathy with national syndicalist aspirations.[28] These *ex-combatientes* would be the party's only hope for political success on the morrow of victory.

* When Francisco Bravo, *jefe territorial* of Salamanca, went to Galicia at the end of the year to drum up more recruits, he was honored with the official Army rank of Major. (*Boletín Oficial del Estado,* No. 54, Dec. 12, 1936.)

† According to Ricardo Nieto, the Falange endeavored to provide two thousand recruits for the Italian "Fleccie Nere" during the winter of 1937. Hedilla says that he himself assisted General Gambara of the Italian General Staff with recruiting in Badajoz.

POLITICAL INTRIGUE IN SALAMANCA

A FTER THE MADRID OFFENSIVE of 1936 failed, the scope of the Civil War widened. Both sides realized that full military and political mobilization would be necessary for victory. However, Franco's headquarters was absorbed with military details and unable to bring order out of political confusion. The Nationalist government had no ideological orientation whatever. Although conflicting political interests were never permitted to interfere with military affairs, as they were in the Republican zone, they nonetheless presented a serious problem. As the war went on, it became clear that some sort of political doctrine was necessary, both to mobilize the civilian population and to provide a viable framework for government. The moderate Right had been discredited, but a political vacuum existed in its place.

The bulk of the officer corps was probably opposed to any non-military political force. Colonel Castejón, who led the first units in Franco's advance from the south, summed up their attitude toward the end of 1936; when asked whether he was a Falangist or a Requeté, he answered,

> *Franquista.* Only that, which already suffices.... I am not informed of political plans ... at the top. That notwithstanding, my personal opinion is that for a long time in Spain's future the delicate and pre-eminent role of being the just, balanced, serene, and imperative arbiter of public affairs is reserved for the Army.[1]

On the other hand, many officers were attracted to some sort of nationalist reform movement and opposed to a mere regrouping of the old conservative interests.

During the first months of the *caudillaje* the Generalissimo's principal political adviser was his brother Nicolás. Nicolás devised a scheme for creating a Franquista Party, based on the followers of the Commander-in-Chief, which could lend political support to the rebel war effort. This notion seems to have been sketched out along the lines of Primo de Rivera's old Unión Patriótica. It would have been a consolidation of all the safe, worn-out, conservative-reactionary forces in Spain, something in the nature of a revival and revitalization of the majority Right of the CEDA. Indeed, the idea seemed to attract some of the less constant members of the CEDA,* such as José Ibáñez Martín, Moreno Torres, the Conde de Mayalde, the journalist Joaquín Arrarás, and the outspoken priest Ignacio Menéndez-Reigada, who was soon to become the Generalissimo's household confessor and advocate of civil war as a sacred Catholic crusade.[2]

The stumbling block before the plan was that all these conservative-patriotic groups had become archaic in the violent and idealistic atmosphere of an ideological war. Nicolás Franco was not the most subtle of men, and he found it impossible to put across another mere conservative front. Evidently Don Nicolás was at first interested in bringing the now-numerous Falange into such a federation, but the party's leaders scoffed at the very idea. They were reluctant to have any dealings with the Generalissimo's brother, whom they considered, with some justification, a corrupt capitalist Mason.[3]

With the orthodox Right now *declassé,* an anti-Republican doctrine could come only from the two political movements actively supporting the rebel war effort: the Comunión Tradicionalista and the Falange. The continuity of the Falange, such as it was, had been irreparably shaken by the tragic events of 1936. Lack of effective leadership and the influx of ex-conservatives had destroyed the relative unity enjoyed by the obscure movement in 1935. After the decree that formally unified the various civilian militia groups in mid-December, the active members of Falange were bound to the code of military discipline whenever the need should arise. This severely undermined the independent political existence of the party.

To make matters worse, factionalism had begun to gnaw at the roots of the Falange command by the beginning of 1937. The reasons

---

* See Zugazagoitia, p. 241. The "orthodox" CEDA had tried to assemble the Right-wing members of the 1936 Cortes in Salamanca, but this was prohibited by the military.

were various. José Antonio had been shot in Alicante on November 20, and although many refused to accept the fact, the Falange was now formally without a head. The pressures of war and the effects of sudden expansion continued to disrupt the few surviving cadres of leadership. As we have seen, Manuel Hedilla did not have the qualities of an outstanding political leader. His personal approach was too open and simple, and lacked the suppleness and maneuverability so necessary in a hectic and disordered political situation. His control was not firm or comprehensive enough to hold the party organization together, and he did not have the cooperation of the other Falange leaders. Faupel, the German ambassador, shared the opinion most common in Salamanca:

> Hedilla was a completely honest person, but by no means equal to the demands imposed on the leader of the Falange. He was surrounded by a whole crowd of ambitious young persons who influenced him instead of being influenced and led by him.[4]

As 1937 wore on, the Falange leaders became divided into three main factions. The first of these, and the strongest within the party, was the official group centered around Hedilla. Hedilla was not entirely lacking in personality, and indeed he had shown more initiative than some of his fellows had expected. When he finally made real efforts to re-establish discipline within the Falange, however, opposition developed. His adherents were characterized by vigorous social conscience and considerable revolutionary impulse. They were supported by the majority of *jefes provinciales,* at least in the northern sector of rebel Spain. Virtually all the party intellectuals supported Hedilla, including the ideological esthetes who comprised the Pamplona clique centered around the propagandizing priest Fermín Yzurdiaga.

However, Hedilla was compromised by his close association with a number of pseudo-fascist journalists and intellectuals, who, as recent converts to *falangismo,* were already under a vaguely Nazi influence. Chief among them was Víctor de la Serna, a Germanophile journalist who had been closely associated with extreme Right-wing interests. Although Hedilla himself was by no means pro-Nazi, there was a general lack of enthusiasm in his group for the less militant foreign fascistic parties, such as the one in Italy; his supporters tended to look to Germany for technical training and support, if not precisely for ideological orientation.

The second faction was composed of the Falange legitimists, the followers of José Antonio in a narrow and legalistic sense. They refused to accept any change in the organization, command, or style of the Falange unless they could find it explicitly outlined in the previous speeches of the *Jefe*. They opposed Hedilla's leadership without having anything very different to offer. They criticized Hedilla's independent initiative and said that he had no right to exercise real authority in the party, being only one among equals on the Junta de Mando.

Augustín Aznar was the principal representative of this group in Salamanca. His chief collaborator from the remnants of the Madrid Falange was José Antonio's former law clerk Rafael Garcerán, who had begun to intrigue incessantly against Hedilla's leadership. Garcerán managed to boost himself into the *jefatura territorial* of Salamanca at the end of 1936 and then ousted one of his rivals to become Secretary of the Junta de Mando. In January 1937, Tito Menéndez, a strong adherent of Garcerán's, was named Chief of Propaganda, under the *Jefe Nacional* of Press and Propaganda, Vicente Cadenas. More or less connected with Garcerán and Aznar were most of the leaders of the Andalusian Falange, which included José Antonio's "family" appointees, such as Sancho Dávila. In times of stress, any of Hedilla's other enemies could be counted on to join forces with this group.

During December 1936 a struggle for power took place in the Valladolid Falange, and Andrés Redondo was expelled from the leadership. In Old Castile, the party tended to fall under the domination of militia leaders from the front, notably Luis González Vicén and José Antonio Girón. These two veteran activists had finally emerged victorious from a two-year struggle with the Redondo brothers.[5] Although relations between Hedilla and Girón had once been pleasant enough, having led to Girón's appointment as *inspector territorial* of Castile, Girón soon began to share Vicén's disenchantment with the political leadership of the party. They probably distrusted the Germanophile intellectuals around Hedilla and questioned Hedilla's own capacity, and they may have feared that the Falange would lose its political independence in Salamanca. At any rate, the new Valladolid leadership tended to support the opposition attitude of Aznar and the Andalusians.

The third faction within the Falange was made up of newcomers, opportunists, ex-conservatives, clericals, monarchists, and the quasifascist technocrats of conservative corporatism. They had their own program, which was simply to take over the party altogether and recast it in a more conservative mold.

The existence of these factions seriously divided the Falange at the very time when the future political structure of Nationalist Spain was about to be determined. The more intelligent observers realized that the present political uncertainty in the rear guard could not endure. Since both the Falange and the Comunión Tradicionalista wanted different forms of authoritarian government, there would not be room for both groups in the state structure of the new nationalist Spain. Some sort of combination or elimination would be necessary, and if the politicians could not accomplish it, the Army would.

The Falangists had always declared that they would never compromise with the Rightiest groups, which should rather disband and come to them. For their part, the Carlists were officially the most intransigent people in the world. Having maintained their anachronistic organization before the resistance of all modern Spain, they felt no need to compromise with a transient group of hypermodernistic fascists.

Formally, however, each party saluted the other as a valiant champion of the Spanish nation. Certain individuals went even further. The more political-minded among the Carlists, who had dragged the Comunión into the rebellion, realized that some kind of adjustment would be necessary. As early as December 19, 1936, Román Ayarzun wrote in *El Pensamiento Navarro,* under the caption "An Idea: REQUETE Y FASCIO":

> Among the things I don't care for in fascism are its banner, whose colors are the same as those of the FAI; its uniform, which is so easily confused with that of Red militiamen (which can even give

rise to dangerous incidents on the battlefield); the habit of calling each other "comrade," a word that sounds ill (for having been prostituted by the Marxists, those Marxists who have hunted down with bullets so many valiant and noble Falangists in our cities); and other things, possibly of greater importance. But such objections should not prevent one from believing that there are many points of coincidence, so that one might judge it convenient to tighten the bonds of union, to soften the points of friction, to smooth over difficulties . . . instead of deepening more and more the divisions, aggravating more and more the bruises and the wounds.

. . .

Both forces have their roots in the people, both draw their support from the masses; in neither of them do the high bureaucratic interests have a place of privilege or positions of command. . . . Both forces confess their belief in God. Between them exists not the slightest fundamental incompatibility.

. . .

Reader . . . : Though you may be opposed to the idea [of union], consider how noble and patriotic is the goal.

There was a definite response from the most clerical sector of the Falange. On January 6, 1937, Fermín Yzurdiaga declared in his paper's large New Year's supplement:

Regarding the tendency toward the formation of a single [political] force, it is undeniable. We think it will be produced by the Falange—whose volume and force of expansion is superior to that of any other party—assimilating those points of Traditionalism that are compatible with the necessities of the movement.

This was not particularly reassuring to the Carlists.

Such sentiments became particularly congenial to the conservatives, clericals, monarchists, *Acción Española* men, and assorted opportunists who lurked on the fringes of the party. They attempted to use the vague possibilities of a Falange-Carlist *entente* to attract the support of the *José Antonistas* who resented the Hedilla leadership. Among the most active proponents of a new Falange combination were the professional men who had infiltrated the party's Technical Services, particularly José Luis Escario, Pedro González Bueno, and Pedro Gamero del Castillo.* Escario and Bueno had both been engineers by profession. Gamero was a very young man from Seville, where he had been the leader of the Catholic students at the university. He had joined the Sevillian Falange when the war began and had done some valuable planning for the technical aspects of party administration in Andalusia.[6] After several months he had moved up into the Technical Services at Salamanca.

The essential aim of these technocrats was to make the Falange the *partido único* in a conservative, authoritarian, corporatist state. The *José Antonistas* had a theoretically different goal, but they were too shortsighted to grasp the true nature of the situation or to comprehend its probable resolution. Distressed over their inability to control Hedilla and deeply resentful over what they considered their secondary place in the party command, they were ready to consider a general shake-up and reorganization. During January Sancho Dávila put out feelers in the direction of the Conde de Rodezno, the most pragmatic and worldly of the Carlist leaders.[7] The results were not discouraging. The technocrats of corporatism and some of the legitimists now decided to join forces. They planned to take advantage of the Carlist command conference in Lisbon during February to discuss terms for an integration of the two movements. All this was done without consulting the official leadership of the Falange.

Dávila, Gamero, and Escario went to Lisbon, and on February 8 they submitted to the Carlists the text of a proposed speech in which the head of the Falange would announce a fusion. The fusion would evidently amount to a mere absorption of the Comunión Tradicionalista by the Falange, although the text also declared that the party would be prepared for "the installation, not the restoration [of a traditionalist monarchy] in the future, at the opportune moment when the interests of the *Patria* may require it." The proposals were extremely vague.

---

* Shortly after the Civil War began, various Technical Services were set up within the party organization to deal with aspects of economics and governmental administration. Many of the leading figures in the national committees of the Services at Salamanca were lawyers and engineers formerly connected with the clerical monarchist review *Acción Española*.

The Carlists replied with a list of "Essential Points for the Union." The second point declared that there could be no question of the absorption of one group by the other; the fusion would have to be equitable and complementary. The third point provided for the establishment of a triumvirate to command the new party, stating that the immediate aim must be to win the war, which still hung in the balance. After peace was proclaimed, a Catholic traditionalist monarchy under the Carlist Regent, Don Javier, was to be installed. A corporative state would be established and a network of national syndicates set up for labor. All vestiges of the old liberal party system would be abolished.

The second note from the self-appointed representatives of the Falange stated that the Comunión ought to join the Falange since

> the Falange declares its intention, always implicit in its program and in its conduct, of installing and maintaining in the future the institutions and political values of Spanish Tradition insofar as they are a guarantee of the continuity of the New State and a basis for its Empire.

On February 17 the Falangists handed a concrete set of "bases for union" to the Carlists. The most important provisions were these: that "The Comunión Tradicionalista enters the Falange Española de las J.O.N.S."; that "The Falange declares its intention of installing the new monarchy at an opportune moment. . . ."; that the Falange would have custody of whatever Crown Prince were proposed; and that the Regent would delegate all his powers to the leadership of the Falange, although the Falange would be required to consult him on who was to be crowned king.

These provisions were completely unacceptable to the Carlists. Fal Conde replied with a "final proposition," which included the following conditions: union, not incorporation, of the two groups, with the resulting formation to be given a new name; a declaration of the principle of monarchy; a declaration of the primacy of Traditionalist principles; a Regency headed by Don Javier as the supreme authority in the new group; active command to be delegated to a Chief named in the pact of fusion, and if not to him, to the heads of the sections of Politics, Culture, and Militia; dissolution of the unified party when the Monarchy was finally set up.

Agreement was impossible, since neither side would give in. Final conversations were held on February 23 and 27. A Regency under Franco was also discussed, but no progress was made. The only understanding reached during these meetings was set forth in a private note stipulating that neither party would have anything to do with any other political group and that both would oppose any government embracing a third political party. The negotiations closed with a letter from the Conde de Rodezno designed to leave the way open for future arrangements of a practical nature.[8]

When the members of the Junta Política first learned that Dávila and his entourage were on their way to Lisbon, reactions were mixed, Some wanted to lend them a private automobile and otherwise assist their efforts; others spoke of expelling the trio from the party, or even of having them shot.[9] Hedilla himself did not learn of the intrigue until it was too late to stop it. His inactivity throughout the whole affair diminished his prestige, especially among political observers at military headquarters.[10]

After this, Hedilla became touchy about any kind of cooperation undertaken with the Carlists without his consent. On February 26 he deprived the *jefe provincial* of Burgos of his party shirt for one day because the latter had permitted Falange militia to alternate with Requetés in an honor guard for the Virgen del Pilar in Zaragoza.[11]

After the beginning of March plans for unifying the party system were rife in rebel Spain, and intrigues multiplied on all sides. Many political formations finally gave up, disbanded, and either tacitly or explicitly threw in their lot with the corporatist new order of the conservative-clerical "technocrats." On March 8 Renovación Española announced its own dissolution and officially petitioned for unification of parties. At a major meeting in Salamanca, Antonio Goicoechea declared:

> Do some organizations concern themselves with the humble and needy, bearing the ideal as a banner? Yes. Yet I say that the solidarity of the war has increased the capacity for sacrifice of the powerful in favor of the humble classes, and that this is a postulate of all the political organizations.
>
> . . .
>
> [We require] a sole party, or better, a patriotic front like that which exists between us and I say that we will carry out all the

sacrifices necessary that this may be attained. . . . A totalitarian system . . . in a purely organic state, in which all have a role to fill.[12]

The abuse of power by Falange leaders like José Moreno, José Muro, Arcadio Carrasco, and Agustín Aznar weakened the prestige of the party in the eyes of non-Falangists. When party bosses commandeered large cars and drove about accompanied by squads of five or six men armed with submachine guns, the general impression could hardly be favorable. Conditions varied from region to region, but the requisitions and insolence which now marked much of the leadership augured ill for the moral influence of the party. Furthermore, there were all sorts of low-level swaggerers who made themselves resented and feared in rebel territory. They made people forget the hard work and modesty of some of the most important men in the party.

The bulk of the civilian population understood that the Falange was an organization with great social demands, but the nature of the demands remained vague in their minds, as it was vague in the minds of most Falangists. The great mass of the party members had virtually no ideological training, even in 1937. Only another José Antonio might have retained some control over this amorphous mass. It was entirely beyond the reach of the less competent men on the Junta de Mando.

Counteragents were now working for both the Cuartel General and the conservatives who were trying to engineer a new political arrangement. They strove to increase the inner tensions among the Falange leadership in order to capture the movement more easily. Although Manuel Hedilla had early escaped from the control of the "legitimists" who hoped to use him, some of the writers and intellectuals in his coterie exercised an equally undesirable influence. Insofar as one may distinguish fact from fiction, the *éminence grise* of these elements was Víctor de la Serna, the journalist of dubious reputation already mentioned. He evidently wrote a good number of the fine-sounding addresses delivered by Hedilla during the winter of 1936–37. He did all he could to impress the Falange chief with the possibilities open to him, flattering his talents (modest though they were) in the hope of leading him to believe that the moment was right for him to assume José Antonio's vacant role. There is little doubt that Serna was also connected with other groups in the political maneuvering then going on in Salamanca. It has even been suggested that he was bribed to incite Hedilla to push his personal leadership to the point where a split in the Falange command would become imminent.[13]

By the spring of 1937 the political direction of the party had fallen into total confusion and uncertainty. A unified direction, with adequate moral and physical authority behind it, was essential if the Falange were not to fall under its own weight. As the establishment of a new *jefatura única* became a practical necessity, the struggle to control its appointment was carried on by the three factions dividing the party.

The intransigent followers of José Antonio held that the election of a new *Jefe Nacional* was illegal, since the death of José Antonio, according to their peculiar manner of reasoning, had not been adequately verified. Their only plan for providing authoritative leadership was to secure the exchange of Raimundo Fernández Cuesta from his cell in a Republican prison. Having been Secretary-General of the party before the war, Fernández Cuesta was next in line for the apostolic succession. That he was lacking in real executive capacity did not seem to disturb those who advocated this move.

The intellectuals around Hedilla, joined by the northern *jefes provinciales,* supported the chairman of the Junta de Mando as a worthy candidate for *Jefe Nacional*. Basically, their plan was to elect Hedilla and hope that a tightening of the reins of party authority would make it possible to steer the Falange into a position strong enough to permit effective bargaining with the Cuartel General.

Some of the militia leaders, especially those from Valladolid, favored a stern and military candidate, such as the "Falange General," Yagüe.[14]

The new Falangists, conservative and opportunistic, wanted to remake the party by nominating a new leader brought in from outside. Even some of the Old Falangists turned against the official party. Prominent among them was Joaquín Miranda, the *jefe provincial* of Seville, who had become the unofficial *jefe territorial* during the spring of 1936, only to be demoted after the return of Sancho

Dávila. Nursing personal grievances against the Falange leadership, he joined forces with those who conspired to overthrow it. Miranda was seconded by Ernesto Giménez Caballero, the bizarre esthete who had sown the seed of national syndicalism among the more unbalanced sectors of the Spanish intelligentsia. Having dropped out of the movement only to have his request for re-admittance refused by José Antonio, Giménez Caballero was also looking for vengeance.

The only difficulty encountered by the various factions was to settle on a candidate. Almost everyone wanted some kind of general, but they did not all agree on which general. The Generalissimo himself was the logical choice, though some of the military would have preferred Mola.

Franco badly needed a political lord chamberlain to help him construct a civil government for the Army dictatorship. His time was largely occupied with military affairs, and his brother Nicolás had met with little success as a political adviser. Don Nicolás had failed completely to get a "Franquista Party" off the ground, and he was inept at handling relations with the Falange and the Carlists.

The political vacancy in Franco's household was filled during March, when Ramón Serrano Súñer, the Generalissimo's brother-in-law, arrived in Salamanca after a long journey from the Dutch Embassy in Madrid, to which he had escaped the previous October.[15] Before falling temporarily into Republican hands, Ramón Serrano had built up a promising political collaboration with Franco, having served as the Generalissimo's chief civilian contact in metropolitan Spain during the troubled spring of 1936. To make things even more convenient for him, relations within the Franco family had become strained over differences between the wives of Francisco and Nicolás.[16] Since the Generalissimo's wife was the sister of Serrano's spouse, the form of the new power alignment could be easily foreseen.*

Besides being very ambitious, Serrano was easily the shrewdest

---

* This was far from the first occasion, although certainly the most significant one, on which his wife's influence made Serrano's opportunity. He had been aided in his bid for freedom at Madrid by her acquaintance with Belarmino Tomás, the Socialist leader. (Antonio de Lizarra, *Los vascos y la República española*, pp. 124–27.)

politician to have appeared in Salamanca during the war. His former post as head of the JAP had given him extensive contacts among the Right. He was also acquainted with members of *Acción Española* and the Comunión Tradicionalista, and his former friendship with José Antonio even lent him some slight standing with the Falangists.[17] As the days passed, Franco tended more and more to place political affairs in his hands.

Personally, Serrano was emotional and highly subjective. He had few friends. He was badly shaken by the execution of his two brothers in Republican Spain. He had barely escaped the same fate, and for some time he felt as though he were virtually in mortgage to the dead, liable to them for an immense debt. Although this pious mood did not last, it provided an initial orientation for his energies. He viewed with immense scorn the "tribe" of narrow opportunists around Franco, which included Don Nicolás and the Foreign Minister Sangróniz, among others. He had more respect for members of Renovación Española, the Rodezno clique, and his own CEDA, but he considered their ideas insufficient for the twentieth century. Serrano knew that some of the generals, notably Mola, were looking forward to the permanent establishment of a military government. He, on the contrary, believed such a government would prove too superficial to last.

Serrano was perhaps the only man at rebel headquarters with a clear notion of what he wanted to do. He wanted to construct a new Spanish state on a juridical basis, essentially authoritarian, which could prevent any future democratic excess like the one that had taken the lives of his two brothers. At the same time, the new state was not to resemble the ineffective monarchist creations of the past. A strong form of organized corporatism, resting on a solid conservative base, would have to be installed in order to dissipate social tensions and hold the country together as a single national unit.[18]

Ramón Serrano had been a close friend of José Antonio's from college days, but he had carefully resisted the latter's persistent requests to join the Falange. The national syndicalists had always seemed to him too demagogic and superficial, a radical party based on an insecure foundation. But after surveying the situation in Salamanca, he decided that there could be but one solution, for there was only one modern corporatist party with any popular support. Its only competitor, Carlism,

> suffered from a certain lack of political modernity. On the other hand, a good part of its doctrine was included in the thought of the Falange, which furthermore had the popular social revolutionary content that could permit nationalist Spain to absorb ideologically Red Spain, which was our great ambition and our great duty.[19]

At that time the Falange was filled "even with masses coming from the Republic and [Anarcho-] syndicalism. . . . Its leaders were old provincial chiefs, usually little known, and extremely young squad leaders, in many cases merely improvised."[20] The Falange must be reorganized on a firm, conservative basis, which would then qualify it to become the state party of nationalist Spain. In this way Serrano hoped to realize the aims of the "true" José Antonio, which he took to be José Antonio the nationalist and party leader, not José Antonio the aspiring revolutionary.

To advance this scheme for reorganization, Serrano made contact with people of every political stripe. The talents of intellectuals from *Acción Española* and the initiative of conservative-minded planners from the party's Technical Services were the most convenient tools. Serrano conferred with young Gamero, with González Bueno, with Alfonso García Valdecasas.[21] Valdecasas had by this time returned to the Falange and was one of the leading proponents of readjustment.[22]

A policy of political unification was being strongly urged both by the military and by the Axis powers. The officers were tired of political parties, and the more vocal among them demanded their abolition. Since the Army had started the war and tightly controlled its half of the country, it would doubtless get what it wanted. Furthermore, the Germans made no secret of their attitude. Both to the Falangists and to the rebel government, Faupel declared that a strong party-state was needed immediately.[23] Although no direct pressure was applied, the qualitative importance of German aid made it inevitable that hints so blunt would have their effect. The Italians were also known to favor the same step, though their ambassador was more cautious and uncertain in his advice.[24]

Reform and reconstruction had been loudly proclaimed by the rebels from the beginning. The Generalissimo had declared to the world that although the nationalists proposed a military dictatorship, a plebiscite would be taken; he added that unions would be sanctioned if they did not preach class warfare. Franco now promised

> All possible reforms within the capacity of the nation's economy. We balk at nothing that the country's economy can stand.
> No use in giving poor land to poor peasants. It is not land alone that counts, but money to work it. Another twenty-five years will see the break-up of the big estates into small properties and the creation of a bourgeois peasantry.[25]

As the war continued, the military stepped up such propaganda. Queipo said to the foreign press: "We realize that the problem of class hatred can be solved only by the removal of extreme class distinctions. We realize, also, that the wealthy, by means of taxation, have to contribute toward a more equitable distribution of money."[26] Mola publicly declared his belief in a "representative" corporatism.[27]

Such statements seemed compatible with some kind of watered-down national syndicalism, and some of the more politically astute provincial leaders of the Falange were coming to accept the inevitable. Confronted with the present vacuum of authority within the party and the complete monopoly of power by the military from without, they began to believe that the only viable policy was to unify the existing political groups under the only real leader then enjoying public confidence—the Generalissimo. Andrés Redondo had already said this during the autumn of 1936, before his ouster from Valladolid. Other leaders privately thought the same while remaining outwardly loyal to the Junta de Mando.

An independent initiative in this direction developed on the part of Ladislao López Bassa, a Falangist and a lieutenant of engineers from the garrison of Mallorca. He propagated the notion of a great Falange of all the nationalist parties under the direction of Franco, and visited Falange groups in various parts of Spain.* These gestures were assisted by dissidents like Miranda and Giménez Caballero.

---

* He was accompanied by a cousin of José Antonio's, one Doctor Orbaneja. Orbaneja, a strange individual, was an accomplished children's specialist who had won a gory reputation for himself in the Falange terrorism on Mallorca.

Meanwhile, Hedilla was urged by his backers to seize the initiative before it was too late. He was even invited several times to the home of General Faupel, who further encouraged him to take the lead for the Falange.[28] Given such a strong incentive, Hedilla met secretly with several Carlist leaders in a small town in Alava province. They realized both the Carlists and the Falangists might soon be presented with a formal degree of fusion by the Cuartel General. It was still impossible to resolve their mutual differences, but it was agreed that none of those present would accept a post in a party created by military fiat.[29]

Meanwhile, in conjunction with Serrano, López Bassa took up residence in Salamanca and worked hard to impress upon Hedilla the importance of unifying all parties under Franco. He intimated that although the Generalissimo might become the nominal head of the unified movement, Hedilla would undoubtedly be made Secretary-General and given extensive powers with which to implement the national syndicalist program. He implied that the independence and internal organization of the Falange would be respected. Although Hedilla never talked directly with the Cuartel General, López Bassa was presented to him as its official representative, and the Falange leader was partly convinced by his talk. He began to speak of Franco with enthusiasm, whereas he had hitherto made it clear that he was no partisan of the Generalissimo.[30]

While Franco's entourage persevered in these political soundings, they also saw the advantages of promoting further confusion and division within the party, which would retard the growth of possible nuclei of resistance among the veterans. To help overcome the present state of disunion, Falange "legitimists" continued to urge the exchange of Fernández Cuesta. When Hedilla was persuaded to speak to Serrano in this regard, Serrano made the most of the situation by declaring that such a transfer would be morally inexcusable, since there were so many other people of equal or greater rank languishing in the Republican zone.[31]

Opposition to Hedilla within the party grew apace. The "legitimists" were determined to take nominal control from his hands, for they feared that he was planning to make himself *Jefe Nacional* under military authority. They wanted to seize control of the party first, so that no single *Jefe* could be proclaimed. Their only concrete aim seems to have been to preserve the party in a continuing state of political limbo, but under their own personal command.

When Hedilla expressed intentions of convoking a National Council, the dissidents made their move at a surprise meeting of the Falange leadership called on April 12. Dávila, Aznar, and Garcerán immediately went to Hedilla's office and read a series of charges against him, among which were the following:

> Manifesting reserve with the official Junta, to which he has never given a full account of his activities, conversations, and political leanings, of which persons alien to the Falange command were informed. . . .
> Submitting docilely to the unofficial Junta, while acting with brusqueness and hostility toward the official Junta. To the former belong opportunists and dangerous men.
> Making inordinate and improper propaganda for himself in order to gain greater authority than is due him, and *orienting his activity* toward the creation of personal followers, employing for this task otiose collaborators who have fabricated articles and speeches of all kinds.
> Engaging in ultimate treason against the Junta de Mando, in order to free himself from its control. . . . Excluding from this forthcoming National Council the names of important comrades whose policies he thinks are opposed to his own, and calling instead only those whom he supposes to be his friends, . . . and therefore capable of making him *Jefe* of the Movement. Among these "friends" are several implacable enemies of José Antonio, traitors to our organization who constantly disfigure it, whose action became so dangerous that an agreement had to be made in a meeting of the Junta de Mando, held in March of this year, to prohibit him [Hedilla] from speaking in public without express permission from the Junta itself.
> Showing manifest ineptitude, heightened by illiteracy, which has caused him [Hedilla] to fall into the hands of the men most dangerous for our Movement, men of whom he feels himself a prisoner.[82]

They even accused Hedilla of plotting with Mola to establish a new rebel government.[83]

According to the party's statutes, if it were necessary for the *Jefe Nacional* to absent himself from Spanish territory for any length of time, the organization would be directed by a triumvirate until his return. Basing their action on this grotesquely inappropriate rule, the rebels simply declared that Hedilla was deposed and would be replaced henceforth by a triumvirate chosen by and composed of themselves. The self-appointed triumvirs were Sancho Dávila, Agustín Aznar, and José Moreno (a former *jefe provincial* of Navarre whom Hedilla had eased into a new position). The opportunistic intriguer Rafael Garcerán became the official secretary for the triumvirate, which announced that it would call a special National Council within fifty days, adding that ten seats on the Council would be held vacant for Falange leaders presumably still detained in Republican territory.

Having thus elevated themselves, the self-styled directors of the party hurried to Franco's headquarters to report on their action. They were kept waiting for some time, but the Generalissimo finally received them in a cordial mood, congratulated them, and advised them to do nothing rash.[34] Next, they delivered a dispatch announcing the new party directorate to the National Radio for broadcast.

The triumvirs at once began to call in supporters from nearby provinces to strengthen their position. Not all of the "supporters" were happy about the move. When Dionisio Ridruejo, the *jefe provincial* of Valladolid, was called to Salamanca and advised that the rebels had acted to forestall a sellout by Hedilla, he protested that the whole business had been an enormous mistake. He believed that what the party needed above all else in that perilous moment of its existence was a united front; and even though old Falangists like Miranda and López Bassa were making deals with the Cuartel General, it was necessary to unite behind Hedilla in order to achieve the best bargain possible.

After recovering from the shock of this *coup* against him, Hedilla apparently decided to attempt a reaffirmation of his leadership, in which he was strongly encouraged by members of his entourage. The proclamation by the triumvirs had not yet been broadcast by the National Radio, and events were hanging fire. On the night of April 14, some sixty hours after the rebellion, José María Goya, a young militia leader and National Counselor of the SEU, asked permission to try to patch things up. Goya, although one of Hedilla's supporters, was also a personal friend of Dávila's, the two having taken shelter together in the Cuban Embassy at Madrid. He proposed to Hedilla that he go to Dávila's house and attempt to persuade the latter to change his attitude and come to terms. Hedilla agreed, adding that Goya should be careful to tread lightly. Goya was accompanied on this mission by another militiaman, Daniel López Puertas, and three companions.

When the group arrived at Dávila's *pensión*, Goya went ahead to talk with Dávila alone. The discussion had hardly begun when it erupted into a brawl; who started the fighting cannot be determined with complete accuracy. A series of shots rang out across the second floor of the building. When the firing ceased López Puertas and his three companions were in control of the situation. They had disarmed Dávila, his male bed partner, and his bodyguards, but Goya and one of Dávila's escorts named Peral lay dead. Civil Guards, attracted by the firing, soon arrived and arrested most of those involved.[35]

This fatal incident played directly into the hands of Serrano Súñer and his collaborators. A howl went up from the General Staff about disorder in the rear guard, which further discredited the Falange with the Army. The affair also seemed to remove all possibility of the Falange leaders agreeing on a common position with regard to the unification about to be thrust upon them.

Within twenty-four hours Dávila, Aznar, Garcerán, and their immediate supporters had been placed under arrest for inciting civil disorder. The way was now clear for the reassertion of Hedilla's leadership. On Saturday, April 16, the chairman called an impromptu session of the Junta de Mando. Dávila and Aznar were temporarily released from jail so that all the members might be present. Hedilla proposed that if his leadership were being questioned, it should be put to a formal vote. Of the seven Junta members, Dávila, Aznar, Moreno, and Jesús Muro voted against Hedilla; only Francisco Bravo and José Sáinz voted for him.[36] The Junta de Mando had obviously broken up.

The next day, after Dávila and Aznar had been sent back to jail, Hedilla posted urgent notices calling a formal session of the Falange National Council for Sunday, April 18. All the available National Councilors appointed in 1935 and 1936 were summoned, as well as several others whose precise status was in doubt.[37] The two-page circular announcing the meeting declared that its object was to clear up questions relating to appointments, dissolve the Junta de Mando, and elect a *Jefe Nacional*. The *Jefe,* it stated, would be named with the understanding that he would serve only until the possible reappearance of José Antonio (in whose death many still refused to believe); should the Secretary-General, Fernández Cuesta, be returned to rebel Spain, the Council would be reconvened to reconsider the problem of legitimacy.[38]

The National Council met on the morning of April 18 in a heavy atmosphere, with the embalmed corpse of Goya, now dead more than seventy-two hours, lending a macabre touch to the scene. There was by no means a feeling of comradeship among those present.* The first six topics discussed dealt with petty points of party personnel and bureaucracy. Only after wrangling for some time over which *jefe* ought to be admitted under what status, or censured for exceeding his nominal authority, could the Council get down to business.[39]

After Hedilla had aired the charges of the dissidents against him, Jesús Muro said that it would be better to forget internal differences and consider the solemnity of the occasion. He referred to Goya's cadaver, which heightened the unreal quality of the meeting. Hedilla then stood up once more to say that he had just been told in the Cuartel General that the Generalissimo was planning to take charge of the command of the Falange, possibly that very night. This news, though not unexpected, had a sobering effect. Francisco Bravo proposed that Hedilla be delegated to talk with Franco about the terms for a unification and reorganization of parties.

With that, the Council finally proceeded to the order of the day, which was the election of a new *Jefe Nacional*. The results of the voting were as follows: 8 blank votes; 1 vote each for Miguel Merino, Martín Ruiz Arenado, Jesús Muro, and José Sáinz; 10 votes for Manuel Hedilla.† Only ten of the twenty-two present voted for Hedilla. There was really no alternative leader, but some members of the Council thought it foolhardy to defy the Cuartel General by

---

* Andino relates that José Sáinz tried to persuade José Moreno, the only one of the new "triumvirs" who had not been arrested, to give up his pistol. Moreno was fearful, and required a good deal of persuasion.

† Merino was the *jefe territorial* of Lower Aragon, and Ruiz Arenado was the *jefe provincial* of Seville.

electing their own *Jefe* when a complete loss of independence threatened.[40]

The new Falange Chief went to call on the Generalissimo that
same evening. According to Hedilla, Franco congratulated him on
the election but refused to discuss more fundamental matters. Later
that night the General made a short speech to a crowd gathered outside his balcony window, and Hedilla also appeared for a few
moments. This touched off a small demonstration by Falange sympathizers, who chanted "Hedilla—Franco."[41] The incident created
great suspicion at military headquarters.

The following day, April 19, Hedilla reconvened the National
Council. The party was already engulfed by the shadow of Franco,
but the Falange leaders went ahead with their title-making. A three-
man board was appointed to investigate the recent internal revolt, and
then the delegates proceeded to elect a new four-man Junta Política.
Apparently incapable of divining the real intentions of the Generalissimo, the delegates proceeded to discuss the significance of his speech
the night before. They decided that clemency ought to be asked for
those being held as prisoners as a result of the Goya affair. Finally,
in a last attempt to rise to the demands of the occasion, the delegates
to the last independent National Council of the Falange Española
decreed that no Council member was entitled to a bodyguard of more
than two men. The old Falange went out with only a whimper.

That night the Cuartel General delivered its *coup de grâce*.
Serrano Súñer had been charged with the preparation of a decree
unifying the Falangists and the Requetés. According to Serrano, both
Mola and Queipo had already been consulted about the text, which
was released at midnight on April 19, 1937. From that hour forward,
the Falangists and Carlists were fused as the official party of the
new Spanish state.*

The new political formation was to be called Falange Española

---

* "It was, in essence, a unilateral act by Franco, even though there were
some previous negotiations with elements of the parties concerned, whose most
outstanding representatives had been notified of the intentions of the Cuartel
General, which nonetheless did not decide to complete what was laboriously
being prepared until prompted by the events that occurred in Salamanca during
the first days of April." (Thus, in a long breath, Ramón Serrano Súñer in
Entre Hendaya y Gibraltar, pp. 30–31.)

Tradicionalista y de las Juntas de Ofensiva Nacional-Sindicalista, a very clumsy title reflecting its eclectic composition.[42] The pragmatic intentions behind the new party were made clear in the official decree:

> The Movement that we lead today is truly that: a movement more than a program. And, as such, it is in the process of elaboration, subject to constant revision and improvement, as reality may counsel. It is not rigid or static, but flexible. Therefore, as a movement it has undergone different stages [of development].
> . . . Abandoning that preoccupation with doctrine, we bring an effective democracy, bearing to the people what really interests them: seeing and feeling themselves governed [by men with] an aspiration for integral justice, as much in the moral order as in the socio-economic realm.[43]

Within forty-eight hours Falangists everywhere had dispatched fervent statements of allegiance to the policy of the Caudillo; they entertained no thoughts of rebellion. The political weakness of the party was never more dramatically exposed. The weak propaganda for Hedilla had never compared with the overwhelming build-up given Franco by the government press. At the moment of unification Manuel Hedilla, the mechanic from Santander, was entirely forgotten.

In Salamanca, Hedilla's support had been completely swept away. Mistakenly believing that there was something to negotiate, he had thought that the new Falange hierarchy would be respected. But there was nothing to negotiate, and no one had any intention of respecting the leaders of his party.

Franco had declared himself the *Jefe Nacional*. As of the moment, there was to be no Secretary-General. Hedilla was named chairman of the new Junta Política of the FET, which was then in process of being organized. That is, Hedilla was expected to find solace as the first among equals on an honorary advisory board composed of opportunists and pliable Carlists selected by the Generalissimo and his brother-in-law.[44] Immediate executive administration would be handled by a new Political Secretariat headed by López Bassa.[45]

Hedilla refused the proffered position. For three days military headquarters cajoled and threatened him, but he remained adamant.[46] Representatives of the Axis powers endeavored to ease the tension by suggesting that Hedilla make a professional visit to one of their countries, but such a solution was not desired by the Cuartel General. On April 25 Hedilla was arrested. To get the uncooperative Falangist out of the way, the political directorate behind the fusion of parties apparently concocted the charge that Hedilla had inspired a plot against the Caudillo. Without further ado, he was handed over to a military judge and placed in solitary confinement.

Among other things, Hedilla was accused of sending telegrams to all the provincial chiefs asking them to assemble in Salamanca to put pressure on the government. There is no real evidence such a telegram was ever sent. José Sáinz has since testified that word was received in Salamanca that, owing to erroneous interpretations of the decree of unification, Falangists and Requetés had begun to snarl each other's chain of command. The only telegrams sent out read as follows: VIEW OF POSSIBLY ERRONEOUS INTERPRETATION UNIFICATION DECREE OBEY NO ORDERS SAVE THOSE RECEIVED THROUGH DIRECT COMMAND HIERARCHY.[47]

The Generalissimo may or may not have been convinced of the truth of these charges. Whatever the case, Hedilla says that he was offered his release if he would accept the post on the new Junta Política. Having proved steadily recalcitrant, Hedilla was swiftly convicted of rebellion by a military court and sentenced to death on two counts. Those Falange leaders who remained at liberty mobilized whatever influence was available to help their vanquished chief. General Yagüe was asked to petition on behalf of the military, and the German ambassador even made a formal intercession with Franco.* Franco apparently remained unmoved, but Serrano Súñer finally decided to intervene. He probably knew all along that Hedilla was innocent of any "plot," but he had no desire to prevent the removal of one of the principal Falange "radicals." However, he did

---

* German pressure was a secondary influence in saving Hedilla from execution. Faupel had earlier suggested to Franco that it would be better to leave a civilian as *Jefe Nacional* of the new party.

After Hedilla's arrest, Faupel did what he could for the man he called "the only real representative of the workers." However, his request for permission to make a formal protest was denied by the Wilhelmstrasse. (*Germany and the Spanish Civil War*, Doc. No. 243, pp. 267–70; Doc. No. 286, pp. 312–13; Doc. No. 296, p. 319.)

ask Franco to commute the double sentence of death to life imprisonment, which might make the remaining Falange chiefs more pliable.
Hedilla was promptly shipped off to the Canary Islands and placed
once again in solitary confinement.

Many lesser Falangists were caught up in the maelstrom and
arrested, but none were actually shot. Ricardo Nieto, the *jefe provincial* of Zamora, was sentenced to twenty years and one day as an
"intransigent" and an accomplice in the "Hedilla plot"; this came
about even though he had not voted for Hedilla and had sent an
immediate pledge of support to Franco. It seems that in the confusion and excitement of those days a young Falangist from Zamora
had informed military headquarters that his *jefe provincial* was working to thwart the unification decree.[48] Nieto had also been blacklisted
for declaring in a public café that when the war was over the Falange
militia would be entitled to give the country its new political orientation.

Virtually all Falange leaders of any importance were detained by
Civil Guards or military police for a few days, as a precautionary
measure. Most of them were swiftly released, but some of the political
stalwarts of the party were strongly encouraged to go off to the fighting front for the duration of the war.

As for the other side in the internal Falange dispute, a government
War Council eventually proclaimed their "absolute innocence." They
were even commended for their "patriotic spirit" and "civic virtues"
in enduring a long test of their feeling for the *Patria*. Dávila, having
been something of a friend of Serrano Súñer's, was released and sent
back to Seville. Garcerán did not fare so well, having been accused
of a clandestine relationship with Indalecio Prieto. Given his penchant for intrigue and Prieto's subsequent interest in fishing among
troubled waters in the Falange, this is quite possible. Garcerán was
not freed for some time and was permanently eliminated from rebel
politics.

Pilar Primo de Rivera, being a cousin of Aznar's fiancée, attempted
to intervene on behalf of the militia leader. Aznar was soon released,
but he was never considered fully reliable, even though he was later
honored with a position on the Junta Política.[49]

The only Falange leader to manage a clean break with the military regime was Vicente Cadenas, the *Jefe Nacional* of Press and Propaganda. He happened to be in San Sebastián, near the French border, when the storm broke. Rather than risk the same fate that befell Hedilla, Nieto, and several others, he fled across the Pyrenees and spent the remainder of the Civil War in Italy.[50]

All the Falangists condemned in this affair were eventually reprieved, most of them within two or three years. The one who suffered most was Manuel Hedilla. At first it was evidently hoped that he would rot to death in prison. For four years he was allowed to see virtually no one save Jesuit confessors. During that time he was often denied food, and at one point his weight dropped to almost eighty-five pounds.[51] His wife went insane over the unjust fate meted out to her husband and later died in an asylum. But Hedilla managed to survive. He may have been shortsighted, gullible, and bereft of political talent, but he had an iron constitution and a very strong moral will. After more than four years of solitary confinement, Manuel Hedilla remained relatively healthy—and more independent than ever. The government finally relented, and in mid-1941 he was moved to comfortable quarters at Mallorca.[52]

The average supporter of the military government received the news of unification with considerable relief and even with joy. Few people beyond the clique at the Gran Hotel in Salamanca had any taste for politics during those months. It was felt that a unification of the two most active civilian groups would solve the political problems of nationalist Spain and close its ranks for the winning of the war. Some professional politicians might murmur, but that was only to be expected.

At the front, news of the unification was accepted by Falange militiamen almost with indifference. The nominal structure of the party meant nothing to them, and since they had little grasp of ideology the politics of the rear guard seemed unreal. During 1937 the Republican war machine began to show signs of real efficiency, and the militia had to concentrate more effort than ever on military affairs.

Everyone who thought seriously about politics had realized that some sort of party unification behind the rebel war effort could be expected. Military control of the Nationalist government made it certain. The *caudillo* heritage from nineteenth-century Spanish politics and the military atmosphere enforced by the war made the leadership of Franco inevitable.

Some Falangists had already admitted this, and the fusion was generally accepted as a natural and unavoidable *dénouement*. Patriotism precluded any other attitude. Furthermore, the official proclamation of the Falange program by the Caudillo seemed to assure the continuity of the party. Many Falangists still clung to the view that the militia would provide the impetus for a reorientation of the nation's political life when the fighting was over. Amid the confusion and tension of the war effort, it was hard to push one's thinking much further than that.

XIV

THE FALANGE AS STATE PARTY
1937-1939

THE FORMAL DECREE of unification settled very little with regard to the structure of the new party. The civil government moved at a very slow pace. Franco and his staff still occupied themselves primarily with military affairs, apparently satisfied that the rudimentary *Gleichschaltung* of April had temporarily shelved all internal political problems. The resulting readjustment was an involved process, and no one seemed to be in a hurry. At first, there was not even much money available.[1] The lack of any clear conception of the new party's mission was suggested by the nature of the first official task given the FET by the Governor General of Salamanca; his order authorized the party to organize nursing courses.[2]

Slowly, the Political Secretariat began to draw the party cadres together, and the incorporation of local auxiliary units got under way on May 11. Under the new dispensation party membership continued to increase, but it was apparent that many of the new members were fair-weather friends who would be with the Falange only for the duration of hostilities. As Serrano Súñer admitted, "A very great number of Party members were never more than nominal affiliates. They were, in reality, members who retained their own individual identities and were more or less cautious representatives of free opinion."[3]

In an *ABC* interview on July 19, Franco proclaimed once again that his aim was "a totalitarian state." He also reiterated that the FET was to serve, in effect, as a great melting pot for such a state:

> There exists in Spain a great unaffiliated neutral mass . . . which has never wanted to join any party. This mass, which might feel hesitant to unite itself with the victors, will find in the Falange Española Tradicionalista y de las J.O.N.S. the adequate channel for uniting itself with National Spain.[4]

However, it would obviously be difficult to make a going concern of the new party with the active support of the surviving leaders of the old Falange. Almost all those who had first been arrested were speedily released, but from this to securing their energetic cooperation in the FET was a long step. An ex-officio committee representing the old Falange had been set up in Salamanca at the house of Pilar Primo de Rivera. There the remaining Falange chiefs met to decide which of them would collaborate with the new party, and under what terms. The most influential voices were those of Agustín Aznar, José Antonio Girón (who represented the militia), and Fernando González Vélez, the serious and intelligent *jefe provincial* of León.[5]

Franco's agent in the negotiations that followed was Ramón Serrano Súñer.[6] The representative of the Falange committee was Dionisio Ridruejo, the twenty-four-year-old *jefe provincial* of Valladolid. Ridruejo was honest and highly intelligent, yet very emotional. His blend of personal qualities somehow won him admittance to the very narrow but extremely intense circuit of Serrano's affection, and the two became good friends.

A vague understanding was soon reached between the Falange committee and the Cuartel General. It was assumed that the Falangists would respect the hierarchy of command being established, and that after the war a sincere attempt would be made to implement the national syndicalist program. The construction of the new state party was to begin immediately.

Some of the Falangists had private reservations about this arrangement. Others, like the National Council delegate and *jefe provincial* of Seville, Martín Ruiz Arenado, were fully convinced of Franco's sincerity. At any rate, they had no choice. Everyone felt that it was better for the FET to be set up and administered by Falangists rather than by a collection of Carlists and conservative opportunitists. Individually, or in small groups, they resolved to build as strong a core of *camisas viejas* (Falange veterans) within the new organization as they possibly could, both to ensure the continuity of the party and to change the nature of the current leadership. González Vélez was given Hedilla's vacant seat on the Junta Política.[7] Later named its chairman, he was a strong advocate of this policy of boring-from-within.

The first party statutes, which were not released until August 4, 1937, preserved in large part the previous structure of the Falange. Twelve special services were set up for the party, taking in every aspect of government activity. It has been suggested that Serrano Súñer's reason for preparing such an elaborate program of service cadres was to compensate for the lack of executive training in the Falange leadership.[8] In effect, the functions of the various Falange services were duplicated at many levels by the government ministries. Thus the Falange's bureaucracy could gain experience without having to face full responsibility. Later, party cadres would be ready to help administer the one-party state. The apparent intention was suggested even more clearly by a law of October 30, 1937, which required the approval of the local Falange and Civil Guard chiefs for anyone recommended to a position in a local or provincial government; it was declared that such double authorization would be necessary until the construction of the "new totalitarian state" was finished.[9]

In the latter part of 1937 there appeared a series of leaflets attacking the capture of the Falange by the Army, signed "Falange Española Auténtica." These made little impression on the old Falangists, who were now rapidly being placed in responsible positions in the FET. The sheets were printed in foreign territory, probably in France. Rumor linked their appearance to Vicente Cadenas, the Falange's former Chief of Press and Propaganda, who had managed to escape from Spain on the morrow of the unification.* It was also suggested, quite logically, that the leaflets were circulated by agents of the Republican minister Indalecio Prieto, who hoped to be able to provoke further dissension within the FET.[10] Having failed in their purpose, the leaflets disappeared after several months.

Chief of Press and Propaganda for the FET was Fermín Yzurdiaga, the bizarre Pamplona priest who had founded the Falange's first daily newspaper. Before the unification he had been a supporter of Hedilla, but he easily made an adjustment to the new situation.

* Cadenas denies that he ever participated in such activities or that, so far as he was ever able to learn, any such organization as "Falange Española Auténtica" ever existed. He dismisses the incident as an anti-Franco maneuver led by unidentified parties.

During the latter half of 1937 *Arriba España* usually ran a front-page caption reading "For God and the Caesar." Appointed to his new post in May, Yzurdiaga chose as his Chief of Propaganda Dionisio Ridruejo; his Press Chief was a veteran Carlist, Eladio Esparza.

During 1937 Falange propaganda was sometimes hampered by military censorship and occasionally quashed outright by the official government information service. Since Yzurdiaga's grasp on reality was slight in any event, it was not surprising that the general effect of his efforts was negligible. In a speech at Vigo on November 28, 1937, Yzurdiaga replied to murmurers in the party. He admitted that there was some truth in the charge that the Falange was no longer revolutionary, saying that one must tread the path to revolution very carefully.[11]

The Falange press was full of praise for the Army.* It carried the customary condemnations of all kinds of liberalism, and flattering articles on Nazi Germany and Fascist Italy. In rare moments of belligerence, some Falange papers still denounced the Franciscan aspects of Catholicism and declared that papal politics were not infallible.[12] There were also occasional diatribes against the virtually nonexistent Jews.[18]

Only occasionally did a really telling blast come from the national syndicalist trumpet. One such instance was Gonzalo Torrente Ballester's slashing critique of a pamphlet being circulated by the privately organized "Provisional Directive Junta of Economic Forces." The pamphlet condemned the vices of a controlled economy and propounded a doctrine of relative *laissez faire*. Torrente Ballester, one of the new party intellectuals, emphasized the need for widespread state control and intervention to ensure a just and adequate functioning of the national economy.[14]

With such statements Falange writers served the military government as an instrument for warning the financial and industrial forces of Spain that they were not to be the sole beneficiaries of the new state. It was implied that those who did not wait patiently on the Caudillo might be fed into the jaws of the national syndicalists. In

---

* Even before its director became Press and Propaganda Chief, Yzurdiaga's *Arriba España* ran in front-page headlines the motto: "The Sound Doctrine: Always With the Army." (May 30, 1937.)

fact, in his own public statements Franco took some pains to pose as a social reformer. He spoke of the "dehumanized banker" and the need for protecting the working classes.[15]

> We are also making a profound revolution in a social sense, which is inspired by the teachings of the Catholic Church. There will be fewer of the rich, but also fewer of the poor. The new Spanish State will be a true democracy in which all citizens will participate in the government by means of their professional activity and their specific function.[16]

Eventually, some sort of executive leadership had to be given the FET, but Serrano and the political directorate were at a loss as to how to proceed. None of the remaining *camisas viejas* had enough talent or prestige to administer the party, and Franco did not consider them trustworthy. The Generalissimo preferred that Serrano Súñer take over direction of the FET. But Serrano (whom political wits dubbed the *cuñadísimo,* or "most high brother-in-law") was a cautious, careful man who strove to act with extreme finesse. He was already unpopular among the veteran Falangists, and he knew that any further power accorded him would increase resentment.

The old guard continued to press for the exchange of Raimundo Fernández Cuesta, the last Secretary of the original party. Before the unification, Serrano had opposed this, not wishing to increase the possible resistance of the *camisas viejas* against the process of coordination then being planned. Now that the power of the old guard had largely been broken, he began to reconsider the matter; Fernández Cuesta's presence might not be harmful and might even have political advantages.[17] Serrano knew well that Fernández Cuesta was not sufficiently energetic as an administrator to be dangerous in the new situation. Furthermore, his eighteen months in Republican jails seemed enough to guarantee his full loyalty to the rebel government.

Feelers were accordingly put out for the exchange of Fernández Cuesta, who had already escaped from prison twice and been recaptured each time. The proposal was favored by Indalecio Prieto, who was still greatly impressed with the papers left behind in José Antonio's cell at Alicante. Prieto had already sent copies of José Antonio's testament into Franco Spain, hoping to provoke a break in the Franco government by exciting the revolutionary aspirations of the Falange old guard. He thought that the return of Fernández Cuesta might possibly rouse the *camisas viejas* to action.*

The ex-Secretary-General arrived in rebel territory in October 1937. He made his first public appearance at Seville on October 29, the fourth anniversary of the founding of the Falange. After thanking Franco for his deliverance from Republican territory, he declared that the aim of the FET was to establish the Spanish economy on a syndical system, which he described as perfectly compatible with capital and private property. Some platitudes about controlling the stock market and financial operations followed, but nothing more.[18] Fernández Cuesta looked like a safe party Secretary for the Caudillo, and he was appointed on December 2, 1937. There was no reaction from the *camisas viejas,* except a general feeling of contentment that no ex-conservative had been imposed on them. In a New Year's Day interview, Fernández Cuesta warned:

> Sincerity and affection oblige me to say to the Old Guard that it must have an understanding spirit, and not lock itself up in exclusiveness or adopt repulsive airs of superiority, but receive with love and comradeship all who come with good faith to Falange Española Tradicionalista.[19]

Fernández Cuesta had a tolerant nature and was not unintelligent, but he lacked initiative and had little administrative talent. Furthermore, being a *camisa vieja,* he was never trusted by Franco. Only Serrano Súñer had the Generalissimo's confidence, and it was Serrano who continued to pull the wires in the Falange. The little lawyer lived and acted on a plane removed from the ordinary servants of the state. Always dressed in a well-tailored black business suit, he was the only important person in Salamanca who felt no compulsion to sport a uniform.

Franco and Serrano Súñer displayed extraordinary skill in balancing off the various incompatible and contradictory elements wedged

---

* Prieto urged Fernández Cuesta to join the still mysterious "Falange Española Auténtica." Fernández Cuesta says that he never doubted the good faith of those who promoted the "FEA," but that after the harsh experiences of 1936 he had no personal desire to reject the leadership of Franco. (Conversation with Raimundo Fernández Cuesta, Madrid, Feb. 13, 1959.)

into the FET. The party itself soon became hopelessly faction-ridden, which was just what the dictator wanted. No one really knew where the Caudillo stood on the long political spectrum reaching from national syndicalist revolution to clerical reaction. The German ambassador noted:

> [Franco] has very cleverly succeeded, with the advice of his brother-in-law, . . . in not making enemies of any of the parties represented in the Unity Party that were previously independent and hostile to one another, . . . but, on the other hand, also in not favoring any one of them that might thus grow too strong. . . . It is therefore comprehensible that, depending on the party allegiance of the person concerned, one is just as apt to hear the opinion in Spain that "Franco is entirely a creature of the Falange," as that "Franco has sold himself completely to the reaction," or "Franco is a proven monarchist," or "he is completely under the influence of the Church."[20]

Serrano Súñer bore the brunt of the enmity aroused by the new political alignment of 1937. His first and bitterest opponents were not Falangists but monarchists, who realized that with the unification he was trying to lay the basis for a corporative, authoritarian, nonmonarchical state. This created an enormous, seemingly insuperable, obstacle to their plans for a restoration. They launched an extensive whispering campaign against Franco's evil genius, the *cuñadísimo*.

In his *ABC* interview of July 19, Franco had already rolled out what was to become his standard line for monarchists:

> If the time for a Restoration should arrive, the new Monarchy would of course have to be very different from the one which fell on April 14, 1931: different in its content and—though it may grieve many, we must obey reality—even in the person who incarnates it. . . . [That person] ought to have the character of a pacifier and ought not to be numbered among the conquerors.[21]

In short, everything was to be postponed indefinitely. There was no reason to hide the fact that the military dictatorship would be necessary for some time after the war was over. Franco ended with the comforting statement that the aristocracy had made great sacrifices and had shown up well in the war, as if to say that this glory and their personal perquisites should be enough for them.

For his part, Serrano Súñer declared to all that his only goals were "to help establish *effectively* the political *jefatura* of Franco, to save and realize the political thought of José Antonio, and to contribute to establishing the National Movement in a juridical regime, that is, to institute a State of Law."[22] A Falange pedigree was quickly built up for Serrano. His dealings with José Antonio were inflated and noised about, in preparation for greater things to come.[23] When the first regular Franco cabinet was set up on January 30, 1938, the *cuñadísimo* became Minister of the Interior and *Jefe Nacional* of Press and Propaganda for the FET. Serrano now ran internal Nationalist politics.

After the new government list was announced, a howl went up from the *camisas viejas* over the appointment of General Gómez Jordana as Foreign Minister. Jordana was a monarchist and had a reputation as an Anglophile. He would be likely to countenance what Falangists termed the "crime of Gibraltar" and to work for a Bourbon restoration. Furthermore, he was not overly fond of the fascist governments admired by most Falangists.

The old guard was soon given compensation for this affront. Since Serrano, the party's nominal Press and Propaganda Chief, was also head of the Ministry of the Interior, this meant that the Falange propaganda machine could now control the official propaganda of the state. This opened the way for the first of Franco's many compromises. In return for accepting a cabinet packed with conservatives and monarchists, the *camisas viejas* would be allowed to control government rhetoric.[24] Two young protégés of Serrano, both super-Falangists, were chosen for the government posts of Chief of Propaganda and Radio Director. They were, respectively, Dionisio Ridruejo and Antonio Tóvar.

Ridruejo, only twenty-five years old, set out to establish a "totalitarian" propaganda machine, and the quasi-revolutionary line of the Falange enjoyed a tight monopoly of information outlets. Young Dionisio was soon nicknamed "the Spanish Goebbels"—a strained analogy, based only on the diminutive physical stature of the two men. Dionisio was the most eloquent speaker in the party since José Antonio, and he strove to maintain the vanished *Jefe's* tone of "poetic fascism."*

It was evident throughout the first half of 1938 that each temporary military crisis was likely to bring a recrudescence of political differences.[25] As the war dragged on without a clear end in sight, the political malaise deepened. General Juan Yagüe, the "Falange General," grew very tired of the war and the political dealings of the Cuartel General. The calculated cruelty and premeditated hatred of the Civil War disgusted him. He saw few signs of a "new Spain" emerging from the political intrigue around Salamanca. Yagüe was so embittered that during a speech on the first anniversary of the unification he lashed out publicly against the actions of the Caudillo's clique.[26] According to von Stohrer, the German ambassador,

> In particular it was felt that the parts of his [Yagüe's] speech in which he gave free recognition to the bravery of the Red Spanish opponents, defended the political prisoners—both the Reds and the "Blues" (Falangists), who were arrested because of too much political zeal—and severely attacked the partiality of the administration of justice, went beyond his authority and represented a lack of discipline; the answer was his recall from command, at least temporarily.[27]

In a major speech at Zaragoza, given on the same day as Yagüe's address, Franco strongly denounced all murmurers and dissenters:

> Efforts to infiltrate the cadres of our organizations multiplied; an attempt was made to sow rivalry and division in our ranks; secret orders were given in order to produce lassitude and fatigue. An effort was made to undermine the prestige of our highest authorities by exploiting petty complaints and ambitions.
>
> These are they who want to sound an alarm to capital with the phantasm of demagogic reforms. . . .
>
> Therefore Spain's constant enemies will not cease in their attempt to destroy our unity, as they did even after the decree of unification, speculating at times with the glorious name of José Antonio, founder and martyr of the Falange.[28]

---

* Ridruejo was a bard in his own right, and a better one than José Antonio. After his propaganda duties ended in 1941 he won well-deserved literary recognition as one of the two or three best neoclassical poets in Spain.

The German ambassador reported that forty per cent of the civilian population in rebel territory were still considered politically unreliable, and were held in place only by the government's policy of ruthless reprisals. All of the more responsible elements in the Franco government were becoming depressed by the sea of blood flowing from the savage police repression intended to guarantee the "internal security" of the Nationalist government. Although precise figures cannot be determined, it is clear that many thousands of people were slaughtered by the White Terror during the Civil War. The first indiscriminate massacres gave way to the more legalistic methods of the military tribunals set up under General Martínez Anido, who became Minister of Public Safety in the 1938 cabinet; but the killing went on unabated. Many people, conservative and Falangist alike, voiced their apprehension over the continuity of a state based on such foundations.*

Martínez Anido had won his spurs as a legalized murderer by arranging the slaughter of Anarcho-Syndicalists in the great Barcelona repression of 1921-22. But that had been child's play compared to what went on after 1936. Many of the *camisas viejas* hated Martínez Anido as a reactionary and a butcher; despite their many errors of thought and deed, the Falangists had never intended the national syndicalist state to pursue a juridical policy of mass murder.[29] In June of 1938, some of the old guard leaders proposed through Serrano Súñer that the Ministry of Public Safety be handed over to them, and that a more limited Ministry of Public Health be created for Martínez Anido.[30] This suggestion was quietly sidestepped. Objections to the policy of brutal repression were not sufficiently widespread in influential circles to be taken seriously. When Martínez Anido died unexpectedly a few months later, Serrano Súñer took over this position

* During the first part of the Civil War many Falangists participated with great abandon in the Rightist repression. The Army, which was responsible for the initiation and execution of this policy of mass murder, preferred to use Falangists for such tasks whenever possible. The complicity of the Falange in this gruesome work was very great. However, the Falange was the only one of the Rightist groups that attempted to restrain its members from arbitrary crime, even to a limited degree, as the liberal lawyer Antonio Ruiz Vilaplana has recorded. (See *Doy fe: Un año de actuación en la España nacionalista*, pp. 168-69.)

as well. Serrano was still oppressed by the memory of his brothers slain in the Republican zone; the killings went on, as they would continue to do long after the Civil War had officially ended.

The full roster of the first National Council was not complete until October 19, 1937.[31] Of its fifty members, twenty could be classified as more or less genuine Falangists; eight were Carlists, five were generals, and some seventeen were assorted monarchists, conservatives, and opportunists. This mixed fry was a good representation of the political heterogeneity behind the Franco regime. There was a sufficient variety of discordant groups to assure that nothing unplanned or original could be accomplished. The regime's favorite tactic of playing critics off against one another was already obvious. The first National Council met only a few times, and its insignificance was extreme.[32]

Little more could be said for the party's first Junta Política. According to Serrano,

> Its labors were rather insignificant, serving only to maintain official contact between the party and the state.
>
> In some cases the meetings (it should not be forgotten that the official party, like the national movement itself, was a conglomeration of forces) were strained and even agitated. The political life of the regime resided principally in the Ministries.[33]

The Ministries, with one exception, were controlled by non-Falangists.

Perhaps the only noteworthy action taken by either the first Council or the first Junta Política of the FET was a deliberation regarding the realignment of party structure undertaken by the National Council in June 1938. All those genuinely concerned with the party realized that unless something were done to strengthen its organization within the structure of the state, it had little hope of projecting any influence in the future. Pedro Gamero del Castillo, Dionisio Ridruejo, and the Carlist Juan José Pradera were appointed to draw up a plan for reorganizing the FET. Gamero and Pradera were both shrewd enough to realize that no bold adjustment would be viewed with favor by the government. But Ridruejo, one of the last of the firebrands in the party, still cherished ambitions of seeing Spain turned into a true totalitarian Falange party-state. His two associates shied away from his proposals but suggested that he draw

them up and present them on his own initiative. Ridruejo ingenu-
ously did so. The proposals he presented at the next meeting of the
National Council would have made the Falange militia autonomous
and increased the party's power throughout the state.

The resistance on the part of the Rightists and the generals was
led by Pedro Sáinz Rodríguez, the Minister of Education. Ridruejo
had already drawn the ire of Sáinz Rodríguez by opposing in the
Junta Política the immense control being given to the Church in educational matters. Sáinz Rodríguez declared that Dionisio's proposals
for radical change demonstrated a lack of confidence in the present
government. The Generalissimo, who was presiding over the meeting, showed considerable anger, announcing that, even worse, they
showed a lack of confidence in the Caudillo. Ridruejo defended
himself by saying that he had simply acted on suggestion of the party,
and that since the Caudillo was *Jefe Nacional* of the party, to strength-
en the authority of the party would be to strengthen the authority
of the Caudillo, but that if the Caudillo did not really consider himself the head of the party, and so on. Nothing came of the proposals,
to be sure, but Ridruejo escaped formal censure.[34]

The only result of this incident was that Franco grew even more
suspicious of the *camisas viejas*. He had already received reports
(completely false) that Agustín Aznar and Fernando González Vélez,
both National Council members, were preparing a plot against him;
he evidently took Ridruejo's proposals as evidence of such feelings of
rebellion.[35] Both Aznar and González Vélez were soon arrested, and
on June 23 and 25 their dismissal from official position was announced.[36] After a brief period the two were released, but they were
exiled to remote provinces for the remainder of the war.[37] González
Vélez's plan to partipate in the FET and work to influence the government from within had accomplished nothing against the authority,
suspicion, and obduracy of the dictator.*

---

* Even before the war ended, Franco was busy removing potential internal
opposition. Eugenio Vegas Latapié, an obstreperous intellectual and a leader
of the *Acción Española* group, was ejected from the National Council on
March 4, 1938, and Fal Conde's day of grace ended forty-eight hours later.
(*Boletín del Movimiento de Falange Española Tradicionalista*, No. 16, Mar. 15,
1938.)

Fernández Cuesta made only weak efforts to save his two comrades. There was really little he could do, but he attempted even less. His failure to attempt a serious defense of Aznar and González Vélez further diminished his prestige, which was already on the wane among the *camisas viejas*. In this matter, as in larger questions, the Secretary-General found himself with little room for maneuver. He was liable to be damned by either side. His only possible recourse would have been to rebel against Franco, but this was impossible during wartime; the Falangists considered themselves too patriotic.

By the beginning of 1938 the rulers of rebel Spain felt the need to begin some sort of work on the nation's social problem. The Italians seemed particularly anxious that the government prepare a labor charter to provide a reformist façade for the Franco dictatorship. The notion was discussed at the beginning of 1938 in the Council of Ministers and was duly approved. Two draft projects were commissioned: one to be prepared by Pedro González Bueno and the clique of conservative "technocrats" to which he belonged, and the other to be drawn up by a pair of young economic-minded academicians, Joaquín Garrigues and Francisco Javier Conde, with the collaboration of Dionisio Ridruejo. This latter draft turned out to be quite radical; it placed the national economy under the control of the proposed syndical system, with its entire program based upon an explicitly anticapitalist concept of property. The Garrigues-Conde project was championed in the Council of Ministers by Fernández Cuesta, but it was immediately rejected.[38] The González Bueno project, on the other hand, was more conservative and of a paternalist-capitalist nature. It was referred to the National Council of the FET for further polishing.

This disposition of the projects brought on a general free-for-all in the National Council. Carlists and representatives of the financial oligarchy offered amendments to make the proposed *fuero* more conservative, and the Falange "Left" countered with amendments to make it more radical.[39] Serrano Súñer, as nominal chairman of the Council, remained neutral. González Bueno, who had been appointed Minister of Syndical Organization in January of 1938, declared that he would resign if the members insisted on seriously revising the project. Serrano then tried to adjust the situation by saying that they were all acting too hastily without specialized knowledge of the matter. He said that the most acceptable result would be merely a general statement of the aims and ideals of the "new Spain" with regard to labor.

Serrano's counsel was decisive. A third draft was drawn up conjointly, paragraph by paragraph. Ridruejo and Eduardo Aunós made the largest number of proposals. Queipo de Llano wanted to insert the phrase "The land belongs to him who works it," but this was vetoed by the conservatives. The final product was a set of platitudes known as the *Fuero de Trabajo,* which became the labor charter of the regime.[40] It merely stated that "capital was an instrument of production," but that labor's rights would be protected and extended through guaranteed employment, unspecified fringe benefits, and general government supervision.[41]

The Ministry of Syndical Organization and Action had already been set up in the general decree of January 30, 1938, which established the first formal Franco government. The new Ministry was to be comprised of five National Services: Syndicates, Jurisdiction and Housing of Labor, Social Security, Emigration, and Statistics.[42] Further details included in the decree of April 31 elaborated the upper echelon of the syndical bureaucracy. A Central Syndical Council of Coordination was provided for and National Syndicalist centers were established in each province.[43] On May 13 provisions were made for the establishment of Labor Magistrates to adjudicate disputes.[44] Needless to say, this entire project was controlled from above.

Raimundo Fernández Cuesta distinguished between the nature of Spanish syndicalism and the Italian corporative state in the following way:

> Neither is the Vertical Syndicate a copy of the Corporation. In those countries in which the governors have encountered, on coming to power, as in Italy, a class syndicalism that they could not dismantle, they have seen themselves forced, as a lesser evil, to convert it into State syndicalism and afterwards to create supersyndical organs of interconnection and self-discipline in defense of the totalitarian interest in production. Those organs are the Corporations. The Corporation, then, had a forced basis in class syndicalism. The Vertical Syndicate, on the other hand, is both the point of departure and of arrival. It does not suppose the

previous existence of other syndicates. Broad horizontal structures do not interfere with it. It is not an organ of the State, but an instrument at the service of its utilitarian economic policy.[45]

The Falangist state, he said, would not be a syndicalist state:

When we say "the National Syndicalist state" we are referring to only one aspect of the State, the economic aspect. We mean that the State, to discipline the economy, employs the instrument of the Syndicates, but we do not mean that the State is mounted solely and exclusively on the Syndicates or that the sovereignty of the State lies in the Syndicates.[46]

Pedro González Bueno was considerably less than successful as Minister of Syndical Organization. Although a professional engineer, he lacked the full capacity for the job. His orders were usually inadequate, contradictory, or unrelated to the problem at hand. Provincial syndicate leaders referred to him as the "Minister of Syndical Disorganization." The *camisas viejas* required a great deal more of González Bueno than he was able to give. Even before the Ministry was set up, Fernández Cuesta had to order that all Falange press and syndicate chiefs "ABSTAIN COMPLETELY FROM PUBLISHING ANY STATEMENT THAT MAY PRETEND TO INTERPRET THE POINT IN QUESTION [on syndicates in the Falange program]."[47] Some of the syndical *delegados provinciales,* such as José Andino of Burgos, simply resigned.[48]

In theory, what González Bueno accomplished was the formation of a thin skeletal chain of syndicates throughout rebel Spain, which were supposed to embrace all workers and all branches of production. The reality was less impressive, and the syndical organization was most rudimentary. A shell was set up, but no results were obtained, nor much flesh added, during the duration of the conflict. Confusion reigned both at the Ministry center and in the provinces. There was not even a guiding philosophy or a well-worked-out theory of syndical organization. With chaos about him, González Bueno was unable to see his way clear to a coherent achievement; he was eventually removed in mid-1939.

The control of capital and agricultural production was beyond the reach of the syndicates. The Ministry of Economics, safely managed by representatives of the financial world, handled these areas largely as it found most prudent. Even before the appearance of the Ministry of Syndical Organization, Economics had taken the initiative in establishing syndicates or cooperative organizations in special areas.[49] On August 23, 1937, the National Wheat Service was established to control grain prices, and it played a significant role in the economy for years afterwards.[50] On July 16, 1938, a special law created the Regulative Commission for Producers, which was to survey and regulate all aspects of business activity; the boards would be named by the various departments concerned, and would thus reflect the several sections.[51] This Commission, basically a political and bureaucratic creation, served as the primary agency of business regulation during the first years of the regime. Various other control agencies were set up in 1937 and 1938, but some of the syndicalization decrees for producers issued by the Ministry of Economics had to be canceled for lack of means to carry them out.[52]

All this commission- and syndicate-naming had nothing whatever to do with the Falange's working-class syndicates, or with the party itself. It merely pointed up their insignificance.[53] After the Falange became the *partido único* it still lacked the influence to intervene directly in economics, but it was given increased powers to confiscate certain types of capital goods and levy certain contributions for its own use. The business world saw no need to submit to such things, and there was much resistance to this arbitrary use of privilege. A series of fines was levied throughout the war on property-holders who refused to cooperate.[54]

Turning to the home front, Falange papers complained of the passive resistance of the "Third Spain"—the old Right and the business groups still in league with the conservative politicians, all of whom were considered arms of the ever menacing internal enemy.[55] In return, the party press was sometimes harassed by military censorship.[56] When conservatives called the Falangists "crazy," they replied:

In your spurious lips we were insane both before the uprising and during it; therefore we died in the streets and fought in the trenches, while you doubted. But listen: materialists of every stripe, our sacred insanity of raising Spain toward God has not ended. We were and are crazy, but we shall not cease to be crazy so long as the Social Justice which this revolution demands is not realized on every level.[57]

The only thing of which the Falangists were masters in the "new Spain" was rhetoric.*

The *camisas viejas* were at least a year in accepting the fact of the *Jefe's* death. All sorts of wild rumors circulated concerning his whereabouts and his physical condition. As late as February 1937 the Italian ambassador was given to believe by Franco that José Antonio was still alive.[58]

The cult of José Antonio officially began on the second anniversary of his death. A government decree of November 16, 1938, declared November 20 a day of national mourning. Plaques commemorating José Antonio and the rebel dead were to be placed permanently on the walls of all Spanish churches. Chairs of political doctrine, named for José Antonio but appointed by Francisco Franco, were to be established at the Universities of Madrid and Barcelona. All sorts of press and propaganda gimmicks were set up under the Founder's honorary patronage. Projects for naming trade schools and special military units for the fallen leader were outlined. All centers of learning were directed to give a special lesson in his exemplary life and works.[59]

Ideal identification with José Antonio provided a necessary and welcome dodge for the Salamanca *camarilla*. The round little Generalissimo led off the act. In a radio message of July 18, 1938, he reported that José Antonio had been ready to hand over the Falange to him in October 1934, which was only part of the truth.[60] On November 20 Franco delivered a special address over the National Radio in honor of *El Ausente,* as the *camisas viejas* called him.[61] José Antonio Primo de Rivera had become the official symbol and patron saint of the new dictatorship. The grand climax came at the end of the war, when José Antonio's remains were removed from the common cemetery at Alicante. A torchlight procession of Falange militiamen bore the vanished *Jefe's* bier over a three-hundred-mile trek to a

---

* Although held in check politically, they undertook a few worthwhile projects. One of the most constructive civil activities of the Falange, in no way political, was the mobilization of young people for the organized reforestation of treeless areas. This work began formally on October 4, 1938, and eventually had a real effect on the face of Spain. (*Boletín del Movimiento de Falange Española Tradicionalista,* No. 33, Oct. 10, 1938.)

grand and solemn burial in front of the altar in the church at El
Escorial, the resting place of Spain's kings.[62]

José Antonio was the hero, the martyr, the troubadour, the transcendent reference, the perfect symbol—in short, everything that the
leaders of the "new Spain" were not.

The overt political fusion promulgated in April 1937 reflected no
real change of heart in either of the two protagonists, despite the high-
sounding pronouncements of government propagandists. An order
of April 30, 1937, established equal representation for each group on
committees of fusion in every province, but this made little impression.[63] Falangists and Requetés preferred to maintain separate headquarters until an order of June 8 declared that in towns with popu-
lations of less than 10,000 it was absolutely mandatory that they occupy
the same quarters.[64] Plans were also made to fuse the respective youth
groups, but these were never carried out.[65] Some veteran Carlists,
as a sign of resistance, simply refused to accept FET membership
cards.

However, the Requetés at the front lines reacted as did their peers
in the Falange. Rear guard politics seemed very unreal in the battle
zone, but unity seemed very reasonable and very necessary. There
was no interparty conflict, for too many other things required immediate attention.[66]

Nonetheless, it was fundamentally impossible to effect a mean-
ingful compromise between the monarchist-regionalist program of
the Traditionalists and the party-minded statism of *falangismo*.
Whenever the opportunity presented itself, animosity flared up in
the rear lines. One French journalist asked a Falange leader what
his group would do if the monarchy were really restored. The Falangist replied: "There would simply be another revolution. And
this time, I assure you, we would not be on the same side."[67] At the
militia review in Burgos on October 12, 1937 (the annual "Día de
la Raza"), the Carlist leader, José María Zaldívar, threatened to withdraw his Requetés if they were not permitted to drill on a separate
half of the field. The Requetés were not marched off, but the festive
event was partially ruined by the long altercation which resulted. In
the chastisement that followed, Zaldívar was expelled from the FET

and several other Carlist chiefs were deprived of party rights for a period of two years.[68]

Franco endeavored to rope in the more recalcitrant Traditionalists when he appointed Fal Conde to the National Council on November 20, 1937. A long correspondence ensued, during the course of which Fal respectfully begged off because of his opposition to *"the idea of the party* as a medium of national union, a base of the state, and an inspiration of the government, which I understand as contrary to our Traditionalist doctrine, to our antecedents, and to our very racial temperament."[69] After Raimundo Fernández Cuesta became Secretary-General of the party in December 1937, he continued this correspondence.[70] It ended when Fal's appointment was finally canceled on March 6, 1938.[71]

Initially, the Carlists had received the *jefatura provincial* in eight of the sixteen provinces of rebel Spain. According to the original understanding, such posts were to be divided evenly between the two groups, and where one received the *jefatura,* the other was to be given the *secretariado.* However, after Fernández Cuesta became Secretary of FET, the Carlists found their initiative increasingly circumscribed by the national command. After a Ministry of Syndical Organization was established at the end of January 1938, whatever influence the Carlists had achieved in syndical organization was progressively curtailed.

When Serrano Súñer became Minister of the Interior and Falange Propaganda Chief early in 1938, the Traditionalists found their propaganda activities more sharply limited than ever before.[72] Dionisio Ridruejo and Antonio Tóvar, who directed state and party propaganda in 1938–39, were determined that national syndicalist ideology, and only national syndicalist ideology, would be expounded in the "new Spain."*

The Carlists' only lasting political satisfaction was achieved

---

* For example, José María Iribarren's 1939 biography of General Mola was blue-penciled whenever any praise of the Carlists appeared. Even a quotation from Shakespeare that Navarre would one day be "the astonishment of the universe" was eliminated. When Iribarren wrote that 14,000 Requetés and 4,000 Falangists had originally reported to Mola, the censor simply switched the proportions. (From José María Iribarren's manuscript, "Notas sobre la gestación y peripecias desdichadas de mi libro *Con el General Mola,*" May 15, 1944.)

through the clerical laws of 1938. When the first regular Franco cabinet was set up in January of that year, Rodezno was given the portfolio of Justice, and he chose Arellano as his Subsecretary. Their main goal was to rewrite Spanish religious legislation, crushing any form of laicism, granting the Church complete educational rights, tying the state to Catholicism, and rigidly circumscribing any of the other Christian churches.[73] With able assistance from Pedro Sáinz Rodríguez in the Ministry of Education, they were overwhelmingly successful. All opposition from the Falange was overridden, and the Jesuits were brought back to Spain within sixty days. The Carlists had finally scored a success within the Franco state, and to many of them this helped greatly to compensate for their other frustrations. It may not have been possible to build either a Carlist or a Falangist party-state in Franco Spain, but in all ordinary civil affairs, the church-state was dominant.

Most veteran Falangists resented the overwhelming triumph of clericalism under the regime. Certain segments of the party became the last respectable strongholds of a certain brand of anticlericalism. A brawl in Seville during the autumn of 1938 between a Falange youth demonstration and a Church procession created a major scandal, which the government tried desperately to cover up.[74]

On the civilian front, the Carlists had nothing to match the Falange's Auxilio Social, set up during the first year of the war. The Carlist civilian auxiliary service of Fronts and Hospitals functioned as a part of the FET.[75] It continued to do valiant work under Carlist leaders, but it was connected only with front-line relief; at the end of the war this service was no longer needed, and the Carlists were left with nothing. Falangist control of the social services of the FET was virtually undisputed. This meant little, however, for by late 1939 the Carlists were deserting the FET *en masse*. The evident degeneration of the party into an office-holding clique did not disillusion them, for Traditionalists had never expected anything of the Franco-Falange in the first place. At the war's end, they simply returned to the mountains they had left in the summer of 1936.

Several of the more loyal Carlist leaders were temporarily arrested or banished during the five years that followed. Fal Conde was permitted to return to Spain when the fighting ceased, but he was placed under house arrest at Seville in 1939 and was sent to internal exile at Mallorca three years later.[76] As isolated and politically impotent as ever, the Traditionalists settled down to survive *franquismo* just as they had survived constitutional Monarchy and Republicanism.

The influence of Germany and Italy on the Falange during the Civil War was never more than secondary. Neither country made a direct effort to intervene in the domestic politics of rebel Spain; each feared it might affront the other if it attempted a politically aggressive policy. At first, the Italians seemed to believe that the Germans were pressing them forward in order to foist upon them any blame for overly ambitious intervention in Spain. Count Ciano informed Roberto Cantalupo, the Duce's first ambassador to Salamanca, that Italy's policy would be to avoid any kind of heavy involvement.[77]

The Germans appeared equally diffident. On December 5, 1936, their Foreign Minister, von Neurath, defined Germany's aims as "predominantly of a commercial character."[78] Two months earlier, Ernst von Weizsäcker, the chief political counselor at the Wilhelmstrasse, had informed the German representative that there was absolutely no authorization for them to press for a National Socialist-type revolution in Spain. The Germans never wavered from this attitude.[79] Hassell, their ambassador in Rome, urged:

> Anyone who knows the Spaniards and Spanish conditions will regard with a good deal of skepticism and also concern for future German-Spanish relations (perhaps even for German-Italian cooperation) any attempt to transplant National Socialism to Spain with German methods and German personnel. It will be easier with Latin Fascism, which is politically more formalistic; a certain aversion to the Italians on the part of the Spaniards, and their resentment of foreign leadership in general, may prove to be a hinderance, but that is a matter for the Italians to cope with.[80]

The Italians demonstrated a complete disinclination to cope with it. They had little interest in or acumen for Spanish politics, and they had never shown any great confidence in the future of Iberian fascism.*

---

* The Marqués de Valdeiglesias declares that during the first week of the Civil War, the current Italian ambassador told him at Biarritz that his last report to Rome had dismissed the possibilities of a successful Rightist rebellion as nil. (Conversation in Madrid, Feb. 17, 1959.)

The only foreign "intervention" of any sort that took place in Salamanca occurred during the spring of 1937. In the months immediately preceding the unification, Faupel had feared that the military dictatorship would discard the fascist party before it even got started. In January 1937 he had written:

> The Government believes at present that by taking over part of the Falange program it can carry out social reforms even without the Falange itself. This is possible. But it is not possible without the cooperation of the Falange to imbue the Spanish workers, especially those in the Red territory to be conquered, with national and really practicable social ideas and to win them over to the new state. For that reason collaboration between the Government and the Falange is still indispensable.[81]

As has been seen, Faupel urged both Hedilla and the Generalissimo to work for political unification and the formation of a revolutionary state party. However, this encouragement never went beyond conversations arranged on the very personal initiative of the German ambassador. Faupel fully realized that the Army was the basic power in rebel Spain; he admitted that it would be impossible to back the party if it ever tried to buck the Army:

> If in his attempt to bring the parties together Franco should meet with opposition from the Falange, we and the Italians are agreed that, in spite of all our inclination toward the Falange and its sound tendencies, we must support Franco, who after all intends to make the program of the Falange the basis of his internal policy. The realization of the most urgently needed social reforms is possible only with Franco, not in opposition to him.[82]

Faupel was not pleased by the results of the April *diktat* and greatly distrusted the "reactionaries" in Salamanca. As previously mentioned, he pressed the Caudillo for leniency in dealing with Hedilla, but his request for a formal protest was denied by the German Foreign Office. In return, both Franco and Serrano came to detest Faupel for his officiousness and gratuitous counsel, even though the German ambassador seems at first to have trusted in the sincerity of the *cuñadísimo*.[83] When he tried to foist on Fermín Yzurdiaga, FET Chief of Press and Propaganda, a plan for a German-directed propaganda and information-exchange institute to be named for Charles V, the Caudillo's annoyance increased.[84] Faupel was finally recalled in October 1937.

Dr. Eberhard von Stohrer, his successor, was more congenial to the rebel leaders. The new ambassador emphasized that Germany should avoid "any interference in Spanish domestic affairs."[85]

> We have thus far confined ourselves to indicating our particular sympathies for that movement in the Falange which is called the "original Falange," the "revolutionary Falange," or the "Camisas viejas," which is closest to us ideologically and whose aims, in our opinion, also offer Spain the best guaranty for the establishment of a new and strong national state which could be useful to us. We have, therefore, readily placed our experience at the disposal of the Falange, have shown our party organizations, social institutions, etc., in Germany to picked representatives of the Falange, and have advised them upon request. We have thereby considerably lightened their task here, but we have naturally not been able to strengthen them to the extent that the victory of this element is assured.[86]

The Falangists naturally felt strongly sympathetic to the German and Italian parties. There was considerable propaganda interchange and the Falange organized pro-German "galas." Many of the first leaders of the party's Auxilio Social were sent to Germany for training in the Winterhilfe.[87] That, however, was the limit:

> On request, the Falange receives from the German press office a wealth of material on German conditions and the organization, etc., of the NSDAP. There is no importunate propaganda or "intervention in the internal affairs" of Spain. Any objection of this type formerly made can at most refer to the beginnings of the Falange (the Hedilla affair).[88]

In Berlin, neither the ambition nor the interest of Nazi leaders was aroused by the Falange. Dionisio Ridruejo recalls that the party was never mentioned on either of the two trips he made to Germany, in 1937 and in 1940. During the spring of 1938 Weizsäcker wrote that it no longer seemed worth while to attempt to cultivate the Falange as an independent entity.[89]

Many of the party's foreign connections depended on Serrano Súñer in the period following unification. His Catholic conservatism drew him more toward the Italian Fascist Party than toward the Nazis, but the Italians took little interest in Spanish internal developments. They had not even a consistent foreign policy. Mussolini could not bring himself to risk a heavy involvement in Spain until the resounding defeat of the Italian expeditionary force at Guadalajara in March 1937. By that time, the Duce was so confused about the real facts of Spanish affairs, misinformed as he was by groups of mutually suspicious intriguers, that he sent Roberto Farinacci on a formal mission to Salamanca; according to his military attaché, Farinacci's main task was to gather accurate information.[90]

A secondary political objective of this mission was to sound out the willingness of Spanish authorities to accept a proposed Italian candidate for the Spanish throne. Such a regime would supposedly be set up with the Falange playing the role of the Italian Fascist Party.[91] However, independently of each other, both Franco and Hedilla rejected this scheme, and it was quickly forgotten.

Immediately following the unification, Signor Danzi, the Italian Fascist Party's representative at Salamanca, offered a copy of his party's statutes to the Caudillo, so that they might be used as a model for the FET. As the German ambassador predicted, these were largely ignored.[92] After that, the Italians seemed to lose interest altogether. They left the FET and its masters quite alone.

When Dionisio Ridruejo accompanied Serrano Súñer on a state visit to Rome in the summer of 1938, he was drawn aside by Ciano and asked which men were of present or potential importance in the Spanish party. Ridruejo replied, "Either Serrano Súñer or Fernández Cuesta." Ciano then closed the matter by saying that the ex-Cedista FET members he had seen reminded him of the elderly, conservative wing of the old Partito Popolare. He indicated that he considered it impossible to build a real fascist party with such material.

A year later, after visiting Spain, Ciano changed his attitude:

The central factor in the country is now the Falange. It is a party which is still only beginning to build up its formation and activity [on the contrary, it was already on the downgrade], but it already has grouped around it the youth, the most active elements, and in particular the women [evidently referring to the special labors of Auxilio Social and the Sección Femenina].[93]

However, Ciano's more positive estimation of the Spanish party came long after Franco and Serrano Súñer had made the Falange their own. The principle of nonintervention in Franco's domestic affairs was already well established, and the Falange would henceforth reflect only those characteristics of the Italian party that were desired by the Caudillo. During the crucial months in Salamancan politics, neither Germany nor Italy had been able to arouse herself for a serious effort at intervention. Italian suspicion, German disinclination, and the mutual hesitation of both nations prevented them from seeking political castles in Spain. Francisco Franco, the only man who ever outplayed Hitler, was left to build his peculiar little system unhindered.

THE "NEW SPAIN" OF THE CAUDILLO

D ON FRANCISCO FRANCO became the principal enigma of twentieth-century Spain. No one better kept himself from projecting a clearly definable political image. A great deal of confusion and contradiction arose about Franco's supposed "aims," chiefly because he had so few of them. The Left cursed him for restoring to power the forces of reaction, but he never showed any real inclination to implement a fully reactionary program. Monarchists reviled him for delaying a restoration, yet he always favored them and eventually even paid a subsidy to their favorite candidate. The conservatives hated his "Falangism," but he never showed the slightest enthusiasm for granting real power to the party.

Franco apparently won an early reputation for bravery in the Moroccan *tercios* of the Legion. At the age of thirty he was so badly wounded that his life was despaired of. However, after his front-line career ended, the young officer from Galicia realized that prudence and caution were the prime requisites to professional advancement. Franco soon showed himself to be a born politician; early in his career it became evident that his major preoccupation was self-advancement. Franco knew that the future of the military lay with nationalist sentiment and with the conservative parties of order. There were no personal predilections behind his politics. The Church meant less than nothing to him as a young man, and his famous brother, Ramón, worked with the Anarchists. During the forlorn Sanjurjo plot of 1932, Franco refused to lift a finger.[1]

Partly because of Franco's good CEDA connections, Gil Robles made him Chief of Staff in 1934. Power affected neither his extreme personal asceticism nor his political perspective. Franco refused to move against the legitimate government both in October 1934 and in February 1936. He fully realized the strength and determination of the Left, and he hesitated long in weighing the prospects of the Mola-UME conspiracy. He joined the military plot only a month or so before the Civil War broke out, and he demanded control of the most efficient segment of the Army as his price. Having thrown in his lot with the rebels, it was no more than natural that he should seek the top command. Authoritarianism was the only program the generals had, and it could function effectively in the Spanish environment only under a *jefatura única*.

As we have seen, the Generalissimo very much lacked an ideological direction. The only element of political idealism in his make-up was expressed in his definite, if vaguely conceived, insistence on the prestige and unity of the Spanish nation. That is, according to his own lights, he was a patriot. This vague concern with national glory had little relation to daily policy. The Generalissimo had only one requirement for the structure of the Spanish state: it had to be workable. He played no favorites; anyone with a safe political record who was willing to cooperate was acceptable to him.

The Falange was accepted as the state party because it seemed the best bet for an authoritarian anti-Leftist military regime in an age of fascism. Franco conceived of the FET as the party of the state, but he never thought of his regime as a real party-state. The Falange, far from controlling the state, was no more than an instrument for holding the state together. Whenever its political pretensions threatened to disturb the internal equilibrium worked out by the Caudillo, he quickly cut the party down to size.

The long continuation of the Falange "line" was essentially a display of hollow rhetoric designed to conceal the intellectual poverty of the conservatives and the generals. It provided an emotional appeal that could distract young idealists and keep them out of the way of their elders. Equally important, nationalist exaltation helped divert attention from serious economic shortcomings. The Caudillo realized that he could never rely fully upon the party, because its own immaturity and the frustrations continuously imposed on it soon robbed it of any popular backing. But the party served admirably for checking monarchists, prelates, and bankers. Franco asked no more of his government than that it continue. He quickly achieved great skill in bribing, balancing off, or discrediting each of the heterogeneous forces behind the "Glorious National Movement."

That national syndicalism should become the Spanish version of the corporative state was practically inevitable; some sort of syndicalism offered the only logical means of reharnessing the national proletariat after the great social conflict of the thirties. The syndical system, however, was carefully trimmed and regulated to fit many of the requirements of capitalists. The financial world received great privileges not because Franco cared for bankers but because he needed the support of the upper middle classes to provide a technical, organized base for a regime of "order." Similarly, the Church got almost anything it asked for. Only the Church could stimulate strong emotional support among wide sectors of the peasantry and the middle classes.

Thus the tangled web of state policy was spun, and the only person who knew where the center lay was the Caudillo. Like a divine right monarch, he was answerable only to God. Chapter XI of the party statutes declared:

> As author of the Historical Era in which Spain achieves the possibility of realizing her historical destiny, and with it the goals of the Movement, the *Jefe* assumes absolute authority in its utmost plenitude.
>
> The *Jefe* is responsible before God and before History.

Virtually everyone of any importance joined the party at one time or other during the Civil War. That is to say, anyone who hoped to find a place in the "new Spain" had to affiliate himself with the "Crusade." All Army officers *ipso facto* became members of the FET; so did all important government employees. In addition, a law of October 1, 1938, declared that anyone who had been jailed for political reasons in Republican territory would automatically become a member of the FET.[2] Instead of a select, energetic political movement, the Falange had become a grand national honorary society.

The structure of the FET had been fully worked out by the end of the Civil War. Only twenty members were necessary to form a *local,* and in the heyday of *falangismo* there were *locales* in most of the villages of Spain. The *jefe local* and *secretario local* were appointed by the *jefe provincial,* who in turn was appointed by the *Jefe Nacional,* Franco. Franco appointed the National Council, which in turn named half of the members of the Junta Política; the other half were appointed directly by the *Jefe Nacional.* This was a tightly circumscribed sphere of command.*

The Caudillo's party served the Caudillo's new state in a number of important ways: First, it provided the ideological rationale and the bureaucratic form by which a new medium could be constructed to contain the Spanish proletariat—the national syndicates. The product of this work was not scrupulously faithful to the spirit of the original Falange, but nothing in the "new Spain" was done with scrupulous fidelity to the spirit of *Joséantonismo.* Begun in 1939, the syndical system was complete by 1944. The syndicates may have been a fraud, but they worked. According to Chapter VII of the party statutes, they were to be staffed and administered by the FET.

The SEU, the Falange student syndicate, was revived on November 21, 1937. Two years later it was given a monopoly on student representation, and in 1944 the membership of all university and secondary school students was made compulsory.[3] This provided a state-controlled student organization with an authoritarian structure somewhat similar to that of the party. More important, it provided the instrument for indoctrinating the most impressionable, and potentially most rebellious, minds in the nation.

Effectively frustrated in all the higher echelons of government, the FET filled in the framework of local government in the provinces. Here the identification of the party and the state was very close, for in 1941 the offices of Civil Governor of the province and *jefe provincial* of the party were in practice fused. All the petty, insignificant posts of local administration were thrown open to the Falange spoils system. This killed two birds with one stone: the Caudillo solved the problem of staffing the local governments, and the Falangists were given jobs, which kept them content and provided compensation for their lack of significant political influence. By introducing Falangists into the bureaucracy, which was for the most part an artificial and arbitrary procedure, Franco bound them

---

* Article 42 of the party statutes declared: "The Caudillo will secretly designate his successor, who will be proclaimed by the Council in the event of [the Caudillo's] death or physical incapacity." Hollow though it was, this was the only provision originally made for the continuity of the Franco state.

to the service of his state, and they could henceforth rebel against him only at the risk of losing their livelihood.

The Falange took over all the social services in Spain through its Sección Femenina. The Sección had been set up in 1934 by family friends of the Primo de Riveras and placed under the direction of Pilar Primo de Rivera, José Antonio's younger sister. By 1936 it was represented in thirty-four provinces and had nearly two thousand members in Madrid and about the same number in the rest of Spain.* The organization's size and scope expanded enormously during the war, and by 1939 it had 580,000 members.⁴ During the war, the women had engaged in any activity that could be of value to the war effort, from cultural work to washing Army uniforms by hand. In the latter part of the war, some sort of service was demanded from every able-bodied unmarried woman in Spain who was not otherwise employed.⁵

Late in 1939 the Sección Femenina was reorganized on a permanent basis, with a formal structure in many ways similar to that of the regular party.⁶ Pilar Primo de Rivera was named *Jefe Nacional* of the organization, which functioned in many fields, including physical education, youth work, and health services. Special attention was given to cultural facilities, especially in the rural areas. Mobile educational units were set up, and many kinds of social assistance were provided. By 1940, 1189 youth centers were said to have been inaugurated.⁷ Under normal circumstances, unmarried women who did not work were formally required to serve six months in the organization's Servicio Social.

Although its efforts were seldom spectacular and fell far short of the immense amount of social work needed in Spain, it can safely be said that the activities of the Sección Femenina proved of much greater benefit to Spain than did those of its masculine counterpart. The Sección provided a modest basis of social achievement with which the young women of the lower classes might identify themselves, at least in the village, and so added an element of strength

---

* In those days most of the girls had to combat family opposition in order to join. Dora Maqueda, the most energetic of the founders, recalls, "The Sección Femenina was our poison and our glory." (Conversation in Madrid, Jan. 10, 1959.)

and solidarity to the Caudillo's regime. The Sección Femenina offered the only direct example of an effort to obtain social justice under a government whose propaganda harped incessantly on *la patria, el pan y la justicia.*

The FET provided the ideological framework for the new state. Vociferous elaboration of the Twenty-six Points offered a rationale for nationalist authoritarianism.[8] With an endless barrage of sneering, ranting adjectives, Falange propaganda struck at the "decadence" and inadequacies of the Western democracies. Endless harping on the "treason" of Spanish liberals of the eighteenth and nineteenth centuries was intended to secure historical identification with the absolute national monarchy of the sixteenth century. Liberalism and relativism, doubt and questioning, were bad; authority and conviction were good. No one was to doubt that the Caudillo had contrived the best of all possible worlds.

This historico-political rationale fitted in nicely with the apotheosis of the reactionary, dogmatic Spanish Catholic Church. The two supplemented each other, *falangismo* employing in political affairs the same reliance on authority and absolute hierarchy that characterized the Church.

Franco's various uses of the Falange were all intended to prove that only political discipline under the Caudillo could assure social justice and economic progress. And what was more important in 1939, the same sort of disciplined development was declared to be the only way for Spain to achieve a rightful place in international affairs. The "new Spain" would be just, powerful, authoritarian, and efficient. Only the third adjective fit.

The end of the war was bound to bring changes in the personnel and the administration of both the party and the government. Some Falange militants still thought that their hour would soon arrive. With the easing of the enormous pressure exerted by military affairs, considerably more time and energy could be devoted to economic and political reorganization. The popular base built up among the Falange combatants could be used as a springboard for launching the real national syndicalist revolution.

However, there is nothing to indicate that the majority of the party's ex-combatants had such positive feelings. Their principal sensation in the spring of 1939 was an overwhelming sense of fatigue. The Civil War had lasted too long. It had been a tremendous ordeal, and everyone was very tired. The veterans asked only to be allowed to return home in peace. Even the ex-militiamen of the Falange, with their few vague ideas of what composed the national syndicalist revolution, had no moral energy left for political reform. Their only deep political sentiment was a rather pitiless hatred of the Republicans who had maintained the strife for the better part of three long years. Few people had any interest in political disputes within the victorious nationalist camp.

Furthermore, the very uncertain international situation of 1939, which reached a climax when Germany began another world war, militated against any domestic quarreling. Spain was socially torn apart and economically prostrate, and every ounce of national energy was needed to set the country back on its feet. During 1939 many wartime Falangists simply dropped out of the party with a quiet feeling of relief. For the first time in the Falange's history, the party membership declined instead of rising.*

Once formally established in Madrid, the dictatorship concerned itself first and foremost with cementing its power. Ramón Serrano Súñer had come out of the political adventures of the war with greater influence than ever. As the primary political architect of the regime, he enjoyed the personal confidence of the Caudillo and was the undisputed Number Two man in Spain. Both Franco and Serrano would have preferred that the latter take over control of the Falange; they were tired of having to deal with the shadow leadership of Fernández Cuesta. However, most *camisas viejas* still resented Serrano and clung to Fernández Cuesta, despite his failings. With characteristic delicacy, Serrano decided not to irritate feelings by pushing himself forward at this time. Another combination was in order.

The long-awaited cabinet shake-up occurred on August 9, four

---

* The first (and last) "purge" of the Falange came at the end of 1938, when a mild effort was made to oust those guilty of petty crimes during the war. This was sporadic and removed few names from the party rolls. (*BMFET,* Nos. 22 and 33, June 15 and Oct. 10, 1938.)

months after the cessation of hostilities, and it further diminished the power of the *camisas viejas*. Serrano retained the Ministry of the Interior and took over the vacant post of González Vélez as President of the party's Junta Política. Fernández Cuesta was sent to Rio de Janeiro as Franco's ambassador, and there was no real Falangist left in the national cabinet.

Brigadier General Muñoz Grande, supposedly a "Falange General," was appointed Secretary-General of the party. As a military man, Franco had somewhat greater trust in him than in Fernández Cuesta. Muñoz Grande also became director of the militia. Pedro Gamero del Castillo, one of Serrano's old favorites and formerly *jefe provincial* and Civil Governor of Seville, was named Minister without portfolio and Vice Secretary-General of the FET.[9]

The dictatorship's control of the party organization was strengthened in 1939 by the reappearance of a number of former Falange leaders from Madrid and elsewhere who had spent the war languishing in Republican prisons. Thirty months of privation had completely removed any doubts they might have had about Franco's rule and the composition of the FET; after their harsh experience the "new Spain" was all sweetness and light by contrast. The liberated Falangists, Rafael Sánchez Mazas, Miguel Primo de Rivera, José María Alfaro, Manuel Valdés, and many others, became unconditional supporters of the new state. Within the party, they backed Serrano Súñer, as the architect of the new Falange, against Fernández Cuesta, who had sporadically but ineffectively been trying to hold the line against the new opportunists. Their status as *camisa vieja* leaders lent them considerable moral prestige within the party, which in turn redounded to the benefit of Franco.[10] When the shake-up occurred, all these new figures were given top jobs. Sánchez Mazas became Minister without portfolio; Alfaro was named Subsecretary of Press and Propaganda and placed on the Junta Política; Valdés became Subsecretary of Labor; Miguel Primo de Rivera was appointed *jefe provincial* of Madrid and also given a place on the Junta Política.

By this realignment Franco evidently hoped to achieve a military-civilian synthesis that would assure a modicum of stability in the new state. Number One was Franco, a general. Number Two was

Serrano, a civilian. Muñoz Grande, the Secretary-General, was a soldier, but his immediate subordinate was civilian. So it went down the line. Balanced representation and mild contentment were what the Caudillo envisaged for the victors in the "new Spain."

The Falange old guard, however, was virtually ignored in the central party hierarchy, although it had several seats on the National Council. Of the nine regular members of the Junta Política, only one, Ridruejo, was an authentic member of the old guard. The other eight chairs were occupied by two monarchists (José María de Areilza and the Conde de Mayalde), two "renovated" Falangists (José María Alfaro and Miguel Primo de Rivera), two renegade Carlists (Esteban Bilbao and José María Oriol), and two outright opportunists who had never professed belief in an explicit political creed of any kind (Demetrio Carceller and Blas Pérez González).

The military hierarchy was determined that nothing like an SA or black shirts' militia organization should arise in the "new Spain." The Falange would never be allowed an effective, independent militia. When Ridruejo had proposed such a thing in the National Council, he was nearly expelled from the party. Before the war ended, Franco stated in one of his infrequent press conferences: "We do not need to maintain a very large permanent Army. A small permanent Army is more suited to our needs." However, that was not really what he meant. He continued, "The efficiency of that Army has to be so great and strong that no other military organization may surpass it. Spain has to organize itself as a 'nation-in-arms.' "[11] There was to be military and premilitary training for everyone.

As it turned out, the permanent Army was large rather than small. This was no more than an old Spanish custom, for the nation had always sustained a military unit much larger than her actual requirements justified. The tensions of the Second World War, added to the disturbing presence of the captive portion of the population, greatly increased the incentive. Universal conscription was maintained, and all military training was handled by the regular Army.

After the Civil War ended the Falange militia was carefully deprived of any independent force. All militia veterans were grouped together in the *ex-combatientes'* organization under the nominal leadership of José Antonio Girón, the most popular of the militia leaders. The *ex-combatientes* were rendered little more than a harmless chowder-and-marching society.

An official Falange militia was reconstituted by a decree of July 2, 1940. It was to be composed of three sections: pre-military trainees, young men who had already served their regular tour of duty, and those over military age. The organization was completely controlled by the regular Army command, which staffed all the important posts, and all members were subject to the official code of military discipline.[12] There was no connection with the party's chain of political command.

Some *camisas viejas* had feared that they would be swallowed up by the victorious military clique after the war ended. A few had even spoken of the desirability of a monarchical restoration, to serve as a moderating influence between them and the Army. However, such fear of the military ignored the nature of Franco's policy of divide-and-rule. He was not likely to give the Army, or anyone else, full satisfaction against the Falange.

At the end of the war the Falange's student syndicate, the SEU, still enjoyed partial autonomy, and *Haz,* the SEU review, was published more or less independently of the bulk of the Falange press. During the war, most of the original SEU leaders were killed or called to the front. New enthusiasts, most of them under military age, stepped in during these three years to help direct the syndicate's propaganda and activities. Prominent among them was the nineteen-year-old Enrique Sotomayor, who took a leading role in the preparation of *Haz* during 1938 and 1939. Sotomayor and his friends were full of ideas for building the future of the SEU. They wanted to reform the syndicate and planned a broad Frente de Juventudes ("Youth Front") designed to diffuse SEU ideals among the youth of Spain and implant a strong national-Catholic-syndicalist spirit in the new generation.

The nominal leaders of the SEU were largely opposed to this project. As far as they were concerned, the war had ended in 1939 and the new order was now established. Satisfied with their own positions and with that of the SEU, they had no desire to see a pleasant bureaucratic situation disrupted by such a disturbing new entity as a militant youth front.

Nonetheless, Sotomayor and his comrades worked out their plans and sent them to Serrano Súñer. To the consternation of the official SEU chiefs, Serrano approved the proposals and sent them to Franco. The Caudillo was also favorably impressed. On August 16, 1939, an appointment was arranged in Burgos between the Generalissimo, Sotomayor, and two other "young Turk" chiefs of the SEU.[13] Afterward, Sotomayor reported that Franco actually wept and declared that all his hope, like that of the nation, lay in the country's youth. The Caudillo said that he looked for an early development of the Frente de Juventudes and that he planned to appoint Sotomayor *Jefe Nacional* of the SEU, which had no official leader at that time.

The word quickly got around and SEU officeholders mobilized their counterattack. Muñoz Grande, Secretary-General of the FET, agreed with them that it would be dangerously imprudent to grant control of the SEU to idealistic, energetic young men. Together they made remonstrances to Serrano and to Franco. The Caudillo evidently had second thoughts; he favored the Frente de Juventudes plan as a means of strengthening the popular support of the regime, but he had no desire to disturb the bureaucratic equilibrium of the party or to create a divisive new influence. He therefore conditionally agreed to appoint as *Jefe Nacional* José Miguel Guitarte, the current *Inspector Nacional* of Juvenile Organizations.[14] The condition was that Sotomayor should be made Secretary-General of the SEU, from which position he was to organize the Frente de Juventudes. Though a *camisa vieja,* Guitarte was one of the pro-Franco group who had only recently been liberated from Republican jails and was therefore a "safe" Falangist.

On August 19, 1939, three days after the conversation between Franco and the Sotomayor group, these modified appointments were announced.[15] Close friends urged Sotomayor not to accept this new post, insisting that his hands would be completely tied. However, Sotomayor felt that this was the only opportunity they would have to develop a youth front and that he should therefore accept the position despite all obstacles.

Shortly afterwards, he began a series of speaking engagements to stir up enthusiasm among young people and propagate the front. He and his collaborators were planning a Frente de Juventudes in twelve sections, which would not be a mere police straitjacket over the young people but would foster their energies and forge them in a national syndicalist mold. Their concept was based on the usual Falange pessimism about the great liberal era of modern history and fortified by a strong dose of Spenglerism. If every civilized epoch were to be ended by a group of barbarians, they reasoned that the task of the new Falange would be to create a disciplined host of national syndicalist barbarians strong enough to destroy the old order from within before alien forces attacked from without. To accomplish its mission, the youth group might have to be harsh and violent, "Catholically barbarous, morally barbarous."[16] But it would be a national, historical, Catholic barbarism which would save the country from the pagan, materialist barbarians on the other side of the walls. If necessary, the young were to be taken from their families for proper training. However, the Youth Front ideologues always took care to bolster their spiritual edifice with strong doses of Catholicism and what they liked to style a return to "primitive Christianity," which must have been primitive indeed.

The essential theme in all of Sotomayor's talks was that the youth and a revolutionary nationalist spirit had been chiefly instrumental in winning the war. If these forces were not united in an energetic, action-bent Youth Front, all the struggle would have gone for nothing—the old divisions and cliques would take over the country once more.

> I know that this proposal for a strong vanguard of the young will seem dangerous and out of line to excessively cautious spirits.
>
> . . .
>
> The same people who were interested in prolonging our war are today desirous of a hungry, rancorous, downtrodden Spain, for the same reasons multiplied a hundred times. The same people who for centuries have come to us enclosing and conquering, those who were counting coin after coin while we were losing man after man, are now waiting for us to lose our enthusiasm in order to begin spreading their old corrosive negations.
>
> The negative slogans return once more. Not this. Not that.
>
> But once and for all, what do they bring? What does the Spanish reaction represent and pretend today?

. . .

Perhaps nothing encourages us so much as the rage of those who oppose us.

. . .

We entertain the immense joy of being hated by them!

Let those who so happily join the chorus of murmurers consider the terrible responsibility they share.

. . .

There is only one road open: Revolution.

. . .

NOW OR NEVER!

. . .

Let all be united in the impetus of a closed front of youth.[17]

Sotomayor's words were eloquent and stimulating. His deeds were effectively squelched by the bureaucratic guard of the regime. He resigned after three months, having accomplished nothing.[18] The Frente de Juventudes idea remained on file, but the directing elements in the party saw to it that nothing was done for the time being. An organization bearing this title was finally established over a year later, on December 6, 1940; it was much more limited in aspiration than the project originally conceived by the Sotomayor circle. The watered-down Frente de Juventudes fitted neatly into Franco's conservative-syndicalist-clerical-military state structure.

As 1939 wore on, those who had expected basic and revolutionary reforms were slowly but surely divested of their illusions. A great deal of pomp and formalism were displayed, the trappings and sounds of Hispanic fascism were everywhere in evidence, all talk of re-establishment and reaction was discouraged, but the institutions of government remained firmly in the hands of select and loyal elements of the government clique.

Whenever Falange leaders asked for extension of the social program, a larger program of nationalization, control of credit, and extension of Falange influence into all sectors of national life, it was replied that the nation was too weak, and in too dangerous a condition, for far-reaching reforms, which were liable to create new antagonisms on the Right among those who had helped to win the war. It was said that the nation was too poor to afford a socialized economic program, and that all the government's effort had to be spent on strengthening Spain's position against the wave of international conflict that was already beginning to roll across Europe.

Many old Falangists felt cheated and betrayed. After losing their leaders and the best men from their ranks in the struggle against the forces of Left-liberalism, they saw themselves being deprived of the fruits of victory. Their attitude was reflected by a German diplomat, who replied to the question "How do you find the new Spain?" by saying, "When I find it I shall tell you."[19] A new political-financial oligarchy, which reminded one of nothing so much as the old order, was arising from the ashes of desolate Spain. The outwardly imposing edifice that had been created for the Falange was indeed to be used as a "totalitarian instrument"—not for "the nation" but merely for the regime.

The Falange was horizontally cut off from the Council of Ministers and had no direct, organic connection with the policy-making bodies of the national administration. While the conservatives and opportunists largely controlled the upper echelons, the party was left to amuse itself with the gigantic bureaucracy that gorged itself on the Franco spoils system. All government employees were supposed to be FET members, but no party leader of doubtful intentions was placed in a position of influence. The only department under Falange control was the Syndical organization, which until 1940 was largely a paper creation.

The ranks of the *camisas viejas* had been badly thinned by the war. It has been estimated that sixty per cent of the original members of the party were killed during the conflict. This further reduced the possibility of any resistance to Franco.

The only parts of the party organization that retained any independent fervor were sections of the veterans' group, the *ex-combatientes*. There the inevitable weariness and apathy conflicted with a desire not to see the fruits of victory rot in the hands of the military-conservative clique. On the whole, the longing for peace and tranquility, combined with a blind instinct to have unity among the victors, won out. However, some of the local leaders of the *ex-combatientes* were not inclined to rest on their laurels. There were still Falangists who thought that the "new Spain" properly belonged to the national syndicalist party in deed as well as in word.

These small groups sent out feelers toward each other, and toward the end of 1939 organized a clandestine "Junta política" in Madrid. Its titular president was Colonel Emilio Tarduchy, a veteran of both the Falange and the UME, an old war horse of radical Spanish nationalism.[20] The secretary was Patricio Canales, a *camisa vieja* leader from Seville, who was currently occupying a high position in Press and Propaganda. Various members sat in the Junta from time to time, representing the several regions of Spain. These were: Ricardo Sanz (Asturias), Daniel Buhigas (Galicia), Ventura López Cotevilla (Santander), Luis de Caralt (Catalonia), José Pérez de Cabo (the Levante), Gregorio Ortega (the Canaries), Antonio Cazañas (Morocco).[21]

Their principal contact within the military hierarchy was General Juan Yagüe, still the "Falange General." A great deal of Yagüe's life since 1936 had been spent in political maneuvering and intrigue. When restored to command some six months after his outburst of April 1938, Yagüe merely picked up where he had left off. He had never been directly disloyal, but he was always maneuvering for some sort of political advantage or rearrangement. In personal affairs, Yagüe was ruthlessly honest, and he had a fairly strong, though nebulous, attachment to the Falange program. He had always been opposed to the composition of the official FET, both because it had blocked his own ambitions for political influence and because it stifled the possibility of an authentic Spanish nationalist revolution.

During the year 1940 the clandestine Junta endeavored to extend its base of support.[22] Its logical ally would have been Yagüe, who had his own network of contacts and followers among the military. However, Yagüe informed the Falange group that although he would be at their disposition in time of need, he did not want to bring the two conspiratorial networks together at that moment. With Yagüe was associated José Antonio Girón, the official leader of the *ex-combatientes*. Girón's personal influence was effective only among the *centurias* of *ex-combatientes* in Castile, but these nuclei could be very important. Canales thus went to Valladolid to talk with Luis Vicén and Anselmo de la Iglesia, who were the local leaders of the party in that area; but de la Iglesia happened to be out of town, and Vicén flatly refused to take part in any conspiracy. Girón himself replied that he would go only so far as Yagüe. Girón and the Falange of Castile therefore remained on the margins of this new intrigue.

Nowhere could the Falange conspirators whip up solid support. The great mass of veterans wanted only to be left in peace, and even the old guard itself was not united in its opposition to Franco. If the conspirators were to be able to pull off an effective *coup* against the Caudillo, they needed outside help.

During the year 1940, members of the clandestine Junta had several conversations with Thomson, the Nazi Party representative in Madrid. They informed him that certain elements in the Falange were interested in obtaining German aid to establish a thoroughgoing national syndicalist regime in Spain. Thomson consulted his superiors in Berlin; he reported that they considered Spanish politics a "bag of flies" in which no one ever knew what would turn up next. The conditions they applied to any possible German assistance were so rigid that the Spanish conspirators could not accept them. Nevertheless, the talks continued. The final session occurred some time in February 1941. The Nazis continued to insist on a set of stringent conditions that would virtually convert Spain into a German satrapy. All this was unacceptable to the Falangists, who were considerably shaken to find that several Spaniards had already offered themselves to the Nazis as quislings for the establishment of a new order in Spain.

Meanwhile, one of Yagüe's adjutants had denounced that general's own machinations to Franco. The Caudillo called Yagüe to his office and broke down the general's defenses. Yagüe emerged broken and weeping. Instead of punishing him, Franco promoted him, employing one of his favorite tactics. This destroyed Yagüe's political independence and greatly reduced his moral authority; he was no longer of any benefit to the Falange conspirators.

Realizing that the government had doubtless learned of its activities, the secret Junta met in Madrid during March of 1941. The members now were Tarduchy, Canales, Caralt, Sanz, and López Cotevilla. During previous months they had concocted a plan to assassinate Serrano Súñer, whom they held responsible for many of the Falange's ills. However, they now rejected this project; another representative would be appointed by Franco, and he might well be more ruthless and less diplomatic than Serrano.

Franco, in fact, was the main problem. There was no longer much chance of building up internal resistance or presenting an alternative to his control. The only thing that might be attempted was to topple him with a single bold stroke; if this could not be done, they might as well disband and accept his leadership. Faced with a hopeless domestic situation and the threat of international involvement, there was little choice. The conspirators did not see how they could control the chaos that would certainly follow Franco's death. When they put to a vote the question of whether to assassinate the Caudillo or obey him, the result was four ballots to none, with one abstention, for the latter course.

By this time, the provincial *ex-combatiente* cells supporting the conspiracy had grown restive and entirely dispirited. They no longer had any appetite for intrigue and wanted to dissolve their little groups. In March 1941 their leaders told the Junta members that the conspiracy was hopeless and ought to be given up. Everyone had reached the same conclusion, for the Junta had already disbanded itself.[23] The plot was soon discovered by the authorities, but since the opposition group had voluntarily come back to the fold, little punishment was meted out. Most of the conspirators were not even touched.*

One of them was executed the following year, but not for treason. José Pérez de Cabo, author of the first book on national syndicalism and the leader of the conspirators around Valencia, was an administrator of the Auxilio Social in the Levante.[24] After being denounced by a leading Falangist for having sold part of the Auxilio's flour supplies on the black market, he became the scapegoat of anti-Falan-

---

* One branch of the conspiracy continued to exist. That was the tiny Catalan section built up by Eduardo Ezquer, who had never ceased to plot since José Antonio expelled him from the Falange in the spring of 1936 for insubordination. Though living in provincial exile, he had contacts with the Barcelona SEU, and may have had five hundred followers at one time. The police doubtless learned of these activities, but they did not move to stop them immediately because of their innocuous nature. However, when his efforts persevered into 1942, Ezquer was arrested once more, and his little band was broken up.

gists in the Army. His only possible moral justification was that he might have used the black market funds to finance the anti-Franco plot, but this merely damned him in another way. A last-minute effort by Falange leaders to obtain a reprieve ended in failure. The Carlist General Varela, the Minister of War, wanted to saddle Falange leaders with heavy responsibility for the widespread black market operations, which in the early nineteen-forties almost supplanted the regular economy and had recently provoked new legal restrictions.[25] The unlucky Pérez de Cabo made an easy target.

The conspirators felt that their operation was in great part frustrated by the campaign waged to attract the *ex-combatientes* to the regime. This effort was organized and led by Pedro Gamero del Castillo, the Vice Secretary-General of the party (1939–41). Many and various government jobs were offered to veterans, and twenty per cent of the winning scores in bureaucratic examinations were reserved for them. Such benefits, added to the scant political indoctrination of the *ex-combatientes,* their general weariness, and their desire for normalcy, drained away whatever revolutionary impetus was left. Amid the pressure of foreign threats and national economic misery, the party's rank-and-file subsided into quiescence, even while the façade of their National Syndicalist state was being ever more elaborately adorned.

The syndical system of the Franco state languished within a morbid sphere of shadow existence until an official *Delegado Nacional* was finally appointed on September 9, 1939. The new syndicate head was Gerardo Salvador Merino, a *camisa vieja* from Madrid who had moved to Galicia in 1935. In 1937, after several months on the Asturian front, Salvador Merino had been named *jefe provincial* of La Coruña by Manuel Hedilla. There he had immediately won a considerable reputation as a champion of national syndicalism and the interests of the proletariat. On one occasion he scheduled a mass rally of Coruña workers at the local bull-ring; when middle-class citizens mounted a lively protest, Salvador Merino had ordered that the workers be permitted to "break the ranks of the bourgeoisie."[26] Such attitudes had cost Merino his first post within a year's time, but they won for him a certain political reputation. He served at the front during the last year of the war and learned the virtues of discretion.

By his own admission, Salvador Merino was an ambitious man. When the fighting ended, he looked for a promising position. His pro-syndical record then stood him in good stead. The government was looking for someone capable of undertaking, with talent and effectiveness, the sizable task of syndical organization. Merino was both intelligent and aware of the need for caution. The *politiques,* such as Serrano Súñer and Gamero del Castillo, found him a likely prospect for the post, and a seemingly reliable one. Few men burn their fingers twice in the same fire, but that is precisely what Salvador Merino eventually did.

He took up his labors slowly and carefully. In 1939 there existed only the bare rudiments of a syndical organization. So far no coherent plan or philosophy of syndicalization had been put together. Merino and his collaborators prepared to build the whole system from the ground up. What they planned was a genuine expression of national syndicalism, equidistant between Marxism and the Catholic "free syndicates" (company unions). According to Merino, there were certain fundamental areas of national life not open to debate: the prerogatives of the Church, the unity of the nation, and so forth. Beyond that, any aspect of economics or politics might be made subject to readjustment. Merino intended to satisfy workers' demands to the full, and to make the syndicates the most powerful civil institution in Spain.

He was badly handicapped by the almost complete lack of preparation among Falangists for handling the technical problems of syndical organization. He found it necessary to prepare his own personal planning staff to establish the cadres and the framework of syndicalism. Merino chose a group of industrious collaborators, some of whom were not Falangists but came from diverse political groups. Together they set to work.

There was a constant need to lull the suspicions of the conservatives, and Salvador Merino was forced into a continual balancing act. He refused to identify himself too clearly with any of the political cliques in the Falange and would not participate in petty conspiracy. He always endeavored to hide from the eyes of other politicians the far-reaching nature of the plans being laid.

Merino felt more sympathetic to the Nazis than did other Spaniards; the revolutionary goals of the German party struck a sympathetic note in him.[27] Similarly, Merino felt more at ease with military Falangists like Yagüe and Muñoz Grande than with the *politique* elements. Although he tried to maintain a position of external equilibrium, the fall of Muñoz Grande early in 1940 left him in an exposed position at the very outset of his work.

To soothe the Right and lay the groundwork of syndicalism, the first task undertaken was to finish the construction of the large industry-wide National Syndicates, which organized the workers in each sector of production. This merely completed the outer frame of syndical organization, and had no social significance. It simply brought together all textile workers, for example, so that they could be dealt with effectively as an economic unit. This was a form of syndicalism that the Right understood and appreciated: organization and administration from above, with no wage pressure from below or any other direction.

On January 26, 1940, the Law of Syndical Unity was proclaimed. Government representation for private economic interests, established by the 1938 laws, was abolished. All economic representation was to take place within the syndicate set up for workers and management in each line of activity. On May 3, 1940, it was announced that the syndicates would soon take over the function of controlling prices and economic standards, formerly exercised by the Regulative Commission established some eighteen months previously.[28] Meanwhile, Salvador Merino informed the Caudillo that the real backbone of the syndical system lay in the *Delegaciones provinciales,* which had to be set up on a firm basis. He wanted to begin the Obras Sociales ("Social Works") of the organization in order to attract and hold the workers' attention. Merino was beginning to move too fast, and he soon committed tactical errors.

On Victory Day, March 31, 1940, the first anniversary of the end of the Civil War, he arranged for several thousand proletarians to march in the gigantic parade which was to move down the Castellana in Madrid.[29] This drew the anger of the Army hierarchy. General

José Enrique Varela—Carlist, reactionary, Minister of War, and one of the principal enemies of labor in the officer corps—vowed that he would have Merino ousted.

The syndical chief planned other demonstrations and benefits, especially for the industrial workers. His basic aim was to set the masses of Spain marching once more, but this time under national syndicalist leadership. He realized that if an authentic and representative syndical system were actually established, it might easily get out of control. Salvador Merino says that he was prepared to risk this, hoping to use the power of the syndicates to exert pressure on governmental authority in other areas. It eventually became impossible to mask his intentions, and competing interest groups grew more and more alarmed. His projects, one after another, were blocked by rival departments.

Serrano, who had at first adopted an interested and expectant attitude, became increasingly apprehensive over the possible growth of Merino's power. He considered having the syndicate boss kicked upstairs, and suggested to Merino that he relinquish direct control of the organization to become Minister of Labor. Merino refused, realizing that such a promotion would greatly diminish his influence over the syndicates and prevent him from realizing his plans. Serrano then asked Merino what other post he would accept. Salvador Merino answered that he would exchange the syndicates only for the Secretary-Generalship of the party, and then only if it were combined with the Ministry of the Interior, where real power lay. Serrano Súñer replied that Merino was hopelessly ambitious, as indeed he was.[30]

By the beginning of 1941, Merino had earned the reputation of being the leader of the opposition group within the government. Nonetheless, he strove desperately to maintain his equilibrium between the various discordant cliques inside the Falange. Merino had hopes that, in a pinch, Franco would see fit to save him from the reactionaries who had begun to shout for his head. He calculated that if he could hold control of the syndicates for another year or two, he would build so strong a position that he could hardly be ousted without causing a major disruption in the state. But this was not to be, for his enemies had begun to combine, and time was running out.

Opposition to Merino came from three sectors: the military Rightists, led by Varela; the political archconservatives, led by Esteban Bilbao (a renegade Carlist, and one of Franco's principal yes-men on the Junta Política);* and the powerful industrial-financial interests, represented by Demetrio Carceller, who also sat on the Junta Política.[31]

Merino survived the political crisis of May 1941.[32] But he lasted only for the few weeks it took the Generalissimo to repair the slight damage inflicted upon his household. All the Rightists were insisting that the syndicate leader was growing more dangerous by the day. They waited until the first opportune moment, and struck when he was fully occupied with personal affairs. On July 7, 1941, Merino was married in Madrid and left the capital on a brief honeymoon. While he was absent, it was charged that he had once been a member of the Masonic Order. This was a serious accusation, for hundreds of Masons had been shot in the "new Spain," of which the Order was felt to be an archenemy. When Merino returned to Madrid, he was dismissed from his post and banished to the Balearic Islands.[33] That was the end of the political career of Gerardo Salvador Merino. It is not clear that anyone except the party's Secretary-General tried to defend Merino, even though he felt that he had contributed enough to the "Movement" to overcome the stigma of his earlier affiliation with the Masonic Order. His removal suited all those made uncomfortable by his presence, and it also marked the end of the last independent syndicalist initiative in Franco Spain.

Merino's only competitor for representation of the working-class interests had been José Antonio Girón, the new Labor Minister appointed two months before the syndical chief's eclipse. For personal reasons, the two were strongly antagonistic, and it appears that Girón worked for his rival's downfall. Girón succeeded Salvador Merino as the nominal champion of Spanish labor. However, from

---

* Bilbao was the typical, grotesque sort of political wordmonger who constantly mixed up famous quotations. However, some Spaniards enjoy this, and Serrano had a certain weakness for him. Bilbao coined the ridiculous epithet "Francisco Franco, Caudillo de España por la Gracia de Dios," which was stamped on all Spanish coins. (Spanish jokesters soon corrupted this to "Francisco Franco, Caudillo de España por una gracia de Dios," which more or less means "Francisco Franco, Caudillo of Spain by a joke of God.")

this time forward immediate direction of the syndical organization was kept in the hands of obedient, unenergetic party hacks, who never threatened to mobilize the Spanish masses. Everything was tightly controlled from above, but there was no protest. The Army and the Bank were very strong.

On September 9, 1939, the government established its Institute of Political Studies. Designed as the brain-trust of FET, it was conceived partly as a training school for certain types of party workers and partly as a general study center for ideology and new projects of every sort. The principal divisions of study were the following: Constitution and Administration of the State; National Economy; International Relations; Social and Cooperative Arrangements. The Director automatically became a member of the Junta Política.[34]

The first head of the Institute was Alfonso García Valdecasas, least significant of the three "founders" of the Falange.[35] Valdecasas had temporarily laid aside the monarchical convictions that he had developed during the last years of the Republic. Some of his fundamental political attitudes were well represented in the speech he made at the Comedia meeting in 1933, when he declared that Spain must repudiate with equal disdain the capitalist materialism of the United States and the Communist materialism of the Soviet Union.

If the Institute had lived up to the role cut out for it, it could have become a very important organization. However, like all the agencies of the party, it was destined to a stunted growth and a warped and insignificant maturity. As Franco had already made clear, a real ideological party-state was not his goal. All that was expected of the Institute was that it properly trim its sails to the wind. This task it accomplished with great success.

A decade later under its third Director, a converted Socialist named Francisco Javier Conde, the Institute almost became a center of covert fascistic liberalism, combating clericalism and inviting foreign socialists to Spain. Conde was both prudent and ingenious, having earlier prepared the principal ideological justification of Franco's peculiar *caudillaje*; he had tried to apply the sophisticated sociological formulas of Max Weber and the notion of political charisma to explain the basis of Franco's power, which otherwise rested on force. Eventually Conde's position became too awkward to maintain; after his replacement the Institute once again dozed in a pleasant state of limbo.

During 1938 and afterward, a host of ex post facto generalizations tricked out as political theory were put forth to rationalize the present and future of the Franco state. The most impressive attempt was José Pemartín's ¿Qué es lo nuevo? (1938), a book of three hundred pages of disquisition and a host of diagrams intended to show just how a model syndicalist corporative state would be put together. Pemartín declared that Spanish fascism should be the translation of Traditionalism into modern terms.[36] Meanwhile, the Falange Left did not cease to inform its readers that "fascism is nothing else than the nationalization of the doctrine of Marx."[37] Spanish capitalists did not take these pronouncements seriously, trusting in the discretion of the Caudillo.

The leading Spanish political theorist in the early heyday of the Franco state was Juan Beneyto Pérez. In *El Partido* (1939) and *Genio y figura del Movimiento* (1940), he foreshadowed what was later refined into the principle of *caudillaje*:

> The concept of the Caudillo is a synthesis of reason and ideal necessity. It is not only force, but spirit; it constitutes a new technique and is the incarnation of the national soul and even of the national physiognomy. As a technique, it is the natural consequence and organic necessity of a unitary, hierarchical, and total regime. As an incarnation it is the exaltation of a mystique. It becomes a new concept by which a man arises as rector of the community and personifies its spirit, a concept which proceeds directly from the Revolution. It has a fully and typically revolutionary context, like the idea that nourishes it.
>
> · · ·
>
> In the totalitarian regimes the Party appears exalted in this precise function of selecting the *Jefe*. [In practice, it would seem to have worked exactly the other way around.]
>
> · · ·
>
> ... As a minority, it is to integrate whatever is healthy and robust in political life. Therefore the unification itself has a task of selection, since it seeks homogeneity even in the solvency of its elements. ... The Party thus becomes the depository of a force

that is continually renewed and knows how to orient each generation in a revolutionary spirit. Thanks to the concept of the permanent revolution, and owing to the instrumentality of the Party,
struggles disappear and all energy is concentrated on the task of
national affirmation.[38]

Beneyto Pérez did not hesitate to proclaim the totalitarian quality
of the Franco state and its similarity to all other fascist regimes,[39]
but a reverse tendency soon appeared, strongly connected with the
vicissitudes of World War II. Early in 1942 García Valdecasas declared:

In the original [Twenty-seven] Points of the Falange, the State
is defined as a "*totalitarian instrument* at the service of the integrity of the *Patria*." It is, then, deliberately expressed that ours
is an instrumental concept of the State. Every instrument is characterized as a medium for something, by a task which it serves.
   No instrument is justified in and of itself. It is worth while
insofar as it fulfills the end for which it is destined. Therefore, the
State is not for us an end in itself, nor can it find its justification
in itself.
   ... The State ought not to pursue ends nor undertake tasks
that are not justified as a function of the integrity of the *Patria*.
On the contrary, its forces are dispersed and wasted in improper
enterprises, which, when attempted, aggravate the process of bu-
reaucratization to which we have previously referred.
   ... In order to justify itself in a positive sense, the State must
act as an instrument for the achievement of ultimate moral values.

· · ·

   ... Genuine Spanish thought refuses to recognize the State
as the supreme value. This is the meaning of the polemical attitude of all classical Spanish thought against the *razón de Estado*
enunciated by Machiavelli.[40]

A few good things were even said for liberalism, and even more
care was taken to differentiate *falangismo* from other antiliberal ideologies. Thus Javier Martínez de Bedoya in 1943:

A worldwide transmutation is being effected. Signs of it are Bolshevism, Italian Fascism, German racist socialism and the other
styles and modes which we have described in previous pages. They
are eruptions, beginnings, already pregnant with what is to come,

but entities in no way definite, permanent, or conclusive. And, of course, Bolshevism, fascism, and racism alike are restricted national phenomena, without worldwide breadth or profundity.

Perhaps the voice of Spain, the presence of Spain, when it is fully worked out and developed, may give to changing reality its most perfect and fertile expression, the forms which can fix it firmly in universal history.[41]

This re-evaluation and re-expression of Falange doctrine reached its climax with José Luis de Arrese's *El Estado totalitario en el pensamiento de José Antonio* (1944). Arrese, then party Secretary-General, declared that José Antonio had early insisted that the Falange concept of the Spanish nation was based on a *destino en lo universal* grounded in Spanish history and in theological truth [*sic*]. "We do not, therefore, seek a totalitarian State."[42] This was not what the party ideologues had said in the early days, but it served the needs of the regime between 1943 and 1946.[43]

The Caudillo did not ask for a rigorously ideological state, but only for a general theory of authoritarianism. His formula was a conservative syndicalism, bounded by all sorts of state economic controls, spiritually tied to Catholicism, ready for any kind of practical compromise, and always backed up by the Army.

XVI

POLITICS DURING WORLD WAR II

UNFORTUNATELY FOR THE manipulators who controlled the Spanish government in 1939, Muñoz Grande did not wear well as Secretary-General of the party. Perhaps because of his military background, Muñoz Grande lacked the kind of skill needed to keep so heterogeneous an outfit running smoothly. He was more of a nationalist than a syndicalist, and he was uncomfortable in his new position from the very beginning. Personally austere and honest, Muñoz Grande had little executive talent, and complaints from several sides were frequent. Effective control of the party continued to remain in Serrano's hands, which only increased Muñoz Grande's sense of futility. Disputes and disturbances were continual, and by the end of 1939 it was plain that such a situation could not endure.

Muñoz Grandes' retirement was announced on March 15, 1940. No successor was named at the time, and the party was left under the nominal direction of Pedro Gamero del Castillo, the Vice Secretary-General.[1] Gamero was fundamentally a Catholic monarchist who hoped to create of the eclectic, heterogeneous membership of the new Falange a strong political movement that could support and help shape the development of the new nationalist state. For this reason he had worked for the unification of parties in 1937 and had consistently supported Serrano Súñer ever since. The incorporation of the *camisas viejas* was especially important in this process of administrative organization, for no effective union could be made without them. After 1939, the remainders of the old Falange were so uncertain and demoralized that, in most cases, there was little active desire to oppose the party leadership, even though some veterans were quite suspicious of Gamero. The Vice Secretary-General had scant sympathy for the original *jonsista* variety of Falangism, but he played a leading role in the development of the syndicate structure, editing the original law of Syndical Unity.

Nonetheless, the role of Gamero was no easier than that of Muñoz Grandes, since real political power continued to rest with Serrano Súñer in the Ministry of the Interior. Leading a heterogeneous membership, eschewing any truly revolutionary measures, closely hemmed in by the other pressure groups of the Franco state, the direction of the party was an extremely frustrating task.[2]

Throughout his term of office, Gamero retained close contact with the monarchists. He was one of the few members of the Spanish government in 1940 who looked favorably on the United States, nourishing as he did private hopes about drawing North American capital into the task of reconstructing Spain. After more than a year as nominal director of the Falange, he despaired of ever accomplishing anything in domestic political administration and resigned in the spring of 1941.

The party limped along in this fashion throughout 1940. The Falange, official and otherwise, once again began to split up into a set of private cliques. There were the in-group circles at Madrid, the unambitious cadres of provincial leaders, the impotent *ex-combatientes* (some conspiring, the others vegetating), the Tarduchy Junta, the local Ezquer conspiracy in Catalonia, and the potentially powerful syndical organization run by Salvador Merino.

By the beginning of 1941 what remained of the old guard in the Falange organization was fed up with Serrano Súñer. The devious policy he had helped originate four years earlier, which he had unfailingly implemented by compromise, corruption, and outright denial of responsibility, had sapped the marrow from the party. There appeared to be nothing left of it but a noisy propaganda machine, an overgrown bureaucracy, and a few immature students.

In Madrid the old guard continued to circle around the home of Pilar Primo de Rivera, the perennial head of the party's Sección Femenina. Early in 1941 they delivered a virtual ultimatum to Serrano Súñer, asking him either to take over direct control of the FET, reuniting the party and re-establishing its influence in the state, or to throw off his pseudo-Falangist pose and go over to the conservatives and reactionaries.

As was his wont, Serrano first reacted in an extremely circum-spect fashion. He knew that things had not worked out in the FET as planned. Instead of producing a strong conservative, nationalistic, corporative party with a firm organization and a consistent ideology, four years of political juggling had produced an amorphous fish-fry. But by this time Serrano was interested in more important things. There were no visible limits to his ambition, and he had been moving constantly upward. After France fell to the Germans, foreign affairs shared primacy with domestic politics. It was to the former sphere that Serrano was now turning his attention.

On October 16, 1940, Serrano Súñer had taken over the Ministry of Foreign Affairs. This new position occupied most of his time and redoubled his political problems. Monarchist opposition to the poli-tician who was regarded as the gravedigger of the restoration and the strong man of the dictatorship had never ceased. Conflict with Se-rrano's Germanophile foreign policy was now added to their resent-ment against his domestic program, for Serrano's new task was to reverse the Anglophile attitudes sometimes displayed by Jordana and Beigbeder, his predecessors. Beneath the surface, there was much antagonism over Spanish neutrality. After the fall of France, Se-rrano believed that the Allies had lost the war on the continent. He felt that the hour of the Axis had arrived, and he was fully prepared to make a deal with Germany. On the other hand, it so happened that Anglophilia was fairly strong among a part of the Spanish upper classes, especially the monarchists. While the extent of such feelings can easily be exaggerated, they did increase internal discontent.

If the hour of the fascist state had definitely arrived in Europe, it would be prudent to increase the fascistic emphasis of the Spanish government as well. Serrano thought that it might be wise to accept the first alternative proposed by the *camisas viejas*: take direct con-trol of the FET and build it up to a position of real influence. This would provide him with the opportunity of creating a party-state with himself at the head of the party. However, it was most doubtful that the Caudillo would or could countenance such an independent increase of his brother-in-law's power. Furthermore, it was Serrano, not Franco, who was compromising his political position by shoul-dering formal responsibility for a clearly pro-Axis policy. At the height of his power, Serrano was in a very delicate situation, where he could not afford either to retreat or stand still.

The latent discontent within the Falange came to a climax in May of 1941. This crisis was precipitated by the appointment on May 5 of Colonel Valentín Galarza as Minister of the Interior, Serrano's old post. Formerly one of the chief leaders of the UME, Galarza was a permanent Army politician whose most recent job had been to remove whatever fangs remained in the Falangist militia. As a careerist who put the officer corps first, he was deemed profoundly antipathetic toward the goals of the Falange. The appointment of this military intriguer 'sparked intense resentment among *camisas viejas*, and within a few days nearly ten *jefes provinciales* had resigned, the most prominent being Miguel Primo de Rivera at Madrid.

Anti-Galarza feeling increased during the next few days with the appearance of an unsigned article in *Arriba*, entitled "El Hombre y el Currinche" ("The Man and the Pipsqueak"). The pipsqueak was not identified, but it was understood to be Galarza. The Army leaders now demanded the head of the Falangist responsible for this insult. The author of the article seems to have been Serrano's personal favorite, the poet Dionisio Ridruejo, who was still the official Director of Propaganda for the Ministry of the Interior. However, Antonio Tóvar, Press Subsecretary of the Falange, was nominally responsible for *Arriba*, and he gallantly took responsibility for the article.

To placate the military, Franco dismissed both Tóvar and Ridruejo, even though they were junior protégés of Serrano.[3] The *cuñadísimo* claimed that he had not even been consulted about the dismissal, which he considered as evidence of a dangerous tendency to bring the Army gang into formal control and disrupt the party-conservative-civilian-military synthesis that he had labored so long to build up. He strongly believed that something had to be done to right the balance and placate the Falangists. It has been said that Serrano was so perturbed that he even sent a private letter of resignation to the Caudillo.

Franco, however, was well prepared to deal with this crisis. It had been necessary to back up the military in the Galarza appointment, but the Caudillo was not ready to let the Army gain the upper hand over the Falange. He decided to appoint a new Secretary-General, José Luis de Arrese, who had previously been *jefe provincial* of Málaga.

By profession an architect, Arrese was a *camisa vieja,* and was related through marriage to José Antonio's mother. Although he had been arrested in the 1937 purge, he had later been found reliable and had made a good record at Málaga, particularly as champion of low-cost housing for workmen.[4] Arrese had at first been a sincere opponent of Franco's tactics of compromise and division. He first met the Caudillo at an official reception during one of Franco's inspection tours; Arrese's sincere, modest manner favorably impressed the Generalissimo, who wanted to win the Málaga *jefe* over to his side. A personal foe of Galarza, Arrese had just resigned as *jefatura provincial* because he felt that it would be impossible to work with the new Minister of the Interior.

After leaving the Málaga post, Arrese went immediately to Madrid, where he received the surprising news of his appointment as Secretary-General. He had a very strong sense of loyalty to the "Movement" and was quite willing to accept the position, but he nevertheless insisted to the Caudillo that more compensation must be given the Falange to offset the recent elevation of Galarza. The mere naming of an old-guard Falangist as Secretary of the Falange meant little.

Franco was quite willing to broaden the base of his cabinet in order to spare the regime any sort of Falangist revolt. At a meeting held in Arrese's home, Serrano Súñer, Miguel Primo de Rivera, and other Falangist leaders prepared a possible cabinet realignment. The proposals were largely accepted, and a government shake-up on May 19, 1941, gave the Falange two new seats in the cabinet: José Antonio Girón, leader of the *ex-combatientes,* became Minister of Labor, and in an appointment ridiculous even for Franco Spain, Miguel Primo de Rivera was named Minister of Agriculture. Furthermore, the services of Press and Propaganda were taken out of the Ministry of the Interior and transferred to the newly created Vice-Secretariat of Education in the FET. Girón and Miguel Primo de Rivera snapped at the opportunity for cabinet rank, and the changes were made with great speed.[5]

Serrano could not but approve of the new alignment, which re-established the equilibrium he had sought. At the same time, however, the new situation reduced his own influence in the Falange. The leadership of the party was still being juggled around just as Franco desired, and there was little prospect that even a conservative Falange would become that institutional force that Serrano had hoped to create. The only leverage left to the *cuñadísimo* was his post as chairman of the Falange's Junta Política, and he wanted to make the most of it.

Arrese was himself interested in delimiting more precisely the zones of authority in the party hierarchy. Since Franco had not fully trusted the previous Secretaries of the Falange, Serrano had exercised inordinate influence. In order to provide adequate administrative leadership, Arrese proposed to Serrano that they make suggestions clarifying their respective functions. Arrese understood Serrano to agree that the Secretary-General would handle appointments and administration within the FET, leaving the chairman of the Junta to deal merely with questions of ideology and general policy. Arrese therefore approved the proposals sent to Franco, who immediately signed them into law. His surprise was great upon finding that Serrano's actual proposals gave the chairman of the Junta power to initiate and review all significant policy, thus reducing the independent authority of the Secretary-General to the vanishing point. Arrese hurried to inform Franco that he had, in effect, been double-crossed.

It was now Franco's turn to be surprised, for he thought Arrese had approved the Serrano proposals. This presented a dilemma. Franco had already been disquieted by Serrano's independent behavior during the May crisis, and he now began to doubt the *cuñadísimo*'s loyalty and selflessness. Serrano's position was becoming awkward, for he had earned the enmity of many people both inside and outside the party. On the other hand, Franco had confidence in Arrese, whom he believed to be a fully loyal administrator. He thus deemed it prudent to nullify the effects of the Serrano proposals. Since he could not immediately cancel what he had just decreed, he permitted Arrese to dictate a series of appointments that otherwise should have been made by Serrano.[6]

The events of 1941 and the rise of Arrese thus brought a definite decline in Serrano's influence. The *cuñadísimo's* star was on the wane. He occupied the Ministry of Foreign Affairs for another year, but his power in the FET faded away during 1941. He had never been so powerful and independent as outsiders had believed; he had simply been Franco's deputy in diluting the revolutionary fascistic impulse generated during the Civil War. Neither of his pretended goals, Catholic corporatism or neo-fascism, had been achieved, and in the end he suffered the customary fate of court favorites and big political fixers. He could well remark, as he did to his friend Ridruejo, that "nothing could undo the ill we have done Spain."[*]

Arrese was not a new Serrano, and he exercised less political initiative. Scrupulously loyal, he blocked all attempts of syndicate leaders to form a "Left-Falangism" around him. The appointees of Salvador Merino hoped to continue planning for a dynamic syndical leadership even after their leader's dismissal, but Arrese regarded them as potentially schismatic and gave them no support. Instead, he brought in safe Franco-Falangists to keep the syndicates quiet.

Arrese regarded disunity within the Nationalist front as tantamount to suicide. Although he was a vehement anti-capitalist and wanted to see the Spanish state implement sweeping social and economic reforms, Arrese did not place the economic goals of national syndicalism ahead of the personal prerogatives of the Caudillo. He believed that Franco's leadership in the Civil War had given him an historical mandate to guide Spain's destinies during the near future. Furthermore, Arrese's strong religious convictions prompted him to

---

[*] Quoted by Ridruejo in an interview conducted by Luis Ortega Sierra, in *Preuves,* No. 76 (June, 1957), p. 14.

In his memoirs, Serrano did not hide the fact that the new party he had helped construct was no more than an ideological facade and an organizational tool, the regime's basic institutional strength lying in the Army. "Neither the legislation nor the governmental policies [of the regime] would ever come to be entirely uniform. In the last analysis, the center of gravity, the true support of the regime (in spite of the appearances which we foolishly forced ourselves to exaggerate) was and would continue to be the Army: the national Army . . . would even be (perhaps fortunately) the substitute for a state that had not completed its being, that had not completed its institutional body and true organic form." (*Entre Hendaya y Gibraltar,* p. 127.)

support a policy of political compromise. Devoutly believing that Christian unity was necessary to save Europe from Communism, he eschewed the violent fascist elements in the Falange's ideology.

The dictator trusted his new choice for Party Secretary because of the latter's honesty and personal decency, but also because Arrese lacked any dangerous talent for independent political intrigue. Franco had calculated that the responsibilities of office would finish the task of bringing Arrese around to his own viewpoint, and in this he was not mistaken. Arrese became a sincere supporter of the Caudillo, and an invaluable executor of his new policy of injecting more religion and less radicalism into the Falange. He openly declared that compromise and moderation were necessary if Spain was to rebuild a prostrate fatherland, heal class division, and escape a world at war. Admitting that all the organs of the Falange did not function with the efficiency desired, he warned of the dangers of demagogy. Arrese never tired of repeating that the Falange was Catholic, and that its ties with the Army were closer than ever.[7] He declared that the party's aims were to "(1) Spiritualize life. (2) Make Spain more Spanish. (3) Implement justice." But he warned that "Spain—and may some who wear the blue shirt but hide the red shirt hear it quite well—will be nothing if it is not Catholic."[8] Evidently the Falangist was to be half monk, half soldier: "We believe in God, Spain, and Franco."[9]

Arrese has conceded that during his first term at the party helm the Falange's policy and propaganda line clearly shifted from a theoretical emphasis on revolution to a more or less self-admitted acceptance of evolution.[10] Although he could declare on public occasions that "without fanaticism and intolerance nothing can be done," his actual role in Spanish politics was characterized by great moderation.[11] The Arrese leadership was Franco's greatest success with the party since Serrano had brought off the unification five years before.

The new cabinet of 1941 definitely broadened the base of the regime. It brought the Falange greater official influence than it had ever enjoyed during the Franco regime, with two seats on the Council of Ministers. However, it was influence given to a docile party. By agreeing to collaborate fully in the new cabinet the Falangists relinquished any right to moral aloofness or personal independence. All plans for a party conspiracy against the regime had ended. Those who did not like the latest phase of the "new Spain" simply packed up and went home.

The role of the FET in the evolution of the Franco state was made more explicit by a decree of November 28, 1941, which abolished the twelve National Services set up for the party in 1938. Serrano may have originally hoped to make the Falange organization parallel and complementary to the regular structure of the government ministries, but the Generalissimo finally decided to discard the entire idea. Instead, four Vice-Secretariats were established within the party: the Movement (executive administration of the Falange bureaucracy); Social Works (syndicates and *ex-combatientes*); Popular Education (which, in effect, took over state propaganda, even on the local level); and Services (which included a number of secondary sections, such as communications, health, and so forth). Outside its work in propaganda and the syndicates, the Falange had no direct contact with national administration. Beyond talking about and administering the labor front, its political significance was secondary and its political initiative non-existent. Of the one hundred and six members sitting on the party's National Council in 1942, no more than about forty could reasonably be considered Falangists of any sort. Approximately twenty were military men, and a half-dozen were Carlists. The rest were miscellaneous Rightists and middle-class opportunists.[12]

The Falange had been tamed. No one really thought about a national syndicalist revolution any more. The Franco formula was unopposed. As one Leftist critic said, "This Falange of the *camisas viejas* took refuge in editorships. It never leaves that sphere. When ordered, it shouts against reaction or against marked Reds."[13] But it took no initiative.

The more ardent spirits in the party hoped to exhaust their frustration and find a radical outlet for their ideological passion by joining the "Blue Division," a Spanish force being organized to succor the German Army on the Russian front. Here disappointed Falangists could once more shoulder arms against atheistic Bolshevism and give vent to their pent-up emotions by ramming a bayonet down a Russian throat. By no means all members of the Blue Division were enthusiastic Falangists, but a great many of them were, and such ardent young fanatics as Dionisio Ridruejo and Enrique Soto-mayor joined. Losses on the Russian front were severe, and scores of promising young Falange leaders never returned to Spain. Some of those who survived the first year refused to give up the fight, even after the Blue Division was officially dissolved. Those who remained were made into a "Blue Legion," which fought on at the eastern front almost to the very end. The veterans who returned to Spain in 1943 were hardly sure that they had done the right thing, for they found the political situation at home worse than ever. Arrese told Ridruejo, "I am a *franquista*," and said that the Caudillo was more clear-headed than any political figure in Spain, which was doubtless true.

One significant change did occur in 1942, however. It began innocently enough with a religious demonstration in Vizcaya. On August 16 of each year it was the custom of local Carlists to attend a special mass at the shrine of the Virgin of Begoña, in Bilbao. Requeté veterans, who always displayed great enthusiasm on such occasions, burst from the church shouting "Long live the King!" and other Carlist slogans, among which were undoubtedly curses hurled at the Falange. Several young Falangists who happened to be in the square outside the church responded violently to what they considered a "treasonous" and reactionary demonstration. The pugnacious Carlists replied to the taunts by throwing themselves on the handful of Falangists, one of whom was a crippled war veteran. To save his comrades from a bad beating or something even worse, a Falangist named Domínguez threw a hand grenade (which he was carrying illegally) into the crowd of Carlists, wounding six of them. The Falangists then went to the local police station to denounce the Carlists.

The matter was complicated by the presence inside the church of General Varela, the Minister of War. A Carlist and a reactionary, Varela was an old enemy of the Falange. Since the Carlists had immediately filed their own complaint against the Falangists, Varela received a telephone call from the vacationing Caudillo, who asked for a personal report. Franco immediately realized that the Begoña incident could have serious repercussions inside the regime. He questioned Varela very specifically as to whether the Falangists had planned a personal attack against him. Varela admitted that this was not the case; it had been merely a street incident between young hotheads.

Widely varying reports of what had occurred were noised about. A Falange pamphlet dated August 18, 1942, and signed by the National Sports Delegate of the SEU claimed that all the Carlists present had sung a verse that ran:

> Tres cosas hay en España
> Que no aprueba mi conciencia:
> El subsidio,
> La Falange,
> Y el cuñado de su excelencia.*

It was further charged that former Basque separatists were now disguising themselves as Carlists, which was doubtless true.

The Carlists circulated a pamphlet entitled "The Crime of the Falange in Begoña—A Regime Found Out." They claimed that the entire incident was planned by the Vizcayan Falange and that a bomb attempt had been made on Varela's life. They called upon their followers "to resist boldly this insupportable situation, equal to that in the Republic during 1936."[14]

Both Carlists and Army leaders were demanding punishment, and so the Falangists involved were tried by a military court. Domínguez was summarily sentenced to death; there were other bad marks on his record, for during the war he had passed over the battle lines and had already been reprieved from one death sentence. Arrese did his best to have the death penalty commuted, for he wanted to avoid the possible consequences of a judicial execution. But Serrano, in one of his last official decisions, ruled that the juridical history of Domínguez, with one previous death sentence on his record, made clemency impossible.

The Carlists and some Army leaders were still not satisfied. The

---

* "There are three things in Spain / That my conscience does not approve: / The subsidy, / The Falange, / And the brother-in-law of His Excellency." (The subsidy, a typical Franco gimmick, was being paid to the main branch of the old Bourbon dynasty.)

Traditionalists bitterly resented their lack of influence in the FET, and ten Carlist chiefs resigned their posts in the "Movement." The most important Carlist, General Varela, identified his Traditionalism with the Church and the Army, not with a political party. Anglophile and anti-fascist, he thought the moment had arrived to put the remaining Falangists on the run. Not content with the death of Domínguez, he and Galarza sent messages to the military Captains-General throughout Spain, asking for their response to the Falangist insolence of having attacked "the Army" in Begoña.

With this move, however, the anti-Falangist reaction overreached itself. Varela and Galarza had no authorization from Franco for their circular, and their action, bordering on insubordination, merely armed the Falangists against them. Franco viewed Varela's action as needlessly provocative and almost subversive; such independent maneuvers could not be tolerated inside the government. Instead of pressuring the Falange, Franco would now have to ease out Varela and Galarza.[15]

At the beginning of September Varela was replaced as Minister of War by General Asensio, one of the three nominal "Falange generals." Galarza was dismissed from the Ministry of Interior, to be replaced by Blas Pérez González, an early protégé of Serrano Súñer and Gamero del Castillo. Pérez was a loyal *franquista* but also had a reputation for pro-Falangism.

The upshot of these cabinet changes was that Serrano Súñer would have to go, Foreign Ministry and all. Franco had been contemplating this move ever since Serrano's opposition during the 1941 cabinet crisis. To the Caudillo, Serrano was not only dispensable, he was becoming a positive liability. Serrano was the "Axis minister," but the geopolitical situation no longer looked so favorable for the fascist powers. The outcome of the 1942 German offensive was in doubt, and an Anglo-American second front could be expected in France or the Mediterranean any day. If the Anglophile Varela went out, the Anglophobe Serrano could not stay. Thus Franco's personal and diplomatic predilections coincided with practical political necessity.

On the whole, the official Falange leaders were pleased with this settlement, which eliminated both Varela and Serrano. To facilitate the maneuver, Manuel Valdés had even fabricated a fake SEU report denouncing Domínguez as a British spy.

Some of the more idealistic *camisas viejas,* who had stuck with the party through thick and thin, were outraged at the moral hypocrisy involved in this latest compromise. Most of them dropped out of active affairs altogether. *Arriba* continued to editorialize about Left-liberals and opportunists within the party, but it now concluded, "In the end, we are all Spaniards." The Iron Age of Franco Spain was nearly over. The age of permissiveness was beginning.*

Indeed, the FET had been maintained as a party only because of the fascist vogue and the great need for a state ideology and a political framework. As the vogue began to disappear in 1943, the political framework also began to change. The party, which had already shrunk in 1939–40, was further depleted in 1943. Its conversion into a tame bureaucratic instrument was complete. Although it grew more artificial and more isolated with each passing season, it survived, like the regime, because its enemies could never agree among themselves on how to remove it or with what to replace it. The confusion of 1936 was never lifted from Spanish politics.

The FET was still valuable to Franco as a bulwark against a monarchist restoration, which would bring a precipitate end to his regime. In 1943, as Italy fell out of the war and German armies were everywhere in full retreat, monarchists built up strong pressure for a change. Several leading monarchists, including members of the Falange's National Council, signed a petition asking that the Caudillo make ready to restore the Bourbon dynasty. It was argued that only such a move could save Spain from eventual Allied intervention and the return of the Left. Franco was incensed by this gesture, and had the six signatories who sat on the National Council, including Gamero del Castillo and García Valdecasas, expelled from their posts. Nonetheless, the monarchist pressure kept growing.

At this juncture, Franco's pawns freely volunteered their services

---

* Three years later, Serrano Súñer wrote: "In reality the Falange was a political effort that never reached full maturity. It was an ideal, a current of thought, of emotion and of action initiated and defended by José Antonio Primo de Rivera, to which some thousands of men tried to be faithful. . . . At certain moments that current has been almost identical with a concrete party. At certain moments it seemed to be on the verge of identifying itself with the present regime in Spain. Then [at other times] that current was something quite different, far from any concrete historical realization." (*Entre Hendaya y Gibraltar,* p. 366.)

to continue his game of divide-and-rule. The Carlists had split into three or four factions after the extinction of their main line, but they were determined never to permit the return of the orthodox "usurpers," even though they might run the risk of foreign intervention. When the monarchist crescendo of 1943 was at its height, a lieutenant serving one of the current Carlist pretenders, Don Carlos (grandson through the female line of the former pretender Carlos VII), made an alternative suggestion to Falange leaders. He proposed that they all create a large diversionary action among Spanish monarchists in favor of Don Carlos. This would deprive Don Juan, the regular Bourbon candidate, of that near-unanimity of monarchist support he would need to impose himself on the regime.

This proposal, first advanced in March of 1943 by a Carlist lawyer from Valencia, was accepted with alacrity. Through the anti-monarchist Falange, the government financed a "clandestine" Carlist campaign in favor of Don Carlos. Within three or four months this raised some doubt in the minds of the middle classes as to the sole legitimacy of the claim of Don Juan. The orthodox monarchists were temporarily forestalled, and the regime survived another threat.

Such inner division and mutual enmity guaranteed the continuity of the pseudo-Falange state under so skillful a maneuverer as Francisco Franco. As the original proponent of this 1943 gambit wrote fifteen years later:

> If we should see ourselves in the same situation one hundred times, we would do the same thing one hundred times, for a hundred years of the government of Franco, with all the corruption of its administration, is preferable to one year of Don Juan, which would be the swift bridge to Communism.[16]

Franco's strength was based on the weakness and mutual hatred of his opponents.

XVII

PLAYING OUT THE STRING

AFTER THE TIDE OF THE WAR turned in 1942-43, the regime began
to make serious efforts to escape the onus of its foreign ideological affiliations. There was no longer much talk in Spain about
supporting international fascism, and the regime's opposition to the
Soviet Union was officially predicated on the need to protect "Christian Europe" from "Asiatic Communism." Hitler made one last
effort to draw Spain into the war in January 1943, when the party
Secretary, Arrese, made a visit to Germany. Arrese's Catholic convictions made him a fully reliable representative of the Caudillo in
such a situation; his lack of enthusiasm for radical fascism would
keep him from lending any support to a mere pro-Nazi front abroad.
He replied to the entreaties of Nazi leaders by saying that Spain was
quite willing to make a contribution to the struggle against Communism, but that such a war must be based on the principles of the
Christian West, which meant that it could not involve hostility to
the Anglo-Saxon powers. Furthermore, there was no logic in alliance
with an Asiatic and pagan power like Japan, which was destroying
all the achievements of Christian civilization in the Far East. In order
for Spain to participate in the Second World War, Arrese said, the
entire system of opposing alliances would have to be changed. All
Spain would offer was increased support on the Russian front after
Hitler had made a separate peace in the West; there was little point
in maintaining one Spanish Blue Division in Russia unless another
were sent to the Philippines to oppose Japanese Shintoist aggression.[1]
By 1943 Hitler may no longer have been opposed in principle to a
separate peace with the West, but his revolution of nihilism had gone
too far to make such a move practical. This being the case, the Spanish regime moved farther and farther away.

During the last year of the war, the Franco regime made a desperate attempt to divest itself of the worst outward trappings of fascism. In such an effort, of course, the Falange was one of the Caudillo's chief liabilities.[2] When the formation of a new cabinet was finally announced on July 20, 1945, only two names appeared from the Falange. General Asensio, a "Falange General," was replaced by an orthodox conservative militarist. Arrese was dismissed from the post of Minister and Secretary-General of the "Movement" (as the party was now innocuously referred to), and his seat was left vacant to point up the insignificance of the party in the new scheme of things.

In a public address the Caudillo declared that the Falange was not really a state political party, but a sort of administrative "instrument of national unification." The party line dropped off very sharply. There was no more talk about the impending doom of the Western democracies or the manifest superiority of martial values and institutionalized violence. On July 27 the Vice-Secretariat of Popular Education, which controlled propaganda, was taken out of the FET party structure and placed under the Ministry of National Education. More and more of the trappings of fascist display were discarded with each passing month. A decree of September 11, 1945, repealed the 1937 law that had made the raised-arm fascist salute mandatory for the nation.[3]

The theoretical significance of the party steadily diminished as a liberalized façade was erected for the regime. Arrese himself had been chiefly instrumental in preparing the decree of July 1942 that restored an official Cortes to Spain in the guise of a fake representative chamber packed with official appointees ratified by means of extremely indirect corporate elections. In 1943 the first elections had been held for *enlaces sindicales,* the local representatives of each syndicate group. These halfhearted attempts to deny the reality of dictatorship were supplemented in mid-1945 by a new municipal election law. This law provided that municipal voters would be allowed on occasion to choose between alternate candidates, both of whom would be nominated by the regime. One third of the municipal representatives were to be elected by the heads of families, another third by members of the local syndicates, and the remainder by the first two-thirds already chosen. Appointments to all significant executive posts were to be made from above.

On July 17, 1945, the Caudillo suddenly announced a Fuero de los Españoles, a Spanish bill of rights, which became the law of the land. The new *fuero* contained a series of provisions ostensibly aimed at guaranteeing the security of citizens from arbitrary procedure; the "guarantees," however, remained in the realm of general principles, and no specific safeguards were given. The main joker in the pack was Article 33, which stated that "the exercise of the Rights recognized in this Bill of Rights may not attack the spiritual, national, and social unity of Spain."[4] On October 22, 1945, growing a bit desperate, Franco promulgated a law by which issues of transcendent national concern could be submitted to popular referendum, naturally at the discretion of the Caudillo.

None of this greatly impressed the Western democracies, who saw fit to withdraw their diplomatic representatives from Madrid. Franco's wartime friendship with National Socialism had made Spain the pariah of the Western world. Her regime was banished from the circle of civilized diplomacy.

But the silent treatment never had its desired effect on Franco. The six years of isolation that the nation endured after the end of World War II possibly did more to solidify the dictatorship than had the six years of internal police terror preceding them. Faced by a hostile world, many Spanish moderates who might otherwise have built an effective opposition had no recourse but to identify their fate with that of the regime.

Although the liberal "reforms" were purely window dressing designed to pacify certain foreign and domestic critics, political repression did begin to diminish in degree. This was because internal resistance, which had never slackened throughout the six years of the World War, commenced to fall off in 1946. The Spanish Left had felt sure that the defeat of the fascist powers in central Europe would foreshadow the end of Franco's rule. When the Western democracies made no direct move against the regime, the Leftist underground began to lose hope. Defections greatly increased in volume.

Seven years of practice had noticeably increased the efficiency of the Spanish political police. Their organization had at first been poor and clumsy, and they had compensated with primitive ferocity for what they lacked in professional control. By 1946 they were able to crack down on the Leftist underground with real effectiveness; a large series of arrests broke the back of the resistance groups. After 1947 sizeable organized underground units ceased to exist.

The index of slaughter also fell off. As Manuel Halcón, the Falange *jefe local* of Seville, had said as early as 1938, "Our Christian principles do not permit us to kill *all* our enemies."[5] There is no way to determine how many political prisoners were killed during the first five or six years following the Civil War, but the figure was in the tens of thousands. In 1944 an official in the Ministry of Justice furnished the Associated Press a slip of paper supposedly indicating that there had been 192,684 political executions in the past five years.[6] In view of all other evidence, this seems an enormous exaggeration, but it nonetheless suggests the spirit of the repression.

Between 1946 and 1950 Franco's regime lived wholly within its own little world. The internal opposition was impotent, and foreigners remained entirely aloof. The brutality and bloodletting of 1936–44, the disappointments of 1945–46, and the internal antagonisms characteristic of Spanish politics had temporarily broken the back of the Left. The regime could afford to ease up.

After mid-1945 the Caudillo's only concern with the Falange was to keep it quiet. He had hit a good balance in domestic affairs, giving economics to the Bank, military affairs (with liberal opportunities for graft) to the Army, moral life and much of education to the Church, subsidies to the monarchists, foreign affairs to Catholic Action, lip-service to the Carlists, tentative security to the middle classes, rhetoric (at least until 1945) and employment to the party, job tenure and promises to the workers. It was stabilization on a very low level, but it worked. The national inertia was enormous.

The party had played its role well, serving as both a mask and an instrument for the dictatorship. It was now an ossified bureaucracy, in which active membership steadily decreased. Most of the veterans registered in the *Vieja guardia* no longer participated in party affairs with the slightest trace of zeal or energy.

The party organization had been left under the caretaker administration of Rodrigo Vivar Téllez, the alternate Vice Secretary-General. Vivar Téllez was said to be an irreproachable gentleman, delicate, honest, and levelheaded, if not brilliant. He had been a judge in Málaga and had come up the power scale with Arrese. Personally, Franco never cared for Téllez because of his frankness, but he trusted in his loyalty. Vivar Téllez was no Falangist, and he could not see why the farce had to be kept up. The FET was clearly a spent force. With the party mired in corruption and bureaucratic pettifoggery, virtually no one believed in it any longer. The sun of fascism had set in Europe, and the continued existence of the party prejudiced the regime in the eyes of the victorious democracies. The Vice Secretary-General suggested that the most logical thing to do would be to disband the whole party structure and dissolve the Falange, hinting that such fossils should be preserved in museums.

Franco refused even to consider the idea. To discard the Falange entirely would disrupt the tight little system he had established. How could "the Crusade" maintain its rationale and coherence without the official instrument of "national coordination"? The lack of an official patronage machine and political façade would leave the regime too naked. The Falange was still much too valuable a pawn to consider removing it from the game. Its very weakness made it more desirable than before.

After 1945 the Falangists found themselves in a definite minority among other Nationalists. They were increasingly resented by Catholics and conservatives, who saw them either as radical totalitarians or as crypto-Reds. The Falange's emphasis on economic reform and its desire to implement the reunion of social classes collided with the immobile conservatism of the dominant Right, with its great distrust of the working class. As one Falangist noted, "As soon as the Cortes began to function, it was curious to observe how those least inclined to discussion, those most authoritarian, were precisely those who were not identified with the Falange."[7] Since Franco had provided a variety of temptations to lure Falangists from active politics, and had frustrated their every initiative, "More than one [Falangist] felt as though he had had his 'wings clipped' and took refuge in professional life, not by choice, but rather out of despair that matters were not following the course that he had desired."[8] During the postwar period Falangism was mainly confined to the field of literary rhetoric.

Members of the old guard who still remained active hoped that the passage of time would strengthen the Spanish economy enough to permit the structural reforms necessary to fulfill the party platform. The last party Secretary, José Luis de Arrese, was closer to Franco than any other *camisa vieja,* and he still cherished the notion that the Caudillo might someday see fit to install a more equitable syndicalist program. Arrese's Falangism, however, was Franco-Falangism; it was not the nihilistic radicalism of Ramiro Ledesma or the humanistic voluntarism of José Antonio. The only one of the Falange's founders who had espoused an orientation similar to Arrese's was perhaps Onésimo Redondo. Arrese professed loyalty to the ideals and plans of José Antonio, but his real political acts seemed to aim at other goals.

As Arrese publicly stressed, the development of the Civil War, the incontrovertible authority of Franco among the Nationalists, and the political growth of the Nationalist front as a coordination of all forces behind the Caudillo had created an entirely new political situation. These developments had made it impossible to fulfill the original party ambitions of the Falange, but there was left nonetheless a body of doctrine and a social program that ought to guide the path of state and society in Spain during the coming decades.

Arrese always liked to talk of the possibility that the regime might socialize much of the economic structure and make the Cortes more representative. He was still opposed to the political Right, writing in 1947 that "in Spain the worst opponent of Falangism has always been the man of the Right."[9] The harmless rhetoric of Arrese condemned capitalism as a cardinal sin of the modern age, and the Falangist leader always talked as though the absolute elimination of usury were imperative. Arrese lent his name to several books, in part written by other theorists, which presented abstract schema by which Spain would be able permanently to transcend class struggle. In the late forties, Arrese's group stressed the old Falange doctrine that labor was not a mere material commodity, but the human aspect of an organic social process of an organic process of production. It was proposed in party propaganda that all members of the productive system ought to feel a common interest in their work, which should be conducted on a cooperative basis, with profits shared by management and labor alike. Arrese declared that he would have liked to see the syndical system evolve into a chain of cooperatives, in which selfish private capitalism would be abolished.[10]

All this was simply whistling in the dark against the reality of the reactionary triumph of Spanish capitalism, a triumph that Franco evidently had no desire to disturb.

However desirable economic transformation seemed to Arrese, he admittedly regarded it as secondary to the preservation of Spanish unity and "Christian principles." Class struggle and economic exploitation were among the primary causes of the breakup of modern society, but to remove the causes was not so urgent as to contain the new Anti-Christ: atheistic, anti-Christian Communism. This was the axis of modern politics, and all other factors must be subordinated to common resistance of the great foe. Security for such a struggle could be found only behind the bulwark of Catholic religiosity, and only the leadership of the Caudillo and the political values of the Movement could avert the dire danger of revolution.

Such an attitude played directly into the hands of the proponents of military dictatorship and big business. Arrese's conundrum (political liberty = disunity = rebellion = anticlericalism = Communism = Anti-Christ) precluded any kind of independent stand against the dictatorship. Arrese's Franco-Falangism was thus truthfully no longer "fascism." It was simply military authoritarianism buttressed on every side by Catholicism and propped up by a state syndical system. It lacked any aggressive, dynamic, or radical overtones. Arrese could honor the old fascism only as a halfway measure:

> Fascism is not a complete formula. . . . It is correct insofar as it searches for a solution to the dilemma of capitalism [versus] communism, but it is mistaken when it does not decide to abandon a materialistic attitude, the only way of achieving the desired transcendence. Furthermore, if fascism had not been silenced by the thunder of cannons it would have ended in failure; better said, it would have failed in its final mission of illuminating a new era.[11]

The trouble with fascism was that it was too materialistic, too nihilis-tically radical. It was not Catholic. Thus it had been unable to save European civilization from Communism and prepare for the post-modern epoch.

During these years, the Falange had only one vital political func-tion—to serve as checkmate to the royalists. This became doubly important when Franco decided to pacify the orthodox Right by providing a means of legal succession for his regime. On July 6, 1947, a Law of Succession was submitted to the Spanish people in national referendum. It recognized General Francisco Franco as Caudillo and rightful Chief of the Spanish State. Further sections stipulated that "when the office of Chief of State was vacant," a Regency Council would take over the national government to prepare the restora-tion of the Monarchy. In the meantime a Council of the Realm, appointed by the Caudillo, would assist him in establishing the rules and procedures whereby the eventual transition might be car-ried out.[12]

The referendum achieved its inevitably overwhelming success, and the Caudillo's government became a sort of pro-Regency. The old-guard Falangists were emphatic antimonarchists and strongly objected to these vague provisions for restoration, but no one listened to them. By 1947 old guard Falangists were something of a laughing-stock in Spain.

Their political stock rose a point or two in the following year, after an unsuccessful interview between the Caudillo and the Pre-tender, Don Juan, in Portugal. Don Juan let it be known that he would not consider the restored Monarchy as a mere legal continua-tion of the Franco regime, adding that he could not approve the present government's state party and its Twenty-six Points. This clouded the political atmosphere once more and left the Caudillo disposed to make another token gesture with the moribund Falange.

In 1948 Raimundo Fernández Cuesta was reappointed Minister and Secretary-General of the Movement, thereby filling a post that had lain vacant for three years. The brief flurry of activity occasioned by the ensuing effort to restore some life to the organization was de-signed only to bring the monarchists up short. It was far too late to inject new life into the party, even if that had been desired.

Spain's isolation came to a close in 1950, when the Cold War against Communism became uncomfortably warm. Official recognition was extended to the dictatorship when a United States ambassador was appointed to Madrid. The resulting tendency to draw the Franco state into an anti-Communist alliance was natural, if ultimately reprehensible.

Economically, in 1950 the country was not very far from where it had been in 1936. Lacking foreign aid, it had taken nearly ten years to repair measurably the destruction wrought by the Civil War. This progress had been further prolonged by the deprivation and isolation accompanying a long international conflict. Living standards had not improved during all this time, and in some areas they had even declined. The nation's economic resources were in the grip of a ruthlessly capitalistic system tempered by state economic controls. Raw materials, import licenses, foreign exchange, international trade, some aspects of credit, and many of the conditions of internal production were fixed by government fiat according to the economic laws and syndical norms first drawn up in 1940-41. Finance, however, was only intermittently affected by state restrictions. The banking world received a free hand in ordinary matters and was, in fact, aided by the government ministries.

The defeat of the Left, the eclipse of the sentimental Right, long years of black market operations, and the shock dealt traditional customs by the total nature of the Civil War, combined with the more sophisticated economic environment of the midcentury, all tended to revitalize the Spanish businessman. By 1950 Spain was much closer to being a capitalist country than ever before. The margin of profit for the possessing groups soon became very high, and the rate of capital formation in established enterprises was great.

During the nineteen-fifties capital investment reached considerable proportions. Spain embarked on her greatest period of industrial expansion since the halcyon years of World War I. According to the Banco Central's Annual Report for 1959, the national index of industrial production increased approximately one hundred per cent between 1951 and 1958. This was made possible by a ruthless policy of wage and price pressure maintained by the major financial and industrial concerns, which still controlled basic economics. Further-

more, the association of government industries (INI), a pet project
of the regime, poured billions of pesetas into a variety of state fac-
tories and government economic projects. Such investment went
ahead so fast that it soon outstripped the actual productive capacity
of the economic system.

Competition within the business world was sometimes strong,
and prices were kept high to assure the rate of capital accumulation.
Costs were often excessive, for Spain lacked the secondary industries,
the engineers, and the skilled workmen to sustain a program of rapid
industrial expansion. The dependence on imports to maintain the
system was extreme. The government itself went off the deep end
to continue an inefficient program of economic expansion. United
States aid, which reached significant proportions by 1953, momentarily helped to stabilize the situation but then aggravated it by
encouraging the business world to risk further imbalance. The natural result of this state of affairs was a process of creeping inflation,
which became serious after 1955.

The only idealism still alive within the party lay among the
"Falanges Universitarias," the student following of the Movement.
Except in the first few years following the war, these young Falangists were never more than a minority among the university youth,
but there was belief and fervor in their ranks. After getting out into
the world, however, even such ardent spirits were liable to lose much
of their enthusiasm. Between 1945 and 1955 a series of student groups
and youth associations connected with the schools attempted to revitalize, and even to rethink, *falangismo* for the young. In a dictatorship influenced by five or six powerful pressure groups, this required
an increasingly greater effort. Such interest was impossible to sustain, and after 1955 the nation's youth sank into political apathy.

This phenomenon was not undesired by the regime. During the
first years of his rule, the Caudillo found that it was going to be
impossible to build a viable ideological state. The instrument—the
party—was both untrustworthy and incapable, while the opposition
from the major powers of the Right was too strong. Thus Franco
had settled for the façade-state, the political farce, in order to provide
a formal framework that might hold the governmental system together. Outside the circle of officeholders and the official party, only

acquiescence was required. Since there was nothing vital for the people of Spain to support, Franco's basic goal was to keep them satisfied to ignore politics. With the Left driven out of sight, the Right absorbed in religion and profits, and the official party a laughing-stock, bread and circuses were the order of the day.

For the first time in fifteen years, bread became more abundant. Real wages increased slightly as production expanded, even though the lion's share of the return went to capital. As for circuses, Spain became one of the most sports-conscious countries in Europe. Newspaper editors who cut the sports content of their journals too low might feel the weight of official displeasure. Madrid was one of the two European capitals to harbor a full-sized daily sports paper, which was also the largest selling newspaper in the country. To top it off, the biggest soccer stadium in the world was erected in the nation's capital.

During the Civil War the official chronicler of the Cuartel General had written: "Let us not deceive ourselves—when this war ends we shall dominate many who have been conquered, BUT NO ONE WHO HAS BEEN CONVINCED."[13] As it turned out, Franco was never so anxious to convince them that he would risk setting their minds to work.

By 1955, if not before, Madrid was politically the most cynical city in Europe. Every political ideology of the modern world had been introduced there during the nineteen-thirties. Each had suffered either physical defeat in the Civil War or moral pollution in the years following. There was no sign that any significant part of the population really believed in anything, beyond the minority that attended church. With each passing year, the vanquished Left seemed to become more divided, rancorous, and ineffective. As production slowly increased, there was more room for economic differentiation, and the attention of ambitious workers inevitably became fixed more on economic than on political goals. There was no political life. The only public issues in Spain were certain economic realities.

Owing to these factors, the only Falangist to win recognition during the years of the long cabinet (1945-57) was José Antonio Girón, the militia leader who had become the Minister of Labor. He took his position seriously and did something to create within the government a greater sensitivity to the workers' needs. The framework of advanced social legislation was installed, although the norms set were too ridiculously low to provide for real well-being. The most attractive feature of the syndical structure was the job security and featherbedding written into it. Underemployment was the norm, but unemployment hardly existed. Girón received credit for trying to improve the situation, even though his underlings were notorious for peculation. He even achieved a certain kind of popularity among such hardened groups as the miners of Asturias.[14]

However, in the inflationary spiral set off during the nineteen-fifties, it was impossible for the workers, urban or agricultural, to keep up. Lest the recrudescence of extreme economic discontent reawaken the political feeling that had lain dormant for eight years, some sort of adjustment was in order. Girón took credit once more for an enormous across-the-board wage increase effected in 1956. Owing to the complicated nature of the Spanish wage system, the real increase was neither so great nor so immediate as it then seemed, but the gesture was obvious. This action had the logical effect of speeding up the inflationary process considerably. A series of illegal strikes occurred in several industrial areas during 1955 and 1956. Even Catholic liberals began to grow restless.

Several *camisas viejas* began to speak their minds once more. Said Carlos Juan Ruiz de la Fuente at the 1956 *Vieja guardia* congress: "Our capitalism fixed its mold in 1936. More and larger. [It is] the only Marxist capitalism still surviving."[15] Some sort of change was obviously called for, since the Ministry of Economics required better management and the state system itself needed strengthening.

In this climate of opinion, the Monarchy, as Franco's titular successor, rapidly gained popularity. Already established by the 1947 law to succeed the Caudillo, it looked like the way out to some conservatives. If they had not been heretofore, all bankers became monarchists. Most functionaries of the regime began to whisper secretly to foreigners that they were really monarchists, not *franquistas*. Just as a conservative Republic had been sanctioned by the Right to prevent a more serious blowup in 1931, so the same elements began to look toward a slightly constitutionalized monarchy for their salvation in 1956. Sniffing danger, the Church hierarchy also began to gather up its collective robes and withdraw from the Caudillo. The regime found itself in narrow straits for the first time in a decade.

Franco thought it prudent to rely on the trustworthy Arrese in such a difficult situation, and in 1956 the latter was once more given the Caudillo's blessing as Secretary-General of the party. Old-guard Falangists were certain that Arrese had been restored in order to accomplish a major institutional change, and within a year the Falange's membership was said to have increased by 35,000, which was the first rise in the number of members since the Civil War. Leaders of the FET suddenly began to realize that this might be their last chance. The Caudillo might need them to help transform his dictatorship into a more viable political system, and if veteran Falangists did not seize the present moment to reorient the Spanish state, it might be forever too late. Accordingly, a commission was appointed to consider revising the statutes of the Movement and to propose an extension of the "Fundamental Laws" to broaden the base of the regime. In addition to Arrese, several former Falangist leaders and National Council members participated, among them such men as Luis González Vicén, José Antonio Elola, Vicente Salas Pombo, Francisco Javier Conde, and Rafael Sánchez Mazas.

The commission, however, was entirely dominated by Franco-Falangists, and little interest was shown in restoring the Falange to a place of primary influence as a party, or even in building up its following among the people. Instead, the commission members were concerned with providing a more viable structure for the Franco state by arranging a little more representation for "safe" elements. This would offer the possibility of continuing the edifice in the future, beyond the life-span of the Caudillo.

The only radical Falangist voice on the commission was that of Luis González Vicén, the former militia leader from Valladolid, who was a friend of Girón, a National Council member, and an anti-guerrilla trouble shooter for the regime. Vicén proposed to construct Spanish political representation through the framework of an expanded Falange, which would become the executor of the new state and would build a more representative and equitable economic system. After engaging in a considerable argument during the course of one meeting, Vicén decided that he could get nowhere against the wishes of the majority and resigned.

In a letter to Arrese, dated June 8, 1956, Vicén tried to explain the criteria for his action. He agreed that after the Civil War the Falange could no longer have aspired to a position as an independent political party. ". . . The party, which was by necessity a movement, ought to have transformed itself into something else a long time ago . . . [something] which I say—I know not if correctly—ought to be transformed into a System." If the party were transformed into a regular structure of government, the arbitrary personal rule of a Caudillo would no longer be necessary.

> A System so conceived not only does not need a *Jefe* but rather finds—which is much more important—that his presence is prejudicial for his rule and for the System itself. The System ought to be one of collective rule with only circumstantial Caudillo-rule. An elective National Council with a precise structure is the axis of everything and the instrument that assumes all the functions of the *Jefatura,* which it can delegate in as many ways as may be thought convenient, either to individual or smaller committees.[16]

The Falange National Council, which should oversee the work of the Spanish state, should be free of either military or clerical influence. Vicén emphasized that he did not deny the right of the Army and the Church hierarchy to be represented in all important national decisions, but he strongly opposed reserving special seats for them on the National Council. "Their proper place . . . is in the Cortes, that is, together with the Spanish people in its legislative activity. There they undoubtedly have their place, together with many other professional groups and strata of the country."[17] Vicén emphasized that Spain was a Catholic country, and that because of that very fact he resented any attempt by the Church hierarchy to establish particularistic privileges. The Spanish people deserved to be spared the possible conflicts resulting from such a situation, since its religious unity was the only form of union wrought by the regime.[18] At the same time, Vicén feared that recent signs of Church withdrawal might indicate a willingness of the Church to help scuttle the regime.[19]

The Army posed an even greater problem than the Church. In any critical situation, Vicén continued, the Army seemed to think itself authorized to act as the political arbiter of Spain, even though it lacked political education or political discipline. Since the only values the Army knew were "heroism, sacrifice, and love for the

Fatherland," it was never prepared for positive political intervention, and whenever it had attempted such intervention it had acted merely as another sectarian political group. If it should attempt to control the transformation of the Spanish state, it would "be regarded by Spaniards as a conquering Army implicated in political work and therefore, as the conqueror of its own country, converted into its political subject. Political armies have failed in every land."[20]

The third member of Vicén's unholy trinity was Spanish capitalism, or the political Right. "The Spanish Right, which has always labored under the influence of the fear and worry caused by its own lack of authentic content, has constantly shouted: Church and Army."[21] Only such spiritual and military authority could save its "precarious position" in Spanish life.

According to Vicén, one of Spain's basic political problems was

> the failure to liquidate the Civil War, which at the present time still finds itself in almost the same condition as in 1939. . . . In this very moment, the difference between being a Red or a non-Red, between having supported the Movement or not, in other words between conquerors and conquered, is a reality in national life and in the administrative decisions of the government. The accessibility of power which is perfectly delimited between conquerors and conquered, the treatment of citizens in which the difference is equally marked, the chance for social influence and many other factors, clearly indicate that this most grave problem still lacks solution. If this is so obvious from our camp you can easily imagine how it appears from the other side. They not only regard themselves as defeated and politically unsatisfied; they see themselves treated as second-class Spaniards and exaggerate the injustice which they receive, building up hatred against the other half whom they think the cause of the evil.[22]

Thus the transition of the nationalist movement from its present dictatorship into a comprehensive political system would have to take some account of the other half of the nation. If the Franco state were equated with the Movement, it would represent only half of Spain and would never be able to build a firm foundation for the future. The danger was doubly great because the Falange, the only organized political force behind the present limited Movement, was not really strong:

Any political action requires a force which the Falange at this moment does not have, and which it must urgently seek if it does not wish to continue waving the flag and representing every interest save its own. This strength can only come from two places, either from a *Jefe* of great prestige, such as the one it presently has, or from its own mass and the strategic position which it gains within the state structure.[23]

Vicén strongly disapproved of permitting the Falange to continue to rely merely on the authority of a personal leader like Franco, for the following reasons:

1. Because of the mortality and mutability of men.
2. Because it [dictatorship] bears within itself an absolute rule that can, in some cases, result in tyranny.
3. Because in it is employed the personal and direct method of naming the commander, with its grave consequences of coercing leaders, [promoting] servility, and denying liberty to men who fulfill functions of judging and acting, and with the danger that when the commander errs (and the commander errs since he is a man, even though he may err less than other men), the error is automatically supported by everyone and can take the dimensions of a cataclysm.
4. Because, unfortunately, men are capricious, above all, the men who are more highly placed, and the country cannot be forced to suffer the caprice and fickleness of any one man no matter how high he may be.
5. Because this procedure of force and command from the top downward unleashes in the nation the activity of all the incorrigibles of unmerited ambition, since one arrives at a position of influence through personal connection and not through work, political service, knowledge, or personal qualities.
6. Because there is no way, in this type of command, to take advantage of a country's wealth of talent, since all nominations have to be made among those who are known by or visible to the one who makes the appointment, and one man, however exceptional he may be, can never have before his sight or imagination more than a limited number of persons, and no filing system can replace personal acquaintance.
7. Because a selection of the worst is made, since only those are seen whose temperament, economic ambition, or lack of employment lead them to make themselves seen.[24]

An exiled Red could hardly have written a more balanced condemnation than Vicén's critique of the political structure that he himself had helped to create. The solution, to Vicén, was not a return to full political democracy on the model of the Republic, but a broadening of the present governmental structure to incorporate all the Spanish people. He proposed that the Falange's National Council be empowered to name candidates for Chief of the Spanish State and to guarantee the honesty of all elections held. Furthermore, the National Council should supervise all functions of the state and exercise a virtual veto power over all government actions. All adult Spaniards would vote in "presidential" elections for a Chief of State among the candidates chosen by the Council.

Vicén outlined concrete structural proposals for reorganizing the entire Spanish state. The new political system would rest on universal suffrage channeled through indirect representation. Local government officials and representatives would be chosen by direct vote of all the local populace, but they in turn would elect the members of the provincial assemblies and part of the national Cortes. One third of the total membership of the Cortes would be chosen in this way, a second third of the members would be chosen by the syndicates (either indirectly or, in the case of the great national syndicates, by direct vote among syndical members), and the final third would be composed of eminent Spaniards from different categories selected by the government. The Cortes would have the power to pass national legislation, to approve the Chief of Government (or Prime Minister) appointed by the Chief of State, to deny its confidence to a cabinet and thus force it to resign, to oversee and criticize the functioning of the government, and to veto all tax bills. Dissolutions and new elections were not to be held more often than every two years.

Parallel to the establishment of more representative government, Vicén proposed that the Falange organization be strengthened and democratized. Each local *Jons* should elect its own leader by vote, although the choice should be approved by the *jefe provincial.* The latter would still be empowered to depose the *jefe local,* but only with the support of the Provincial Council. The local *Jons* could also present a vote of censure against its *jefe,* although the resolution of such a matter lay in the hands of the Provincial Council.

The total membership of the Falange in each province was to elect the members of its Provincial Council, which would then select the *jefe provincial,* the choice of whom might always be vetoed by the party's National Council, if it saw fit. The National Council itself would be in part composed of the fifty *jefes provinciales,* themselves chosen through indirect election. The second third of the Council members would be elected directly by the party members. The remaining members of the Council would be appointive officeholders and outstanding individuals chosen by the national leadership. The National Council would then select the party's *Jefe Nacional* and would also designate the members of the Junta Política. It would be the Council's duty to oversee the political purity of the Spanish state, having the right to veto laws, to criticize and force reforms, and to purge the party membership.

The political vacuum that surrounded the Franco regime simply could not continue. As Vicén wrote to Arrese, "Gauge as precisely as you can the fact that the mass of Spaniards have been turned out into complete chaos, without leaders, standards, or organization. . . ." If the attempt to turn the Falange "movement" into a "system" should fail, "One cannot even calculate what the reaction might be."[25] It would be catastrophic for the remaining Falange leaders to await the demise of Franco before reorganizing their forces, which were nearing exhaustion already. After the end of Franco, the Army and the monarchists would try to eliminate the Falange altogether. It would then be too late to construct a viable system. Vicén asked Arrese,

> Do you think that it could [then] be done? It is more probable that we would be cast out by the monarchists and the king himself, who very logically would wish to remove the presence of a Falange in large part imposed, but not loved. We would remain with the leaflets that you are now editing in our hands and with the memory of our present lack of vision, if not of our cowardice and conformity.[26]

It would take some years to put a "system" into functional operation, and each passing month thus became precious. The remaining days of the Caudillo's rule ought to be used in building up all the prestige and strength obtainable:

> One must do everything very rapidly in order to take advantage of the years remaining to the Caudillo, in order that he may leave the future of the Patria secure, and not leave us in the tremendous uncertainty that we know today.[27]

Vicén's proposals were considered too extreme by the other members of the commission. They thought it would be impossible to re-Falangize Spain; all that might be accomplished was the safeguarding of the political goals of the Movement by the National Council, whose composition would not, however, be very Falangist. The commission members were only concerned about transforming the present absolute dictatorship into a "system" under a quasi-constitutional monarchy.

After some months of deliberation the commission prepared a report and several "Anteproyectos," or draft laws. The theoretical "Bases" of the report stressed that the continuity of the Movement would be founded upon certain basic and incontrovertible political principles. Once these were accepted, differences in emphasis and execution might be tolerated so long as that did not result in the return to a political party system. At any rate, a formally integrated juridical structure must be built for the Spanish state, because the *caudillaje* could not continue after Franco's death: "The authority of the Caudillo is only lifelong. . . . By its very nature the authority of the Caudillo *is not susceptible to succession.*"[28]

The notion of a constitution was too formalisic and material, tending toward juridical relativism. State law ought instead to evolve through a successive series of Fundamental Laws. These Laws provided for the eventual transition of the Spanish state into a Monarchy through the guidance of a Council of the Realm.

Once the transition to monarchy was firmly established, the resulting problem was how to incorporate representation of the people. The Law of Succession was not to be interpreted as simply handing the Spanish state over to the King; this Law was to be interpreted simply as one of the Fundamental Laws, and it would be bound by their collective content. Thus, in accordance with the letter of these Laws, the Spanish state under the Monarchy must be representative. The "Bases" noted that the democratic tendency might not always be desirable, but that it was "irreversible."[29]

The National Movement, of course, was to be the basic reality behind any political representation. The unity of the Movement could not be destroyed in favor of a return to the old party system. The regrowth of parties, even on the basis of limited and controlled suffrage, would be a disaster. A restricted franchise would merely create the opportunity for campaigns of demagoguery by disaffected elements, who would represent the excluded to themselves as constituting the *pays réel* as opposed to the *pays officiel*.

Representative government should not be interpreted to deny the King political power. The concept that "the King reigns, but does not govern" should not be employed to rob him of all influence. The King (or Chief of State) would name the Chief of Government (or Prime Minister) by himself, and would also appoint most of the representatives of the Movement. The cabinet should thus be responsible primarily to the Chief of State, not to the Cortes.

According to the proposed "Anteproyecto de Ley de Ordenación del Gobierno," the Chief of Government would be responsible to the Chief of State, and would be appointed for a period of five years, after the Chief of State had consulted with the president of the Cortes and the Secretary-General of the Movement. The Chief of Government could be removed either by the Chief of State or by the reiterated censure of the National Council of the Movement, to whom he would always be answerable for interpellation.

Cabinet ministers, on the other hand, because of their administrative functions, would be responsible to the Cortes itself. Three adverse votes by the National Council would defeat the Chief of Government himself. Censure by the Cortes would force resignation of any minister, unless the Chief of Government continued to support him, in which case the problem would be thrown into the lap of the National Council.

There would be no change in the composition of the Cortes, however, and decree laws would still be operative in some cases. It would be the duty of the Cortes to deal with legislation and not with political questions of basic orientation, which would be handled by the National Council. Under this new system, the people would be represented in three ways: by national referendums, by the Movement, and by the Cortes. No changes were to be made in the Fundamental Laws without a national referendum.[30]

The Commission also prepared an "Anteproyecto" to redefine the doctrinal principles of the Movement. The text made it clear that the original fascistic Twenty-six Points were obsolete. There was not a word about "Empire," and Spain was pledged to cooperate with all countries sincerely working for an international community.

There was no more mention of violence or radical projects, but only an emphasis on maintaining an army "in order that a military sense of life may inform all Spanish existence." That was as close as anyone could come in 1956 to the "sacred violence" of Onésimo Redondo. Otherwise, the proposed political catechism stressed the pre-eminence of Catholicism, national unity, social justice, and the viability of a moderated capitalism.

Arrese made a strong speech in favor of the proposed new Laws at an august gathering in Salamanca on September 29, 1956, the twentieth anniversary of Franco's rise to power. The proposed laws were circulated among members of the National Council and other interested parties, and they drew a wide variety of replies, many quite hostile. The Army, the Church, and the financial interests were strongly opposed to the new proposals, which they feared would dangerously increase the influence of Falangists. The only change they would countenance lay in the direction of an authoritarian monarchy. They preferred the present benevolent dictatorship to any revival of Falangism.

Twenty years of Francoism had brought nothing of the "new Spain" that José Antonio had once dreamed of, and the more intelligent *camisas viejas* were acutely aware of it. On the night of the twentieth anniversary of José Antonio's death, José Luis de Arrese read the following text over the National Radio:

José Antonio: . . . Are you satisfied with us?
I do not think so.
And I think not because you struggled against materialism and egotism, while today men have forgotten the grandeur of your words only to run like thirsty madmen down the path of materialism and egotism.
Because you wanted a Fatherland of poets and of dreamers eager for a difficult glory, while men seek only a catering, round-bellied Fatherland, full of starch, though it possess neither beauty nor gallantry.
Because you preached sacrifice, while men look from one side to the other in order to hide themselves.
Because you despised money, while men lust for money, and business is superimposed on duty, and brother sells brother, profiteering with the humble and the trials of the Fatherland.
Because men confound your slogan of being better with getting along better.

Because spirit becomes carnal, sacrifice becomes gluttony, and brotherhood becomes avarice.

Because you called a cortege of thousands of martyrs that they might serve us as standard and guide, and yet men have not seen in the blood of your followers an example, and they find its memory uncomfortable, and they are annoyed when we repeat in their ears, closed to all generosity, our monotonous insistence on the example of our martyrs, to the extent that some exploit the fallen as a platform on which to climb or a springboard for business and self-indulgence.

José Antonio, you are not satisfied with us. You who watch us from your place, from your twentieth of November, with a profound sense of melancholy and scorn.

You cannot be satisfied with this mediocre, sensual life.[31]

Arrese went on to pledge that things would go better in the future, that the Falange and all of Spain would know how to live up to the vision of José Antonio and the founders of the party. His exposition of the dismal situation then prevailing, however, had a greater ring of truth and carried with it little hope for the future.

On December 29, 1956, Arrese presented a final report on the new Fundamental Laws to the Falange National Council. He announced that of the 151 Council members consulted, a total of 3, 16, and 14 had declared themselves entirely opposed to the "Anteproyectos" Nos. 1, 2, and 3, respectively. Among the other Council members "there was every kind of opinion, ranging from advocacy of a presidential-type Republic to support for a Constitution entrusted to the custody of the Armed Forces."[32]

"One of the most facile and monotonously repeated objections made by opponents of the Laws is that they represent an effort to construct a totalitarian regime. The Falange, precisely because it desires a Catholic state, repudiates the totalitarian state."[33] The opportunity for representation of a variety of interests would prevent any tendency toward undemocratic centralism. To show how little danger there was of excessive Falange influence, Arrese read off the following list of old-guard Falangist officeholders serving under the Franco system:

2 of the 16 ministers
1 of the 17 subsecretaries
8 of the 102 directors-general

        18 of the 50 civil governors
         8 of the 50 presidents of the provincial deputations
        65 of the 151 national councilors of FET y de las JONS
       137 of the 575 deputies in the Cortes
       133 of the 738 provincial deputies
       766 of the 9,155 mayors
     2,226 of the 55,960 municipal councilmen

"That is to say," Arrese commented, "that the original Falange occu-
pies approximately five per cent of the posts of leadership in Spain."[34]

Precisely because the Falange possessed so little effective power,
its chances for getting the proposed new laws adopted were very
slim. The final decision was up to the Caudillo, but he received an
ever-increasing number of protests from bishops, military governors,
and bankers, who strongly protested any quasi-representative Falan-
gistization of Spain. After waiting two months more, he made his
decision; the new laws were quietly buried and a major governmental
shake-up was carried out in February 1957. The changes showed that
there was never to be any reversion to the Falange, for the party was
pushed almost completely out of the government. For example, José
Antonio Girón had been Minister of Labor for sixteen years; it had
been said that with his demagogic radio speeches and his injurious
but impressive wage increases, he was building too strong a position
ever to be ousted. But Girón was ejected and obviously would not
be coming back. He was replaced by Fermín Sanz Orrio, a syndical
chief who was entirely lacking in political initiative or personality.
At the same time, Arrese was superseded by José Solís Ruiz, who
had begun his career as a syndical zealot in the nineteen-forties and
had ended up as a clever and capable party hack.

To defend himself and the party from the barrage of criticism
leveled against them, Arrese found the courage to circulate a clandestine pamphlet in which it was declared that the Falangists had
been "cast aside by the priests and the military, who are the ones who
have governed from the very beginning." He went on to cite his
report to the National Council meeting in which he had listed the
number of old-guard Falangists who still occupied political positions,
thus attempting to prove that "the Falange cannot be responsible
for the situation of our *patria*."

However, Franco had already deprived Arrese of his personal independence by retaining him in the innocuous position of Minister of Housing. This made it impossible for Arrese to identify himself with political protest and further condemned him in the eyes of the opposition.

The new mainstay of the regime was its collaboration with leaders from the secret Catholic religious order and laymen's association "Opus Dei." This extremely hermetic and mysterious formation was founded by an Aragonese priest in 1929. Designed primarily to make Catholicism effective in the secular world, its membership was largely composed of laymen. The formal structure and composition of the group were wrapped in the darkest secrecy. Vows were strict, and the organization's growing number of lay members were held to very rigid standards.

Opus Dei had received its first impetus from the religious outburst attending the Civil War, and in 1939 it began to reach noticeable proportions. Its first opportunity to exert some influence within the government came when José Ibáñez Martín, an ex-Cedista, replaced Pedro Sáinz Rodríguez as Minister of Education in that year. The group continued to grow during the next two decades, and by 1957 it controlled large sections of Spanish education and was very influential in the financial world. It harbored several prominent political theorists and economic specialists, who advocated a strongly Rightist, even reactionary, political orientation. The financial experts of Opus Dei decried slipshod methods in government and in private economic circles. They advocated authoritarian rule without further ado, and preached a heavy-handed economic doctrine.[35] Since they were the spearhead of Spanish Catholicism, Franco turned to the "grupo Opus" as his logical alternative on the Right. Two Opus Dei men were brought into the 1957 cabinet, where they occupied the Ministries of Finance and Commerce.

The opposition began to cry that Franco had finally discarded the Falange mask and had now sold himself to the Catholic reaction. By no means. It was true that the FET had very nearly come to the end of the road. By 1957 no one belonged to the party who did not in some way make a living from it. The organization was rarely referred to as "the Falange," but more customarily as "the Movement," the euphemism commonly employed to alternate with "the Crusade" as a label for the group that won the Civil War. Many Spaniards had their own ideas about what kind of a movement it was. Nevertheless, the "grupo Opus" was not invited to partnership with the Caudillo in order to replace the Falange. The Opus group was merely being used by the Generalissimo as his latest pawn in a twenty-year-old game. The dictatorship needed to officially incorporate new support so that the responsibility for future policies could be shared by other shoulders. The Caudillo had once more arranged to sidestep potential difficulty by broadening his cabinet.

It took the Opus people two years to discover this, proving that they were hardly the practical men they claimed to be. When it finally became apparent that the Opus group had been brought in only to fill vacant seats in the latest round of musical chairs, and that it had fully compromised itself with the dictatorship without acquiring any important political influence, a spirit of revolt set in. During the winter of 1959 there was talk of an Opus-Army understanding about bringing back the Monarchy. This had very little basis in reality, however. The majority of Catholics did not support Opus Dei. Indeed, Catholic Action distrusted, and even despised, the arrogance and harshness of the Opus people.

Although it was next to impossible to gain concrete information about the group, the Opus drive seemed to be leveling off. Its economic representatives proved to be something less than the tough-minded geniuses they were supposed to be. Indeed, as the Caudillo doubtless planned, they were being saddled with much of the blame for Spain's rising inflation and continued economic squeeze. By the spring of 1959 it was rumored that the Opus people were becoming more lenient in their attitude toward liberalism; they probably realized that it might later be convenient if their enemies felt more liberal-minded toward them.

During 1958–59 prices rose more rapidly than ever, and the level of investment did not keep pace. Exports fell off, currency reserves reached the vanishing point, and the maze of government controls frustrated all attempts to stabilize the situation. The rate of small business failures increased alarmingly, and heavy industry began to lay off workers. The regime was on the verge of bankruptcy. Underground opposition began to stir once more, and a series of strikes threatened to break out in the coming months.

Franco's time-worn economic system had finally run out of gas. In July 1959 a program of "liberalization" was begun. The peseta was drastically devalued and a wide variety of government controls and restrictions were removed. The administration of this new policy was for the time being left in the hands of the Opus ministers who had so zealously directed the old system. This prevented any disturbance of the current political *status quo* and deprived those particular Opus men of their remaining vestiges of political independence.

During these years the foreign press was full of stories predicting the imminent collapse of "the little world of Don Caudillo." Such stories had little basis in reality. The dictatorship had issued from and capitalized on a series of profound divisions in the Spanish body politic, and in a certain sense, it had survived only by fanning these flames. So long as the Right feared and hated the Left, it would never dream of participating in a concerted effort to overthrow the regime. Not only were Right and Left divided against each other, but, as has been seen, they were divided within themselves. Economic affairs ultimately could influence this situation very little. The workers, who suffered most, were tightly corralled. The industrial and financial interests certainly could not complain; indeed, the dictator had always sheltered them from certain realities of the modern world. The Right could never rebel, while the Left still suffered the rigors of the police state.

For twenty years Franco had carefully fostered all the hatreds, enmities, divisions, and infantile fixations which beset Spanish politics in 1936. They were vital to him; they had been the permanent foundation of the "new Spain."

As for the Falange, after 1957 it was almost doubtful whether it was still alive, even in a technical sense. No one was sure what its name was. Not even the few thousand party members who still paid their trifling dues would argue that the Falange counted for anything. Whatever support the Falange or its former membership had lay outside the bounds of the shrunken, evaporated "Movement."

The only enthusiasts *falangismo* was able to muster were a handful of young people enrolled in the Guardias de Franco youth squads. Some of the more rebellious among them formed secret cells, and one group began to hearken back to Ramiro Ledesma and the JONS as the authentic expression of Spanish national syndicalism. These lads even began to prepare clandestine propaganda proselytizing their own version of the JONS. Early in 1958 they made a major effort to distribute material at the railway station of Atocha in Madrid, where most of them were arrested. Although the group was forced to disband, some of their fellows kept the feeling of dissent alive. In one case, an entire *centuria* of the Madrid Guardias de Franco was composed of young men who called themselves Hedillistas, in honor of Manuel Hedilla, the former head of the independent Falange's Junta de Mando.

Hedilla had finally been released from prison in 1947. The Archbishop of Valencia had privately declared that next to Jesus Christ, Manuel Hedilla had suffered more things unjustly than any other man in the world. The Church helped to make amends. Through the clerical contacts he had formed during his incarceration, Hedilla eventually became established in the lower levels of the industrial world, taking up partnerships in several enterprises.

He did little to encourage support among the young. He struck no political attitude, nor did he appear fundamentally interested in politics. The young rebels who chalked "Hedilla-JONS" slogans on walls in Madrid during 1958–59 were, as was customary in the party, very young and immature. They had nothing concrete to offer, and were very confused among themselves.

Nonetheless, a few party veterans wanted to use the sincere and incorruptible Hedilla, the only Falange leader still alive who was not compromised by the regime, as the focus for a new rally. In his native province of Santander, a group was formed which called itself Haz Ibérico. The program of this new clandestine formation was a sort of watered-down, technocratic form of national syndicalism, less extreme in its national claims and more moderate in its economic demands. It attracted several thousand followers scattered throughout northern Spain, but on a national level it had no significance.

The Haz Ibérico was not the only semiclandestine neo-Falange group in Spain. There were several others, partly interconnected. No single unit was homogeneous, and the division of opinion among the units was extreme. All they had in common was a belief that some form of national syndicalism was necessary to shape and control the Spanish body politic. In his own way each member affirmed the importance of "restoring" *falangismo,* done to death by the compromises and distortions of the Caudillo. One spokesman declared that these scattered, loosely organized, neo-Falangist nuclei had some 25,000 affiliates by the spring of 1959. This was, of course, no more than a drop in the bucket, and no one could say whether or not such neo-Falangism would be in a position to influence seriously the future political organization of Spain.

By 1960 there was nothing to contradict the contention that *falangismo,* as an organized living force, was entirely dead. The same confusion and contradiction that had marked its beginnings now characterized its end. Neoclericalism and neo-Socialism prepared to contest the political stage, and most Spaniards could hardly recall that the Falange had ever existed.

Amid the unpleasant realities of *franquismo,* it seemed almost unreal to recall the political career of José Antonio Primo de Rivera. That the regime itself invoked his memory on every occasion appeared a trifle incongruous. As the Socialist Rodolfo Llopis said, José Antonio had been the victim of his own contradictions; his twisted and confused career led him to deny his basic instincts. José Antonio's greatest asset was an extremely fine sense of style. He was a very singular fascist, so different, in fact, that the term hardly suits him. His rhetoric was frequently wholesome and sometimes even sublime. His career was inherently tragic, and he has proved an ideal political martyr.

It is very difficult to trace the direct effect of José Antonio's ideas on the dictatorship that arose from the Civil War. Much of the form is there, but woefully little of the content. Considering the immaturity of the national syndicalist movement, it could hardly have been otherwise.

The Falange did contribute to the outbreak of the Civil War. Its fascist intransigence and hyperbole further strained the tense nerves of Spanish radicalism, which were already near the breaking point. But beyond this, the Falange was not in any large sense guilty of provoking the conflict. The Civil War was the product of profound social, political, and economic antagonisms, and to these the Falange merely reacted as a secondary catalyst. The Falange was by no means the most important group plotting open rebellion, and from the time the fighting began it was under the control of the militarists. Indeed, with its *Jefe* gone and its internal leadership confused, the Falange would probably have fallen into obscurity if Franco and the military had not found it a useful tool for conquest.

It was not simply by chance, however, that the Right hung on to the Falange and made it the *partido del Estado*. In the Western world, some sort of corporatism has become a logical response whenever the revolutionary demands of workers cannot be resolved by ordinary economic means. Something very similar to national syndicalism was the only device that could be used to harness the Spanish working class after the outbreak of the war in 1936. This was the indispensable contribution of *falangismo* to the Franco regime. To be sure, the syndical system was organized entirely as the government saw fit, but it was vital nevertheless.

The Falange itself never really had a plausible opportunity to grasp power, particularly after the dynamism of the *Jefe* was lost in the party's great hour of need. To try to achieve a synthesis of Left and Right without being able to enlist the support of either was impossible. While trying to fight the Left, the Falange was irresistibly swallowed up by the Right and by the master-maneuverer, Franco. Had it not been for the delicate nature of the Caudillo's juggling act, the party would never have retained a semi-independent identity as long as it did.

It was the emotional quality of their dialectic that led the Falangists to their doom. Once an all-embracing myth of national glory and unity had informed the totality of Falange doctrine, the possibility of maneuver and compromise, of adjustment to political reality, was lost. Faith in the effectiveness of political idealism had been a prime characteristic of European ideologies since the middle of the nineteenth century. Perhaps nowhere more than in Spain, the decade ending in 1945 brought on a cataclysmic disillusion. There remained only a nostalgic and ambiguous afterglow of the passions that once burned so fiercely.

NOTES

CHAPTER I

1. See Gutiérrez-Ravé; Fernández Almagro, p. 210; Sevilla, *Antonio Maura*.
2. *El pensamiento de Primo de Rivera* (ed. Pemán), p. 53.
3. In *La Nación* (Madrid), August 6, 1927, quoted in Pemán, p. 65.
4. From an address at a banquet in honor of Alfonso XIII, January 22, 1925, quoted in Pemán, p. 203.
5. Ratcliff, p. 59.
6. Guillén, *Los que nacimos*, p. 121. Guillén Salaya was a collaborator on the *Gaceta*.
7. Giménez, *Genio de España*, pp. 34–35.
8. *Ibid.*, p. 35.
9. *Informaciones* (Madrid), No. 3790, quoted in Mendizábal, p. 183.
10. Quoted in Mendizábal, p. 178.
11. Cited in Basaldúa, p. 13.
12. Giménez, *La nueva catolicidad*, pp. 143–44.
13. Quoted in Basaldúa, p. 81.

CHAPTER II

1. Albiñana, *Confinado en las Hurdes*, p. 113.
2. The official program is given in Albiñana, *Después de la dictadura*, pp. 242–46.
3. *Albiñana, Prisionero de la República*, p. 60.
4. Albiñana, *Confinado en las Hurdes*, pp. 170–71. It is not at all clear that Albiñana ever read Charles Maurras, but Léon Daudet tried to start an international press campaign in his behalf during 1932. He enlisted the aid of Italian Fascist writers and eventually went to the League of Nations. (*Ibid.*, pp. 210–16, 326–28, and José Calvo Sotelo in *La Nación* [Madrid], Feb. 8, 1933.)
5. As Albiñana says in his *España bajo la dictadura republicana*.
6. Aparicio, *La Conquista del Estado*, pp. vii–ix; Aparicio, *Ramiro Ledesma*, pp. 13–18; Arrarás, *Historia de la Cruzada española*, I, 385 (hereafter cited simply by volume and page).
7. Later collected in *Los escritos filosóficos de Ramiro Ledesma*.
8. It has been observed that the proper Spanish form is *Sindicalismo nacional*, not Ledesma's *Nacional-Sindicalismo*, which reads more like a direct corruption of *Nazionalsozialismus*.
9. There is an especially strong pronouncement in *El Sol* (Madrid), Dec. 6, 1930, and a Socialist critique by Julián Besteiro in *El Socialista*, Jan. 6, 1930.
10. Roberto Lanzas (pseud. of Ledesma), *¿Fascismo en España?*, p. 52; *La Conquista del Estado*, No. 10, Mar. 16, 1931.
11. Aparicio, *La Conquista del Estado*, p. xi.

12. *La Conquista del Estado*, No. 1, Mar. 14, 1931.

13. *Ibid.*, No. 2, Mar. 23, 1931; No. 11, May 23, 1931. This contradiction may be reconciled if one bears in mind that these were the two Spanish political groups that opposed most vigorously the legacy of the eighteenth and nineteenth centuries.

14. *Ibid.*, No. 13, June 6, 1931.

15. Quoted in Guillén, *Historia del sindicalismo español*, p. 141.

16. Quoted in Aparicio, *La Conquista del Estado*, p. xviii.

17. See Foltz, p. 63, and Ledesma, *¿Fascismo en España?*, pp. 54–57.

18. Narciso Sánchez, "Onésimo Redondo," *Temas españoles* (Madrid, 1953), No. 39, pp. 5–6.

19. It is said that Redondo did spiritual devotions daily and read the Bible every night, certainly a strange preparation for totalitarian agitation. *Cf.* Arrarás, I, 423. Redondo's strong clerical background is noted in Fernández Almagro, pp. 210–12; Marcotte, pp. 60–61; Pattee, pp. 305–6; and Hughes, p. 31. For Ledesma's remarks, see below.

20. "Onésimo Redondo y el Sindicato Remolachero," *SP*, Mar. 8, 1959, p. 10.

21. *Libertad*, No. 7, July 27, 1931.

22. *Ibid.*, No. 3, June 27, 1931, and *JONS*, June 2, 1933.

23. Quoted in Basaldúa, p. 11.

24. A modern use for the emblem had first been mentioned by Fernando de los Ríos, Socialist Professor of Law at the University of Granada, in a class attended by Juan Aparicio, who later became Ledesma's secretary. The device was also on the city shield of Guadix, Aparicio's home town. Fernández Almagro, p. 212; Guillén, *Los que nacimos*, p. 96.

However, the symbol had also been mentioned by such nationalist writers as Giménez Caballero and Rafael Sánchez Mazas in articles dating from 1927–28, according to Jato, p. 49.

25. According to Ledesma in *Discurso*, p. 14.

26. *Libertad*, Nos. 38–40, Feb. 29, Mar. 7, and Mar. 14, 1932.

27. *Ibid.*, No. 36, Feb. 15, 1932.

28. *¿Fascismo en España?*, p. 78.

29. Guillén, *Los que nacimos*, pp. 112–14. Conversation with Anselmo de la Iglesia (one of Redondo's most loyal followers) in Madrid, May 26, 1959.

CHAPTER III

1. Lizarza, p. 16; Arrarás, I, 485.

2. These maneuverings are described in detail in Galdino, pp. 95–182.

3. Ansaldo, p. 54.

4. A very interesting appraisal of the role of Catholicism during the Republic is given in Iturralde, pp. 239–408.

5. The external vicissitudes of the Right during the Republic are dealt with in Fernández Almagro; Arrarás, Vol. I.

6. Valdecasas later claimed to have been disillusioned with the Republican constitution at the very outset (conversation in Madrid, Nov. 18, 1958). Valdecasas had taken a leading role in the effort to write the construction of "Tech-

nical Councils" into the Constitution. This was designed to place economic policy in the hands of experts, and thus remove it from the reach of political haggling. See Smith, pp. 120-27, 167-68, 191-93, 271-73, 303-4.

7. Capella's *Primo de Rivera* gives a fairly good presentation of the dictator's personality.

8. As even the Socialist José Antonio Balbontín admits (*La España de mi experiencia,* pp. 306-7).

9. Ximénez, *José Antonio,* is the standard propaganda biography; José Antonio's early life is dealt with on pages 1-56. Other biographical information may be found in Pavón, pp. 15-29, and articles by José's early friends and relatives Nieves Sáenz de Heredia, Lula de Lara, and Raimundo Fernández-Cuesta in *Dolor y memoria,* pp. 174-82.

10. Conversations with Emilio González López, New York, October 27, 1957, and Jesús Prados Arrarte, Madrid, May 22, 1959. As students these two men held opposite political views, but they agree on José Antonio's position. Further details, distorted in interpretation, are given in Ramón Serrano Súñer, *Semblanza de José Antonio, joven* (Madrid, 1959), pp. 19-20, and Serrano Súñer's articles in *Dolor y memoria,* pp. 197-200; Francisco Bravo Martínez, *José Antonio: El hombre, el jefe, el camarada* (Madrid, 1939), p. 10; Jato, p. 27.

11. Pemartín, pp. 597-601.

12. Some of his last literary efforts are contained in *Blanco y Negro* (Madrid), Dec. 8, 1929, and *La Nación* (Madrid), Nov. 28, 1929.

13. Ratcliff, pp. 80-81.

14. *El Heraldo de Madrid,* Mar. 13, 1930.

15. The corruption and turpitude of the UP-UMN clique is touched on in Aunós, *España en crisis,* pp. 300-310, and Maura. Aunós was Primo de Rivera's Minister of Labor.

16. *Diario de Jerez,* July 1, 1930, quoted in *Textos inéditos y epistolario de José Antonio Primo de Rivera* (Madrid, 1956), pp. 25-26 (hereafter cited as *Epistolario*).

17. *La Nación,* Feb. 12, 1930; *Unión Patriótica* Bulletin, Feb. 18, 1930.

18. *La Nación,* Feb. 18, 1930, reprinted from the *Diario de Albacete.*

19. *Textos de doctrina política. Obras completas* (Madrid, 1952), pp. 6-7 (hereafter cited as *Obras*). José Antonio had first sought support for such a seat in his home district of Cádiz during May 1930, when there was talk of elections to be held by the Berenguer government. (Letter from José Ma. Pemán to Ximénez de Sandoval, Dec. 11, 1941, in Ximénez, pp. 472-73.)

20. This was most true of the monarchist *ABC.* See Ximénez, pp. 103, 107. *Cf.* the Jesuit *El Debate,* Oct. 1-5, 1931.

21. According to Ximénez (pp. 109-10), José Antonio concentrated his reading on the extremists: Hitler, Rosenberg, Mussolini, Farinacci, Lenin, and Trotsky. The only liberal whose works he read was the elitist Ortega. The only other Spaniards he considered were extreme Rightists, such as Donoso Cortés, Menéndez Pelayo, and Ramiro de Maeztu.

22. *Epistolario,* pp. 36-80.

23. *ABC,* Mar. 16, 1931.

24. In *La Nación,* Jan. 17, 1931.

25. José Antonio had recently found a nonpolitical outlet for his energies

by courting the heiress to one of Spain's oldest dukedoms. Since the girl was an only child, her father, the current duke, insisted that José Antonio renounce his own title, Marqués de Estella, in order to continue the direct line of his future fiancée. José Antonio was too concerned with his own family's glory ever to consider this. There is some evidence that José Antonio, who never married, was troubled by this unhappy attachment to the end of his days. *Cf.* José Ma. Villapecellín, *José Antonio: En la cárcel y a hombros de sus camaradas,* in Ximénez, p. 493. (The writer has talked with several people reputed to know about José Antonio's grand attachment and has received four varying sets of details.)

26. Arrarás, I, 423.

27. Ledesma claims that 130,000 copies of the first number were ordered in advance (*¿Fascismo en España?,* p. 87). This figure seems exaggerated. However, there was definite interest in the financial world; Juan Pujol, the influential Catalan financier, even contributed an essay under a pseudonym.

28. Hughes, p. 29.

29. Arrarás, I, 594; *¿Fascismo en España?,* pp. 88–89. One of the contributors, Sánchez Mazas, had been frightened into withdrawing his article beforehand.

30. *Obras,* pp. 43–47.

31. Quoted in Dávila and Pemartín, p. 19.

32. According to Prieto in *El Socialista,* May 19, 1949.

33. Ansaldo, p. 89; conversation with José Plá, Llofriu (Gerona), Apr. 28, 1959. Plá had the reputation of being one of the best-informed political commentators in Madrid during the Second Republic.

34. Quoted in Ximénez, p. 127.

35. Dávila and Pemartín, p. 24.

36. Ruiz de Alda, Julio, and Ramón Franco, *De Palos al Plata* (Madrid, 1927).

37. Prologue to Ruiz de Alda, *Obras completas,* pp. 13–26.

38. *Ibid.,* pp. 27–28.

39. *Ibid.,* p. 34.

40. Further leaflets were distributed by a handful of students in Oviedo and Seville (Jato, p. 54).

41. The figure may even have reached several thousand. *Ahora* (Madrid), July 23, 24, 26, 1933.

42. Arrarás, I, 604.

43. See the correspondence in José Antonio's *Epistolario,* pp. 125–42.

44. *El Sol,* Oct. 25, 26, 1933.

CHAPTER IV

1. Ximénez, pp. 131–35; Ansaldo, p. 64; and Valdecasas in *Dolor y memoria,* pp. 257–59.

2. *Obras,* pp. 63–69.

3. *El Sol,* Oct. 29, 1933.

4. *Acción Española,* No. 43, Dec. 16, 1933.

5. Quoted in Díaz, *Cómo llegó Falange,* p. 15.

6. Ximénez, pp. 131–32, 148; Arrarás, I, 681. *Cf.* Albiñana, *Las Hurdes,*

p. 111. Giménez Caballero claimed credit for it in the 1938 Zaragoza edition of *Genio de España*.

7. Ansaldo, p. 63.

8. Conversation with Valdecasas, Madrid, Nov. 18, 1958. See also Guillén, *Anecdotario*, p. 100, and Hughes.

9. *Obras*, pp. 177–78.

10. "Ensayo sobre el nacionalismo," in Juan Aparicio, ed., *JONS* (Madrid, 1943), p. 146.

11. As he himself admitted to friends. Bravo, *José Antonio*, p. 52. *Cf.* José Ortega y Gasset, *Obras completas*, I, 265–308.

12. Ximénez, p. 612.

13. The campaign was full of incidents, which are recorded in *El Sol*, Nov. 14, 16, 18, Dec. 2, 1933; Mauger, pp. 61–66; Dávila and Pemartín, pp. 36–38, 43–50.

14. Ansaldo, pp. 81–82.

15. *¿Fascismo en España?*, p. 91.

16. *Ibid.*; Arrarás, I, 593; Jato, pp. 54–55.

17. Guillén, *Sindicalismo español*, p. 55. The subsequent street-fighting is chronicled in *¿Fascismo en España?*, pp. 101–3; Guillén, *Anecdotario*, p. 88, and *Los que nacimos*, pp. 129–30; Jato, p. 56.

18. Guillén, *Los que nacimos*, p. 128.

19. *¿Fascismo en Espana?*, p. 145.

20. *Ibid.*, p. 143.

21. *Ibid.*, pp. 145–46.

22. The nine groups were from Madrid, Barcelona, Valencia, Bilbao, Zaragoza, Valladolid, Granada, Santiago de Compostela, and Zafra.

23. For further details, see Arrarás, II, 19–23, and Ximénez, pp. 228–29.

24. Letter of Mar. 12, 1934, quoted in *¿Fascismo en España?*, p. 149.

CHAPTER V

1. Ansaldo, p. 89.

2. The phrase is Ledesma's (*¿Fascismo en España?*, p. 129). Sánchez Mazas had been *ABC*'s correspondent in Rome, where he had picked up his Italianate estheticism and his interest in fascism. (See Giménez, *La Falange*, p. 4.) Sánchez Mazas was one of the few figures in the old Falange who lacked both physical and moral courage.

3. Agustín de Foxá in *Dolor y memoria*, pp. 216–20.

4. Bravo, *José Antonio*, pp. 11, 31–32, *Historia de Falange*, p. 87; Marcotte, pp. 75, 88.

5. See the prologue to Torrente, *Panorama*, and Castellano (pseud.), "La Falange," in *Cuadernos*, No. 31, pp. 24–30.

6. Jato, p. 62.

7. Prologue by Manuel Valdés to Jato, p. 10; Valdés was one of the two who helped Ruiz de Alda.

8. Fernández Almagro, p. 209.

9. Ruiz de Alda, pp. 217–28.

10. *FE*, No. 1, Dec. 7, 1933.

11. Letter to Julián Pemartín, Apr. 2, 1933, in *Obras*, pp. 49–50.

12. For the purported "confessions" of one of the *pistoleros* of the Socialist Party, see Vicente Reguengo, *Guerra sin frentes* (Madrid, 1954), pp. 24–68.

13. *El Sol*, Nov. 3, 4, 1933. (*El Sol* will be cited throughout as the most impartial news source then available in Spain.)

14. *Ibid.*, Dec. 5, 1933.

15. *Ibid.*, Jan. 12, May 3, 1934.

16. *Ibid.*, Jan. 19–21, 1934; Bravo, *José Antonio*, p. 40.

17. Jato, p. 69.

18. *El Sol*, Feb. 10, 1934. Montero was possibly killed in revenge for a raid he had led on the FUE center in the Faculty of Medicine two weeks earlier. (Ximénez, pp. 207–8.) The assassin was later caught and found to be a member of the Socialist Youth. Though disavowed by the head of the latter group, he was seized carrying a list of persons "dangerous" for Socialism and sentenced to twenty-one years in prison. *El Sol*, Feb. 20, 1934.

19. As shown by his article in *FE*, No. 12, Feb. 22, 1934.

20. Ximénez, p. 211.

21. *ABC*, Nov. 18, 1933.

22. Quoted in Bravo, *Historia de Falange*, p. 38.

23. Bravo, *José Antonio*, p. 45.

24. *El Sol*, Jan. 4, 1934.

25. Ximénez, p. 203.

26. *ABC*, Feb. 13, 1934.

27. Ledesma, *¿Fascismo en España?*, pp. 138–40.

28. *Ibid.*, pp. 135–36.

29. Guillén, *Sindicalismo español*, p. 62.

30. Bravo, *Historia de Falange*, pp. 26–27.

31. *Obras*, pp. 194–95, 197.

32. *El Sol*, Mar. 6, 8, 1934. On the day of the Valladolid meeting, the Socialists held an "anti-fascist" meeting in Toledo.

33. Bravo, *Historia de Falange*, p. 29.

34. José Antonio Primo de Rivera was evidently first referred to simply as José Antonio in an article in *La Nación*, Aug. 25, 1933.

35. *El Sol*, Mar. 9, 28, 1934.

36. *Ibid.*, Apr. 11, 1934.

37. Published in *FE*, No. 11, Apr. 19, 1934.

38. According to Ansaldo, pp. 71–78.

39. See the Marqués de Valdeiglesias in *Dolor y memoria*, pp. 249–51.

40. *El Sol*, June 24, 1934.

41. Ledesma, *¿Fascismo en España?*, pp. 174–75.

42. *El Sol*, July 9, 1934.

CHAPTER VI

1. *El Sol*, Apr. 15, 1934; Dávila and Pemartín, pp. 65–74.

2. Letter to Francisco Bravo, May 24, 1934, in Bravo, *José Antonio*; Dávila and Pemartín, pp. 75–81.

3. One of them had already died of a self-inflicted wound caused by an accident while on sentinel duty. *El Sol*, June 17, 1934.

4. *Ibid.*, July 4, 1934; *Obras*, pp. 259–68.

5. Bowers, p. 87; Arrarás, II, 83–85.

6. *Cf.* Bravo, *José Antonio*, p. 87.

7. Jato, p. 112.

8. Ansaldo's own account is in *¿Para qué?*, pp. 85–87. Other details are in *¿Fascismo en España?*, pp. 179–89; *El Sol*, Aug. 10, Sept. 1, 1934; Jato, pp. 99–114.

9. *¿Fascismo en España?*, pp. 170–71n.

10. Buckley, p. 129.

11. As in the case of the JONS, the chief contact was José Félix de Lequerica. Manuel Aznar in *Dolor y memoria*, pp. 190–92.

12. Remarks of Giménez Caballero to Hughes, pp. 32–33; the indirect statements of Ximénez, pp. 264–65; Gannes and Repard, p. 59.

13. Bravo, *José Antonio*, p. 69; Ansaldo, pp. 80–81.

14. Hughes, *loc. cit.*

15. Copies of both documents are in the possession of the writer. Their authenticity is beyond doubt. The description of the pact given in Ansaldo, p. 89n, seems to be incorrect.

16. Conversation with Pedro Sáinz Rodríguez, Lisbon, May 1, 1959. The Falange must have been badly pressed for funds, because in the second round of these financial intrigues José Antonio felt forced to offer the recently evicted Ansaldo his old job back with increased authority. Ansaldo, however, refused. (Ansaldo, p. 89.)

17. These materials are drawn from the files of José Andino in Madrid.

18. *El Sol*, Sept. 4–5, 1934.

19. See Zayas, pp. 51–56, and Meleiro, pp. 114–20.

20. *Cf.* Castrillo, p. 188. José Antonio also proposed to establish a Confederación de Empleadores Nacional Sindicalistas. (*La Nación*, Nov. 1, 1934.) Employers were notably uninterested, and the project was never undertaken.

21. Interview in *Luz*, April 19, 1934.

22. Ledesma, *¿Fascismo en España?*, p. 168.

23. Prologue to Ruiz de Alda, p. 36.

24. Ledesma, *¿Fascismo en España?*, p. 188.

25. Bravo, *José Antonio*, pp. 183–85.

26. Conversations with Felipe Sanz Paracuellos, Bilbao, Dec. 10, 1958, and Jesús Suevos, Madrid, Feb. 8, 1959. Both voted for the measure. Suevos, being the youngest district leader (Galicia), served as secretary and voted last, casting the deciding vote.

27. Arrarás, II, 282; Zayas, p. 38; Mauger, p. 79.

28. *Obras*, pp. 293–96.

29. Bravo, *Historia de Falange*, pp. 77–79; Núñez, I, 128.

30. Letter to Francisco Bravo, Nov. 3, 1934, in Bravo, *José Antonio*, p. 81.

31. *Obras*, p. 326.

32. Vegas, pp. 104–11.

33. It appears Ruiz de Alda wanted to admit Calvo, but Ledesma logically sided with José Antonio in this encounter with the Right. (*¿Fascismo en España?*, pp. 166–67.)

34. According to Ansaldo, p. 56.

35. Mauger, p. 122.

36. Dec. 19, 1934. Quoted in Jato, p. 67.

37. Two priests were particularly prominent: Manuel Gutiérrez in Oviedo (Jato, p. 65), and Fermín Yzurdiaga, who became Falange Chief of Press and Propaganda in 1937, in Pamplona.

38. His political ideas, further developed, were later expressed in *Autoridad y libertad* (Madrid, 1945).

39. The events surrounding Eliseda's secession are discussed in Bravo, *Historia de Falange*, pp. 76-77; Ximénez, pp. 361-62; Jato, p. 123.

40. Quoted in Galindo, p. 358. Calvo had talked with Mussolini and was a great admirer of the Italian system. His political ideas are presented in Vegas; Aunós, *Calvo Sotelo*; Calvo, *Mis servicios al Estado, La voz de un perseguido*, and *El capitalismo contemporáneo y su evolución*.

41. Some interesting remarks by the party secretary are recorded in Harold McCoy, "Gil Robles: Scourge of Liberal Spain," *Current History*, 40: 682-88 (September 1934).

Gil Robles had taken a summer vacation in central Europe, where he was much impressed by the clerical fascism of the Dollfuss regime in Austria. However, the corporative, authoritarian elements in the CEDA received their greatest encouragement from the October revolt in Spain, which greatly speeded the polarization of political groupings.

42. Prologue to Ruiz de Alda, pp. 36-38.

43. Bravo, *Historia de Falange*, p. 85; Marcotte, pp. 74-75.

44. Ledesma, *¿Fascismo en España?*, pp. 216-17; Ansaldo, p. 101.

45. Ledesma's account of his last days in the party is in *¿Fascismo en España?*, pp. 218-21. See also Ximénez, pp. 372-76.

CHAPTER VII

1. "Many of those who enlisted would have preferred to follow, without pressures and interruptions, an intellectual vocation. Our time gives no opportunity. We have been met with a martial destiny into which one must throw himself with heart and soul. Through fidelity to our destiny we go from place to place withstanding the shame of exhibitions, having to proffer with cries what we conceive in the most silent austerity, suffering defamation from those who do not understand us and those who do not want to understand us, spending ourselves in this absurd daily farce of conquering 'public opinion.' " *Haz* (the SEU journal), No. 12, Dec. 5, 1935, in *Textos*, p. 745.

2. Bravo, *José Antonio*, p. 114.

3. The American ambassador recorded the figure José Antonio presented to his acquaintances in these months: "José [Antonio] Primo de Rivera . . . was young and darkly handsome. His coal-black hair shone glossily. His face was slender and of Andalusian hue. His manner was courtly, modest, deferential. The passion of his life was the vindication of his father. . . . A good speaker, his speeches [were] rich in substance, well-phrased, but with an irrepressible Andalusian weakness for floridity. . . . [In the Cortes] he would become a thorn in the side of many hypocrites with whom he was allied. Incapable of dissimulation, with a gift for the barbed phrase, he was to arouse the

bitter enmity of many, and to live dangerously, going about with a reckless abandon that was the despair of his friends. He loved the crowds and refused to shun them. One night when riding in Madrid he was fired upon from the shadows. Stopping his car, he sprang out in pursuit, alone, unarmed, heedless of possible enemies lurking in the dark. A little later he appeared smiling and jubilant at the Bakanik, where fashion went for cocktails, and those to whom he told the story found him delighted as a child. He was of the breed of Dumas' Musketeers. I shall always remember him as I saw him first, young, boyish, courteous, smiling and dancing that afternoon in the villa in San Sebastián." Bowers, pp. 28–29.

4. Prieto and Azaña are the best examples, but the Socialist José Antonio Balbontín later wrote: "There is no doubt that José Antonio Primo de Rivera carried a dream in his head, a dream dangerous for him and for our people, . . . but a dream which, in the end, it would not be just to confound with the bastard covetousness of those 'new' Falangists of Franco Spain. . . ." *La España de mi experiencia*, pp. 306–7.

5. Quoted in *El Día Gráfico* (Barcelona), Jan. 28, 1934, from an interview published in *Luz*.

6. *Obras*, p. 420.

7. José Antonio Primo de Rivera, *Epistolario*, pp. 145–61.

8. Speech in the Ateneo of Zaragoza, Feb. 17, 1935. *Ibid.*, p. 283.

9. As Bravo, in a letter of Oct. 12, 1934. (*José Antonio*, p. 218.)

10. *Ibid.*, p. 104.

11. Interview in *La Voz* (Madrid), Feb. 14, 1936.

12. "Don't forget that the chief responsibility is yours and that after having gone so far with so many dead no one can turn back." Letter from Bravo to José Antonio of Jan. 18, 1935. (Bravo, *José Antonio*, p. 255.)

13. *El Sol.*, May 22, 1935.

14. Buckley, p. 128.

15. *¿Fascismo en España?*, pp. 186–88.

16. Guariglia, *Ricordi*, pp. 203–4.

17. The date was October 9, 1933. Solmi, p. 69; Mauger, p. 51; Foltz, p. 68.

18. According to an interview in *Blanco y Negro*, Nov. 11, 1934.

19. This is what he told Dionisio Ridruejo and others in the winter of 1935–36. Conversation with Ridruejo, Madrid, Nov. 17, 1958. (Ridruejo was the Falange propaganda chief from 1938 through 1941).

Onésimo Redondo was more explicit: "Nor does it suit us to accept the dialectic—which ought to be called dialectic rather than doctrine—of Mussolini, on relations between the state and individuals: what in this is called *fascist doctrine* is, in our judgment, a transitory tactic, incongruous as a fixed entity, which the combative and constructive talent of Mussolini has been adopting to fit his particular and very personal inspiration in order to govern Italy during recent years. . . . What there is not, rightly speaking, is a doctrine of public law, however much there may appear to be; *fascism* changes its course, as the calendar changes, in the passage of a year; we cannot even be sure that the 'doctrine' which appears most characteristic and fundamental, that of the semi-pantheistic supremacy of the state over everything else, will be maintained by Mussolini until his death." (*El Estado Nacional*, May, 15, 1933.)

20. Foltz, p. 71; Ximénez, pp. 288–91, 859; Pavón, p. 192.

21. So he told Ansaldo (Ansaldo, p. 78).

22. *Obras*, p. 165.

23. José Antonio's last public acceptance of the term seems to have been in an *ABC* interview of Apr. 11, 1934.

24. *Obras*, p. 266.

25. At Callosa de Segura (Alicante), on July 22, 1934. *Obras*, pp. 386–87.

26. *El Sol*, Feb. 6, 1934.

27. Hughes, p. 30.

28. Speech in Madrid, May 19, 1935. *Obras*, p. 558.

29. Such as the agronomist Florense. (Plá, IV, 140.)

30. *Obras*, pp. 409–12, 483–508.

31. Buckley, p. 127.

32. *Obras*, pp. 555–56.

33. José Antonio was evidently in full agreement with Onésimo Redondo's definition of the myth of Empire, made in 1931:

"We believe in the imperial power of our great culture. And in order that those who take fright or smile before this great *imperial* concept may dismiss the belief that to say 'empire' is to mean the conquest of lands and nations by means of physical war, we use this occasion to define somewhat the effective vigor and scope of this word.

"Empire is, of course, domination, or, at least, superiority exercised among a group of peoples.

"But the importance—and even the utility—of the *Empire is positive and multiple*: It means, certainly, a desirable hegemony, a glorious sensation of power which benefits and exalts the race that exercises it before others. It is also—and here, without doubt, is its greatest and truest public utility—a source of positive national aspirations, and the supreme motor of the great energies latent in each race: it is the maximum ideal for a people, and, by the same token, the greatest stimulant for outstanding individualities, a goad and a platform at the same time, in order that great men may arise and exercise their beneficial influence. . . .

"And *the Empire,* so understood, does not presuppose, *is not,* an exterior enterprise, which would require the consecration of energies fully necessary for living in peace and prosperity within one's own home. This is the primitive deception of domestic temperaments, of the cowardly, torpid, and indigent." (*Libertad*, No. 2, Aug. 31, 1931.)

34. This estimate was given by Mariano García, the former administrative secretary of the party. (Conversation in Madrid, Jan. 8, 1959.) The exact figures were later lost, but José Luis de Arrese (in early 1936 *jefe provincial* of Granada) has recalled the number of cardholders before the Popular Front elections to have been approximately 8,000. (Conversations with Prof. Juan J. Linz, Madrid, December 1960.) Raimundo Fernández Cuesta, then the Secretary-General, has expressed doubt that there were even that many, estimating that the *primera línea* as of February 1936 numbered no more than 5,000. (Conversation in Madrid, Feb. 13, 1959.)

The most judicious estimate of the Falange's registered strength in 1936, by province, would indicate the following enrollment:

Madrid	1500	Valencia	400
Valladolid	1500–1800	Málaga	300
Estremadura	1200	Catalonia	300
Seville-Cádiz	1200	Granada	200
Santander	800	Vizcaya	200
Burgos	500	Mallorca	200
Galicia	500	Other areas	1000

The sources for these figures, by province, are as follows:

Valladolid. The records of the local Valladolid JONS are in the possession of Anselmo de la Iglesia.

Estremadura. Extrapolated from the membership figures later given in González Ortín, p. 208.

Seville-Cádiz. The records of the JONS of Seville are in the possession of Patricio González de Canales in Madrid. See also Beltrán.

Santander. Conversation with Manuel Hedilla, Madrid, Jan. 4, 1959. Hedilla insists on a higher figure, but the writer has scaled down his estimate.

Burgos. Florentino Martínez Mata, *jefe provincial* of Burgos from 1938 to 1942, says, "In February we were almost nothing in Burgos." (Conversation in Madrid, Jan. 22, 1959.) José Andino, however, would put the figure somewhat higher. (Conversation in Madrid, Dec. 4, 1958.)

Galicia. Conversation with Enrique Tajuelo (formerly an organizer in that province), Madrid, May 7, 1959. On Orense, see Meleiro, p. 33. Jesús Suevos, *jefe territorial* in 1935, would put the figure higher. (Conversation in Madrid, Jan. 22, 1959.) However, Suevos exaggerates notoriously. *Cf.* Moure-Mariño, pp. 99–128.

Valencia. Conversations with Ricardo Palmí Sancho (former *jefe provincial*), Valencia, Mar. 4, 1959, and Juan Ferrer de Diego, Valencia, Mar. 5, 1959. See also Pérez and Higón.

Málaga. *Cf.* Gollonet and Morales, *Sangre y fuego—Málaga.*

Catalonia. Conversations with Luys Santa Marina, Barcelona, Dec. 21, 1958, and Luis Fontes de Albornoz (a former triumvir in Catalonia), Barcelona, Dec. 22, 1958.

Granada. Gollonet and Morales, *Rojo y azul en Granada,* p. 99. Conversation with Santiago Cardell (*jefe provincial,* 1934–36), Granada, Mar. 20, 1959.

Vizcaya. Conversations with Felipe Sanz, Bilbao, Dec. 10, 1958, and José Ma. Valdés, Bilbao, Dec. 12, 1958. Both are former *jefes provinciales.*

Mallorca. Bernanos, p. 104; Zayas.

35. Jato, p. 95; letter of José Antonio in Bravo, *José Antonio,* p. 73; Schempp, *Das Autoritäre Spanien,* p. 12.

36. A special Feminine Section was organized in June 1934 by friends of José Antonio's younger sister, Pilar. This formation had no significance prior to the Civil War.

37. As stated above, the students accounted for more followers than all other classes combined but could not ordinarily be listed as official members. Nevertheless, a few were so enrolled, perhaps because they were over-age.

38. Bravo, *Historia de Falange,* p. 87. José Antonio might have retorted that they had received good training in accordance with the precepts of Una-

muno himself, citing the latter's former dictum, "Shoot first and aim afterward." (Noted by Jato, p. 169.)

39. *Obras*, p. 566.

40. José Antonio Girón and Luis González Vicén, the leaders of the Valladolid schism, played prominent roles in the Falange after 1936. The foregoing account of the dispute is based largely on conversations with Luis González Vicén, Madrid, Feb. 27, 1959, and Anselmo de la Iglesia, Madrid, May 26, 1959, the latter being a strong *partidario* of Onésimo Redondo.

41. In Santander, violence was narrowly averted when José Antonio came to expel the crypto-Rightists. Montes, pp. 134–39; Jato, p. 140; "Diary" for 1935 of Florentino Torre Bolado (*jefe provincial* of press and propaganda in Santander during 1937).

42. Frank Jellinek, who knew the CNT well, says: "It is certain that there was close cooperation between some irresponsible individuals and the Falange Española. . . . It is equally certain that these individuals were completely disapproved by the responsible committees." (Jellinek, pp. 259–60.)

43. Castillo and Alvarez, pp. 132–34; conversation with Luys Santa Marina, Barcelona, Dec. 20, 1958.

44. In *El Heraldo de Madrid*, quoted in Bravo, *Historia de Falange*, p. 23.

45. Letter to Dávila, in Dávila and Pemartín, pp. 80–81.

46. From the prologue to Pérez de Cabo.

47. *Arriba*, No. 11, May 30, 1935.

48. Ximénez, pp. 635–36. José Antonio continued to plead with local leaders to encourage members to pay their dues. *Epistolario*, pp. 271, 311–12.

49. Hughes, pp. 31–32; Pavón, p. 77.

50. Cacho, p. 13.

51. Ansaldo, p. 81.

52. *Obras*, pp. 313–21.

53. Bravo, "Early Days of the Spanish Phalanx," *Spain*, 1:10 (October 1938), pp. 6–7; Aznar, p. 20.

54. Gonzalo Torrente Ballester, his anthologist, calls the plan "José Antonio's madness." (*José Antonio*, p. 32.)

55. Comandante B. Gómez Oliveros, with General Moscardó, *General Moscardó* (Barcelona, 1956), p. 104.

56. Cacho, pp. 23–25.

CHAPTER VIII

1. Andino, pp. 21–22. José Antonio later presented a formal proposal to the Junta Política, and the participation was ratified by a plebiscite of *jefes provinciales* arranged in a circular of Jan. 6, 1936.

2. *Obras*, pp. 618–19; *ABC*, July 31, 1935.

3. See Plá, IV, 180–95, 228–34.

4. Bowers, p. 169.

5. Jato, pp. 134–35, 209–10.

6. Guillén, *Sindicalismo español*, p. 63.

7. Interview with José María Gil Robles, Madrid, May 14, 1959.

8. Meleiro, pp. 141–61; Gutiérrez, p. 93.

9. Bravo, *Historia de Falange*, p. 150.

10. Meleiro, pp. 161–65.

11. Andino, pp. 31–32.
12. *Obras, pp.* 854–58.
13. Bernanos, p. 185.
14. *Obras,* p. 420.
15. *Ibid.,* pp. 831–32.
16. *Ibid.,* p. 840.
17. *ABC,* Feb. 14, 1936. Similar sentiment was expressed the same day by *Informaciones* and *La Nación,* both hitherto the only Madrid journals more or less friendly to the Falange.
18. Dávila and Pemartín, pp. 116–18.
19. *Textos,* p. 872.
20. Conversation with José María Gil Robles, Madrid, May 14, 1959.
21. Venegas, *Las elecciones,* p. 28.
22. *Blanco y Negro,* Dec. 25, 1935.
23. Patricio González de Canales, on page 5 of a questionnaire report given to the writer on Jan. 24, 1959.
24. *Arriba,* No. 17, Oct. 31, 1935.
25. *Obras, p.* 840.
26. *Arriba,* No. 33, Feb. 23, 1936.
27. *Obras,* p. 886.
28. He talked with General Franco for the first time at the home of Serrano Súñer on March 8. (Serrano, *Entre Hendaya y Gibraltar,* p. 18; Arrarás, *Franco,* pp. 186–87.) Furthermore, the Falange's Servicio EE was still in touch with the UME in various parts of the peninsula.
29. Canales, p. 5.
30. All information on this maneuver comes from the Socialists. Zugazagoitia, pp. 7–8; Rodolfo Llopis, "Spain Awaits her Hour," Part III, *Iberica,* Vol. 5, No. 7 (1957), pp. 4–6.
31. Plá, IV, 282.
32. Canales, p. 3.
33. *Ibid.,* p. 9. Falange writers cite various instances in which local leaders chafed at the restrictions against reprisals which José Antonio tried to impose on them.
34. Bowers, p. 210; Pavón, pp. 113–14.
35. *El Sol,* Mar. 12, 1936.
36. *Ibid.,* Mar. 15, 1936; Plá, IV, 332.

CHAPTER IX

1. *Cf.* Gil Robles in *Paris-Soir,* July 30, 1936; conversation in Madrid, May 14, 1959.
2. See especially Beltrán, *Preparación y desarrollo;* Lizarza, *Memorias de la conspiración;* Maíz, *Alzamiento en España.*
3. *Epistolario,* p. 358.
4. Andino, p. 42.
5. Bravo, *Historia de Falange,* p. 189; Díaz, pp. 33–37.
6. *The Times* (London), Apr. 15, 1936.
7. The number of Falangists killed is given in Bravo, *Historia de Falange,* pp. 164–65.
8. *Mundo Obrero,* Mar. 13, 1936.

9. Ruiz de Alda, pp. 40, 261–63.

10. Quoted from *El Defensor de Cuenca* in *Mundo Obrero*, May 11, 1936.

11. *El Sol*, Apr. 17, 1936.

12. *Claridad*, May 7, 1936; *El Sol*, May 15, 1936.

13. According to Mariano García, who kept the files. Conversation in Madrid, Jan. 8, 1959.

14. This can best be followed in *El Sol* and also in the Leftist press, especially in the issues of *Claridad* (the new organ of the Largo Caballero faction of the Socialist Party) for May 8, 16, 28, June 20, 23, 27, 1936, and in *Mundo Obrero*, Jan. 9, 10, 18, 21, 31, Feb. 1, 14, 24, Mar. 10, 11, 13, May 8, 1936.

The number of killings has often been exaggerated. *El Sol* tended to underplay the incidence of violence, while the radical Left press overdid it, trying to stir up the workers. The Communist daily charged that the leaders of the conservative newspapers in Madrid (such as *ABC, El Debate, Informaciones*) were ignoring the essentials of the problem. These journals only printed lists of Falangists arrested in the provinces with the conventional comment "The causes for these detentions are unknown," while constantly playing up the disorder springing from the Left.

José Peirats, the chronicler of the CNT, declares that in the five months from February 17 to July 17 there were 213 attempted assassinations, 113 general strikes, and 228 partial shutdowns. In these affrays 269 people were killed and 1287 wounded, according to his *La C.N.T. en la revolución española*, I, 121.

15. See Beltran, *Preparación y desarrollo*, pp. 126–28. There are many other versions of these plans. *Cf.* pp. 755–57. Ansaldo also had a plan to free his old friend Ruiz de Alda, but the latter refused to try to escape. (Ansaldo, pp. 116–17).

16. The Falange had made no effort to contest the municipal elections held in April. José Antonio said that they would inevitably be won by the Left, but that abstention would spoil their plebiscitary effect. Letter to Onésimo Redondo, Mar. 23, 1936, in *Epistolario*, pp. 476–77.

17. At one point José Antonio even authorized Goicoechea to be his wandering representative to the radical Right. Letter from José Antonio to Goicoechea, June 16, 1936, a copy of which is in the possession of the writer.

18. According to Eugenio Vegas Latapié, who says that Gil Robles told him. (Conversation in Madrid, Nov. 25, 1958.)

19. Maíz, p. 82.

20. Pattee, p. 179.

21. *El Sol*, May 12, 1936.

22. *No Importa*, No. 2 (n.d.); Montes, p. 289; Alcázar, p. 81; Arrarás, II, 494–95.

23. Bravo, *Historia de Falange*, p. 180.

24. *El Sol*, May 5, 1936.

25. *El Sol*, Apr. 5, 1936; *Claridad*, May 8, 1936; *Obras*, pp. 911–18; Ximénez, pp. 747–48.

26. Ximénez, pp. 759–62.

27. Ansaldo, p. 121.

28. *Ibid.*

29. *El Pensamiento Alavés* (Vitoria), May 17, 1936.

30. *La Unión* (Seville), July 18, 1937. The Conde de Rodezno, head of the Carlist organization in their stronghold of Navarre, visited José Antonio "repeatedly" in the Modelo. (Beltran, *Preparación y desarrollo,* p. 130.)

The Carlist leadership was divided between the national command, in exile with the Prince Regent at St. Jean de Luz, and the local leaders of Navarre, headed by Rodezno and José Martínez Berasáin, a Pamplona banker. As it happened it was the shallow and opportunistic Rodezno clique that actually brought about active Carlist participation in the military rebellion, which Fal Conde, from France, opposed to the last. Rodezno and Berasáin were no party to the Fal–José Antonio commitment, which they ignored. Conversations with José Martínez Berasáin and Desiderio Jiménez, Pamplona, Dec. 16, 1958.

31. Canales, p. 9. See José Antonio's laments in Zugazagoitia, pp. 7–8.

32. Pavón, pp. 165–66.

33. Maíz, p. 129.

34. Andino, pp. 49, 52. Mariano García, who worked long hours in the secret party headquarters, declares that relations between the Falange and the military in Madrid were "very bad." (Conversation in Madrid, Jan. 8, 1959.)

35. According to Dionisio Ridruejo, who saw the letter. (Conversation in Madrid, Dec. 2, 1958.)

36. *Obras,* pp. 935–36.

37. According to Maura himself. (Conversation in Barcelona, Dec. 23, 1958.)

38. From the original copy in Maura's files.

39. Andino, p. 63.

40. During his 1935 maneuvers with the UME, José Antonio had prepared a cabinet list for a government to be formed after a *coup* against the Republic. It contained the following names:

National Defense: General Franco.

Justice: Ramón Serrano Súñer.

Education: Eduardo Aunós (former Labor Minister for Primo de Rivera). Subsecretary: Manuel Valdés (former *Jefe Nacional* of the SEU).

Economics: Demetrio Carceller (capable and corporativistic, but strictly representing the financial world).

Interior: General Mola.

Navy and Colonies: General Goded.

Communications: Julio Ruiz de Alda. Subsecretary: José Moreno (Falange *jefe provincial* of Navarre).

Corporations: Manuel Mateo (head of the CONS). Subsecretary: Rafael Garcerán (José Antonio's former law clerk).

See José Antonio's *Epistolario,* p. 199; there is a photostat in Alcázar, p. 169. As this list reveals, two cabinet posts represented the practical limit of the Falange's ambitions in 1935, which were no higher a year later.

41. Andino, pp. 67–69.

42. *El Socialista,* July 12, 1936.

43. Pavón, pp. 167–68.

44. Andino, pp. 64–65.

45. Iribarren, *Con el general Mola,* p. 42.

46. Beltrán, *Preparación y desarrollo,* pp. 135–36.

CHAPTER X

1. The most detailed account is in Fernández, pp. 101 ff.

2. The slowly increasing alarm manifest in the official communiqués is traced by Alessi, pp. 97–103.

3. Owing to the many rumors of rebellion, Largo Caballero's *Claridad* made this demand as early as July 16.

4. *Cf.* Iribarren, *Con el general Mola*, pp. 107–8.

5. Two personal, impressionistic accounts of this action are: for the Right, Cuadrado Alonso, pp. 38–39; for the Left, Barea, III, 117–21.

6. See Lladó; Lacruz, pp. 1–178.

7. For a synopsis of the outcome of the rebellion in each part of Spain, see Orizana and Liébana, pp. 124–275.

8. Aznar, p. 81.

9. Iribarren, *Con el general Mola,* pp. 69, 135–36.

10. *Documents on German Foreign Policy,* Series D, Vol. III, *Germany and the Spanish Civil War* (Washington, D.C., 1950), Editor's Note, pp. 1–2.

11. Conversation with the Marqués de Valdeiglesias, Madrid, Feb. 20, 1959.

12. See Lizarza, Appendix; *How Mussolini Provoked the Spanish Civil War: Documentary Evidence* (London, 1937).

13. Or so Ciano told the first Italian ambassador to rebel Spain. Cantalupo, p. 63.

14. Three of the bombers were forced to crash-land in Algeria because of lack of fuel, thus creating a premature international scandal. *The Times* (London), Aug. 1, 1936.

15. It appears that the most significant agent in promoting German intervention was Admiral Canaris, head of the Intelligence Service. The Admiral had carried out several missions in Spain during his earlier career, when he had made the acquaintance of Franco. On Canaris, see Abshagen, pp. 30–32, 58–59, 111–14; Colvin, pp. 30–37; Bartz, p. 20.

16. See Beumelburg; Hoyos.

17. *The Times* (London), Aug. 6, 1936; Solmi, p. 143.

18. The German ambassador, Schwendemann, in his dispatch of July 25, expressed grave pessimism as to the rebels' chances. *Germany and the Spanish Civil War*, Doc. No. 11, pp. 11–13.

19. Cattell, in *Communism and the Spanish Civil War*, shows that the first Russian aid began to reach the Republic in October.

20. This entire campaign is very ably studied in Colodny's *The Struggle for Madrid.*

21. *El Heraldo de Aragón* (Zaragoza), Aug. 27, 1936.

22. According to the information then current in Burgos. Ruiz Vilaplana, pp. 58–59.

23. As the rebels' Italian allies noted. Volta, pp. 57–58.

24. According to the files of José Andino, Bilbao banks offered the Burgos Falange a credit of 100,000 pesetas shortly after the beginning of hostilities. This offer was refused.

25. Conversation with Ricardo Nieto, Madrid, Jan. 17, 1959. Nieto was *jefe provincial* of Zamora and had the difficult task of trying to organize some thousands of newcomers into some sort of shape.

One pro-rebel correspondent wrote: "Actually I found there were very few of them who had even taken the trouble to inquire into the doctrines of the party. Many of the younger ones had joined up because the smart blue uniform gave them a decided advantage over Red youth in the matter of their girl friends. The greatest number had undoubtedly joined up as being the simplest way to help their country. I have questioned dozens of them here, there, and everywhere; I found them on duty on the roads, guarding post-offices, banks, etc., and none of them was clear about anything except that they were anti-Red. One of them told me quite simply he 'guessed it was a kind of Communism, only much better expressed.'" Gerahty, pp. 17-18.

26. Canales, p. 6. There is a rather similar statement by the Falange in *El Adelanto* (Salamanca), Aug. 7, 1936.

27. *Hoy* (Badajoz), Aug. 30, 1936; *La Unión* (Seville), Aug. 30, 1936.

28. Or so Miranda would have us believe. Conversation in Seville, Mar. 9, 1959.

29. Most of this material comes from Miranda; from Pedro Gamero del Castillo (Vice Secretary General of the party, 1939-41), in Madrid, Dec. 6, 1958; and from Luis González Vicén (National Counselor, 1941-46), in Madrid, May 18, 1959.

30. Volta, pp. 87-88.

31. *Arriba España* (Pamplona), Jan. 1, 1937.

32. Quoted by Beltrán, *Preparación y desarrollo,* p. 221. Later, the last independent interview of Manuel Hedilla was published under the title "Spain will be a gigantic syndicate of producers." *Arriba España,* Apr. 16, 1937.

33. Bergamo, pp. 40-41.

34. *FE* (Seville), January 1937; *Arriba España,* Jan. 28, Feb. 2, 1937.

35. Even by Hedilla himself. *Arriba España,* Apr. 16, 1937.

36. Reprinted by *Arriba España,* Jan. 6, 1937.

37. On the attitude of the Church see Cardenal Gomá y Tomás, *Pastorales de la guerra de España.*

38. *Arriba España* Jan. 6, 1937.

39. Conversation with Patricio Canales, Madrid, Jan. 6, 1959.

40. According to Ignacio González de Migoya, of the Asturian Falange. Conversation in Oviedo, Jan. 25, 1959. Dionisio Ridruejo has estimated that some twenty per cent of the new members came from the Left. (Conversation in Madrid, Nov. 17, 1958.) In Seville, a prosperous and conservative publisher was warned by an Army friend, "Have nothing to do with the Falange. That is where the avalanche is going. Since they require no guarantees, their greater percentage is of Marxists." (Bahamonde, pp. 5-6.)

41. According to Bahamonde, p. 15.

42. *La Gaceta Regional* (Salamanca), Aug. 9, 1936.

43. *Arriba España,* Feb. 2, 1937.

44. Clark, I, 653.

45. So say Eugenio Vegas Latapié and José María Gil Robles. (Conversations in Madrid, Feb. 19 and May 14, 1959.)

46. On Yagüe's political background, see I. García Escalera, "El General Yagüe," *Temas españoles* (Madrid, 1953), pp. 1-26.

47. According to José María Iribarren, Mola's secretary.

48. Kindelán, pp. 51-59. The dates are adjusted in Vigón, p. 253.

49. According to his successor in Valladolid, Dionisio Ridruejo. (Conversation in Madrid, Nov. 17, 1958.)

50. Canales, p. 13.

CHAPTER XI

1. *Obras,* pp. 945–46.

2. Jato, p. 182.

3. According to the typescript of José Antonio's trial, pp. 62, 74. There were few Falangists in Alicante, and five were killed in the rescue attempt. (Gutiérrez, p. 245.)

4. These and other papers of José Antonio's were published in a Socialist Party pamphlet entitled "El Testamento de Primo de Rivera," prepared by Indalecio Prieto in Mexico (no date). They first appeared in an article by Prieto in the Mexican journal *Mañana,* May 24, 1947. A partial presentation was later given by Rodolfo Llopis in his *Los puntales del régimen de Franco se quiebran.*

5. Trial typescript, p. 87. This is corroborated by his note to Echeverría dated Aug. 9, 1936, in the files of Martínez Barrio, in Paris.

6. Several letters on the topic and on prison conditions are preserved in the files of the Republican Government, kept by Martínez Barrio.

7. Jato, pp. 246–47.

8. Telegram from the Chargé Voelcher, Oct. 17, 1936. *Germany and the Spanish Civil War,* Doc. No. 102, pp. 114–16.

9. Canales, p. 12.

10. *Ibid.*

11. Conversations with Hedilla, Jan. 20, 1959; Anselmo de la Iglesia, May 26, 1959; Luis González Vicén, Feb. 23, 1959; Narciso Perales, Feb. 12, 1959; Carlos Juan Ruiz de la Fuente, Nov. 30, 1958. "In my judgment they were merely slow and ineffective." (Canales, p. 12.)

12. According to Hedilla; Ximénez, pp. 784–85, 828; Schempp, p. 10; Conde de Romanones in *Dolor y memoria,* pp. 307–8; Bray, p. 78. Despite the accusations of certain Falangists, there exists no evidence to substantiate suspicion of Franco in this matter. Even the Germans, who distrusted many of the rebels as reactionaries, seem never to have questioned this.

13. The London *News Chronicle,* Oct. 24, 1936, quoted in Bravo, *José Antonio,* pp. 138–42. José Antonio's version was given three weeks later at the trial. Trial typescript, pp. 20–21. He contests only minor points.

14. *Cómo y por qué salí del Ministerio de Defensa Nacional* (Mexico City, 1940), p. 61.

15. Trial typescript, p. 23.

16. Quoted in Ximénez, pp. 800–802. Other accounts are in *Solidaridad Obrera* (Barcelona), Nov. 17, 18, 1936, and Pavón, pp. 185–201.

17. Largo, pp. 208–9. Other accounts were found in a conversation with Julio Just (Republican Minister of Public Works in November 1936), Paris, Oct. 2, 1958; Zugazagoitia, pp. 246–49; Schulz-Wilmersdorf, p. 104.

18. *Epistolario,* pp. 517–30.

19. Miguel was later exchanged together with his wife and taken to Mallorca aboard a British warship. Schulz-Wilmersdorf, p. 104.

20. See Ximénez, pp. 809-25; Pavón, pp. 217-18; Mauger, pp. 163-68; Manuel Serrante Esplá in *Dolor y memoria*, pp. 311-15.

21. Mauger, p. 171.

CHAPTER XII

1. Iribarren, *Con el general Mola*, p. 344.

2. Conversation with Luis González Vicén, Madrid, May 21, 1959.

3. Canales, pp. 13-14.

4. *Boletín Oficial del Estado*, No. 64, Dec. 22, 1936. (Hereafter cited as *BOE*.)

5. *BOE*, No. 96, Jan. 24, 1937. No full commander was appointed, but the cavalry officer, General Monasterio, was named second-in-command, with temporary authority.

6. *Ibid.*, Nos. 100 and 104, Jan. 28 and Feb. 1, 1937.

7. All this is explained in the following chapter.

8. Conversations with Luis González Vicén, Madrid, May 6, 1959, and José María Valdés, Bilbao, Dec. 13, 1958.

9. Kemp, p. 21. These are the memoirs of a volunteer British officer who served with the Spanish Legion.

10. Jato, p. 243.

11. Such as the Centuria Cánepa and the Second Centuria, both of Seville, which were virtually wiped out in the fighting inside the Ciudad Universitaria. Patricio Canales, from the script of a Madrid television interview, Nov. 23, 1958.

12. García Mercadal, p. 336.

13. Conill, *Codo*.

14. Alonso Bea, *Ecos de la gesta de Teruel* (Zaragoza, 1940); García Mercadal, II, 201; Cirilo Martín Retortillo, *Huesca vencedora* (Huesca, 1938); Antonio Algarra Ráfegas, *El asedio de Huesca* (Zaragoza, 1941), p. 196.

15. *BOE*, No. 139, Mar. 8, 1937; Juliá, pp. 100-101.

16. García Mercadal, I, 322: Esperabé, pp. 32-33, 95-96.

17. *Arriba España*, Jan. 6, 1937.

18. *The Times* (London), Dec. 9, 1936; G. M. Godden, *Conflict in Spain* (London, 1937), p. 104.

19. According to Dionisio Ridruejo, who was sheltered by Monasterio during the crisis of April 1937.

20. The first bandera from the distant Canaries sailed on September 5, 1936. The Army was so short-handed that three hundred of the ablest men were converted into shock troops. *Hoy* (Las Palmas), Sept. 6, 1936; Doreste, *Ocho meses*.

21. According to Ricardo Nieto, *jefe provincial* of Zamora.

22. According to Canales, who was then editing the Falange paper in Oviedo. Other *camisas viejas* concur with these figures.

23. Von Stohrer, the second German ambassador, thought that sympathy for national syndicalism was widespread throughout the fighting front. *Germany and the Spanish Civil War*, No. 529, pp. 590-99.

CHAPTER XIII

1. Ortiz, p. 21.
2. *Cf.* Menéndez-Reigada, *La guerra nacional española ante la Moral y el Derecho.*
3. According to Patricio Canales.
4. Report of Apr. 14, 1937. *Germany and the Spanish Civil War,* Doc. No. 243, pp. 267–70.
5. See Chapter VI.
6. Gamero was first the secretary of the *Jons* of Seville, and then *asesor tecnical.*
7. According to his own declaration, quoted in the *Diario de Burgos,* May 24, 1937.
8. All documents pertaining to these negotiations are in the files of the Carlist historian, Melchor Ferrer, in Seville.
9. According to Pedro Gamero.
10. So Franco told Faupel on Apr. 11, 1937. *Germany and the Spanish Civil War,* Doc. No. 243, pp. 267–70.
11. According to Andino. (Conversation in Madrid, Feb. 6, 1959.)
12. *ABC,* Mar. 9, 1937.
13. There is no clear proof of this, but it is the belief of most of those connected with these events, including Hedilla himself.
14. Dionisio Ridruejo, then the new *jefe provincial* of Valladolid, says that they boosted Yagüe because he possessed a forceful temperament, great capacity for organization, and abundant energy, even if he lacked certain other qualities.
15. *Entre Hendaya y Gibraltar,* p. 19; Schulz-Wilmersdorf, pp. 222–23.
16. Or so Serrano told Dionisio Ridruejo, of whom he became a close friend.
17. "I had maintained friendly relations with the Falange, Traditionalists, and monarchists, with Sáinz Rodríguez, Rodezno, Hedilla, . . . Gomá [the primate], . . . Mola." *Entre Hendaya y Gibraltar,* p. 26.
18. Serrano was considerably impressed by Italian Fascism, although he was repelled by the crudeness and insolence of the Nazis. *Cf.* Sencourt, p. 340.
19. *Entre Hendaya y Gibraltar,* p. 32.
20. *Ibid.,* pp. 25–26.
21. *Ibid.,* pp. 63–64.
22. The foregoing sketch of Serrano Súñer's attitudes and aspirations is in part based on the remarks of Dionisio Ridruejo, collected by the writer in a series of conversations.
23. *Germany and the Spanish Civil War,* Doc. No. 248, pp. 277–79.
24. Cantalupo, pp. 211ff.
25. *Chicago Daily Tribune,* July 27, 1936.
26. *The Times* (London), Apr. 18, 1937.
27. *Ibid.,* Mar. 8, 1937.
28. According to Hedilla.
29. Hedilla dates this meeting as toward the end of March 1937.
30. Cantalupo, p. 118.

31. According to Hedilla.

32. Quoted in Alcázar, pp. 64–66.

33. *Ibid.*, pp. 68, 70. This, of course, was quite absurd.

34. According to Luis Pagés Guix' pamphlet, "La Traición de los Franco," p. 13.

35. This account of the events of the night of April 14–15, 1937, is based on conversations with Daniel López Puertas, Madrid, Jan. 5, 1959, and letters from Luis Ortiz de Hazas, June 9, 1947, Víctor de La Serna, June 10, 1947, and Tomás Rodríguez López, June 13, 1947, all addressed to Manuel Hedilla, published in the clandestine "Cartas entrecruzadas entre el Sr. D. Manuel Hedilla Larrey y el Sr. D. Ramón Serrano Súñer" (Madrid, 1948).

The version given by Zugazagoitia in his history was evidently based on Pagés Guix' pamphlet and is erroneous.

36. According to Hedilla. See also Alcázar, pp. 58–59; Dávila later claimed that only Hedilla had voted for the chairman. *Diario de Burgos,* May 24, 1937.

37. It has been said de la Serna incited Hedilla to "pack" the National Council meeting. There is no confirmation of this. Six new Council members were invited over and above the 1936 list, but they were not all Hedillistas.

38. Original copies of the circular are in the possession of Hedilla and of José Andino.

39. The substance of this account of the National Council meetings of April 18 and 19 is based on the personal memos of José Andino, prepared on the spot. Hedilla pronounces them substantially accurate.

40. For example, Ricardo Nieto, of Zamora, has explained that he cast a blank vote because he considered it less provocative merely to send an official representative, not a new *Jefe Nacional,* to talk with Franco. He and a number of other delegates thought that Franco's leadership was inevitable and that the Falange could only bargain for reasonable terms.

41. Hedilla says that he does not know who, if anyone, organized the demonstration.

42. Hedilla has claimed that he himself suggested the title when his opinion was first asked on the matter. Letter to Luis Carrero Blanco, Mar. 24, 1947, in "Cartas entrecruzadas."

43. Franco, *Palabras del Caudillo,* pp. 10–11, 14.

44. The first appointments were made public in less than three days. *BOE,* Apr. 22, 1937.

45. Joaquín Miranda, who became vice-secretary, admits that he was the only more or less authentic Falangist in this body.

46. Hedilla says that Aznar, José Antonio's sister Pilar, and all the Madrid "legitimists" urged him not to compromise with Franco.

47. From a letter written by José Sáinz to Hedilla, May 17, 1947. Mariano García, former head of the party secretariat, confirmed this in a letter of May 20, 1947. After ten years, Ramón Serrano Súñer admitted to Hedilla that the accusation must have been false. Letter of May 31, 1947. (All these letters are reproduced in "Cartas entrecruzadas.")

48. Or so Franco told Faupel on May 1. *Germany and the Spanish Civil War,* Doc. No. 248, pp. 277–79.

49. On the immediate fate of these people, see the Pagés Guix pamphlet.

50. Conversation with Vicente Cadenas, Madrid, Feb. 23, 1959.

51. Or so at least he alleged in a letter to Ramón Serrano Súñer of June 18, 1947.

52. *BOE*, No. 199, July 18, 1941.

CHAPTER XIV

1. As of April 30, 1937, the financial resources of the two groups forming the state party were as follows:

Falangists: cash on hand, 5,157.40 pesetas; in the Banco de España, 4,064.30 pesetas; in the Banco de Bilbao, 50,000.00 pesetas; total, 59,221.70 pesetas.

Requetés: cash on hand, 1,439.70 pesetas; in the Banco Español de Crédito, 30,500.00 pesetas; other funds, 520.19 pesetas; total, 32,459.89 pesetas.

According to a receipt signed by Pablo de Legarreta, treasurer of the Falange, in the files of José Andino.

2. *BOE*, April 22, 1937.

3. *Entre Hendaya y Gibraltar*, p. 60.

4. *Palabras del Caudillo*, p. 167.

5. This is according to Dionisio Ridruejo.

6. He says, "Some rebellious Falangists who had remained at liberty formed a small group hostile to the official Secretariat in order to continue to influence their own masses. I understood that the Secretariat was not sufficiently representative and that, on the other hand, dealing with these dissidents would be useful in order to achieve the cordial entry of the most authentic into the new organization. I endeavored to give them the impression we wanted talks and understanding. My labors of patience were infinite, but that was the only sure way to learn the viewpoint of the Falangists and to gain an idea as to which were the persons in whom they had most faith, or who were really the most valuable. In Salamanca that group established its headquarters in a small house on the Plazuela de San Julián where resided Pilar Primo de Rivera, a priestess who offered every sacrifice and remembrance to the great thought and intentions of her absent brother. That pure and rigorous—almost sublime— loyalty greatly moved me. Falangists from nearly every province passed by that house to receive orders or transmit worries, and all that was cast upon the Cuartel General with considerable impertinence." Serrano, p. 42.

7. *BOE*, No. 205, May 13, 1937.

8. Clark, II, 622.

9. *Ibid.*, II, 639.

10. Serrano, p. 75.

11. *Unidad* (Santander), November 30, 1937.

12. *Unidad* (Santander), May 23, 1937; *Sur* (Málaga), Dec. 12, 1937; *FE* (Seville), Jan. 1, 1938; *Hierro* (Bilbao), Mar. 7, 1938.

13. Even by so broad-minded a writer as Pío Baroja. *FE*, Jan. 8, 1938.

14. *Amanecer* (Zaragoza), Dec. 14, 1937.

15. In a speech of July 18, 1937, reprinted in *Palabras del Caudillo*, p. 28; and in a United Press interview of the same month, in *ibid.*, p. 149.

16. *Ibid.*, p. 196.

17. According to Serrano, "In the first months there was not in reality a viable candidate [for Secretary-General] in the Falange, either because of ex-

cessive youth, scant importance in the history of the party, or the suspicion excited at headquarters." When the possibility of Fernández Cuesta's candidacy became known, "it was presented immediately for that post not only by the Falangists but also, with great energy, by other groups and sectors who maintained the most passionate opposition to me." *Entre Hendaya y Gibraltar,* p. 59.

18. Fernández Cuesta, pp. 51–57.

19. Quoted from *La Voz de Galicia* (La Coruña) by *FE,* Jan. 4, 1938.

20. Report from von Stohrer of May 19, 1938. *Germany and the Spanish Civil War,* Doc. No. 586, pp. 657–63.

21. *Palabras del Caudillo,* pp. 168–69.

22. *Entre Hendaya y Gibraltar,* p. 31.

23. *Cf.* Alcázar, p. 145. It was explained that Serrano's brother Fernando had been *secretario provincial* of the Falange in the Balearics before the war. Zayas, pp. 29–31.

24. The only party representative was Fernández Cuesta as Minister of Agriculture, a position for which this gentleman was utterly inadequate.

25. In his May 19 report, von Stohrer wrote: "When military reverses occur political differences come to the fore. . . . This phenomenon is now also appearing in the course of the present slowdown in the military operations." *Germany and the Spanish Civil War,* Doc. No. 586, pp. 657–63.

26. *El Pueblo Gallego* (Vigo), Apr. 23, 1938, quoted by Venegas, *Verdad y mentira de Franco,* p. 267.

27. *Germany and the Spanish Civil War,* Doc. No. 586, pp. 657–63.

28. *Palabras del Caudillo,* pp. 46, 52–53.

29. As difficulties between Falangists and the military continued, the German ambassador in Moscow gained the distinct impression from the Russian press that the Communists thought an understanding with elements of the Falange was possible. Report of Count von der Schulenburg, June 20, 1938. *Germany and the Spanish Civil War,* Doc. No. 615, pp. 698–99.

30. According to von Stohrer's communication of July 1. *Ibid.,* Doc. No. 626, pp. 709–11.

31. *Arriba España,* October 22, 1937.

32. Serrano observes wryly, "Its life was not precisely intense." *Entre Hendaya y Gibraltar,* p. 65.

33. *Ibid.,* p. 66.

34. The account of this incident is taken from Ridruejo's own verbal narrative to the writer.

35. At this time González Vélez had already been relieved of his former rank on the Junta Política.

36. *Boletín del Movimiento de Falange Española Tradicionalista,* No. 23, July 1, 1938 (hereafter cited as *BMFET*).

37. González Vélez' health was already poor, and he died within a few months. Aznar was finally restored to circulation in November 1939, but he never again figured in politics.

38. According to Ridruejo, González Bueno was violently jealous of Garrigues, who was Professor of Mercantile Law at the University of Valladolid. Later in the year he helped magnify an innocent remark by Garrigues concerning the possibility of ending the war by mediation into a charge of treason which cost the latter several months in prison.

39. That is, the alignment was between Sáinz Rodríguez, Aunós, Arellano, Esteban Bilbao, José Yanguas Messías, and José María Valiente, *et al.* on the one hand, and Fernández Cuesta, Aznar, Ridruejo, *et al.* (aided by Queipo de Llano) on the other.

40. This account of the writing of the *Fuero de Trabajo* is according to Dionisio Ridruejo, conversations in Madrid of Jan. 10 and 19, 1959.

41. *BMFET*, No. 16, Mar. 15, 1938.

42. Clark, II, 731–32.

43. *BMFET*, No. 19, May 1, 1938.

44. Clark, II, 747–50.

45. *Intemperie, victoria y servicio: Escritos y discursos*, p. 91.

46. *Ibid.*, pp. 101–2.

47. *BMFET*, No. 11, Jan. 1, 1938.

48. According to Andino. This gentleman had been ousted from his *jefatura provincial* after the fusion, because Burgos was reserved for the Carlists. Andino had refused to accept the *secretariado provincial*, and was unemployed until assigned to the syndicates.

49. Clark, II, 726.

50. *BMFET*, No. 3, Sept. 1, 1937; *Actividad* (Palma de Mallorca), Aug. 21, 1937.

51. Clark, II, 752–53.

52. *Ibid.*, II, p. 727.

53. *Cf. El Pensamiento Navarro*, Jan. 11, 1938.

54. McCullagh, pp. 61–62; *Sur*, Sept. 11, 1937; *Alerta* (Santander), Sept. 12, 1937; *Arriba España*, Dec. 1, 1937; *El Heraldo de Aragón*, Dec. 1, 3, 1937; *El Ideal Gallego* (La Coruña), Dec. 14, 18, 1937; *El Pueblo Gallego* (Vigo), Jan. 7, 1938; *La Rioja* (Logroño), Feb. 26, 1938.

55. *Arriba España*, Jan. 9, 1938; *Amanecer* (Jerez), Sept. 27, 1937; *FE*, Dec. 21, 1937; *El Pueblo Gallego*, Jan. 11, 16, 1938; *Arriba España*, Apr. 9, 1938.

56. On at least two occasions, over-zealous censors took to blotting out the very word "Falange." *Hierro*, Jan. 13, 1938; *El Ideal Gallego*, Feb. 4, 1938.

57. *La Rioja*, Jan. 14, 1938.

58. Cantalupo, p. 117.

59. *BOE*, Nov. 17, 1938.

60. *Palabras del Caudillo*, pp. 77–79.

61. *Ibid.*, pp. 132, 139.

62. See Ros and Bouthelier.

63. *BMFET*, No. 2, Aug. 15, 1937.

64. *Ibid.*

65. Political Secretariat Circular No. 1, July 5, 1937.

66. *Cf.* Colmegna, p. 53.

67. Oudard, p. 251.

68. *BMFET*, No. 7, Nov. 1, 1937. There was even unreconciled animosity between "Falange priests" like Fermín Yzurdiaga, who became Chief of Press and Propaganda for FET, and the regular Carlist curates. Some of this is noted by the Basque priest Iñaki de Aberrigoyen, in *Sieben Monate und sieben Tage in Franco-Spanien*, pp. 114–15.

69. Letter to General Franco of November 28, 1937, in Melchor Ferrer's

documentary collection, "El General Franco y la Comunión Tradicionalista," pp. 38–41.

70. See the following chapter.

71. *BMFET*, No. 16, Mar. 15, 1938.

72. The same thing happened to other Rightist groups. Members of the *Acción Española* band, themselves principal proponents of the fusion of parties, found their propaganda activities reduced almost to nothing by the short-lived Ridruejo policy. According to Eugenio Vegas Latapié, they were not even permitted to publish an anthology of material first printed several years earlier under and against the Republic itself.

73. According to Arellano.

74. Report of the German ambassador, von Stohrer, Nov. 17, 1938. *Germany and the Spanish Civil War*, Doc. No. 699, pp. 796–801.

75. Political Secretariat Circular No. 12, July 19, 1937.

76. This is recounted in a letter from Fal Conde to Franco dated Aug. 19, 1945, in the Ferrer file.

77. Cantalupo, pp. 62–65, 83–86.

78. *Germany and the Spanish Civil War*, Doc. No. 142, pp. 152–53.

79. However, when General Faupel, the first German ambassador, went to Salamanca in November 1936, he was accompanied by a propaganda assistant and by one expert "for questions of organization of the Falange." *Ibid.*, Doc. No. 125, p. 134.

80. *Ibid.*, Doc. No. 157, pp. 170–73.

81. *Ibid.*, Doc. No. 207, p. 229.

82. *Ibid.*, Doc. No. 243, pp. 267–70.

83. Serrano, pp. 47–51; *Germany and the Spanish Civil War*, Doc. No. 254, pp. 284–86.

84. According to Yzurdiaga.

85. In a report of February 1938. *Germany and the Spanish Civil War*, Doc. No. 529, pp. 590–99.

86. *Ibid.*, Doc. No. 529, pp. 590–99.

87. *Cf.* Marcel Sauvage, *La corrida* (Paris, 1938), pp. 203–4.

88. *Germany and the Spanish Civil War*, Doc. No. 455, pp. 480–84.

89. *Ibid.*, Doc. No. 565, p. 640.

90. Interview with Gen. Emilio Canevari, Rome, Apr. 6, 1959.

91. Mira and Salvatorelli, pp. 805–6.

92. *Germany and the Spanish Civil War*, Doc. No. 248, pp. 277–79.

93. Notes from his conversation with Franco of July 19, 1939, in Malcolm Muggeridge (ed.), *Ciano's Diplomatic Papers*, pp. 290–95.

Furthermore, the Italians emphatically approved the Falange's opposition to vaguely Anglophile foreign ministers like Sangróniz and Jordana. *Ciano's Hidden Diary, 1937–1938*, p. 48.

CHAPTER XV

1. No satisfactory biography of the Caudillo has ever been written. On details of his early career Coles, *Franco of Spain*, is sometimes helpful.

2. *BMFET*, No. 33, Oct. 10, 1938.

3. Clark, II, 635, 653. The SEU had never been strong on theory or the inculcation of academic virtues. However, its original statutes (1933) had insisted on the primacy of state-directed lay education. Under the Sáinz Rodríguez–inspired education laws of the Franco state, lower education was handed over lock, stock, and barrel to Church norms and clerical supervision. There were few complaints, save in the freer atmosphere of wine-shops frequented by party veterans.

4. *La Sección Femenina: Historia y organización*, p. 20.

5. *BMFET*, No. 6, Oct. 15, 1937.

6. Clark, II, 652.

7. *La Sección Femenina*, p. 32. A sympathetic impressionistic account is in Corthis, pp. 84–108.

8. The Twenty-seventh Point, prohibiting alliances with other political groups, had understandably been dropped.

9. *BOE*, Aug. 10, 1939.

10. Miguel Primo de Rivera's status was vicarious; he had played no role in the Falange prior to the war. On the benefits to Franco, see Serrano, p. 122.

11. *Palabras del Caudillo*, p. 299.

12. Clark, II, 659.

13. Telegrams of Aug. 2 and 15, 1939, from Sotomayor to Carlos Juan Ruiz de la Fuente, in the latter's personal files. Ruiz de la Fuente was Sotomayor's principal collaborator in these plans.

14. He had been appointed some four months previously. *BMFET*, May 10, 1939.

15. *Ibid.*, Aug. 20, 1939.

16. From an undated programmatic sketch prepared by Ruiz de la Fuente.

17. From a speech before the Falange of Madrid early in November 1939, published in pamphlet form.

18. *BMFET*, Nov. 20, 1939. Sotomayor was killed two years later while serving in Russia with the Blue Division. The principal source on these maneuvers for the Frente de Juventudes is Carlos Juan Ruiz de la Fuente. Conversations in Madrid, Nov. 30, 1958; Feb. 8, 1959.

19. Report of von Stohrer, Feb. 19, 1939. *Germany and the Spanish Civil War*, Doc. No. 740, pp. 843–51.

20. See Chapter IV.

21. Caralt says that the conspirators could have counted on about 900 *excombatientes* in Catalonia during 1940. However, over half of these supported Eduardo Ezquer, the former *jefe provincial* of Badajoz, then undergoing internal exile at Gerona. Ezquer had built his own private little system of conspiracy, with which the larger network had little direct contact. Conversation with Luis de Caralt, Barcelona, Mar. 31, 1959.

22. It was necessary to expel Buhigas and Cazañas, because of their involvement in peculation of public funds.

23. The principal source for this account of the 1939–41 conspiracy is the conversation and notes of Patricio Canales. The reader should bear in mind that personal recollections are easily subject to exaggeration.

24. See Chapter VI.

25. General Valera's attitude has been thus described by Arrese. Conversation in Madrid, December 1960.

26. According to Merino himself. Conversation in Barcelona, Apr. 2, 1959.

27. He eventually made an inspection trip to view German labor in the spring of 1941. *Arriba,* Apr. 3, 1941.

28. Clark, II, 764, 775.

29. *Arriba,* Apr. 1, 1940.

30. This is all according to the remarks of Gerardo Salvador Merino.

31. Carceller was one of the smartest capitalist managers in Spain and one of the most successful financial opportunists connected with the regime. As such, he deserves a word apart. Carceller came from a very humble family and in his early years was sponsored by the Conde de Egaña. He received training as an industrial technician and managed several small enterprises before going into the financial world. After becoming head of a petroleum company in the Canaries, Carceller began to dabble in politics. During the Republic he was a member of the financial group that provided monetary aid to Calvo Sotelo and José Antonio (see Chapter II), eventually becoming a Falangist leader in Barcelona.

Carceller was both an intelligent businessman and a skillful politician. By the end of the Civil War he sat on the Falange's National Council. He went on the 1940 Serrano Súñer mission to Berlin and became Minister of Industry and Commerce in 1941. Carceller's policy in that office was to exploit to the hilt the needs of the war economies of the Axis and the Allies. (*Cf.* Herbert Feis, *The Spanish Story,* New York, 1950.) He is customarily given credit for having initiated corruption on a grand scale in the regime after 1941. In 1944 he helped start the switch in Spanish policy back toward courting the Anglo-Saxon nations, harping on the theme that capitalists throughout the world should understand each other. There is some disagreement about his attitude toward the Falange. After the fall of Merino, he did cooperate with the syndicates on certain matters. Carceller was dismissed in 1945.

32. See the following chapter.

33. According to Arrese, January 1961.

34. Clark, II, 646.

35. *BMFET,* Oct. 1, 1939.

36. See the comments in Pettinato, p. 84–96.

37. Gutiérrez, p. 62.

38. Beneyto and Costa Serrano, pp. 150, 156, 169.

39. Especially in *El nuevo Estado español* (Madrid, 1939), pp. 39, 59–68.

40. Alfonso García Valdecasas, "Los Estados Totalitarios y el Estado Español," *Revista de Estudios Políticos,* Vol. II, No. 5 (Jan., 1942), pp. 5–32.

41. Javier Martínez de Bedoya, "El Sentido de la Libertad en la Doctrina Falangista," *Revista de Estudios Políticos,* Vol. III, No. 10 (July-August, 1943), pp. 313–34.

42. Arrese, *Escritos y discursos,* pp. 211–31.

43. José Antonio had been ambiguous in his use of such terms as "fascist" and "totalitarian." Both were employed during the first months of the Falange, but the *Jefe* later backed away from the word "fascist," and also tried to disassociate the party from the concepts of "pan-statism" and "totalitarianism."

CHAPTER XVI

1. The interpretation of Gamero del Castillo's administration given on pp. 225–26 of an earlier printing of this volume was partially incorrect. The present text has been revised.

2. As Gamero himself declared at one point: "Our finest comrades and many other people in Spain are daily asking a basic question. The question is about the present status of the Falange, about the proportion between the present problems of Spain and the actual possibilities of the Party.

"For the truth is that the Falange neither rules a State of its own—which hasn't yet been built—nor combats an opposing State, which has been destroyed.

. . .

"At the present time the Falange has been called upon to perform a dangerous duty of partial eclipse. It has to work in the most difficult circumstances, weakened by a deep substratum of political heterogeneity that at times reduces the visible result to zero." *Arriba,* Jan. 19, 1941.

3. The appointment of Galarza and the dismissal of Tóvar and Ridruejo occurred within less than a fortnight. *BOE,* Nos. 126 and 138, May 6 and 18, 1941.

4. This is partly treated in his pamphlet, "Málaga desde el punto de vista urbanístico" (Málaga, 1941).

5. *BOE,* Nos. 140 and 142, May 20 and 22, 1941. This account of the political crisis of May 1941 is largely based on a series of interviews with Diónisio Ridruejo in 1958-59 and with José Luis de Arrese in January 1961.

6. This version of the Serrano-Arrese dispute is based on the latter's personal recollections.

7. Arrese, *Escritos y discursos,* pp. 41–47, 89–95, 137–79, *et passim.*

8. Arrese, *La revolución social del Nacional Sindicalismo,* pp. 36, 41.

9. *Escritos y discursos,* pp. 207–10.

10. Interview with José Luis de Arrese, Madrid, Feb. 9, 1959. (Arrese was at that time Minister of Housing.)

11. Quoted in Bray, p. 114.

12. From the *Anuario Español del Gran Mundo* of 1942.

13. García Hinojosa, p. 80.

14. Both these pamphlets are drawn from the files of Melchor Ferrer in Seville.

15. This account of the aftermath of the Begoña affair is based largely on the personal recollections of José Luis de Arrese. *Cf.* Jato, pp. 322–23.

16. From a letter written by Carmelo Paulo y Bondía to the writer, Mar. 2, 1959.

CHAPTER XVII

1. This is according to Arrese's own recollection in January 1961. *Cf.* the prologue to his *Capitalismo, comunismo, cristianismo.*

2. Diehard young Falangists refused to renounce their visions of a fascist new order in Europe, even though the Nazi Empire was being battered down

from three directions. During 1944 a number of party veterans organized a group called the Círculo Nosotros ("Circle of Ourselves"), which pledged never to surrender the original totalitarian goals of the Falange. The pressure of circumstances forced the group to disband in 1945, but on leaving the Círculo the members dropped most of their Falangist activities as well. Jato, pp. 337–38.

3. Clark, II, 719–21.

4. *Ibid.*, II, 519.

5. *Hierro*, Jan. 25, 1938. (Italics supplied by the writer.)

6. Foltz, p. 97. This figure represented only executions under the regular legal administration from April 1939 to June 1944 and did not include special Army executions.

7. Jato, p. 328n.

8. *Ibid.*, p. 339.

9. In 1945 it was rumored that Arrese was trying to form an anti-Rightist bloc in the Movement. *Cf.* Letter to Rodrigo Vivar, Luis González Vicén, and Fermín Zelada, Nov. 20, 1945, in *Boletín de la Guardia de Franco*, No. 20, Dec. 25, 1945, printed in Arrese, *Hacia una meta institucional* (Madrid, 1957) pp. 1–20.

10. Arrese, *Capitalismo, comunismo, cristianismo.*

11. *Ibid.*, p. 104.

12. Clark, II, 573.

13. "Tebib Arrumi," in *Domingo,* Sept. 5, 1937, quoted by Ruiz Vilaplana, p. 235.

14. *Cf.* Francotte, pp. 78–83.

15. *Vieja Guardia,* January–June 1956.

16. Letter from Vicén to Arrese, June 8, 1956, p. 2.

17. *Ibid.*, p. 3.

18. "Perhaps that is the only one which remains to it after these years of our regime, during which in the name of unity there has been carried out a grave process of disunion through class privilege." *Ibid.*, p. 3.

19. "On the other hand I fear that the movement of withdrawal which the Church has already clearly initiated during recent months might be accelerated by our own action and cause a critical situation for the regime before that was desirable." *Ibid.*, p. 3.

20. *Ibid.*, p. 4.

21. *Ibid.*

22. *Ibid.*, p. 5.

23. *Ibid.*, p. 6.

24. *Ibid.*, p. 7.

25. *Ibid.*, p. 10.

26. *Ibid.*, p. 9.

27. *Ibid.*, p. 9.

28. "Informe del Instituto de Estudios Políticos, en relación con los Anteproyectos de Leyes Fundamentales sometidos a la consideración del Consejo Nacional," p. 23.

29. *Ibid.*, p. 12.

30. According to the proposed "Anteproyecto de Ley Orgánica del Movimiento Nacional," the National Council would be composed of at least 150

councilors, some of whom would be chosen by the Chief of State, but at least half of whom were to be elected by the party members at large. The National Council was to meet at least once each year and would have the duty of watching the passage of new laws to prevent ideological deviation, as well as to supervise the Movement. The Secretary-General of the Movement would be elected by the National Council and ratified by the Chief of State for a term of six years. An adverse vote by the Council would force his resignation within twenty-four hours. It was the prerogative of the Council to veto any dangerous law proposed by the Cortes Commissions before it should come to a vote. The Council's Action Committee could make whatever further recommendations on administration that it chose.

As to the final disposition of these proposals, the "Anteproyecto de Ley Orgánica del Movimiento Nacional" stated that whether or not this project was immediately authorized and promulgated by the government, it should come into effect on the succession of a new figure as Chief of State.

31. *Hacia una meta institucional,* pp. 191–92.

32. *Ibid.,* p. 212.

33. *Ibid.,* p. 215.

34. *Ibid.,* p. 213.

35. Their leading ideologue was a bizarre reactionary rhetorician called Rafael Calvo Serer, who set forth a vague elitist theory in several books.

BIBLIOGRAPHY

The following bibliography includes only materials used directly in the preparation of this study; it is not intended as a guide to modern Spanish history. The many individual conversations with participants that contributed so much to the development of this study have been, for the most part, cited in the footnotes and will not be repeated here.

Aberrigoyen, Iñaki de. Sieben Monate und sieben Tage in Franco Spanien. Herausgegeben und übersetzt von Maximilian Helffert. Lucerne: Vita Nova Verlag, 1939.
Abshagen, Karl Heinz. Canaris. Translated by Alan Houghton Brodrick. London: Hutchinson, 1956.
Aguado, Emiliano. Ramiro Ledesma en la crisis de España. Madrid: Editora Nacional, 1943.
Albiñana Sanz, Doctor José María. Confinado en Las Hurdes. Madrid: El Financiero, 1933.
———. Después de la dictadura: Los cuervos sobre la tumba. Madrid: Compañía Iberoamericana de Publicaciones, 1930 (?).
———. España bajo la dictadura republicana. Madrid: El Financiero, 1932.
———. Prisionero de la República. Madrid: El Financiero, 1932.
Alcázar de Velasco, Angel. Serrano Súñer en la Falange. Barcelona, Madrid: Ediciones Patria, 1941.
Alessi, Marco. La Spagna dalla monarchia al governo di Franco. Milan: Istituto per gli Studi de Politica Internazionale, 1937.
Andino, José. Memorias (unpublished).
Ansaldo, Juan Antonio. ¿Para qué? (De Alfonso XIII a Juan III). Buenos Aires: Vasca Ekin, 1953.
Anuario Español del Gran Mundo. Madrid, 1942.
Aparicio, Juan. Ramiro Ledesma, Fundador de las JONS. Madrid: Vicesecretaría de Educación Popular, 1942.
——— (ed.). La Conquista del Estado. Barcelona: Ediciones Fe, 1939.
——— (ed.). El Estado Nacional. Madrid: Editora Nacional, 1943.
——— (ed.). JONS. Madrid: Editora Nacional, 1943.
Arrarás Joaquín. Franco. Santiago de Chile: Zig-Zag, n.d.
——— (ed.). Historia de la Cruzada española. Eight volumes. Madrid: Ediciones Españolas, 1940.
Arrese, José Luis de. Capitalismo, comunismo, cristianismo. Madrid: Ediciones Radar, 1947.
———. Escritos y discursos. Madrid: Vicesecretaría de Educación Popular, 1943.
———. El Estado totalitario en el pensamiento de José Antonio. Madrid, 1945.

——. Hacia una meta institucional. Madrid: Ediciones del Movimiento, 1957.

——. Málaga desde el punto de vista urbanístico. Málaga, 1941.

——. La revolución social del Nacional Sindicalismo. Madrid, 1940.

Aunós, Eduardo. Calvo Sotelo y la política de su tiempo. Madrid: Ediciones Españolas, 1941.

——. España en crisis (1874–1936). Buenos Aires: Librería del Colegio, 1942.

Aznar, Manuel. Historia militar de la guerra de España (1936–1939). Madrid: Ediciones Ideas, 1940.

Bahamonde y Sánchez de Castro, Antonio. Un año con Queipo de Llano. Mexico City: Ediciones Nuestro Tiempo, 1938.

Balbontín, José Antonio. La España de mi experiencia. Mexico City: Porrúa, 1952.

Barea, Arturo. La forja de un rebelde. Three volumes. Buenos Aires: Losada, 1951.

Bartz, Karl. The Downfall of the German Secret Service. London: William Kimber, 1956.

Basaldúa, Pedro de. En España sale el sol. Buenos Aires: Editorial Orden Cristiano, 1948.

Beltrán Güell, Felipe. Preparación y desarrollo del alzamiento nacional. Valladolid: Santarén, 1937.

——. Rutas de la victoria. Barcelona: Farré y Asensio, 1939.

Beneyto Pérez, Bartolomé, and José Ma. Herrero Higón. Falange en Valencia antes del alzamiento. Valencia: Domenech, 1939.

Beneyto Pérez, Juan. Genio y figura del movimiento. Madrid: Aguado, 1940.

——. El nuevo Estado español. Madrid: Biblioteca Nueva, 1939.

——, and José Ma. Costa Serrano. El partido. Zaragoza: Colección Hispana, 1939.

Bergamo, Duca di. Legionari di Roma in terra iberica (1936 xiv–1939 xvii). Rome, 1940 (?).

Bernanos, Georges. Les grands cimetières sous la lune. Paris: Plon, 1947.

Beumelburg, Werner. Kampf um Spanien: Die Geschichte der Legion Condor. Berlin: Gerhard Stalling, 1940.

Bowers, Claude G. My Mission to Spain: Watching the Rehearsal for World War II. New York: Simon and Schuster, 1954.

Bravo, Francisco. "Early Days of the Spanish Phalanx," Spain, Vol. I, No. 10, pp. 6–7.

Bravo Martínez, Francisco. Historia de Falange Española de las JONS. Madrid: Editora Nacional, 1943.

——. José Antonio: El hombre, el jefe, el camarada. Madrid: Ediciones Españolas, 1939.

Bray, Coronel Arturo. La España del brazo en alto. Buenos Aires: Editorial Ayacucho, 1943.

Brenan, Gerald. The Spanish Labyrinth: An Account of the Social and Political Background of the Civil War. New York: Macmillan, 1943.

Buckley, Henry. Life and Death of the Spanish Republic. London: Hamish Hamilton, 1940.

Burgo, Jaime del. Requetés en Navarra antes del alzamiento. San Sebastián: Editorial Española, 1939.

Cacho Zabalza, Antonio. La Unión Militar Española. Alicante: Egasa, 1940.
Calvo Sotelo, José. El capitalismo contemporáneo y su evolución. Madrid: Galo Sáez, 1935.
———. Mis servicios al Estado. Madrid: Imprenta Clásica Española, 1931.
———. La voz de un perseguido. Two volumes. Madrid: Galo Sáez, 1933.
Canales, Patricio G. de. Cuestionario, January 24, 1958 (unpublished).
Cánovas Cervantes, S. Apuntes históricos de "Solidaridad Obrera." Barcelona: CNT, 1937.
Cantalupo, Roberto. Fu la Spagna: Ambasciata presso Franco, Febbraio-Aprile 1937. Verona: Mondadori, 1948.
Capella, Jacinto. La verdad de Primo de Rivera. Madrid: Hijos de Tomás Minuesa, 1933.
Cartas entrecruzadas entre el Sr. D. Manuel Hedilla Larrey y el Sr. D. Ramón Serrano Súñer. Madrid, 1948 (privately printed).
Castellano, J. (pseud.) "La Falange: Mitos y realidades," Cuadernos, núm. 31 (July–August 1958), pp. 24–30.
Castillo, José del, and Santiago Alvarez. Barcelona, objetivo cubierto. Barcelona: Timón, 1958.
Castrillo Santos, Juan. Revolución en España. Buenos Aires: Librería La Facultad, 1938.
Cattell, David T. Communism and the Spanish Civil War. Berkeley and Los Angeles: University of California, 1956.
Ciano, Count Galeazzo. Ciano's Diplomatic Papers. Edited by Malcolm Muggeridge. Translated by Stuart Hood. London: Odhams Press, 1948.
———. Ciano's Hidden Diary, 1937–1938. Translated and Annotated by Andreas Mayor. New York: E. P. Dutton, 1953.
Clark, Clyde L. The Evolution of the Franco Regime. Three volumes. Washington, D.C. (?), n.d.
Coles, S. F. A. Franco of Spain. London: N. Spearman, 1955.
Colmegna, Hector. Diario de un médico argentino en la guerra de España, 1936–1939. Buenos Aires: Espasa-Calpe, 1941.
Colodny, Robert G. The Struggle for Madrid. New York: Paine-Whitman, 1958.
Colvin, Ian. Master Spy: The Incredible Story of Admiral Wilhelm Canaris . . . New York: McGraw-Hill, 1952.
Conill y Mataró, Antonio, Codo: De mi diario de campaña. Barcelona, 1954.
Consejo Nacional de FET y de las JONS. Anteproyecto de Ley definadora de los principios que informan el Movimiento Nacional (1956).
———. Anteproyecto de Ley de Ordenación del Gobierno (1956).
———. Anteproyecto de Ley Orgánica del Movimiento Nacional (1956).
Corthis, André (pseud. of Andrée Husson). L'Espagne de la victoire. Paris: Fayard, 1941.
Cuadrado Alonso, Arturo, presbítero. Mis diez meses de Madrid rojo. Melilla: Postal Exprés, 1938.
Dávila, Sancho, and Julián Pemartín. Hacia la historia de la Falange: Primera contribución de Sevilla. Jerez: Jerez Industrial, 1938.
Díaz, Guillermo. Cómo llegó Falange al poder: Análisis de un proceso contrarrevolucionario. Buenos Aires: Aniceto Lopez, 1940.
Documents on German Foreign Policy: 1918-1945. Series D, 1937-1945, Vol.

III, Germany and the Spanish Civil War: 1936–1939. Washington, D.C., 1950.

Dolor y memoria de España en el segundo aniversario de la muerte de José Antonio. Barcelona: Ediciones Jerarquía, 1939.

Doreste Morales, Prudencio. Ocho meses de campaña. Las Palmas: Falange, 1941.

Eliseda, Marqués de la. Autoridad y libertad. Madrid: González, 1945.

Esperabé de Arteaga, Enrique. La guerra de reconquista española que ha salvado a Europa y el criminal comunismo. Madrid: R. de San Martín, 1940.

Fernández Almagro, Melchor. Historia del Reinado de Don Alfonso XIII. Barcelona: Muntaner y Simón, 1934.

———. Historia de la segunda República española. Madrid: Biblioteca Nueva, 1940.

Fernández de Castro y Pedrera, Rafael. Hacia las rutas de una nueva España. (De cómo se preparó, y por qué hubo de comenzar en Melilla el glorioso Movimiento Nacional salvador de la Patria.) Melilla, 1940.

Fernández Cuesta, Raimundo. Intemperie, victoria y servicio: Discursos y escritos. Redactado por Agustín del Rio Cisneros. Madrid: Ediciones del Movimiento, 1951.

Ferrer, Melchor. El Generalísimo Franco y la Comunión Tradicionalista. Seville, n.d. Also consulted was Ferrer's collection of Carlist documents in Seville.

Foltz, Charles, Jr. The Masquerade in Spain. Boston: Houghton Mifflin, 1948.

Franco, El Generalísimo. Palabras del Caudillo, 19 abril 1937 – 31 diciembre 1938. Madrid: Ediciones Fe, 1939.

Francotte, R. A. L'Heure de l'Espagne. Brussels: Visscher, 1947.

Galindo Herrero, Santiago. Los partidos monárquicos bajo la segunda República. (Biblioteca del Pensamiento Actual, núm. 61.) Madrid: Rialp, 1956.

Gannes, Harry, and Theodore Repard. Spain in Revolt. Second Edition, Revised. New York: Alfred A. Knopf, 1937.

García Escalera, I. "El General Yagüe," *Temas españoles* (Madrid, 1953), núm. 42.

García Hinojosa, A. Garabatos del fascismo español. Buenos Aires: Patronato Hispano-Argentino de Cultura, 1943.

García Mercadal, J. Aire, tierra y mar (los más gloriosos episodios de la gesta española). Three volumes. Zaragoza: Colección Hispania, 1938–39.

García Valdecasas, Antonio. "Los Estados totalitarios y el Estado español," *Revista de Estudios Políticos,* Vol. II, No. 5 (January 1942), pp. 5–32.

García Venero, Maximiliano. Historia de nacionalismo catalán (1793–1936). Madrid: Editora Nacional, 1944.

———. Historia del nacionalismo vasco (1793–1936). Madrid: Editora Nacional, 1945.

Gerahty, Cecil. The Road to Madrid. London: Hutchinson, 1937.

Giménez Caballero, Ernesto. La Falange—hecha hombre—¡conquista el Estado! Salamanca, 1937.

———. Genio de España. Madrid: La Gaceta Literaria, 1932.

———. La nueva catolicidad. Madrid: La Gaceta Literaria, 1933.

Gollonet Megías, Angel, and José Morales López. Rojo y azul en Granada. Granada: Prieto, 1937.

――――. Sangre y fuego―Málaga. Granada: Prieto,' 1937.

Gomá y Tomás, Cardenal Isidro. Pastorales de la guerra de España. (Biblioteca del Pensamiento Actual, núm. 51.) Madrid: Rialp, 1955.

Gómez Oliveros, Comandante B., with the collaboration of General Moscardó. General Moscardó. Barcelona: AHR, 1956.

González Ortín, Rodrigo. Extremadura bajo la influencia soviética. Badajoz: Gráfica Corporativa, 1937.

González Vicén, Luis. Letter to José Luis de Arrese, June 8, 1956 (mimeographed).

――――. Proyecto de Bases que presenta el Consejero Nacional, Camarada Luis González Vicén a la Ponencia encargada del estudio y redacción de las Leyes Fundamentales (1956).

Guariglia, Raffaele. Ricordi, 1922–46. Naples: Edizioni Scientifiche Italiane, 1950.

Guillén Salaya, Francisco. Anecdotario de la JONS. San Sebastián: Editorial Yugos y Flechas, 1938.

――――. Historia del Sindicalismo español. Madrid: Editora Nacional, 1943.

――――. Los que nacimos con el siglo (Biografía de una juventud). Madrid: Colenda, 1953.

Gutiérrez, Ricardo. Memorias de un azul. Salamanca: Imprenta Comercial Salmantina, 1937.

Gutiérrez-Ravé, José. Yo fuí un joven maurista. Madrid: Libros y revistas, 1946.

How Mussolini Provoked the Spanish Civil War: Documentary Evidence. London: 1938.

Hoyos, Oberleutnant Max Graf. Pedros y Pablos Fliegen, Erleben, Kämpfen in Spanien. Munich: F. Bruckmann, 1941.

Hughes, Emmet John. Report From Spain. New York: Henry Holt, 1947.

Instituto de Estudios Políticos. Informe del Instituto de Estudios Políticos, en relación con los Anteproyectos de Leyes Fundamentales sometidos a la consideración del Consejo Nacional (1956).

Iribarren, José María. Con el general Mola. Zaragoza: Heraldo de Aragón, 1937.

――――. Mola: Datos para una biografía y para la historia del alzamiento nacional. Zaragoza: El Heraldo de Aragón, 1938.

――――. Notas sobre le gestación y peripecias desdichadas de mi libro con el general Mola. Pamplona, May 15, 1944.

Iturralde, Juan de (pseud.). El Catolicismo y la cruzada de Franco. Paris: Egui-Indarra, 1955.

Jato, David. La rebelión de los estudiantes (Apuntes para una historia del alegre SEU). Madrid: Cies, 1953.

Jellinek, Frank. The Civil War in Spain. London: Victor Gollancz, 1938.

Juliá Téllez, Eduardo. Historia del Movimiento libertador de España en la provincia gaditana. Cádiz: Cerón, 1944.

Kemp, Peter. Mine Were of Trouble. London: Cassell, 1957.

Kindelán, Alfredo. Mis cuadernos de guerra 1936–39. Madrid: Editorial Plus-ultra, 1945.

Lacruz, Francisco. El alzamiento, la revolución y el terror en Barcelona. Barcelona: Arysel, 1943.

Largo Caballero, Francisco. Mis recuerdos. Mexico City: La Alianza, 1954.

Ledesma Ramos, Ramiro. Discurso a las juventudes de España. Madrid: Ediciones Fe, 1939.

————. Los escritos filosóficos de Ramiro Ledesma. Madrid, 1941.

————. ¿Fascismo en España? (Sus orígenes, su desarrollo, sus hombres.) Madrid: Ediciones La Conquista del Estado, 1935.

Lizarra, Antonio de. Los vascos y la República española. Buenos Aires: Vasca Ekin, 1944.

Lizarza Iribarren, Antonio. Memorias de la conspiración: Cómo se preparó en Navarra la Cruzada, 1931–1936. Pamplona: Gómez, 1957.

Lladó i Figueres, J. M. El 19 de juliol a Barcelona. Barcelona: Biblioteca Política de Catalunya, 1938.

Llopis, Rodolfo. Los puntales del régimen de Franco se quiebran. Toulouse: 1958.

————. "Spain Awaits Her Hour," Part IV, Ibérica, Vol. V, No. 7 (July 1957), pp. 4–6.

McCoy, Harold. "Gil Robles: Scourge of Liberal Spain," Current History, No. 40 (September 1934), pp. 682–88.

McCullagh, Francis. In Franco's Spain. London: Burns, Oates & Washbourne, 1937.

Maíz, Félix B. Alzamiento en España (De un diario de la conspiración). Pamplona: Gómez, 1952.

Marcotte, V. A. L'Espagne Nationale-Syndicaliste. Brussels, 1943.

Martínez de Bedoya, Javier. "El sentido de la libertad en la doctrina falangista," Revista de Estudios Políticos, Vol. III, No. 10 (July–August 1943), pp. 313–34.

Mauger, Gilles. José Antonio, Chef et martyr. Paris: Nouvelles Editions Latines, 1955 (?).

Maura Gamazo, Gabriel. Bosquejo histórico de la dictadura. Two volumes. Madrid: Javier Morata, 1930.

Meleiro, Fernando. Anecdotario de la Falange de Orense. Madrid: Ediciones del Movimiento, 1958.

Mendizábal, Alfred. The Martyrdom of Spain: Origins of a Civil War. New York: Charles Scribner's Sons, 1938.

Menéndez-Reigada, R. P., Fr. Ignacio G., O.P. La guerra nacional española ante la Moral y el Derecho. Bilbao: Editora Nacional, 1938.

Mira, Giovanni, and Luigi Salvatorelli. Storia del Fascismo. Rome: Edizioni Novissime, 1949.

Montes Agudo, Gumersindo. Vieja guardia. Madrid: Aguilar, 1939.

Mora, Constancia de la. In Place of Splendor: The Autobiography of a Spanish Woman. New York: Harcourt, Brace, 1939.

Moure-Mariño, Luis. Galicia en la guerra. Madrid: Ediciones Españolas, 1939.

Núñez, Ignacio. La revolución de octubre de 1934. Two volumes. Barcelona: José Vilamala, 1935.

"Onésimo Redondo y el Sindicato Remolachero," SP, March 8, 1959.

Orizana, G., and José Manuel Martín Liébana. El Movimiento Nacional. Valladolid: Francisco G. Vicente, 1937.

Ortega Sierra, Luis. Ridruejo interview, *Preuves,* No. 26 (June 1957), pp. 13–16.
Ortega y Gasset, José. Obras completas. Five volumes. Madrid: Revista del Occidente, 1946.
Ortiz de Villajos, C. G. De Sevilla a Madrid: Ruta libertadora de la columna Castejón. Granada: Prietom, 1937.
Oudard, Georges. Chemises noires, brunes, vertes en Espagne. Paris: Plon, 1938.
Ossorio, Angel. Mis memorias. Buenos Aires: Losada, 1946.
Pagés Guix, Luis. La traición de los Franco. Madrid: Sánchez, 1938.
Pattee, Richard. This is Spain. Milwaukee: Bruce, 1951.
Pavón Pereyra, Enrique. De la vida de José Antonio. Madrid: Editora Nacional, 1949.
Peirats, José. La CNT en la revolución española. Three volumes: Toulouse: Ediciones CNT, 1951–53.
Pemartín, José. ¿Qué es lo nuevo? Madrid: Espasa-Calpe, 1940.
Pérez de Cabo, José. ¡Arriba España! Madrid, 1935.
Pettinato, Concetto. La Spagna di Franco. Milan: Istituto per gli Studi di Politica Internazionale, 1939.
Plá, José. Historia de la segunda República española. Four volumes. Barcelona: Gráficas Marco, 1941.
Prieto, Indalecio. Cómo y por qué salí del Ministerio de Defensa Nacional. ... Texto taquigráfico del informe pronunciado el 9 de agosto de 1938 ante el Comité Nacional del Partido Socialista Español. Mexico City: Impresos y Papeles, 1940.
——. Palabras de ayer y de hoy. Santiago de Chile: Ediciones Ercilla, 1938.
——. El testamento de Primo de Rivera. Toulouse: Partido Socialista Obrero Español, n.d.
Primo de Rivera, José Antonio. Obras completas de . . . (Edición cronológica.) Madrid: Publicaciones Españolas, 1952.
——. Textos inéditos y epistolario de . . . Madrid: Ediciones del Movimiento, 1956.
Primo de Rivera, Miguel. El pensamiento de Primo de Rivera. Sus notas, artículos y discursos. Edited by José Ma. Pemán. Madrid: Sáez, 1929.
Proceso de José Antonio Primo de Rivera. November 17–18, 1936.
Ramos Oliveira, Antonio. La revolución española de octubre. Madrid: Editorial España, 1935.
Ratcliff, Dillwyn F. Prelude to Franco: Political Aspects of the Dictatorship of General Miguel Primo de Rivera. New York: Las Americas, 1957.
Reguengo, Vicente. Guerra sin frentes. Madrid: Cañizares, 1954.
Ros, Samuel, and Antonio Bouthelier. A hombros de la Falange: Historia del traslado de los restos de José Antonio. Barcelona, Madrid: Ediciones Patria, 1940.
Ruiz de Alda, Julio. Obras completas. Barcelona: Ediciones Fe, 1939.
——, and Ramón Franco. De Palos al Plata. Madrid: Editorial Ibero-africano-americana, 1927.
Ruiz Vilaplana, Antonio. Doy fe: Un año de actuación en la España nacionalista. Paris: Imprimerie Cooperative Etoile, n.d.
Sánchez, Narciso. "Onésimo Redondo," *Temas españoles* (Madrid, 1953), No. 39.
Schempp, Otto. Das Autoritäre Spanien. Leipzig: Wilhelm Goldmann, 1939.

Schulz-Wilmersdorf, P. A. Spanien: Politiker und Generale. Berlin: Steiniger, 1939.

La Sección Femenina: Historia y Organización. Madrid, 1952.

Sencourt, Robert. Spain's Ordeal: A Documented History of the Civil War. London: Longmans, Green, 1940.

Serrano Súñer, Ramón. Entre Hendaya y Gibraltar. Mexico City: Epesa Mexicana, 1947.

———. Semblanza de José Antonio, joven. Madrid: Aguilar, 1959.

Sevilla Andrés, Diego. Antonio Maura: La revolución desde arriba. Barcelona: Aedos, 1953.

Smith, Rhea Marsh. The Day of the Liberals in Spain. Philadelphia: University of Pennsylvania, 1938.

Solá, Victor María de, and Carlos Martel. Estelas gloriosas de la escuadra azul. Cádiz: Cerón, 1937.

Solmi, Arrigo. Lo stato nuovo nella Spagna di Franco. Milan: Istituto per gli Studi di Politica Internazionale, 1940.

Torre Bolado, Florentino. Diary for 1935 (unpublished).

Torrente Ballester, Gonzalo. Panorama de la literatura española contemporánea. Madrid, 1956.

———. (ed.). José Antonio Primo de Rivera (Antología). (Breviarios del Pensamiento Español.) Madrid: Ediciones Fe, 1940.

Vegas Latapié, Eugenio. El pensamiento político de Calvo Sotelo. Madrid: Cultura Española, 1941.

Venegas, José. Las elecciones del Frente Popular. Buenos Aires, 1942.

———. Verdad y mentira de Franco (La rebelión según sus autores.) Buenos Aires: La Vanguardia, 1938.

Vigón, General Jorge. General Mola (El conspirador). Barcelona, AHR, 1957.

Volta, Sandro. Spagna a ferro e fuoco. Florence: Vallecchi, 1937.

Ximénez de Sandoval, Felipe. José Antonio (Biografía). Second Edition. Madrid: Lazareno-Echaniz, 1949.

Zayas, Marqués de. Historia de la Vieja guardia de Baleares. Madrid: Sáez, 1955.

Zugazagoitia, Julián. Historia de la guerra de España 1936–1939. Buenos Aires: La Vanguardia, 1940.

NEWSPAPERS AND PERIODICALS

ABC (Madrid and Seville), 1930–40.

Acción Española (Madrid), 1933.

El Adelanto (Salamanca), 1936.

Ahora (Madrid), 1931–36.

Alerta (Santander), 1937–40.

Amanecer (Jerez), 1936–39.

Arriba España (Pamplona), 1936–39.

Blanco y Negro (Madrid), 1929–36.

Boletín del Movimiento de Falange Española Tradicionalista, 1937–42.

Boletín Oficial del Estado, 1936–42.

Claridad (Madrid), 1936.

La Conquista del Estado (Madrid), 1931.

El Debate (Madrid), 1930–36.
El Día Gráfico (Barcelona), 1934.
El Diario de Burgos, 1934–39.
El Estado Nacional (Valladolid), 1932–33.
FE (Madrid, Seville), 1933–34, 1936–39.
La Gaceta Regional (Salamanca), 1936–39.
El Heraldo de Aragón (Zaragoza), 1936–39.
El Heraldo de Madrid, 1930–36.
Hierro (Bilbao), 1937–39.
Hoy (Badajoz), 1936.
El Ideal (Granada), 1936.
El Ideal Gallego (La Coruña), 1937–38.
Informaciones (Madrid), 1932–36.
Libertad (Valladolid), 1931–32, 1936–39.
Luz (Madrid), 1934.
Mensaje (New York), Vol. II, No. 6, 1958.
Mundo Obrero (Madrid), 1934–36.
La Nación (Madrid), 1929–36.
No Importa (Madrid), 1936.
Paris-Soir (Paris), 1936.
El Pensamiento Alavés (Vitoria), 1936.
El Pensamiento Navarro (Pamplona), 1936–39.
El Pueblo Gallego (Vigo), 1938.
La Rioja (Logroño), 1938.
El Socialista, 1930–31, 1936, 1949.
El Sol (Madrid), 1930–36.
Solidaridad Obrera (Barcelona), 1936.
Sur (Málaga), 1937.
The Times (London), 1936.
Unidad (Santander), 1937.
La Unión (Seville), 1936–37.
Vieja Guardia, June–July, 1956.
La Voz (Madrid), 1936.

INDEX

ABC, 31, 53 f., 68, 70, 78, 90, 93, 174, 180, 273
Abyssinia, 79
Acción Española, 41, 153 f., 160 f., 185 n., 293
Acción Popular, 11, 22
Acosta, Rodríguez, 124
Africa, 43, 90, 120
Agrarian problems, Falange and, 79
Aguilar, Luis, 142
Alava, 108 f., 111, 163
Alberti, Rafael, 57 n.
Albiñana y Sanz, José María, Dr., 10–11, 12, 42 n., 269
Albiñanistas, 42, 54
Alcalá Zamora, Niceto, 92
Alcubierre, 146
Alfaro, José María, 49, 206 f.
Alfonso XIII, 7 ff., 21, 26, 62
Algeciras, 117
Alicante, 138, 140 f., 178, 286; José Antonio in, 107 f., 115, 132, 135 f., 150
Allen, Jay, 137 f.
Allied powers, 227, 237, 239, 295
Alvargonzález, 54–55
Anarchists, 7, 10, 13, 23, 29, 35, 84, 105, 198; in Army revolt, 117
Anarcho-Syndicalist movement, 8, 12, 14, 183
Andalusia, 5, 44, 92 f., 97, 119, 122, 125, 128, 131, 145, 151 f., 154
Andino, José, 115, 129 n., 188, 292
Ansaldo, Juan Antonio, 34, 42, 45, 60 n., 65, 99 n., 275; organizes Falange terrorist units, 57 f.; expelled from party, 61
"Anteproyectos," 257–59, 297–98
Anti-Semitism, 126
Aparicio, Juan, 13, 270
Aragón, 116, 142, 145 f., 167 n.
Areilza y Rodas, José María de, 207
Arellano (Subsecretary of Justice), 193
Army, Spanish: political ally of Falange, 86–87; conspiracy begun, 101–2, 110–15; and revolt of July 17, 1936, 116–22 *passim;* in new Spain, 207–8
Arrarás, Joaquín, 149
Arredondo, Colonel, 54

Arrese, José Luis de, 224, 239 f., 243–45, 251, 256, 261 f., 278, 297; as Secretary-General, 229–34; on José Antonio, 259–60
Arriba, 84 f., 94, 96, 138, 228, 237
¡*Arriba España!,* 82 n., 237
Arriba España (Pamplona), 127, 177
Asensio Torrado, General José, 236, 240
Assault Guards, 104, 132; assassination of Calvo Sotelo by, 114–15; in Army revolt, 117
Association of Catholic Students, 50
Asturias, 71, 128, 146 f., 213
Aunós Pérez, Eduardo, 7, 187
Austria, 31, 276
Auxilio Social, 193, 196 f., 215
Axis powers, 161, 169, 227, 295
Ayarzun, Román, 152
Azaña y Diaz, Manuel, 30, 45 f., 51, 85, 94, 96, 99
Aznar, Agustín, 13, 122 ff., 125, 131 f., 142, 144–45, 151 ff., 157, 164, 171, 289, 291; triumvir of Falange, 165; arrested, 166; in old-guard clique, 175, 185 f.
"Azorín" (José Martínez Ruiz), 56

Badajoz, 81, 147 n., 294
Balbontin, José Antonio, 277
Balearic Islands, 220, 291
Barba Hernández, Captain, 86 ff.
Barcelona, 5, 84, 103, 117, 183, 215 n., 295; University of, 190
Baroja y Ness, Pío, 49
Basques, 3, 80 f., 96, 235
Beigbeder (Foreign Minister), 227, 293
Beneyto Pérez, Juan, 222–23
Berlin, 77 f., 118 f., 196
Bernhardt, Johannes, 118
Bilbao, 16, 32 f., 36, 45 n., 49, 62, 125, 234, 284
Bilbao, Esteban, 207, 220
Bloque Nacional, 70, 72, 95 n.
Blue Division, 233–34, 239, 294
Bolshevism, 90, 119, 233
Bravo, Francisco, 46 n., 75, 147 n., 166 f.
Buckley, Henry, 80, 99 n.
Buhigas, Daniel, 213, 294

Burgos, 42 n., 81, 92, 111, 115, 120, 128 ff., 135, 144 ff., 156, 188, 191, 209, 292

Businessmen: and fascist movement, 32–35, 45; support to Falange, 61–63; under Franco, 247–48

Cabanellas y ferrer, General Miguel, 102, 120, 129 f.
Cáceres, 81, 92
Cadenas, Vicente, 125 n., 151, 172, 176
Cádiz, 33, 36 f., 44, 53, 81, 93 f., 116, 119, 271
Calvo Serer, Rafael, 298
Calvo Sotelo, José, 7, 68, 70, 95, 107, 109, 275 f., 295; assassinated, 114–15
Cambó, Francesc, 34
Camisas viejas, 175, 178–88 *passim,* 205 f., 208, 212–13, 227, 237, 244, 250; and cult of José Antonio, 190–91
Canales, Patricio González de, 131, 213 f.
Canaris, Admiral Wilhelm, 284
Canary Islands, 33, 106, 146, 171, 213, 287, 295
Cantalupo, Roberto, 194
Capitalism, 79, 247–48, 253
Caralt, Luis de, 213 f.
Cárcel Modelo (Madrid), 100, 103 f., 107–8
Carceller, Demetrio, 33, 207, 220, 295
Carlists, 4, 8, 21, 41, 109–10, 128, 159, 161, 163, 186, 283, 292; in Army revolt, 115, 117 f., 121; and plans for Falange union, 152–56; role in FET, 168–69, 175, 191–94, 234–36, 238. *See also* Requetés
Carlos, Don (Pretender), 238
Carranza, Ramón, 44 n.
Carrasco, Arcadio, 157
Carretero, José María, 41, 90 n.
Carrión de los Condes, 104 f.
Casa del Pueblo, 104
Castaños, Ramón, 108–9
Castejón Espinosa, Colonel Antonio, 148
Castelló (militia leader), 143, 145
Castile, 2 f., 50, 55, 146, 213 f.
Castillo, Lt. José, 114
Catalonia, 3, 16, 67, 80 f., 84, 213, 215 n., 226, 294
Catholic Action, 16, 22, 263
Cazañas, Antonio, 122 f., 213, 294
CEDA, *see* Confederación Española de Derechas Autónomas
Cedo-Radical coalition, 59, 71, 90

Censorship, 127
Church, 22, 204, 252; Falange attitude toward, 69–70, 127; clerical laws of 1938, 192–93
Ciano, Count Galeazzo, 194, 197–98
Círculo Nosotros, 297
Civil Guards, 116 f., 166, 171, 176
CNT, *see* Confederación Nacional del Trabajo
Communism, 239, 246–47
Communist Youth, 99
Comunión Tradicionalista, 21, 42, 102, 121, 149, 160; and plans for union with Falange, 152, 154 f. *See also* Carlists
Confederación de Obreros Nacional-Sindicalistas, 63–64, 72, 91, 123
Confederación Española de Derechas Autónomas, 15, 22–24, 36, 59, 66, 68, 70, 85, 91, 95, 149, 160, 199, 276
Confederación Nacional del Trabajo, 14, 44 n., 84, 97 f., 280
La Conquista del Estado, 10, 13 ff., 17 f., 30, 51
CONS, *see* Confederación de Obreros Nacional-Sindicalistas
Córdoba, 116
Cossío, Bartolomé Manuel de, 28
Covadonga, 8
Cuartel General, 144 f., 157 f., 163, 165, 167 f., 170, 175, 182, 249
Cuenca, 106

Daimiel, 52
Danzi, Guglielmo, 197
Daudet, Léon, 68, 269
Dávila, Sancho, 33, 92, 125, 131, 151, 154, 156, 158–59, 164, 171; triumvir of Falange, 165; arrested, 166
El Debate, 22
Delbos, Yvon, 137
Delgado Barreto, Manuel, 30–31, 77
Dollfuss, Engelbert, 52, 276
Domínguez (Falangist), 234 ff.
Donoso Cortés, 271

Echeverría, Martín, 135, 138
Economic reforms, Falange and, 79
Egaña, Conde de, 295
Elections of 1936, 90–96
El Ferrol, 117
Eliseda, Marqués de la (Francisco Moreno Herrera), 60, 62, 69–70
Elola, José Antonio, 251
Escario, José Luis, 153 f.

Esparza, Eladio, 177
Estella, Marqués de Estella, see Primo de Rivera
Estremadura, 128, 146 f.
Ethiopia, 119
Ezquer, Eduardo, 215 n., 226, 294

Fal Conde, Manuel, 102, 109, 143 n., 155, 185 n., 192 ff., 283
Farinacci, Roberto, 197, 271
El Fascio, 30–32, 34, 35 n., 77
Faupel, General Wilhelm von, 143 n., 150, 161, 163, 170, 195–96, 293
FE, 49, 52 ff., 57 ff., 68 f., 131
Federación Universitaria Española, 51, 53
Fernández Cuesta, Raimundo, 92, 114 f., 186, 197, 205, 278, 291; Secretary-General of Falange, 82, 103; imprisoned, 121; plans for release of, 158, 163, 167, 178–79; on Spanish syndicalism, 187–88; Secretary-General of FET, 192; ambassador to Brazil, 206; reappointed Secretary-General, 246
Fernández Silvestre, 146
Foltz, Charles, 128 n.
Foxá, Agustín de, 49
France, 31, 52, 75, 80, 109, 115, 137, 176, 227, 236
Franco y Bahamonde, Generalissimo Francisco, 87, 94, 102, 106, 144, 148 f., 156, 281; and Army rebellion, 118–20; becomes Generalissimo, 129–31; and attempts to save José Antonio, 136–37; and Serrano Súñer, 159 f.; promises reforms, 162 f.; strengthens hold, 165–68; declares himself Jefe Nacional, 169; consolidates power, 170–73; aims at totalitarian state, 174 f.; relations with camisas viejas, 78–86; and cult of José Antonio, 190; relations with Carlists, 192–93; relations with Germans and Italians, 195, 197 f.; early career, 199; ideas on Spanish state, 200–204; cabinet shake-up, 205–8; and SEU, 209–11; plot against, 212–15; syndical system under, 216–20; establishes Institute of Political Studies, 221–22; authoritarianism, 223–24; pro-Axis policy, 227; appoints Arrese, 228–31; reduces influence of Falange, 232–33; capitalizes on factionalism in FET, 234–38; opposes Soviets, 239; dictatorship solidified, 241–45; Law of Succession, 246; nature of Franco state, 248–49; names com-
mission to study Fundamental Laws, 251; government shake-up of 1957, 261 ff.; program of liberalization, 264
Franco y Bahamonde, Nicolás, 130, 159 f.; plans for Franquista Party, 148–49
Franco y Bahamonde, Ramón, 34, 199
Freemasonry, 41 n., 120, 129, 149, 220
Frente de Juventudes, 208–11, 294
Frente Español, 24, 36
FUE, see Federación Universitaria Española

Gaceo, Vicente, 125 n.
Gaceta Literaria, 7 f., 11
Galarza, Colonel Valentín, 228 f., 236, 296
Galicia, 80 f., 117, 128, 146 f., 199, 213, 216, 275
Gambara, General Gastone, 147 n.
Gamero del Castillo, Pedro, 154, 161, 184, 206, 216 f., 225–26, 236 f., 288
Ganivet, Angel, 49
Garcerán Sanchez, Rafael, 110, 115, 123, 151, 164 f., 171; arrested, 166
García, Mariano, 103, 278, 283
García Escámez e Iniesta, Colonel Francisco, 118
García Valdecasas, Alfonso, 32, 36, 161, 221, 237, 270; and liberal movement, 23–24; and founding of Falange, 38, 42; quoted, 223
Garrigues, Joaquín, 186, 291
Generation of Ninety-Eight, 5, 49
Germany, 143, 150 f., 177; National Socialism in, 31, 52; José Antonio in, 77; intervenes in Civil War, 118–19, 130; declines to aid José Antonio, 136; and rebel government, 161, 170; and Falange, 194 ff., 198, 214; in World War II, 205, 227, 233, 236 f., 239
Gerona, 294
Gibraltar, 80, 181
Gijón, 67
Gil Robles y Quiñones, José María, 11, 22, 30, 59 n., 69, 85, 106 f., 114, 128, 199, 276; and elections of 1936, 90 f., 94 f.; on terrorists, 104–5
Giménez Caballero, Ernesto, 7–8, 11, 15, 31, 34, 41 n., 46 n., 75, 85 n., 128, 159, 162, 270
Girón, José Antonio, 143, 146, 151, 175, 208, 213–14, 229, 251, 280; Labor Minister, 220, 249–50, 261
Goded Llopi, General Manuel, 102

Goicoechea Coscuéluela, Antonio, 45 n., 106, 156–57, 282; pact with José Antonio, 62–63
Gómez Jordana, General, 181
González Bueno, Pedro, 153 f., 161, 186, 188, 291
González Vélez, Fernando, 175, 185 f., 206, 291
Goya, José María, 165–68
Granada, 116, 144, 278
Great Britain, 75, 80
Groizard, Manuel, 58
Group for the Service of the Republic, 23
Guadalajara, 119, 197
Guariglia (Italian envoy), 77
Guitarte, José Miguel, 209
Gullino, Cesare, 78 n.
Gutiérrez, Father Manuel, 276

Halcón, Manuel, 242
Hassell, Ulrich von, 194
Haz, 208
Haz Ibérico, 265–66
Hedilla Larrey, Manuel, 92, 137, 143, 147 n., 150–52, 154, 175 f., 195, 197, 216, 265, 285, 289; Jefe Nacional, 124–27; plots against, 150–53, 156–64; deposed, 165; reasserts leadership, 166–68; supplanted by Franco, 169; imprisoned, 170–72
Herrera y Oría, Angel, 22, 95
Hitler, Adolf, 16 n., 30, 32, 45, 77, 198, 239, 271
Huesca, 146

Ibáñez Martín, José, 149, 262
Ifni, 90
Iglesia, Anselmo de la, 213, 280
Informaciones, 85 n.
Institute of Political Studies, 221
Intellectuals, 8, 23; disdain for Falange, 50–51
Iribarren, José María, 192 n.
Italian Fascism, 1, 7, 126, 151, 196 f., 288; José Antonio and, 77–79
Italy, 7, 21 n., 177, 237; aids Franco, 119, 130, 147; and rebel government, 161, 186, 193; and Falange, 194, 196–98, 293

Jaén, 68
JAP, see Juventudes de Acción Popular
Japan, 239
Javier, Don (Carlist Regent), 155

Javier Conde, Francisco, 186, 221–22, 251
Jellinek, Frank, 280
Jesuits, 22, 45 n., 172, 193
Jews, 17, 126, 177
Jiménez de Asúa, Luis, 27 n., 100
JONS, see Juntas de Ofensiva Nacional Sindicalista
Jordana, General Gómez, 181, 227, 293
Juan, Don (Pretender), 238, 246
Junta de Defensa Nacional, 120, 130
Junta de Mando, 124–25, 143, 151, 157 f., 162, 166 f., 265
Junta Política, 68–69, 72, 82, 87, 125 n., 156; members of, arrested, 100; new four-man (Franco's), 168 f., 206
Juntas Castellanas de Actuación Hispánica, 17
Juntas de Ofensiva Nacional Sindicalista, 30, 34, 36, 41, 50, 62, 72, 275; founding of, 18–20, 42; student units of, 45, 51; merged with Falange, 46–48, 55–56, 265
Juventudes de Acción Popular, 70, 85, 98, 104, 160
Juventudes Mauristas, 4

Keyserling, Count Hermann, 25
Kindelán y Duary, General Alfredo, 130
Knobloch, von, 136

La Coruña, 216
Largo Caballero, Francisco, 75, 98, 105, 140
Larios, Margarita (wife of Miguel Primo de Rivera), 139 f.
Las Hurdes, 11
Ledesma Ramos, Ramiro, 10, 17, 24, 28 n., 30–36 passim, 44 f., 49 ff., 61, 67, 71 f., 77, 86, 97, 244, 265, 270, 272, 275; political philosophy, 11–15; and founding of JONS, 18–20; and founding of Falange, 38, 46–48; at Valladolid meeting, 55 f.; and CONS, 63; disagrees on tactics, 64–65; president of Junta Política, 68–69; expelled from Falange, 72; later career, 73 n.; opinion of José Antonio, 76
Left: beginnings of violence in battle with Right, 51–58; Falange attempts to draw support from, 84; victory in 1936 elections, 94–97; renewal of violence, 98–100, 103–5; members in Falange, 128–29; loss of hope, 241–42
Leiza, 21

Lenin, Nicolai, 25, 271
León, 146, 175
Lequerica y Erquiza, José Félix de, 45 n., 275
Lerroux García, Alejandro, 59 n., 90
Levante, 117, 121, 131, 213, 215
Liberals: attempts of to save Republic, 23–24; students as, 50–51
Libertad, 17
Lisbon, 154, 156
Llopis, Rodolfo, 266
Logroño, 111, 128
López Bassa, Ladislao, 162 f., 165, 169
López Cotevilla, Ventura, 213 f.
López Puertas, Daniel, 166
Luca de Tena, Juan Ignacio, 31 f.

MacDonald, Ramsay, 45
Machado, Antonio, 5, 56
Madrid, 16, 35 f., 55, 72, 74 n., 101 f., 206; Spanish nationalism in, 10; Teatro Comedia meeting, 38; JONS merger, 46 f.; José Antonio's circle at Ballena Alegre, 49; raid of Falange HQ, 54; violence in, 56–58; Falange HQ closed, 59; First National Council meeting, 66; Falange members in, 81–84; Second National Council, 89; 1936 elections, 92–94; street fighting, 99–100; on eve of Army rebellion, 111–15 *passim*; rebel drive on, 117 ff., 146, 148; prison massacre, 141; Sección Femenina, 203; political cynicism in 1950's, 249
Madrid, University of, 11, 25, 45, 51, 53, 190, 287
Maeztu y Whitney, Ramiro, 45, 271
Málaga, 84, 125, 128, 147, 229, 243
Malaparte, Curzio, 8
Mallorca, 162, 172, 194
Maqueda, Dora, 203 n.
March Ordinas, Juan, 45 n., 62, 85 n., 92, 150
Martel, Carlos, 117 n.
Martínez Anido, General, 183
Martínez Barrio, Diego, 41, 116, 138
Martínez Berasáin, José, 283
Martínez de Bedoya, Javier, 223–24
Marx, Karl, 25, 222
Marxism, Marxists, 12, 19, 29, 52, 96, 216, 285
Mateo, Manuel, 72
Maura y Gamazo, Miguel, 112
Maura y Montaner, Antonio, 4
Maurras, Charles, 68, 269

Mayalde, Conde de, 149, 207
Medina, Elena, 115
Melilla, 118
Menéndez, Tito, 151
Menéndez Pelayo, 271
Menéndez-Reigada, Father Ignacio, SJ, 149
Merino, Miguel, 167, 295
Merry de Val, Alfonsito, 58 n.
Middle class: lethargy of, 2–4; conservatism of, 22–23
Militia, Falange, 104; attempts to free José Antonio, 132; training schools for, 142–44; as fighting force, 145–47; under Franco, 207–8
Millán Astray y Terreros, General José, 130
Miranda, Joaquín, 122 ff., 158–59, 162, 165, 289
Mola Vidal, General Emilio, 129 f., 132, 142, 159 f., 162, 164, 168, 192 n., 200; and Army conspiracy, 101–2, 110, 113 ff.; directs rebellion, 116–20 *passim*
Monarchists: financial support of Falange by, 62–63; renewed activity of, 250–51. *See also* Carlists
Monasterio, General, 146
Montero Díaz, Santiago, 47
Montero Rodríguez de Trujillo, Matías, 51, 53, 274
Montes, Eugeneo, 50, 137
Monzón, Jesús, 138
Mora y Maura, Constancia de la, 104 n.
Moreno, José, 124, 157, 165 f., 167 n.
Moreno Torres, 149
Morocco, 5, 99 n., 101 f., 122, 146, 213; Army rebellion in, 115–19 *passim*, 129 f.
Mundo Obrero, 66 n., 99 n., 104
Muñoz Grande, General, 206 f., 209, 218, 225 f.
Muro, Jesús, 92, 124, 166 f.
Muro, José, 157
Mussolini, Benito, 7, 12, 24, 32, 45, 79, 194, 197, 271, 276 f.; José Antonio's opinion of, 77; aids Army in Morocco, 119

La Nacion (Madrid), 30, 85 n.
Nanclares de la Oca, 109
National Council of Falange, 66, 89, 123, 125; in Salamanca, 164–67
National Front, Falange's interest in, 89, 92

Nationalism, 3–5, 10 ff., 18; and Falange, 80–81
National Socialism (German), 1, 7, 15–16, 31, 77, 194
National syndicalism: germs of, 15; economic theory, 79. *See also* Juntas de Ofensiva Nacional Sindicalista
Navarre, 21, 128, 165, 192, 283
Navy, Spanish, 117
Nazi Party, 7, 12, 15, 31, 52, 118, 126, 136, 150, 177, 214, 218, 239, 288, 296; José Antonio and, 75, 77 f.; Falange and, 196 f.
Negrín Lopez, Juan, 97
Neurath, Constantin von, 194
Nieto, Ricardo, 147 n., 171 f., 284, 289
No Importa, 49 n., 104 f., 111

Old Castile, 11, 15 f., 116, 122, 151
Opus Dei, 262–63
Orbaneja, Dr., 162 n.
Orgaz y Yoldi, General Luis, 130
Oriol, José María, 207
Ortega, Gregorio, 213
Ortega y Gasset, José, 2, 11 f., 23, 25, 29, 43, 49 f., 75, 137, 271
Ossorio y Gallardo, Angel, 36 n.
Oviedo, 67, 70, 125, 272, 276

Pamplona, 52, 70, 101, 115 f., 125, 127, 150, 176, 276, 283
Pedro Llen, 143 ff.
Pemartín, José, 222
Pemartín, Julián, 33
El Pensamiento Navarro, 152
Perales, Narciso, 99 n.
Pérez de Cabo, José, 82 n., 213, 215–16
Pérez González, Blas, 207, 236
Pestaña, Angel, 84
Philippines, 239
Plá, José, 272
Police reprisals under Franco, 183–84
Il Popolo d'Italia, 77
Popular Front, 89, 105; victory in 1936 elections, 94, 96, 98, 101
Portela Valladares, Manuel, 92–93, 98
Portugal, 2, 12, 44, 101, 115, 246
Pradera, Juan José, 184
Pradera, Victor, 41
Prieto y Tuero, Indalecio, 32–33, 44, 60, 75, 79, 137 f., 140 n., 171, 176, 178 f., 286; refuses to join Falange, 97–98
Primo de Rivera, General Francisco (Marqués de Estella), 24

Primo de Rivera y Orbaneja, General Miguel, 24–28 *passim,* 30, 86, 149; seven-year regime, 5–8
Primo de Rivera y Saenz de Heredia, Fernando, 103, 111, 141
Primo de Rivera y Saenz de Heredia, José Antonio, 123 ff., 142, 157, 167, 178, 181 f., 237 n., 244, 259, 265–66, 271–72, 275, 279 f., 282, 295; early career and philosophy, 24–30; writes for *El Fascio,* 31–32; proposes to run for office, 33–37; and founding of Falange, 38–48; esthetic preoccupations, 49–51; and outbreaks of violence, 52–54; at Valladolid meeting, 55–56; attempts on life, 57–58; called for impeachment, 59–60; expels Ansaldo, 61; pact with monarchists, 62–63; tactical struggles, 65–66; *Jefe Nacional,* 67–68; and Twenty-seven Points, 69–70; gains control of Falange, 71–73; liberal "elitist" attitudes, 74–76; and other fascist parties, 77–79; ideas as party leader, 79–85; attempts union with Army, 86–88; and 1936 elections, 89–96; seeks negotiations with Left, 97–98; renews battle with Left, 99–100; imprisoned, 102; and terrorism, 103 ff.; in Cuenca run-off election, 106; trial and conviction, 107; transferred to Alicante, 107–8; considers alliances with Carlists and Army, 109–11; and Army conspiracy, 111–15, 121; final manifestos, 132–36; last interview, 137; formal charges and trial, 138–40; execution, 141, 150; followers of, 151, 153 f., 158–61; cult of, 190–91; described, 276–77; proposed cabinet, 283
Primo de Rivera y Saenz de Heredia, Miguel, 106, 138 ff., 206 f., 228 f., 286
Primo de Rivera y Saenz de Heredia, Pilar, 171, 175, 203, 226, 279, 289 f.
Pujol, Juan, 272

¿Qué es lo nuevo?, 222
Queipo de Llano y Serra, Gonzalo, 102, 120, 162, 168, 178
Quiroga, Casares, 105

Radical Party, 59, 90
Redondo y Ortega, Andrés, 122 ff., 131, 151, 162
Redondo y Ortega, Onésimo, 15–17, 72 f., 78, 83–84, 92, 126, 244, 259, 270, 278,

280; and JONS, 18–20; and Valladolid meeting, 55 f.; killed, 121; on Mussolini, 277
Renovación Española, 21–22, 42, 45 n., 57, 68, 156, 160; pact with Falange, 62–63
Requetés, 21, 109, 156, 191, 234, 290; in Civil War, 120 f., 143 n., 145 f.; fused with Falange, 168, 170
Revista de Occidente, 11
Reyes, Roberto, 125 n.
Rico, Juanita, 58 n.
Ridruejo, Dionisio, 49, 82 n., 177, 186 f., 196 f., 207, 228, 231, 285, 288, 293, 296; *jefe* of Valladolid, 165, 175; FET Subsecretary of Propaganda, 181–82, 192; plans reorganization of FET, 184–85; joins Blue Division, 234
Right: National Front of, 89; and 1936 elections, 90–96; swing toward fascism, 107
Rio de Janeiro, 206
Ríos, Fernando de los, 270
Rodezno, Conde de (Tomás Domínguez Arévalo), 154, 156, 160, 193, 283
Rome, 7, 194, 197
Ros, Samuel, 49
Rosenberg, Marcel, 271
Ruiz Arenado, Martín, 167, 175
Ruiz de Alda y Miqueleiz, Julio, 51–52, 55, 61, 78, 80, 84, 86, 89, 92, 110, 275; early fascist activities, 34–36; and founding of Falange, 38, 41 f., 46–48; Valladolid meeting, 56; tactical disagreements with José Antonio, 65, 71 ff.; imprisoned, 104, 108, 121
Ruiz de la Fuente, Carlos Juan, 250, 294
Ruiz Vilaplana, Antonio, 183

Sáinz, José, 92, 113, 124, 166 f., 170
Sáinz Rodríguez, Pedro, 44 n., 62, 185, 193, 262, 294
Salamanca, 46 n., 50, 79, 125, 127 ff., 179, 182, 190, 194 f., 197, 290, 293; Falange activities in, 143–76 *passim*
Salas Pombo, Vicente, 251
Salazar de Olivera, Dr. Antonio, 12
Salvador Merino, Gerardo, 216–21, 226, 231
Sánchez Mazas, Rafael, 31, 41, 47 n., 49 f., 92, 206, 251, 270, 272 f.
Sangróniz y Castro, José Antonio, 160, 293

Sanjuro Sacanell, General José, 71, 101, 107, 198
San Sebastián, 21, 172
Santa Marina, Luys, 84
Santander, 81, 84, 92, 124 f., 213
Santiago de Compostela, University of, 47
Sanz, Ricardo, 213 f.
Sanz Orrio, Fermén, 261
Sanz Paracuellos, Felipe, 275
Schwendemann, Dr. Karl, 284
Sección Femenina, 197, 203–4, 226, 279
Second Carlist War, 24
Separatist movement, 3. *See also* Basques
Serna, Víctor de la, 150, 157 f.
Serrano Súñer, Fernando, 291
Serrano Súñer, Ramón, 163, 168, 170 f., 281, 288 ff., 295; leader of JAP, 104, 106 f.; beginning of political powers, 159–61; political role in FET, 174–87 *passim*; Minister of Interior, 192, 195–98, 205 ff., 209, 214–15, 217, 219, 225–30; decline of influence, 231–32, 235 ff.
SEU, *see* Sindicato Español Universitario
Seville, 33, 59, 95, 99, 116, 120, 122, 125, 131, 146, 158, 167 n., 171, 175, 179, 193, 206, 213, 242, 272, 285; University of, 51, 53, 154; militia training at, 137, 143 f.
Sindicato Español Universitario, 51 ff., 57, 81, 83, 91, 99 f., 104, 109 n., 165, 202, 208–9, 215 n., 235 f., 294
Sindicatos Libres, 54, 63–64, 91
Socialist Party, 33, 52, 66, 97, 105, 121, 274
Socialists: attempts at working-class representation, 23; students as, 50–51; and beginnings of violence, 52–58
Socialist Youth, 99; acts of terror involving, 57–58, 274
El Sol, 41
Solá, Víctor María de, 117 n.
Solís Ruiz, José, 261
Sotomayor, Enrique, 208–11, 234, 294
Spanish Nationalist Party, 10
Spengler, Oswald, 25, 210
Stohrer, Dr. Eberhard von, 180, 182 f., 196, 287, 291
Street fighting, 103–5
Students: JONS syndicates, 45, 47; supporters of Falange, 50–51, 81–83; political violence, 52–53; loyal to José Antonio, 74 n.; apathy, 248
Suevos, Jesús, 275

Syndicalism, in Franco state, 216–21. See also National syndicalism
Syndical Organization and Action, Ministry of, 187–88

Tarduchy, Captain (later Colonel) Emilio, 54, 86, 213 f., 226
Technical Services, of Falange, 154, 161
Tenerife, 106, 118
Tercios, 117, 130, 198
Teruel, 146
Thomson (Nazi Party representative in Madrid), 214
Toledo, 87, 92, 113, 274
Tomás Alvarez, Belarmino, 159
Torquemada, Tomás de, 16
Torrente Ballester, Gonzalo, 177
Tóvar, Antonio, 181, 192, 228, 296
Traditionalists, see Carlists
Trotsky, Leon, 271
Tudela, 52
Twenty-seven Points (of Falange program), 68–70

UGT, see Unión General del Trabajadores
UME, see Unión Militar Española
Unamuno Jugo, Miguel de, 5, 49 f., 56, 75, 82, 279
Unión General del Trabajadores, 6–7, 64
Unión Militar Española, 86, 88, 97, 101, 111, 114 f., 200, 213, 228, 283
Unión Monárquica Nacional, 26, 28
Unión Patriótica, 6, 30, 149
United States, 221, 226, 247 f.
Universities: JONS syndicates in, 45, 47; Socialists in, 50–51; political violence in, 53
Upper Aragon, 92
U.S.S.R., 221, 294; war in, 233–34; Franco's opposition to, 239

Valdeiglesias (Marqués de Portago), 118, 194 n.
Valdés, Manuel, 206, 236

Valencia, 45, 72, 111, 114, 117, 132, 215, 238
Valladolid, 15, 17, 63, 74, 83–84, 94, 116, 121 f., 125 f., 151 f., 165, 175, 213, 280; JONS in, 18; Falange rally, 55–56, 78, 274; Falange strength in, 81; National Council meeting, 123; support to Falange militia, 143 f., 146, 158; University of, 291
Valladolid province, 16, 19
Vaquero, Eloy, 71 n.
Varela, General José Enrique, 216, 218–19, 220, 234–35
Vegas Latapié, Eugenio, 185 n., 293
Vicén, Luis González, 143, 145, 151, 213, 280; on reorganization of Falange, 251–57
Vienna, 52
Vigo, 177
Violence: between Falange and Left, 52–58, 282; renewal of, after 1936 elections, 98–100, 103–5
Vivar Téllez, Rodrigo, 242–43
Vizcaya, 16, 234; Bank of, 45 n.

Weber, Max, 221
Weizsäcker, Ernst von, 136 n., 194, 196
Workers: in CONS, 63–64; position of, in fifties, 249–50
World War I, 1, 8, 247
World War II, 207, 223, 239, 241

Ya, 107
Yagüe Blanco, Colonel (later General) Juan de, 130, 143, 158, 170, 182, 213 f., 218, 288
Yzurdiaga, Father Fermín, 127, 150, 153, 176–77, 195, 276, 292

Zaldívar, José María, 191
Zamacola, Fernando, 146
Zamora, 11, 146, 171, 284
Zaragoza, 63, 116, 121 n., 125, 144, 146, 156, 182; University of, 45, 53